Everyman, I will go with thee,
and be thy guide

THE EVERYMAN
LIBRARY

*The Everyman Library was founded by J. M. Dent
in 1906. He chose the name Everyman because he wanted
to make available the best books ever written in every
field to the greatest number of people at the cheapest possible
price. He began with Boswell's 'Life of Johnson';
his one-thousandth title was Aristotle's 'Metaphysics',
by which time sales exceeded forty million.*

*Today Everyman paperbacks remain true to
J. M. Dent's aims and high standards, with a wide range
of titles at affordable prices in editions which address
the needs of today's readers. Each new text is reset to give
a clear, elegant page and to incorporate the latest thinking
and scholarship. Each book carries the pilgrim logo,
the character in 'Everyman', a medieval mystery play,
a proud link between Everyman
past and present.*

Geoffrey Chaucer

TROYLUS AND CRISEYDE

Edited by
MALDWYN MILLS
University of Aberystwyth

EVERYMAN
J. M. DENT · LONDON
CHARLES E. TUTTLE
VERMONT

Introduction and other material © J. M. Dent 2000

First published in Everyman's Library 1953
This new edition first published 2000

J. M. Dent
Orion Publishing Group
Orion House
5 Upper St Martin's Lane
London WC2H 9EA
and
Turtle Publishing
Airport Industrial Park
364 Innovation Drive
North Clarendon
VT 05759-9436
USA

Typeset by SetSystems Ltd, Saffron Walden, Essex
Printed in Great Britain by
The Guernsey Press Co. Ltd, Guernsey, Channel Islands

British Library Cataloguing-in-Publication Data
is available upon request.

ISBN 0 460 87610 4

CONTENTS

NOTE ON THE AUTHOR AND EDITOR

GEOFFREY CHAUCER, the son of a wine merchant in London, was born about 1343 or 1344. He was an omnivorous reader of Latin, French and Italian literature, and of works of science, philosophy and religion. Apart from the *Canterbury Tales* he wrote several long and distinguished poems – the *Book of the Duchess*, the *House of Fame*, the *Parliament of Fowls*, *Troylus and Criseyde* and the *Legend of Good Women*. He also made a prose translation of the *Consolation of Philosophy* by Boethius and of a treatise on the astrolabe. Yet the writing of poetry and prose was often a spare-time occupation for Chaucer, who was successively a member of the King's Household, a soldier, a diplomatic envoy to France and Italy, a high customs official, a justice of the peace, a member of parliament, and Clerk of the King's works. The knowledge of men and women gained from these activities is reflected in the psychological complexity of the principal characters in *Troylus and Criseyde*.

MALDWYN MILLS is an Emeritus Professor of English in the University of Wales, Aberystwyth. His chief research interests are in Chaucer and in the Middle English Romances; among his publications are editions of *Lybeaus Desconus* (1969), *Guy of Warwick* fragments (with Daniel Huws, 1974), *Horn Childe* (1988), and, in Everyman, *Six Middle English Romances* (1973), and *Ywain and Gawain, Sir Percyvell of Gales, The Anturs of Arther* (1992).

CHRONOLOGY OF CHAUCER'S LIFE

Year	Life
c. 1312–13	Birth of Chaucer's father, John Chaucer
c. 1343–4	Birth of Chaucer, son of John and Agnes Chaucer, in London
1357	In service as a page in the household of Elizabeth, Countess of Ulster (wife of Lionel, Earl of Ulster, second surviving son of Edward III)
1359–60	Service in the retinue of Lionel on campaign in France; ransomed after being captured at the siege of Reims

CHRONOLOGY OF HIS TIMES

Year	Literary and Historical Events
1313	Birth of Boccaccio
1321	Death of Dante, soon after the completion of the *Divina Commedia*
1327	Accession of Edward III, aged 14
1337–1453	The Hundred Years' War between England and France
1338	Completion of Boccaccio's *Il Filostrato* (main source of Chaucer's *Troylus and Criseyde*)
1341	Completion of Boccaccio's *Teseide delle Nozze d'Emilia* (main source of the *Knight's Tale*)
1346	English victory at the battle of Crécy
1348–9	About one third of the population of England dies in the Black Death
1350s	Beginnings of the revival of alliterative poetry in the West and North-West of England
1356	English victory at the battle of Poitiers; capture of King John of France, who lives at the English court, 1357–60
1360	Treaty of Brétigny brings peace between England and France until 1369
1361–7	Jean Froissart, the French chronicler and poet, present in the household of Queen Philippa (wife of Edward III)
1364	Death of King John of France; accession of Charles V
mid 1360s	William Langland begins *Piers Plowman* (the 'A-text')

Year	Life
c.1365–66	Marries Philippa Roet, eldest daughter of the Flemish knight Sir Paon de Roet, and sister of Katherine (later Katherine Swynford, mistress, then wife of John of Gaunt)
1366	Death of Chaucer's father; his mother shortly remarries. Philippa Chaucer mentioned as a 'domicelle' of Queen Philippa, wife of Edward III
1367	In service as an esquire in the household of Edward III; granted an annuity for life by the King
c.1367	Birth of a son, Thomas
late 1360s	Translates part of the *Roman de la Rose*; possibly also writing poetry in French at this time
1368–9	Writes the *Book of the Duchess* on the death of Blanche, Duchess of Lancaster
1368–70	Travels to the Continent on the King's business
1369	Serves in campaign of John of Gaunt in Northern France
c.1372–7	Writes the poems later adapted as the *Second Nun's Tale* and the *Monk's Tale*
1372	Philippa Chaucer in service in the household of John of Gaunt
1372–3	Travels to Genoa (to establish an English port for Genoese trade) and to Florence (to negotiate a loan for the King)
1374	Granted a pitcher of wine daily by the King and an annuity of £10 by John of Gaunt. Appointed Controller of Customs for hides, skins, and wools in the port of London; leases a house above Aldgate

Year	Literary and Historical Events
1367	January: birth of Richard of Bordeaux, later Richard II, second and only surviving son of Edward, the Black Prince (eldest son of Edward III) Battle of Najera, in which the Black Prince supports Pedro of Castile The King addresses Parliament in English for the first time
1368	September: death of Blanche, Duchess of Lancaster, first wife of John of Gaunt (third son of Edward III)
1369	Assassination of Pedro of Castile. Renewal of war with France August: death of Queen Philippa
1370	Sack of Limoges in the final campaign of the Black Prince
c.1370	Katherine Swynford becomes the mistress of John of Gaunt
1371	September: John of Gaunt marries Costanza (Constance) of Castile, daughter of Pedro
1374	Death of Petrarch
1375	Death of Boccaccio
1376	June: death of the Black Prince

Year	*Life*
1377–81	Various journeys to France and Flanders in connection with matters including peace negotiations between England and France and a proposed marriage between King Richard and a French princess
1378	Travels to Lombardy on diplomatic business with Bernabò Visconti, Lord of Milan. Richard II confirms Edward III's annuity of 20 marks; Edward's grant of a pitcher of wine daily is commuted to a second annuity of 20 marks
c.1378–81	Writes the *House of Fame*, *Anelida and Arcite*, the *Parliament of Fowls*, and *Palamon and Arcite* (later adapted as the *Knight's Tale*).
1380	Accused, and acquitted, of the *raptus* (probably more rape than abduction) of Cecily Champain
1381	Birth of a son, Lewis, who was ten when Chaucer wrote the *Treatise of the Astrolabe* for him. Death of Chaucer's mother, Agnes
c.1382–86	Writes *Troylus and Criseyde* and the *Legend of Good Women*, and translates Boethius's *De Consolatione Philosophiae*
1385–6	Serves as Justice of the Peace for Kent
1386	Elected Knight of the Shire for Kent; retires from Controllership of Customs and relinquishes lease on house in Aldgate
1387	Death of Chaucer's wife, Philippa
c.1387–1400	Writes the *Canterbury Tales*
1388	May: Chaucer's exchequer annuities transferred to John Scalby
1389	Appointed Clerk of the King's Works; responsibilities included construction at Westminster and the Tower of London
1390	Appointed Commissioner of Walls and Ditches, responsible for works on the Thames between Woolwich and Greenwich

Year	Literary and Historical Events
1377	June: death of Edward III; accession of Richard II, aged 10
1378	Beginning of the Great Schism: popes in Avignon and Rome. First record of mystery plays in York
late 1370s	Langland revising *Piers Plowman* (the 'B-text')
1381	May: marriage of Richard II to Anne of Bohemia June: the Peasants' Revolt
early 1380s	Langland revising *Piers Plowman* (the 'C-text')
early 1382	Arrival of Queen Anne in England
1382	Official condemnation of the heretical views of John Wycliffe
1385	Death of Joan of Kent, mother of Richard II
1386	Richard II suffers a loss of power
c.1386	John Gower begins his English poem, *Confessio Amantis*, which contains a passage in praise of Chaucer
1388	The Lords Apellant remove some of the King's closest advisers
1389	Richard II regains power

Year	*Life*
1391	Retires from Clerkship of the King's Works. Appointed Deputy Forester of the Royal Forest of North Petherton, Somerset (a post later held by his son, Thomas). Writes the *Treatise of the Astrolabe*
1393	Awarded £10 by the King for services rendered
1394	Granted an annuity of £20 for life by the King
1394–5	Revises the Prologue to the *Legend of Good Women*
1395	Chaucer's son Thomas marries the heiress Maud Burghersh
1397	Granted a tun (252 gallons) of wine yearly by the King
1399	Confirmation by Henry IV of Richard's grant, with an additional annuity of 40 marks. Leases a residence in the garden of the Lady Chapel of Westminster Abbey
1400	Death; burial in Westminster Abbey (remains subsequently moved to 'Poets' Corner')

Year   *Literary and Historical Events*

1394   June: death of Queen Anne

1396   John of Gaunt marries Katherine Swynford

1399   February: death of John of Gaunt
                  September: deposition of Richard II; accession of Henry IV

INTRODUCTION

Troylus and Criseyde is Chaucer's greatest and most complex poem, and remained the most popular and influential single work of his from the time of its writing (c. 1385–6) until the first part of the eighteenth century, when it was overtaken by certain of the *Canterbury Tales*. This shift owed something to the influence of Dryden, who in the Preface to his *Fables Ancient and Modern* (1700) dealt with the *Tales* as a whole at much greater length than *Troylus*, spoke of the *Knight's Tale* – also a translation from Boccaccio – as his favourite Chaucerian work, and included a modernized text of it in the *Fables*.

During the twentieth century however *Troylus*, while never quite supplanting the *Tales* in popular and critical esteem, has come into its own again, both as a constant source of pleasure to the reader, and as the object of a very wide range of critical approaches.[2] Some of these have been longer established than others: concern with the psychological depth and insight of the poem; the symmetry of its plan; its philosophical and theological aspects; the tangled relationships between the sixteen major texts of it that have survived, and the possibility that it may more than once have been revised by Chaucer; the unusual complexity of its language; the relationship of Chaucer to the Narrator of the poem; the ways in which the poet had reworked his principal sources in the first place. More recently, these concerns have been supplemented by other ways of reading it, most notably, perhaps, in terms of gender, and of sociological and historical context. But any general study, however brief, is bound to take some account of the relation of the poem to the medieval story of Troy in general, and of Troylus in particular, and this is where we shall begin.

Near the beginning and the end of his text, the Narrator makes it plain that his story of the love of Troylus and Criseyde is part of a much larger one that had chronicled the whole of the siege of Troy (I.141–7) and had also had much to say about the prowess of Troylus in battles fought in the course of it (V. 1765–71). But the chroniclers that he mentions – Dares and Dictys, the self-professed eye-witnesses of the Trojan war[3] – had in fact said nothing of the love of Troylus for Criseyde. That was left to Benoit de Ste Maure, who in the twelfth century worked the latter part of the lovers' story into his enormous *Roman de Troie* (RT). An abbreviated version of this was translated into Latin by Guido delle Colonne in the thirteenth century, but it was not until the following century that a version of the story was created that was both genuinely and generically new. This was *Il Filostrato* (F),[4] composed by Giovanni Boccaccio (c. 1335?), in which Benoit's long descriptions of battles and truces were reduced to a handful of small-scale allusions, and the story of the hero's separation from the heroine, and gradual loss of her love was preceded by a new and equally lengthy account of his winning and enjoyment of it. In a lengthy *Proemio*, Boccaccio claimed that he had deliberately chosen this particular story because of its relevance to his own situation as a lover who had to endure separation from his beloved. Few now take seriously the personal relevance asserted here: even so his attempts at passing off fiction as fact are hardly in the Dares and Dictys class.

When Chaucer took over the story some fifty years later, he kept the temporal limits of Boccaccio's poem, together with its heavy concentration upon the central love affair, and much of its detailed content. But he wrote at significantly greater length (8239 lines of verse to Boccaccio's 5704, plus a prose introduction), and in the process brought in a great deal of fresh incident and detail. Some clearly defined parts of this extra material were drawn from other notable authors: from Benoit himself, from Boethius, from Petrarch, but most of it seems to have been his own. His Narrator is of special interest to all of this, since he is at once a distinctive new creation, having much in common with the equally remarkable Pandarus, and a (none too reliable) guide to the use that Chaucer actually made of such earlier writers.

The Narrator is of course there from the very beginning, and quickly establishes his distance from his opposite number in Boccaccio by disclaiming any real experience of his own as a lover; instead he puts himself wholly at the service of other more deserving ones (I.15–21, 47–51). This deficiency goes with an uncritical enthusiasm in reacting to the consummation of the affair in the third book, and with the greatest respect for what he finds written about love in his 'authoritative' sources. His lack of moderation makes the reader cautious about accepting his own views as being necessarily those of Chaucer himself, although some of them quite certainly will be, and the line of demarcation is not always easy to draw.

We are better able to assess his accuracy when he is speaking of his source, and of his relation to it; here at least detailed comparisons are possible. One surprise for the modern reader is that he never mentions by name either of his principal sources, Boccaccio and Benoit. Instead, he twice cites a mysterious 'Lollyus'[5] as his 'auctor' (I.394, and V.1653); on the first of these occasions the context makes plain that the name is being used as an alias for Petrarch, on the second, for Boccaccio. What he has to say about Chaucer's handling of his composite source is less completely misleading, but while it contains some truth, it is still quite often inadequate.

In I.393–8 he maintains that he has kept not only the general sense ('sentence') of his original, but – after allowances have been made for the difference of language – every word in this as well;[6] in II.12–18, that everything in his own poem goes back to this source, without adulteration from his own emotional experience ('sentement'). But only a little further on he suggests that he has allowed himself a greater freedom of approach, when he admits that he may sometimes (considerably) abbreviate the text before him (II.1071, 1083, and 1219–20), or keep only the general drift of it, with occasional expansions of his own (III.1324–30). This last[7] is a massive understatement, since only a short time before we were given Chaucer's enormously varied expansion of Boccaccio's account of the lovers' first night together (TC III.741–1533; F III.24–52).

What the Narrator never hints at is the freedom with which Chaucer has moved stanzas, characters, and incidents that he found in *Filostrato* to an earlier point in *Troylus*. This of course implies that he had possessed an overall knowledge of Boccaccio's poem well before he began the writing of his own. The most straightforward example of the process is found in the Proem to the third book, where the exalted praise of love in III.1–38 that precedes the consummation of the affair is actually a close translation of a similar run of stanzas[8] found at a much

later point in *Filostrato* (III.74–9), where they are sung by the
hero after his first nights of love. They are unexpected in their
new position: not only do they dramatically interrupt the narrative flow, but their lofty assurance is far removed from the
Narrator's usual tone of worried humility at such points (though
this puts in a belated appearance at the end of the Proem).
When, at the other end of the book, Chaucer reaches the point
corresponding to *Filostrato* III.74, he provides his hero with a
new song (III.1744–71), as elevated in tone as the original, but
here entirely dependent on a passage from the *Consolation of
Philosophy* (CP) of Boethius (II, metrum 8), which he translated
during the same period that he was working on *Troylus*.

In other examples of transposition, parts of the original scene
may be kept at the same point in *Troylus*, and parts moved to
an earlier point in the story, where they are combined with quite
new material. In V.1234–41 the hero's dream of his lady
embracing a boar (Diomede) keeps much of the detail given at
the same point in *Filostrato* (VII.23–4), but says nothing about
the creature's rooting out of the lady's heart with his tusks, or
how this had seemed to please rather than distress her. But
something like the missing details appear in a much earlier
dream of Chaucer's own creation in II.925–31, in which Criseyde dreams of a white eagle that removes her own heart and
leaves its own in exchange, without giving her any fear or pain
at all.

Further on in the seventh part of *Filostrato* we have a much
longer passage that is again in part retained *in situ*, in part
moved back to Chaucer's second book. In this Troiolo, now in
despair that his lady will ever return to him, falls sick and is
visited by his brother Deiphebus, as well as by the ladies of the
royal house, one of whom (Cassandra), alarms and angers him
by revealing his love for Criseida (which he had thought a
secret), and disparaging her social status (VII.77–103). At the
same point in his own story, Chaucer keeps the hero's sickness
and the visit, and angry dismissal, of Cassandra (V.1436–540),
but makes the real point of the episode his sister's long-winded
interpretation of the dream of the boar; this ends with the
identification of the latter with Diomede (which Troiolo had
managed to work out for himself). The most notable absentees
from the scene are now Deiphebus and any other women of the
Trojan royal family besides Cassandra.

But some of these missing characters turn up in a quite new scene of a bedridden Troylus that straddles the second and third books of *Troylus* (II.1540–III.231); this, deliberately contrived by Pandarus, takes place at the house of Deiphebus as part of an elaborate plot to give Troylus and Criseyde their first chance of speaking together privately and at length. In the course of this elaborate scene the sympathetic concern for Criseyde that is only implied at the end of the Italian episode, is very firmly expressed; she is highly praised by both Deiphebus and Helen. Nor is Cassandra allowed in to upset such unanimous approval; the malevolent fairy is kept away from what is, metaphorically, the christening of the love affair.

It is worth noting that the example drawn from Chaucer's third book ascribes to him a power of 'invention' quite different from the other two. It implies, in fact, the usual medieval sense of the word ('the action of coming upon or finding' (OED 1)), whereas the second and third suggest the usual modern one ('the power of mental creation' (OED 4)). This combination of the two ways of expanding a source-text can be seen at all points in *Troylus* and contributes to its endless vitality and fascination.

The doublet statements created by these acts of transposition are wholly characteristic; the generally linear progress of the narrative is crisscrossed by a network of parallels which sometimes closely resemble, sometimes strongly contrast with each other. The two dreams are especially interesting from this last point of view, with the hoggish (presumably post-coital) slumbers of the boar, and the one-sidedness of Criseyde's show of affection standing in grotesque opposition to the elegant, quasi-surgical mastery of the eagle, and the precisely balanced exchange of hearts. And all these examples help to emphasise the symmetrical pattern of the hero's story.

The centre of this pattern is the third book, which is almost entirely enclosed by the closely-related Proem and Song noted above. Between these points Troylus achieves the summit of his happiness in this world, despite some fraught moments caused by the over-elaborate scheming of Pandarus (III.1051–92); the need for temporary separation from Criseyde (1520–33 and 1695–708); and covert warnings of what will happen in the fifth book, when the heroine laments the uncertainty of human happiness, and the misery that jealousy can cause (III.813–40,

1009–36). These become forgotten in the experience of the supreme excellence of love, which goes beyond the power of words to express it (1315–16, 1688–94). With so much achieved between them, the Proem and the Song can be seen, metaphorically, as the outer defences of the Trojan garden of love and friendship against all the hostile forces that would invade and destroy it.

The centrality of this third book to the meaning as well as the structure of Chaucer's poem is enhanced by the balanced relationship of those which surround it. From Troylus's point of view, the two that follow are the mirror images of the two preceding; his progressive optimism in the second book finds its reversal in the fourth; the despair into which he falls near the beginning of the first, its counterpart near the end of the fifth. And the symmetry inherent in this movement 'fro wo to wele and after out of joye' (I.4) is further enhanced by the fact that his despair is preceded in the first book and followed in the fifth by its complete antithesis. In I.183–273 we have the arrogance of a hero who deliberately sets himself above the amorous follies of other mortals; in V.1807–27, the flight of that hero's soul to a celestial vantage point from which it can both see and put into perspective the suffering left behind it on earth.

The course traced by the life of Troylus could also have suggested to a medieval reader that the hero was not just alternately unlucky and lucky in love, but that this story from the moment at which he falls in love until his death was controlled by a single large-scale revolution of the wheel of Fortune.[9] As the story progresses, the agency of this goddess becomes increasingly explicit, and by the time we reach Book Four, at the beginning of the end of the love-affair, her part in the action could not have been made more plain (see IV.8–11).

But the symmetrical pattern defined above is not the only one that can be discerned. An alternative one exists, as relevant to Criseyde as the first is to Troylus, and which, like the first, is thrown into relief by some striking doublets of character and incident. But this time, the common features link the beginnings of the first and fourth books, and involve, first, an action performed by (or at the instigation of) the heroine's father Calkas; second, her own extreme distress at the thought of what may follow; third, an attempt by Hector – a much more attractive father-figure – to set matters right (successful in

I.106–26, but not in IV.176–217). These introductory sections are followed by what are best termed narrative 'moves',[10] which – as far as the heroine is concerned – follow broadly the same course, but differ greatly in their length, in the character of the hero who affords her protection (III.479–80, V.1026–7), and in their long-term consequences for her reputation. For a time this Second Move is as unwanted and dispiriting to her as it is to Troylus, but from the point of view of the narrative – and, finally, from her own as well – it represents a fresh start. Like her father, she is able to adapt and survive, to escape from the fixed doom of Troy (and of Troylus as well).

The co-existence and overlapping of these two narrative patterns justifies the title (*liber Troili et Criseide*) that is given to it at the end of the Pierpont Morgan text. What should not be inferred from this title, however, is that Troylus and Criseyde are simultaneously present throughout the work; with rare and very limited exceptions they appear alternately rather than together throughout the whole of Books I, II, and V, and for nearly the first two thirds of Book IV. Only in the centre of the narrative do they share long and important scenes, and the two most weighty of these (III.953–1526 and IV.1128–687) generate between them yet another set of correspondences, by describing how emotional shock causes one of the lovers to fall into a state of suspended animation (to the great distress of the other), and how the heroine attempts, with variable success, to set the hero's mind at rest.[11]

The Troylus- and Criseyde-patterns also, to a limited extent, define the characters to which they are attached, with the closed and involuted symmetries of the first reflecting the stability, predictability, and ultimate frustrating of its hero; the openness and capacity for renewal of the second, the pragmatism and adaptability of its heroine. But both characters have a great deal more to them than this, and Criseyde is especially noteworthy for the way in which diverse aspects of her personality are brought into play by the company she keeps. This is most obvious when the two moves of her story are contrasted (she is a different person when she is Diomede's Criseyde from when she is Troylus's), but is hardly less so when she is with Troylus and when with Pandarus. With the first she is the pattern of a courtly mistress; by the end of the second book, indeed, she seems close to being made royal by association, since Deiphebus treats her as his friend, and Hector praises her in the highest terms (II.1452–4). Troylus, predictably goes still further, and in the best traditions of love-service, treats her not as his equal, but as his superior, and explicitly gives up his 'estat royal' to her in I.432–4 and becomes her vassal. For her part, she insists that his royal birth shall give him no more dominion over her in their relationship than is proper (III.169–75). The qualification is important, for in their next meeting, the consummation of their love sees them achieve a real balance as he gains confidence, and becomes dominant in his turn (III.1184–414). On the other hand, while her more exalted persona is never wholly effaced in her dealings with Pandarus – the urgency with which he pleads his friend's cause can be thwarted by her 'Daunger', or holding back (II.408–28) – she is very much more relaxed, expressing even her most serious feelings differently, and elsewhere well able to joke with and tease him (II.98–9, 113–19), or respond to his own familiarity in kind (II.1154–69).

Something of this variety comes over in the lengthy account given of her reactions to Pandarus's account of Troylus's love for her (II.701–812). But at other times we are deliberately left uncertain about such private thoughts (I.492–4; III.967–70). This uncertainty is most acutely felt in the fifth book, when she transfers her affections from Troylus to Diomede, and finds its most memorable expression in the Narrator's own puzzlement about her real feelings for her new love (V.1050). It is hardly surprising that a key (or bunch of keys) to her decline from grace should often have been looked for. One favoured explanation has always been the timidity ('she was the ferfulleste wyght' (II.450)) that made a protector of flesh and blood essential to her, and attention has more recently been drawn to the fact that this is hardly surprising in surroundings that, whether Trojan or Greek, are predominantly masculine. There is a war on, and even the Trojans can turn unpleasant when the successful conduct of it seems threatened (I.90–1, IV.183–96).

By contrast Troylus, although occupying a good deal of narrative space, and impressive as a warrior as well as a lover, is much less complex. Once he has abandoned his earlier persona as an arrogant scorner of love, he becomes very much what Pandarus had predicted: the convert who accepts without question the rules of his new religion (I.995–1008). Even in the progressively darker world of the final books, he continues to play by the rules; to give way to his mistress in all things, and – even when most sorely tried – to venture little or nothing in the way of reproach. Before he has positive proof of her infidelity, it is only in his reaction to the dream of the boar that we have violent and sustained criticism of his lady (V.1247–67), and this is again very muted in the letter that he subsequently writes to her (V.1345–51); Boccaccio's Troiolo had been much more outspoken at the same point (F VII.53–4, 58, 61).

Pandarus, on the other hand is obtrusively present and extremely various. As noted, he has important points in common with his niece, but even more perhaps with the Narrator, for all that he functions at the very heart of the love story, while the latter has, of necessity, to remain on the sidelines of it. And from here – and in the Proems in particular – his knowledge of the story as a whole allows him to anticipate what is yet to happen in it, whether at long (I.1–5, 53–6), medium (IV.8–21, 27–8) or short range (III.46–9). But both are fussy, verbose, hyperbolic and tortuous, and even their radical differences of function within the story can sometimes be eroded by the mimetic immediacy of the Narrator's manner; compare the accounts which he and Pandarus give of Criseyde's beauty in I.100–5 and 882–9. Here, as elsewhere he seems actually to be seeing the events that he describes, not retelling what he has found written about them in the best authorities. He claims to have no first-person experience of the joys of love (again like Pandarus, though not, in that case, for want of trying), but his third-person experience can seem almost embarrassingly immediate: like Pandarus again, in III.1135–41, he seems physically in the bedroom with the lovers. He is however more indulgent towards Criseyde once her infidelity has been proved beyond all doubt; compare his temporising in V.1086–92 and 1050 with Pandarus's rejection of his niece in V.1723–43.

The essential function of Pandarus, of course, is to be the agent of the plot that Boccaccio and Chaucer have devised between them, furthering it by advising, bullying, or reassuring the lovers, and carrying messages from one to the other. As such he raises the interesting problem of the dependence of character upon plot in romance fictions. From one point of view a character nearly as complex as Criseyde, Pandarus can from another seem so much the sum of his frenetic activity on the lovers' behalf, as to have little real existence outside it. Even though a lover himself, he is a very unsuccessful one, and allusions to this role are largely subordinated to his relation to the hero and heroine (I.621–37, II.54–77, 94–105).

But at the beginning of the fourth book the control of the plot shifts away from him, and back to Calkas (who, in the medieval sense of the word, had invented it through his prophetic gifts). All is now changed; tortuous and leisurely schemes of the kind that he had loved to contrive are put out of court by the near-immediacy of the exchange of Antenor for Criseyde. He can still arrange for the lovers to meet (IV.650–8), and instruct them how to behave with each other (IV.915–38), but beyond this can do no more than devise alternative scenarios of a fairly basic kind for coping with the new situation: that Troylus should find someone else to love (IV.400–27), or that he should abduct Criseyde by force before she passes over into the Greek camp (IV.526–39 and 582–630). But in this emergency the lovers themselves are as prone as he is to desperate off-the-cuff plotting, with each of them more conscious of the (very real) defects in the suggestions of others than of those in their own. Troylus of course rejects the first of Pandarus's suggestions out of hand, and will only agree to the second if Criseyde consents to it (IV.540–74, 631–7): he would prefer them to steal away together (IV.1499–526). But Criseyde has some very different scenarios of her own, all of which – like Pandarus's first suggestion – start from the acceptance of the coming exchange: for the moment, meaningful activity must give way to passive endurance (IV.1303–9, 1611–14). This marks the beginning of the kind of life that Troylus will be forced to lead in the final book.

Criseyde outlines her scenarios at some length (IV.1296–1414), and the more she says about them, the less convincing they become. Her bright optimism is so clearly misplaced that the Narrator feels it necessary to add a stanza asserting his belief in her good faith, as he had earlier done after Pandarus's outrageous suggestion that Troylus should love somebody else (IV.428–34). What she has to say provides a further example of how character may be created by the demands of plot, since these scenarios depend heavily on her ability to dupe her father, and in the process of outlining them, she recreates him in her own terms. From being the sinister and powerful figure of IV.113–26, who really has the ear of the gods, he becomes an old man, blinded by avarice, who is easily persuaded of their unreliability, or even non-existence, and made doubtful of his own ability to understand them (IV.1366–414). Troylus, no less than the Narrator, finds this new Calkas wholly unconvincing, and goes on to create another of his own who is a rabidly anti-Trojan matchmaker; he also voices the prophet's own certainty that the city will be destroyed (IV.1450–84).

He is not alone in doing this. Diomede too (who conforms exactly to Troylus's notion of a sexually predatory Greek), cites Calkas's prophecy of the coming doom of Troy as part of his second attempt at winning Criseyde's love, in a passage derived from *Filostrato* VI.15–18 (TC V.876–910). But what Chaucer did not find in Boccaccio's poem was his earlier attempt at courting Criseyde, when he led her to the Greek camp from Troy (TC V.85–189). In this scene nothing is said about the fate of Troy, but a great deal about the service of Love, and almost all of it is taken from *Roman de Troie* 13529–712, in which Diomede exhibits a degree of submissiveness and uncertainty that brings him unexpectedly close to Chaucer's Troylus. [12] This might seem wholly out of phase with the confident brutality shown in the later scene, but Chaucer brings the two into a single focus by ruthlessly cutting down Benoit's account, and setting at its head two stanzas that render Diomede's courtliness of diction premeditated and suspect. In consequence, he becomes a creation at once composite and complex. He is composite in being a somewhat downmarket synthesis of Troylus and Pandarus (a lover who makes his advances to the lady himself), and complex in being a most skilful fusion of his namesakes in Benoit and Boccaccio. Shakespeare was to be less successful in his attempt at fusing the two Ajaces into a single character in his own *Troilus and Cressida*. [13]

Chaucer's presentation of Criseyde is also modified by his use of Benoit in this fifth book, but this time the end-product is more impressionistic than clear-cut. In *Roman de Troie* her relationship to Diomede is dealt with in three clearly defined and widely separated passages, each set within a period of truce. The first comes after the seventh battle; the second, after the eighth battle; the third not until after the fifteenth battle. As a result, her decline into infidelity seems a relatively slow process, and indeed, from information given by Benoit, it has been calculated that it must have taken about two years.[14] No such exactness is possible in *Filostrato*, where the first of the above scenes is wholly absent, and the only battle described is the one in which Antenor is captured; the only truce, the one in which the return of Criseida is agreed (F IV.1–13 (=TC IV.29–147)). Chaucer however, after making use of the first of Benoit's three scenes in his V.85–189, later brings together detail from the second and third, which describe her gifts to Diomede and later sympathy for him when wounded (V.1037–50).[15] *Roman de Troie* 20229–340 also provided him with the five stanzas following, in which Criseyde laments her infidelity, predicts her notoriety to come, and determines at least to be faithful to Diomede and to think well of Troylus (V.1051–85). The Narrator then adds two stanzas of mildly sympathetic (but inconclusive) comment of his own.

These inserted passages are explicitly associated with history (Chaucer's 'story') not romance, but are set apart from the measured kind of history that Benoit had written by the accelerated tempo of the first, and the leaping far ahead in time of the third, before returning, in V.1100–6 to a mere nine days after Criseyde's departure from Troy in order to describe the hero's unrest. This jump forward in time undercuts any optimism about her return that the reader might otherwise have felt in the scenes that follow, while the compression of the 'historical' time-scale undermines the Narrator's claim that no 'auctor' tells us how long Criseyde took to be unfaithful to Troylus (V.1086–92): while we are actually reading the passage, her fall seems all too rapid.

If Diomede (deliberately) and Troylus (accidentally) repeat the prophecies of Calkas, and Criseyde briefly proves herself her father's own daughter by voicing a prophecy of her own, Cassandra, the one other character in Troylus who is traditionally a prophet proves something of a disappointment in that respect in V.1457–519. In *Roman de Troie* 10417–54 she had so upset her Trojan audience that they had had her imprisoned, but Boccaccio omits any such displays of her powers in the one scene in which she appears (F VII.84–102), and Chaucer, while alluding to her as 'Sibille' in V.1450, and having Troylus denounce her 'fals gost of prophesie' in V.1521, never allows her to voice any prophecies either. Her most important contribution to the story is to interpret the dream of the boar (which Troiolo had done for himself in F VII.27–8); her most substantial one, to read to the sick hero – a captive audience if there ever was one – a lecture on recent Classical history. And this proves surprising too, since unlike Calkas in IV.120–6 she is not here concerned with any past misdeeds of the Trojans that might explain their present misfortunes, but instead delves into the (only slightly earlier) history of the siege of Thebes, together with its own supernatural causes. But while this particular 'story' has little or nothing to do with the imminent downfall of Troy, it could not be more relevant to the downfall of Troylus. For not only does it serve to establish Diomede as the boar, but as it goes on generates an energy and sense of certainty – for this is assured history, not doubtful prophecy – that carries over into this identification, and especially into its astonishing final line: ' "This Diomede is inne and thow art oute" ' (V.1519).

From Diomede's point of view, however, it is Troylus who is in, but this time in prison with the rest of the Trojans, and destined never to get out alive (V.883–9). Imprisonment is not often mentioned in Troylus, and, in contrast to Antenor and his companions (IV.50–6), Troylus never once becomes a prisoner of the Greeks except hypothetically, as part of an oath (III.379–82). In this respect he contrasts sharply with Palamoun or Arcite, the lover-heroes of the Knight's Tale. Chaucer's rewriting of Boccaccio's Teseida.[16] Nor, at first glance, is there anything to match the juxtaposition of prison and garden (of love) that is so important in that tale.[17] In Troylus the juxtaposed and contrasted locations are those of the walled city of Troy and the plains outside it, on which the Greeks have pitched camp, and where the battles take place. But the words of Diomede suggest an even more startling relationship of garden to prison; essentially, one will become the other.

For by the third book Troy has become for the lovers a protectively walled Garden of Love in which their affair can develop in safety and at leisure; a further link with the best Romaunt of the Rose (RR) tradition is that the flight of Calkas has removed the one person described as having the kind of qualities inimical to love.[18] At the same time the extra-mural world of battle and siege offers a useful proving-ground for the hero's valour, and so reinforces his excellence as a lover within the walls. But once things begin to go seriously wrong for Troy and Troylus together, the walls serve to keep the Trojans in rather than the Greeks out, until such time as they are finally breached by the latter, and the city itself is turned into an (extermination) camp.

A different kind of prisoner and a different kind of imprisonment are evoked by IV.953–1078 which present in verse form part of the prose translation that Chaucer had made of the *Consolation of Philosophy*, (CP) written in the sixth century by Boethius after being imprisoned by the barbarian king Theodoric.[19] In the passage taken over, Troylus argues the case for and against supposing the loss of Criseyde to have been preordained by the God who had foreseen it. This breaks off before he gets to Boethius's resolution of the problem, and despairingly concludes that all that happens on earth comes 'by necessité' (IV.1050). But God's apparent foreseeing (which is really seeing) is not the only supernatural force held to restrict human freedom of action; another is presented, in appropriately pagan terms, at the very beginning of the fifth book, when it is said that Jove has entrusted the carrying out of his decrees to the three Fates, and even on a more hopeful occasion, earlier in the narrative, Troylus had remarked that these 'fatal sustren' had spun his destiny for him from his very earliest days (III.733–4).

This remark is very characteristic of *Troylus* as a whole, in that the supernatural forces to which allusion is made there are overwhelmingly pagan. Sometimes however there are some curious amalgams, as in III.1254–74, when the hero gives thanks for his enjoyment of Criseyde, with the help of a remarkable blending of pagan and Christian allusion.[20] This last could serve either to bring to mind the revelation that the Trojans inevitably lack, or to suggest that their own virtues may yet lead them to salvation. Both possibilities find support near the end of the poem: the first in the Narrator's ferocious dismissal of the pagan pantheon in V.1849–55; the second in the passage drawn from Boccaccio's *Teseida*, in which the hero, guided by one of these discredited gods,[21] attains to 'the pleyn felicité / That is yn hevene above' (V.1818–19).

This second passage is also remarkable in that it quite brilliantly provides an escape for Chaucer as well as for Troylus. Throughout most of the fifth book Chaucer had seemed as constrained by the forces of literary authority as his hero and heroine had been by the forces of historical necessity and supernatural control. However much he might have modified the plot and the characterisation in the first three books, he now seemed unable to make any significant alterations that were not in accordance with the new pessimistic drift of the narrative; the use of the *Roman de Troie* was of this kind. But here, at the very end of his hero's life, he achieves the seemingly impossible by moving out of the *Filostrato* to the *Teseida*, assigning to Troylus the heavenward flight of Arcita, that he found at the beginning of the eleventh book of the latter, and which he did not reproduce in the *Knight's Tale*. With a bound his hero is freed from what Theseus would term 'this foule prisoun of this lyf' (CT, A 3061), and Chaucer is freed with him. The end of the story has in fact been even more radically altered than the middle of it, to escape from those restraints, imposed by history and foreshadowed by prophecy, that had become progressively more dominant throughout this fifth book.

Something must finally be said about the style of the poem, which is extraordinarily varied in its range, and flexible in its pacing. Its variety has been explained in terms of the blending of two distinct literary and linguistic traditions: the one proper to fabliau, the other to courtly literature,[22] with the first most apparent in Pandarus, the second, in Troylus, and the two combined in Criseyde. But sudden changes of register may occur at any time, fostered to some extent by Chaucer's choice of the rhyme royal stanza as his medium. This, at once syntactically flexible within itself, and self-contained in relation to its immediate context, is almost equally adaptable to narrative and lyrical writing. In V.638–44 one of the hero's songs is contained within the limits of a single stanza; elsewhere, three stanzas are grouped to form more elaborate lyrics, whether these are explicitly designated as such (as in the Petrarchan *Canticus Troili* of I.400–20), or not (as in the extraordinary foreshadowing of Metaphysical poetry in the hero's dawn song ('alba') of III.1450–70). The very different poetic textures of these reflect the development of Troylus as a lover as well – prophetically and in very condensed form – as of the progress of English poetry in the sixteenth and seventeenth centuries.

A comparable diversity of style can be seen in some of the accounts given of the letters written by the lovers to each other. There are four major examples, which divide into two sharply contrasted pairs: II.1065–85 and II.1219–25, and V.1317–421 and V.1590–631. The first two, which are explicitly linked, are given in very summary form; the second two, which are not, are given in full, and this agrees with marked differences in the situation of the writer at the time. The early ones are written at a time of hope, things are on the move, there is no time to waste; furthermore, what is said in them is or can be supplemented by Pandarus, who brings them to their addressees. The later ones cannot be supplemented in this way, and so have to be free standing, and although both are largely formal, they are markedly different in style. That of Troylus is self-consciously correct, both muted and submissive; that of Criseyde begins in much the same register (its first stanza is in fact largely based on that of Troiolo's first letter to Criseida (F II.96)), but soon modulates into deviousness; it is perhaps the most disquieting item in the whole poem.

Most interesting of all is the presentation of the first letter written by the hero, since the voice that dominates here is not really his own at all, but an amalgam of those of Pandarus and the Narrator. Pandarus supplies the preliminary instructions and cautions, anticipating in the process Dr Johnson's critique of the alleged mismatch of style to content in some Metaphysical love poetry (II.1037–43). But on this score, at least, he need not have worried, for when the Narrator then takes over, it is clear that here, no less than in V.1317–421, the appropriate conventions are being observed, and at great length. But this time the length – together with the hero's self-abasement – is not conveyed by direct quotation, but by brief and throwaway comments (II.1067–8, 1071, 1083). These last fuse with the Narrator's précis of the letter itself to create an effect at once complex and comic, and a good deal more absorbing than the full text of the same letter supplied in *Filostrato* II.96–107.

References

1 It will often be helpful to consult the Text Summary on pp. 289–92.
2 See the Suggestions for Further Reading.
3 See the note to I.146.
4 The title signifies 'the man overcome and struck down by love'.
5 See the note to I.394.
6 As is possible in *Le Roman de Troilus et Cressida*, a prose transla-

tion of *Filostrato* by Pierre or Louis de Beauvau; a short excerpt (which corresponds to F II.1–25) is given in Rickard 1976: 89–92. It has been suggested that Chaucer made use of this version as a help to his own redaction of Boccaccio's poem, but the evidence is not conclusive: see Windeatt 1984: 19–24.

7 It takes up the first of a pair of stanzas placed before III.1324 in some manuscripts, before III.1415 in others.

8 While the two stanza-forms are not quite identical – the Italian is of eight lines, rhyming *ababababcc*; the English, of seven, rhyming *ababbcc* – they are sufficiently alike to have encouraged the translation of quite long runs of stanzas in *Filostrato* on a one-to-one basis, to produce new sequences of roughly equal length in *Troylus*. Compare, for example, *Troylus* I.421–546 and *Filostrato* I.38–57. The two stanza-runs can be studied in parallel in Windeatt 1984: 114–20; for a translation of the Italian stanzas, see Havely 1980: 28–30. It should be noted that the arabic numerals in all references to *Filostrato* indicate stanzas and not lines (as in TC).

9 See the notes to I.138–40 and 890–6.

10 V. Propp noted that when, in a Russian folk tale, 'an initial villainy is repeated, sometimes in the same forms as in the beginning, [this] new villainous act creates a new "move".' (*Morphology of the Folktale*, 1968: 58–9). A. C. Bradley had found something similar in Shakespeare's tragedies: 'the fourth and fifth [acts] repeat … the movement of the second and third, working towards the catastrophe as the second and third worked towards the crisis.' (*Shakespearean Tragedy*, 1905: 51–2).

11 See the note to III.1086–92.

12 He cannot be compared with Benoit's Troilus, since we are given no account of this hero's courtship of Briseida.

13 See Muir 1994:18.

14 See the note to V.1086–8.

15 See the notes to V.1037 and 1044–50.

16 See the notes to V.1–14, 1809.

17 See Kolve 1984:86–109.

18 See the note to IV.1368–9.

19 For an earlier use of Boethius by Criseyde see the note to III.813–33.

20 See the note to III.1254–67.

21 See the notes to V.321 and 1827.

22 See Muscatine 1960: 132–61.

NOTE ON THE TEXT AND ITS PRESENTATION

The text used is that of Pierpont Morgan Library MS M 817 (formerly Campsall), which contains only *Troylus*. It was copied near the very beginning of the fifteenth century, and bears the arms of the Prince of Wales (the future Henry V) on the recto of its first leaf. It is one of the two earliest texts to have survived; the other, which belongs to the same manuscript group, is Cambridge, Corpus Christi College MS 61, copied a few years earlier; this has supplied the illustration for the cover of the present edition. Although carefully written in a formal hand the Morgan text contains many minor slips of copying, which may affect both sense and metre, together with a handful of individual readings which do neither of these things. In the present edition such readings are kept wherever they make reasonable sense and are not metrically impossible. Words or letters essential to the sense or metre but missing from the MS copy are supplied between square brackets without further comment in the notes. Words or letters that damage the sense, metre, or rhyme are replaced, within square brackets, by variant readings (as before, these are mostly drawn from Corpus), and the MS readings noted at the foot of the page. Superfluous words or syllables in the MS are dropped from the text, but are also noted. Punctuation is modern, if sometimes rhetorical; MS þ is rendered by *th* throughout; consonantal *u* by *v*.

Of all Chaucer's works this poses the most difficulties both for the present day reader and for the editor who seeks to gloss it. Throughout the text most of the glosses of phrases or sentences are supplied at the foot of the page; these are especially full in respect of Troylus's complicated Boethian soliloquy in the fourth book. The majority of the glosses of single words are given, on their first appearance, in the margin; it should be remembered however that the semantic range of the medieval and modern words thus associated will quite often not be identical, and that the gloss supplied may represent no more than the best available compromise.

Chaucer's handling of verse is flexible and endlessly varied, and few authors gain more from being read aloud. However, radical changes in the sounds of English between the late fourteenth and the late twentieth centuries mean that, when given a contemporary pronunciation, his poetry may sound clumsy in both metre and rhyme. Fortunately, help of various kinds is available. H. Kökeritz's *A Guide to Chaucer's Pronunciation* (New York, 1962) is a useful general guide to the sounds of Chaucer's English, while the Chaucer Studio Recordings made over the past decade not only convey these sounds directly (and often dramatically), but the movement of the verse as well.

TROYLUS AND CRISEYDE

BOOK ONE

[*Incipit prohemium libri primi*]

The double sorwe of Troylus to tellen,   *relate*
That was the Kyng Priamus sone of Troye
(In lovynge how his aventures fellen
Fro wo to wele, and after out of joye)
5 My purpos is, er that I parte fro ye.
Thesiphone,* thow helpe me for t'endite   *compose*
These woful vers, that wepen as I write!

To the clepe I, thow goddesse of torment,   *invoke*
Thow cruel Furie, sorwyng evere yn peyne,
10 Help me that am the sorwful instrument
That helpeth lovers (as I kan) to pleyne.   *lament*
For wel sit it, the sothe forto seyne,
A woful wight to han a drery feere,   *have*
And to a sorwful tale, a sory cheere.   *countenance*

15 For I, that god of Loves servauntz serve,
Ne dar to Love, for myn unliklynesse,
Preyen for sped, al shold I therfor sterve:
So fer am [I] fro his help in derknesse.
But natheles, if this may don gladnesse   *give pleasure*

3–4 fortunes changed from sorrow to happiness, and later out of happiness. 12
For, to speak truly, it is very fitting for. 13 sorrowful person . . . gloomy
companion. 15 who am at the service of those who serve. 16–17 Dare not,
because of my inability to please, pray to Love for success, even if I were to die
as a result.

20 Unto ony lovere, and his cause avayle –   *advance*
    Have he my thank, and myn be his travayle.

    But ye loveres, that bathen in gladnesse,
    If ony drope of pité in yow be,*
    Remembre yow on passed hevynesse   *sadness*
25 That ye han felt, and on the adversité   *hardships*
    Of other fo[l]k, and thenketh how that ye
    Han felt that Love dorst yow displese –
    Or ye han wonne hym with to grete an ese.   *If not*

    And preyeth for hem that ben yn the cas   *them, are, situation*
30 Of Troylus, as ye may after here,
    That Love h[e]m brynge in hevene to solas;   *joy*
    And ek for me, preyeth to God so dere   *also*
    That I have myght to shewe in som manere
    Swych peyne and wo as Loves folk endure,
35 In Troylus unsely aventure.   *unhappy*

    And biddeth ek for hem that ben despeyred   *pray too*
    In love, that nevere nyl recovered be,*
    And ek for hem that falsely ben apeyred   *damaged*
    Thorough wykked tonges, be it he or she.   *malicious*
40 Thus biddeth God, for his benignité   *graciousness*
    So graunte hem soone out of this world to pace   *pass*
    That ben despeyred out of Loves grace.

    And biddeth ek for hem that ben at ese,
    That God hem graunte ay good perseveraunce,   *always*
45 And sende hem myght hire loves [so] to plese   *their*
    That it to Love be worship and plesaunce: *honour, delight*
    For so hope I my soule best avaunce,
    To preye for hem that Loves servauntz be,
    And write hire wo, and lyve in charité.

50 And forto have of hem compassioun,
    As though I were here owene brother dere.   *their*
    Now herkeneth with a good entencioun,   *? fair mindedly*
    For now wol I gon streyght to my matere,

21 May he receive the thanks due to me, and let me labour for him. 27 was bold enough to. 31 *hem*: *hym*. 36, 42 *despeyred*: *desespeyred*. 42 Who have cut themselves off from Love's grace by falling into despair. 45 *so*: *for*. 47 I believe it will most profit my soul. 53 move on directly to my story.

In whiche ye may the double sorwes here
55 Of Troylus, in lovyng of Criseyde,
And how that she forsok hym er she deyde.

[*Explicit prohemium primi libri*]

[*Incipit liber primus*]

Yt is wel wyst how that the Grekes stronge   *known*
In armes with a thousand shippes went
To Troyewardes, and the cité longe
60 Assegeden – neigh ten yer er thei stente;
And in diverse wyse and oon entente,
The raveshyng to wreken of Eleyne
By Parys don, thei wroughten al hire peyne.

Now fil it so that in the toun ther was   *it happened*
65 Dwellyng a lord of gret auctorité:
A gret devyn, that cleped was Calkas,   *prophet*
That in science so expert was that he
Knew wel that Troye sholde destroyed be   *must*
(By answere of his god that high[t] thus: *was called*
70 Daun Phebus or Appollo Delphebus).*   *Lord*

So whanne this Calkas knew by calkulynge,
And ek by answere of this Appollo,
That Grekes sholden swych a peple brynge   *host*
Thorugh which that Troye moste ben fordo,   *destroyed*
75 He caste anoon out of the town to go –   *decided*
For wel wyst he by sort that Troye sholde   *divination*
Destroyed ben – ye, wolde whoso nolde.

For which forto departen softely
Took purpos ful this forknowyng wyse,
80 And to the Grekes ost ful pryvely   *army, secretly*
He stal anoon; and they in curteys wyse   *stole*
Hym deden bothe worship and servyse,

---

60 Besieged ... left off. 61 different ways ... single end. 62 abduction ...
avenge. 63 did their utmost. 77 like it or not. 78-9 this far-sighted sage
determined to leave unobtrusively. 82-3 Treated him with great honour,
believing he was able to advise them; *bothe: bothen.*

In trust that he hath konnyng hem to rede
In every peril which that is to drede.   *be feared*

85 The noyse up ros whanne it was first aspied
Thorugh al the town, and generally was spoken   *by all*
That Calkas, traytour, fled was and allyed
With hem of Grece; and casten to ben wroken   *avenged*
On hym that falsly hadde his feith so broken,
90 And seyden he and al his kyn at on[e]s   *same time*
Ben worthi forto brennen, fel and bones.   *burn, skin*

Now hadde Calkas left in this meschaunce,   *misfortune*
Al unwist of this fals and wikked dede,
His douhter, which that was in gret penaunce,   *distress*
95 For of hire lyf she was ful sore in drede,   *her*
As she that nyst what was best to rede;
For bothe a wydowe was she and allone   *lacking*
Of ony frend to whom she dorst hire mone.

Criseyde was this lady name al right:
100 As to my dome, in al Troyes cyté   *judgment*
Nas noon so faire, forpassyng every wyght –
So angelyk was here natyf beauté   *her*
That lyk a thing inmortal semed she,
As doth an hevenysh parfit creature
105 That down were sent in scornyng of nature.   *to put to shame*

This lady, which that alday herd at ere   *perpetually*
Hire fadres shame, his falsnesse and tresoun,
Wel nygh out of here wit for sorwe and fere,   *Almost mad*
In widewes habit large of samyt broun,   *full, silk*
110 On knees she fil byforn Ector adoun;   *fell*
With pitous voys and tendrely wepynge,
His mercy bad, hereselve[n] excusynge.   *implored*

Now was this Ector pitous of nature,
And saw that she was sorwfully bigon,
115 And that she was so fair a creature;
Of his goodnesse he gladed here anoon,

---

85 rumour spread. 87 *traytour: traytour fals.* 90 *ones: onys.* 93 Quite
unaware. 96 a woman quite at a loss as to what was best to do. 98 dared
reveal her sorrow; *dorst: dorst make.* 101 surpassing every living creature. 114
in a wretched state. 116 goodness (of heart), he promptly comforted her.

And seyde, 'Lat youre fadres treson gon
Forth with mischaunce, and ye yourself in joye
Dwelleth with us, whil yow good lyst, in Troye.

120 'And al th'onour that men may don yow have,
As ferforth as youre fader dwelled here,   *fully*
Ye shul han, and youre body shal men save –   *respect*
As fer as I may ought enquere or here.'
And she hym thonked with ful humble chere,
125 And ofter wolde, and it hadde ben his wylle,   *if*
And took hire leve home and held hire stille.

And in hire hous she abod with swych meyné   *retinue*
As to hire honour nede was to holde;
And whil she dwelled yn that cyté
130 Kept here estat, and bothe of yong and olde   *position*
Ful well beloved, and wel men of here tolde –
But whether that she hadde children or noon,
I rede it nought, therfore I late it goon.   *dismiss it*

The thinges fellen as thei don of werre
135 Bitwixen hem of Troye and Grekes ofte,
For som day boughten they of Troye it derre   *more dearly*
And ofte the Grekes founde nothing softe   *not at all*
The folk of Troye; and thus Fortune* on lofte   *on high*
And wonder ofte, gan hem to w[h]eylen bothe   *very*
140 After hire cours, ay whil [that] thei were wrothe.

But how this toun com to destruccion
Ne falleth nought to purpos me to telle,
For it were a long digression
Fro my matere, and yow to longe to dwelle;
145 But the Troiane gestes as thei felle,   *exploits*
In Omer, or yn Dares, or in Dite,*
Whoso that kan may rede hem as thei write.   *is able*

But though that Grekes hem of Troye shetten,   *cooped up*
And hire cyté bisegede al aboute,   *around*

---

118 with a curse. 119 as long as pleases you. 125 would have gone on doing
so. 126 lived quietly. 128 her position made it necessary to maintain. 134
turned out as is usual in war. 139–40 turned them round and round, in
accordance with her custom, as long as they were at enmity. 142 Is no part of
my narrative intention. 144 subject . . . delay.

150 Hire olde usage wolde thei not letten,
    As forto honoure hire goddes ful devoute;
    But aldermost yn honour, out of doute,   *most of all*
    Thei hadde a relyk hight Palladion*   *named*
    That was hire tryst aboven everichon.

155 And so bifell, whan come was the tyme
    Of Aperil, whan clothed is the mede   *meadow*
    With newe grene of lusti ver the pryme,
    And swoot smellen floures white and rede: *sweetly*
    In sondry wyses shewed, as I rede,
160 The folk of Troye hire observaunces olde,
    Palladion[e]s feste forto holde.   *celebrate*

    And to the temple yn al here beste wyse,   *their*
    In general there went many a wight,   *Together*
    To herkenen of Palladion the servyse,
165 And namely, so many a lusti knyght,   *especially, lively*
    So many a lady fresch, and mayden bright,
    Ful wel arayed, bothe meene, meste and leste:
    Ye, bothe for the seson and the feste.   *festival*

    Among these othere folk was Criseyda,
170 In widewes habite blak – but natheles,   *for all that*
    Right as oure first lettre is now an A,*   *Just*
    In beauté first so stode she makeles.   *peerless*
    Hire goodly lokyng gladede al the prees: *cheered, crowd*
    Nas nevere yet thing seyn to ben presed derre,
175 Nor under cloud blak so bright a sterre,

    As was Criseyde, as folk seyde, everichone
    That here bihelden in here blake wede.   *dress*
    And yet she stod ful lowe and stille allone,   *humbly*
    Byhynden othere folk, in litel brede,   *space*
180 And neigh the dore, ay under shames drede,   *fear of*
    Symple of atyr and debonaire of chere,   *gracious, look*
    With ful assuryd lokyng and manere.   *composed*

---

150 Would not give up their ancient customs. 157 fresh green at the beginning
of the fruitful Spring. 159–60 In various ways the Trojans . . . performed their
traditional rites. 162 *here: here goodly.* 167 Splendidly dressed, whatever their
rank. 168 *and: and for.* 174 Nothing has ever been seen worthy of higher
praise.

This Troilus, as he was wont to gyde   *accustomed*
His yonge knyghtes, ladde hem up and doun
185 In thilke large temple on every syde,   *that same*
Byholdyng ay the ladyes of the toun –
Now here, now there, for no devocioun   *commitment*
Hadde he to noon, to reven hym his reste,   *deprive*
But gan to preyse and lakken whom hym leste.

190 And yn his walk ful fast he gan to wayten   *watch*
If knyght or squyer of his companie
Gan forto sike, or lete his eien b[a]yten   *sigh, eyes feast*
On ony woman that he koude aspye;
He wolde smyle and holden it folye,
195 And sey hym thus: 'God wot, she slepeth softe   *comfortably*
For love of the, whan thou tornest ofte.

'I have herd told, pardieux, of youre lyvynge,
Ye lovers, and youre [lewed] observaunces,   *foolish*
And [which a labour] folk han yn wynnynge
200 Of love, and yn the kepyng which doutaunces;
And whan youre prey is lost, woo and penaunces.   *suffering*
O verrey [fool]es, nyce and blynde be ye!   *real, stupid*
Ther nys not oon kan war by other be.'   *warned*

And with that word he gan cast up the browe,
205 Ascaunces: 'Lo, is this nought wysly spoken?'   *As if to say*
At which the god of Love gan loken rowe   *roughly*
Right for despit, and shop forto ben wroken,
And kyd anoon his bowe nas not broken: *soon showed*
F[or] sodeynly he hit hym at the fulle –   *squarely*
210 And yet as proud a pekok can he pulle.   *pluck*

O blynd world, O blynd entencion!   *purposes*
How ofte falleth al th'effect contraire
Of surquidrie and foul presumpcion;   *arrogance*
For caught is proud, and caught is debonaire.
215 This Troylus is clomben on the staire,   *has climbed*

---

183 *he*: he that. 189 find fault with whomever he pleased. 192 *bayten*: beyten.
199–200 what hard work it is to win love, and what fear there is in holding on
to it; *which a labour*: swych labour as. 202 *fooles*: loves. 206 *gan*: gan to. 207
In pure anger, and made up his mind to be avenged. 209 *For*: Ful. 212–13 is
exactly the opposite effect produced by; *surquidrie*: suriquidrie.

And litel weneth that he moste descenden –   *imagines*
But alday falleth thyng that foles ne wenden.   *don't expect*

As proude Bayard* gynneth forto skyppe   *prance*
Out of the wey, so priketh hym his corn,
220 Til he a lassh have of the long whippe,
Than thenketh he, 'Though I praunce al byforn,
First yn the trays, ful fat and newe shorn –
Yet am I but an hors, and horses lawe
I moot endure, and with my felawes drawe.'   *equals*

225 So ferd it by this fers and proud knyght –
Though he a worthi kynges sone were
And wende nothing hadde had swych myght   *power*
Ayens his wil that sholde his herte dere,   *do harm to*
Yet with a lok his hert wax afere,
230 That he that now was most in pride above   *recently*
Wax sodeynly most subget unto love.*

Forthi ensample taketh of this man,   *And so*
Ye wyse, proude, and worthi folkes alle,
To scornen Love, which that so soone kan
235 The fredom of youre hertes to hym thralle;   *enslave*
For evere it was, and evere it shal bifalle,
That Love is he that alle thing may bynde –   *fetter*
For may no man fordo the lawe of Kynde.   *subvert, Nature*

That this be soth hath preve[d] and doth yet,
240 For this trowe I ye knowen alle or some:
Men reden not that folk han gretter wit   *intelligence*
Than thei that han be most with love y-nome,   *conquered*
And strengest folk ben therwith overcome,
The worthiest and grettest yn degre: *status*
245 This was, and is, and yet men shal it se.

And trewelych it sit wel to be so,
For alderwisest han therwith ben plesed,   *wisest of all*
And thei that han ben a[l]dermost in wo
With love han ben comforted most and esed;
250 And ofte it hath the cruel herte apesed,

219 way he should go, as his full belly prompts him. 221 *thenketh: thenketht.*
222 At the head (of the team). 229 after a (single) glance . . . took fire. 239
preved: preves. 246 is very right that it should. 248 *aldermost: addermost.*

And worthi folk maad worthier of name,   *reputation*
And causen most to dreden vice and shame.

Now sith it may not goodly be withstonde,   *reasonably*
And is a thyng so vertuous yn kynde,   *innately powerful*
255 Refuseth not to Love forto be bonde,
Syn as hymselven lyste he may yow bynde.
The yerde is bet that bowen wole and wynde   *bough, bend*
Than that that brest, and therfor I yow rede   *counsel*
To folwen hym that so wel kan yow lede.   *guide*

260 But forto tellen forth yn special
[As] of this kynges sone of which I tolde,
And letten other thing collateral,
Of hym thenk I my tale forto holde,   *intend, continue*
Bothe of his joyes and of his cares colde,   *bitter sorrows*
265 And al his werk, as touchyng this matere,
For I it gan, I wil therto refere.   *began, return*

Withinne the temple he went hym forth pleynge,   *making sport*
This Troylus, [of] every wyght aboute;   *around*
On this lady, and now on that, lokynge,
270 Whereso she were of towne or of withoute;   *Whether*
And upon cas bifel that thorugh a route   *crowd*
His eye p[er]cede, and so depe it wente
Til on Criseyde it smot, and there it stente.   *rested*

And sodeynly he wax therwith astoned,
275 And [gan] hire bet biholde yn thrifty wyse.   *carefully*
'O mercy God,' thoughte he, 'where hastow woned,
That art so fair and goodly to devyse?'   *describe*
Therwith his hert gan to sprede and ryse,   *open, grow*
And softe sighed lest men myghte hym here,
280 And caught ayen his firste pleynge chere.

She nas not with the leste of here stature,
But alle here lymes so wel answerynge   *conforming*
Weren to womanhode, that creature

---

262 abandon other subordinate topics. 268 *of*: *and*. 270 Whether she came from the city or from outside it. 271 it happened by chance. 272 *percede*: *procede*. 276 been keeping yourself? 278 *Therwith*: *And therwith*. 280 assumed again his earlier mocking tone. 281 was not one of the least tall of women.

Was nevere lasse mannyssh in semynge;
285 And ek the pure wyse of here me[v]ynge
Shewed wel that men myght yn here gesse   *clearly, suppose*
Honour, estat, and wommanly noblesse.   *(high) rank*

To Troylus right wonder wel withalle   *indeed*
Gan forto lyke here me[v]ynge and here chere,   *expression*
290 Which somdel deynous was, for she leet falle   *scornful*
Here look a lite aside in swych manere   *slightly*
Ascaunces: 'What, may I not stonden here?'
And after that here lokynge gan she lyghte,   *looked down*
That nevere thought hym seen so fair a sighte.

295 And of here look yn hym there gan to quyken   *kindle*
So gret desire and such affeccioun,
That in his hertes botme gan to stiken
Of here his fixe and depe impressioun;
And though he erst hadde poured up and doun,   *stared*
300 He was tho glad his hornes yn to shrynke –
Unnethes wyst he how to loke or wynke!   *Scarcely*

Lo, he that leet hymselven so konnynge,   *considered*
And scorned hem that Loves peynes dryen,   *endure*
Was ful unwar that Love hadde his dwellynge
305 Withinne the subtile stremes of here eyen;
That sodeynly hym thoughte that he sholde dyen
Right with hire look the spirit yn [his] herte: *vital force*
Blyssyd be Love that kan thus folk converte!

She, this in blak, lykynge to Troylus   *delightful*
310 Over al thyng, he stood [for]to byholde;
Ne his desir, ne whe[r]for he stod thus,
He neither chere ne made, ne word tolde;
But from afer, his maner forto holde,   *keep up*
On other thing his look somtyme he caste,
315 And eft on here, while that the servise laste.   *again*

And after this, not fullyche al awhaped,
Out of the temple al esilyche he wente,   *nonchalantly*
Repentynge hym that he hadde evere y-japed   *made fun*

---

284 less masculine in appearance. 285 very way in which she bore herself;
mevynge: menynge (also 289). 301 whether to keep his eyes open or shut. 312
explained by word or look. 316 completely cast down.

Of Loves folk, lest fully the descente
320 Of scorn fille on hymself – but what he mente,
L[e]st it were wyst on any maner side,
His wo he gan dissimulen and hide.

Whan he was fro the temple thus departed,
He streyght anoon unto his paleys turneth,
325 Right with here look thurgh-shoten and thurgh-darted –
Al feyneth he yn lust that he sojorneth;
And al his speche and cher also he borneth,   *controls*
And ay of Loves servantz every while,
Hymself to wre, at hem he gan to smyle,   *cover*

330 And seyde, 'Lord, so ye lyve al yn l[e]st,   *how pleasantly*
Ye loveres, for the konnyngest of yow,
That serveth most ententiflych and best,   *sincerely*
Hym tyt as often harm therof as prow;   *befalls, profit*
Youre hire is quyt ayeyn, ye, God wot how!   *wages, repaid*
335 Nought wel for wel, but scorn for good service –
In feith, youre ordre is ruled in good wyse!

I[n] noun-certeyn ben alle youre observaunces,
But it a sely fewe poyntes be;   *trivial*
Ne nothing asketh so grete attendaunces
340 As doth youre lay, and that knowe alle ye.
But that is not the worste, as mot I the!   *may thrive*
But tolde I yow the worste poynt, I leve,   *am sure*
Al seyde I soth, ye wolden at me greve.

'But tak this: that ye loveres ofte eschuwe,   *avoid*
345 Or elles don of good entencioun,   *. intent*
Ful ofte thi lady wole it mysconstrue,
And deme it harm yn hire opinyoun;   *consider*
And yet yf she for other enchesoun   *reason*
Be wroth, than shalt thou han a groyn anoon;   *complaint*
350 Lord, wel is hym that may be of yow oon!'   *fortunate*

---

321 For fear it were known anywhere; *Lest: Lyst.* 325 pierced and transfixed.
326 Even if he pretends to be cheerful. 329 *he: her.* 330 *lest: lyst.* 336
(religious) order is a well-regulated one! 337 No fixed rule governs your rites.
339–40 No religion demands such constant devotion as yours. 343 Even if . . .
reproach.

But for al this, whanne he say his tyme,   *saw, chance*
He held his pes – noon other bote hym gayned;
For love bygan his fetheres so to lyme,   *clog*
That wel unnethe unto his folk he feyned
355 That other besye nedes hym destrayned;
For wo was hym, that what to done he nyste,   *didn't know*
But bad his folk to gon wher that h[e]m lyste.   *they pleased*

And whan that he yn chaumbre was allone,
He down upon his beddes feet hym sette,
360 And first he gan to syke and [eft] to grone,   *sigh*
And thoughte ay on here so withouten lette,   *unceasingly*
That as he sat and wok, his spirit mette   *awake, dreamed*
That he here saw a-temple, and al the wyse
Right of hire lok, and gan it newe avyse.   *took note of*

365 Thus gan he make a myrrour of his mynde,
In which he saugh al holly hire figure;
And that he wel koude yn his herte fynde,   *that which*
It was to hym a right good aventure   *fortune*
To love swych on, and yf he dede his cure   *a one, best*
370 To serven here, yet myght he falle in grace,
Or elles for on of hire servantz pace;

Ymagynynge that travaylle nor grame   *labour, pain*
Ne myghte for so goodly on be lorn
As she, ne hym for his desir no shame,
375 Al were it wist, but yn prys and up born
Of alle lovers wel more than byforn:
Thus argumented he yn his gynnynge,
Ful unavysed of his wo comynge.   *unaware*

Thus toke he purpos loves craft to suwe,   *determined, follow*
380 And thoughte he wolde werken prevely,   *covertly*
First to hide his desir yn muwe   *keep penned up*
From every wyght y-born, al outrely,   *absolutely*
But he myght ought recovered be therby;
Remembryng hym that love to wyde y-blowe   *broadcast*
385 Yelt bittre fruyt, though swete [seed] be sowe.   *Yields*

---

352 there was no other remedy. 354 with great difficulty. 355 he was troubled by other urgent concerns. 357 *hem*: *hym*. 361 *lette: ony lette*. 371 be accepted as. 375–6 esteemed and exalted above. 377 at the beginning of his love. 383 be at all relieved.

And over all this, yet muche more he thoughte   *beyond*
[What forto] speken and what to holden inne;   *keep back*
And what to arten hire to love he soughte,   *urge on*
And on a song anoon right to bygynne,
390 And gan loude on his sorwe forto wynne –   *overcome*
For with good hope he gan fully assente   *consent*
Criseyde forto love, and nought repente.

And of his song nought only the sentence,   *sentiments*
As writ my[n] auctour called Lollyus,*
395 But pleynly, save oure tonge[s] deference,
I dar wel sayn in al that Troylus
Seyde yn his song, lo, every word right thus
As I shal seyn; and who[so] lyst it h[e]re,
Lo, nexst this vers he may it fynden here.

[Canticus Troili]*

400 'If [no] love is, O God, what fele I so?
And if love is, what thyng and wh[ich] is he?
If love be good, from whens cometh my wo?
If it be wykke, a wonder thenketh me,
Whenne every torment and adversité
405 That cometh of hym may me so goodly thynke: *seem*
For ay thurst I, the more that I it drynke.

'And yf that at myn owene lust I brenne,   *will, burn*
Fro whennes cometh my waylyng and my pleynte?
If harm agree me, wherto pleyne I th[e]nne?   *pleases, complain*
410 I not; ne whi unweri that I feynte.
O quyke deth! O swete harm so queynte!   *living, strange*
How may of [the] yn me swich quantité
But if that I consente that it so be?

'And if that I consente, I wrongfully
415 Compleyne, iwys; thus possed to and fro,   *indeed, tossed*
Al sterles withinne a bot am I
Amyd the see, bytw[ix]en wyndes two

---

387 *What forto: For what to.* 395 in full detail, as far as the difference of
languages will allow. 398 wishes to hear it; *here: to hire.* 401 *which: what.* 409
thenne. thanne. 410 I do not know; nor why when not tired. 416 without a rudder.

That yn contrarye stonden evere mo.   *perpetually*
Allas, what is this wonder maladye?
420 For hete of cold, for cold of hete, I dye.'*

And to the god of Love thus seyde he
With pitous voys: 'O lord, now youres is
My spirit, which that ought youre[s] be.
Yow thank I, lord, than han me brought to this:
425 But whether goddesse or womman, iwys,
She be, I not, which that ye do me serve;   *compel me to*
But as here man I wole ay leve and sterve.   *die*

'Ye stonden yn hire eyen myghtily,   *are set*
As yn a place unto youre vertu digne;
430 Wherfore, my lord, if my servyse or I
May lyke yow, so beth to me benygne;   *please, favourable*
For myn esta[t] royal here I resigne
Into hire hond, and with ful humble chere
Bycome here man, as to my lady dere.'   *vassal*

435 In hym ne deynede sparen blood royal   *condescended*
The fyr of love – the wherfro God me bl[e]sse! –
Ne hym forbar in no degre, for al   *spared*
His vertu or his excellent prowesse,
But h[e]ld hym as his thral lowe yn distresse,
440 And brend hym so in sondry wyse ay newe,
That sixty tyme a day he loste his hewe.   *colour*

So muche, day by day, his owene thought
For lust to here gan quyken and encres[s]e,   *kindle*
That every other charge he sette at nought;   *duty*
445 Forthi ful ofte his hote fyr to cesse,
To seen here goodly look he gan to pres[s]e,
For therby to ben esed wel he wende –   *comforted*
And ay the ner he was, the more he brende!   *closer*

For ay the ner the fyr, the hotter is –
450 This, trowe I, knoweth al this companye;   *I am sure*
But were he fer or neer, I dar seye this,
By nyght or day, for wysdom or folye,

420 *dye: deye.* 429 worthy of your power. 432 *estat: estal.* 436 from which
may God protect me; *blesse: blysse.* 439 *held: hold.* 440 so consumed him in
many, always different, ways.

His hert, which that is his brestes eye,
Was ay on hire that faire[r] was to sene   *always (fixed)*
455 Than evere was Eleyne or Polixene.*

Ek of the day ther passed nought an houre
That to hymself a thousand tymes he seyde,
'Good goodly, to whom serve I and laboure
As I best kan, now wolde God, Criseyde,
460 Ye wolden on me rewe er that I deyde.   *take pity*
My dere herte, allas, myn hele and hewe   *health, complexion*
And lyf is lost but ye wole on me rewe.'

Alle othere dredes weren from hym fled,   *fears*
Bothe of the assege and his salvacioun;
465 Ne yn hym desir noon othere fownes bredde
But argumentz to this conclusioun:
That she on hym wolde han compassioun,
And he t[o] be here man whil he may dure –   *survive*
Lo, here his lyf, and from the deth his cure.

470 The shoures sharpe f[e]lle of armes preve,
That Ector and hise othere bretheren diden,   *performed*
Ne made hym oonly therfore ones meve;*
And yet was he wherso men wente or riden,
Founde oon the best, and lengest tyme abyden   *most enduring*
475 Ther peril was, and dide ek such travayl   *so laboured*
In armes, that to thenke it was mervayle.

But for non hate he to the Grekes hadde,
Ne also for the rescous of the town,   *help, city*
Ne made hym thus yn armes forto madde,   *to fight madly*
480 But oonly, lo, for this conclusioun: *purpose*
To lyken hire the bet for his renoun.   *please, better*
Fro day to day yn armes so he spedde,   *was so successful*
That the Grekes as the deth hym dredde.   *? plague*

And fro this forth tho refte hym love his sleep,
485 And made his mete his foo, and ek his sorwe
Gan multeplie, that [w]hoso took keep,   *increase, note*
It shewed in his hewe bothe even and morwe.   *night, morning*

---

454 *fairer*: fairest. 458 Most excellent (lady). 460 *deyde*: deyede. 463 *dredes*: dredres. 464 his (personal) safety. 465 produced any other offspring. 468 *to*: te. 470 deadly attacks, the test of prowess; *felle*: fille. 472 Not once drew him (to fight). 484 this time on, love took away. 485 his food repugnant to him.

The[r]for a title he gan hym forto borwe
Of other syknesse, lest of hym men wende   *guessed*
490 That the hote fyr of love hym brende,

And seyde he hadde a fever and ferd amys –   *felt unwell*
But how it was, certayn, kan I not seye,
If that his lady understod not this,
Or feyned here she nyste – oon of the tweye;   *didn't know, two*
495 But wel I rede that by no maner weye
Ne semed it [as] that she of hym roughte,   *cared about*
Nor of his peyne, or whatsoevere he thoughte.

But thanne felt this Troylus such wo,
That he was wel nei[g]h wood, for ay his drede   *mad*
500 Was this: that she som wyght hadde loved so   *(other) man*
That nevere of hym she wolde have taken hede.
For [whi]ch hym thought he felt his herte blede,
Ne of his wo ne dorst he not bygynne
To tellen it, for al this world to wynne.

505 But whanne he hadde a space fro his care,   *respite*
Thus to hymself ful ofte he gan to pleyne:
He seyde, 'O fool, now art thow yn the snare,
That whilom japedest at loves peyne;   *made jokes*
Now artow hent, now gnaw thin owene cheyne!   *imprisoned*
510 Thow were ay wont eche lovere reprehende   *reproach*
Of thing fro which thow kanst the nought defende.   *yourself*

'What wole now every lovere seyn of the,   *say about*
If this be wist, but evere yn thyn absence   *known*
Laughen yn skorn, and seyn, "Lo, there gooth he
515 That is the man of so gret sapience,   *wisdom*
That held us loveres lest yn reverence.
Now, thonked be God, he may goon in the daunce   *company*
Of hem that Love lyst febely forto avaunce."

'But O thow woful Troylus, God wolde,
520 Syn thow most l[o]ve thurgh thy destené,
That thow beset were on swych oon that sholde
Knowe al thi wo, al lakkede here pité;

488–9 alleged a different kind of illness. 502 *which*: such. 504 if it would have
gained him the whole of. 513 constantly behind your back. 518 it pleases Love
to help very little. 520 *love*: leve. 521 had set your heart on such a lady.

But also cold yn love towardes the   *as*
Thi lady is as frost yn wynter mone,
525 And thow fordon as snow yn fyr is soone.   *destroyed*

'God wolde I were aryved in the port   *landed*
Of deth, to which my sorwe wil me lede!
A, Lord, to me it were [a] gret comfort –
Then were I quyt of langwysshyng yn drede!   *free from*
530 For, b[e] myn h[idde] sorwe i-blowe on brede,
I shal byjaped ben a thousand tyme   *made fun of*
More than that fol of whos folye men ryme.   *make verses*

'But now help, God, and ye, swete for whom
I pleyne, i-caught, ye, nevere wyght so faste!   *firmly*
535 O mercy, dere herte, and help me from
The deth, for I, whil that my lyf wole laste,
More than myself wole love yow to my laste;
And with som frendly look gladeth me, swete,
Though nevere more thyng ye me byhete.'

540 This[e] wordes and ful manye an other to,   *as well*
He spak, and called evere yn his compleynte
Hire name, forto tellen hire his woo,
Til neigh that he in salte teres dreynte.   *drowned*
Al was for nought – she herd nought his pleynte;   *complaint*
545 And whan that he bithought on that folye,
A thousand fold his wo gan multeplie.

Bywaylyng yn his chambre thus allone,
A frend of his that called was Pandare*
Com onys yn unwar and herd hym grone,   *unexpectedly*
550 And sey his frend yn swych distresse and care.
'Allas,' quod he, 'who causeth al this fare?   *behaviour*
O mercy God, what unhap may this meene?   *misfortune*
Han now thus soone Grekes maad yow lene?

'Or hastow [som] remors of conscience,
555 And art now fallen yn som devocioun,   *act of piety*
And waylest for thi synne and thyn offence,

---

530 became common knowledge; *be myn hidde: by myn hed.* 534 *ye: yet.* 539
you never promise me any greater favour. 545 realized how foolish that was.
547 While he was lamenting. 553 made you lose weight.

And hast for ferd caught attricioun?
God save hem that byseged han oure toun,
That so kan leye oure jolyté on presse,
560 And bryng oure lusty folk to holynesse!'   *spirited*

(These wordes seyde he for the nones alle,
That with swych thing he myghte hym angry maken,
And with an angre don his wo [to] falle,
As for the tyme, and his corage awaken;
565 But wel he wiste, as fer as tonges spaken,
Ther nas a man of grettere hardinesse   *bravery*
Thanne he, ne more desirede worthinesse.)*   *honour*

'What cas,' quod Troylus, 'or what aventure   *fortune, chance*
Hath gided the to se my langwysshynge,
570 That am refus of every creature?   *rejected by*
But for the love of God, at my preyinge,   *request*
Go hens away, for certes my deyinge   *death*
Wol the disese, and I mot nedes deye:
Therfor go wey; ther is no more to seye.

575 'But if thou wene I be thus sike for drede,
It is not so, and therfor scorne nought;
Ther is another thing I take of hede
Wel more than ought the Grekes han [yet] wrought,   *achieved*
Which cause is of my deth for sorwe and thought.   *anxiety*
580 But though that I now telle [it the] ne lest,   *don't wish*
Be thow nought wroth – I hide it for the beste.'

This Pandare, that neigh malt for sorwe and routhe,   *dissolved*
Ful often seyde, 'Allas, what may this be?
Now, frend,' quod he, 'yf evere love or trouthe   *loyalty*
585 Hath ben, or is, bytwyxen the and me,
Ne do thou nevere such a cruelté
To hide fro thi frend so gret a care:
Wostow nought wel that it am I, Pandare?   *Don't you know*

'I wole parten with the al thyn peyne   *share*
590 (If it be so I do the no comfort)   *Even if*

557 through your fear become contrite? 559 have succeeded in putting away
our cheerfulness. 561 only with the purpose. 563 cause his grief to lessen. 564
rouse his spirits. 573 upset, and I am bound to die; *disese: dishese.* 580 *it the:*
the it. 581 *Be: Ne be.*

As it is frendes right, soth forto seyne,
To entreparten wo as glad desport.   *share, joy*
I have and shal, for trewe or fals report,
In wrong and right i-loved the al my lyve:
595 Hyd not thi wo fro me, but telle it blyve.'   *promptly*

Than gan this Troylus sorwfully to syke,
And seyde hym thus: 'God leve it be my beste
To telle it the; for sith it may the lyke,   *since*
Yet wole I telle it thowh myn herte breste
600 (But wel wot I thow mayst don me no reste);   *give, relief*
But lest thow deme I trust not to the,
Now herke, frend, for thus it stant with me.

'Love, ayens the which whoso defendeth
Hymselven most, hym alderlest avayleth,
605 With desespeir so sorwfully me offendeth
That streyght unto the deth myn herte [s]ayleth;   *directly*
Therto desir so brennyn[g]ly me assaylleth,
That to ben slayn it were a grettere joye
To me than kyng of Grece ben and Troye.

610 'Suffiseth this, my fulle frend Pandare,   *complete*
That I have seyd, for now wostow my wo;
And for the love of God, my cold care
So hyd it wel – I telle it nevere to mo;   *any others*
For harmes myghte folwen mo than two   *misfortunes*
615 If it were wyst; but be thou in gladnesse,
And lat me sterve, unknowe, of my distresse.'   *die*

'How hastow thus unkyndely and longe   *unfeelingly*
Hid this fro me, thow fool?' quod Pandarus;
'Paraunter thow myght after swych on longe
620 That myn avys anoon may helpen us.'   *speedily*
'This were a wonder thyng,' quod Troylus: *marvel*
'Thow koudest nevere yn love thynselven wysse –   *guide*
How devel maystow bryngen me to blysse?'

'Ye, Troilus, now herke,' quod Pandare,
625 'Though I be nyce, it happeth ofte so   *ignorant*

602 this is how things are with me. 604 it profits him least of all. 606 *sayleth*:
ffayleth. 607 In addition . . . so fiercely attacks me. 619–20 Perhaps the woman
you desire is one which my advice.

That on that excesse doth ful yvele fare,
By good counseyl kan kepe his frend therfro.   *guard, against it*
I have myself ek seyn a blynd man go   *moreover*
Theras he fel that koude loke wyde:
630 A fool may ek ofte a wys man gide.

'A whetston is no kervyng instrument,   *cutting*
But yet it maketh sharpe kervyng tolys;
And there thow wost that I have ou[gh]t myswent,   *gone wrong*
Eschewe thou that, for swych thyng to the scole is;
635 Thus ofte wyse men ben war by folys!
If thou do so, thi wit is wel bywared –   *employed*
By [his] contrarie is every thing declared.

'For how myght evere swetnesse have be knowe
To hym that nevere tasted bitternesse?
640 Ne no man may be inly glad, I trowe,   *deeply happy*
That nevere was yn sorwe or som distresse;
Ek whit by blak, by shame ek worthinesse,   *Likewise*
Eche set by other, more for other semeth,
As men may se, and so the wyse it demeth.   *judge*

645 'Sith thus of two contraries is [o] lore,
I, that have in love so ofte assayed   *endured*
Grevaunces, oughte konne (and wel the more)   *Hardships*
Counsayllen the of that thow art amayed.   *dismayed*
Ek the ne oughte not ben yvel apayed   *displeased*
650 Thow[h] I desire with the forto bere
Thyn hevy charge – it shal the lasse dere.   *burden, harm*

'I wot wel [that] it fareth thus by me
As to thi brother, Parys, an hierdesse   *shepherdess*
Which that i-cleped was Oenone,*   *named*
655 Wrot yn a compleynt of hire hevynesse;   *sorrow*
Ye say the lettre that she wrot, I gesse?'   *saw*
'Nay, nevere yet, ywis,' quod Troylus.
'No[w],' quod Pandare, 'herkene – it was thus:

---

626 lack of moderation brings to misfortune. 629 who was able to see all
round him. 634 Avoid ... a lesson to you. 637 Everything is defined by its
opposite; *his: eche.* 643 appears more (intense) on account of the other. 645 a
single lesson proceeds from two opposites; *o: a.* 652 that things stand with me.

    ' "Phebus, that first fond art of medecyne,"   *Apollo, invented*
660 Quod she, "and koude yn every wyghtes care
    Remede and red by erbes he knew fyne:
    Yet to hymself his konnynge was ful bare,   *skill, lacking*
    For love hadde hym so bounde yn a snare,
    Al for the doughter of the kyng Amete,
665 That al his craft ne koude his sorwe bete."   *alleviate*

    'Ryght so fare I, unhappily for me:
    I love oone best, and that me smerteth sore,   *torments*
    And yet paraunter kan I rede the,
    And not myself – repreve me no more!   *reproach*
670 I have no cause, I wot wel, forto soore   *exalt (myself)*
    As doth an hauk that lysteth forto pleye;
    But to thyn help yet somwhat kan I seye.

    'And of o thyng right siker maystow be: *quite certain*
    That certayn, forto deye yn the peyne,   *under torture*
675 That I shal nevere more discoveren the;   *betray*
    Ne, by my trouthe, I kepe not restreyne   *don't wish to*
    The fro thi love, they that it were Eleyne*   *even if*
    That is thi brotheres wyf, if ich it wyste:
    Be what she be, and love hire as the liste!   *pleases you*

680 'Therfore, as frend, fullych yn me assure,   *trust, completely*
    And telle me plat what is thyn enchesoun   *straight, reason*
    And final cause of wo that ye endure;
    For douteth no thyn[g], myn entenciown
    Nys nought to yow of reprehencioun
685 To speke as now, for no wygh[t] may bireve   *prevent*
    A man to love tyl that hym lyst to leve.

    'And weteth wel that bothe two ben vices: *know*
    Mystrusten alle, or elles alle leve;   *believe*
    But wel wot I, the meene of it no vice is,   *middle course*
690 For to trusten sum wight is a preve   *proof*
    Of trouthe; and forthi wolde I fayn remeve   *take away*

---

661 Cure and help through subtle herbs known to him; *he: she.* 665 *koude: koude al.* 679 Whoever she may be. 680 *as: as a.* 682 *final: finally.* 683–5 Don't be at all afraid that I want to reproach you, at this present time. 686 he (himself) is ready to give up.

Thy wrong conceyte, and do the som wyght tryste
Thi wo to telle, and telle me, yf thow lyste.

'Thise wyse seyth, "Wo hym that is allone,
695 For, and he falle, he hath noon helpe to ryse";   *if*
And sith thou hast a felawe, tel thi moone!
For this nys not, yn certeyn, the nexst wyse   *quickest way*
To wynnen love, as techen us the wyse,
To walwe and wepe as Niobe the queene,*
700 Whos terys yet yn marbel ben y-seene.   *visible*

'Lat be thi wepyng and thi drerynesse,   *gloom*
And lat us lyssen wo with other speche;   *alleviate*
So may this woful tyme seme lesse –
Delite not in wo thi wo to seche,   *seek*
705 As don these foles that hire sorwes eche   *increase*
With sorwe when they han mysaventure,   *misfortune*
And lysten nought to sechen other cure.   *take no trouble*

'Men seyn, "To wrecche is consolacioun   *one in misery*
To have another felawe yn his peyne";
710 That ought wel ben oure opynyoun,
For bothe thow and I of love we pleyne!
So ful of sorwe am I, soth forto seyne,
That certaynly no more harde grace   *further misfortune*
May sitte on me, forwhi ther is no space.   *come upon, room*

715 'If God wole, thou art not agast of me,   *afraid*
Lest I wold of thi lady the bygyle;
Thow wost thiself whom that I love, pardé,
As I best kan, gon sithen longe while;
And sithe thow wost I do it for no wyle,   *guile*
720 And sithen I am he thou tristest most,
Tel me sumwhat, syn al my wo thow wost.'

Yet Troylus for al this no word seyde,
But longe he lay stylle as he ded were;
And after this with sikynge he abreyde,   *sighing, recovered*
725 And to Pandarus voys he lente his eere,
And up his eyen caste he, that in feere

---

692 Your mistaken idea, and make you. 696 a close friend, tell (him) what is
wrong! 704 *to: forto.* 716 lure away from you. 718 for a very long time now.
720 *he: he in whom.*

Was Pandarus lest that yn frenesye
He sholde falle, or elles soone dye;

And cride, 'Awake!' ful wonderly and sharpe;
730 'What, slombrestow as yn a lytargie?   *coma*
Or artow lyk an asse to the harpe,
That hereth soun whan men the strenges plye,   *manipulate*
But yn his mynde of that no melodye
May synk yn hym to glade, for that he
735 So dul is of his bestialité?'   *animal nature*

And with that Pandare of his wordes stente,   *stopped talking*
And Troylus yet hym no word answerde,
Forwhy to telle na[s] not his entente   *Because*
To nevere [no] man, for whom that he so ferde;
740 For it is seyd, 'Man maketh ofte a yerde   *rod*
With which the makere is hymself [y-]beten
In sondry maneres' – as this[e] wyse treten;   *maintain*

And namely yn his counseyl-tellyng   *especially*
That toucheth love, that ought be secre,
745 For of hymself it wol [ynough out] sprynge
But yf that it the bet governed be;   *better repressed*
Ek som tyme it is a craft to seme fle
Fro thyng which yn effect men hunte faste –
Al this gan Troylus yn his herte caste.   *consider*

750 But natheles, whan he had herd hym crye
'Awake', he gan to syke wonder sore,
And seyde, 'Frend, though that I stille lye,   *motionless*
I am not def – now pes, and cry no more!
For I have herd thi wordes and thi lore;   *instructions*
755 But suffre me my myschef to bywayle,   *harm*
For thi proverbes may me nought avayle.   *help*

'Nor other cure canstow noon for me;
Ek I nyl not be cured; I wol deye.
What knowe I of the queene Niobe?
760 Lat be thyne olde ensamples, I the preye!'

737 *answerde: answerede.* 738 *nas: nat.* 739 on whose account he suffered.
745 (soon) enough come to light; *wol ynough out: wolde not ought.* 747–8
skilful to appear to run away from what is actually being pursued. 760 No
more of your moth-eaten exemplary tales.

'No,' quod tho Pandarus, 'therfore I seye
Such is delit of foles to bywepe
Here wo, but seken bote thei ne kepe.

'Now knowe I that reson yn the fayleth;   *is enfeebled*
765 But telle me, yf I wyst what she were
For whom that the al this mysaunter ayleth: *afflicts*
Dorstestow that I telle in hire eere
Thi wo, sith thow darst not thiself, for feere,
And hire bysought on the to han som routhe?'   *implored*
770 'Why, nay,' quod he, 'by God and bi my trouthe!'

'What, not as bisily,' quod Pandarus,   *earnestly*
'As though myn owen lyf lay on this nede?'
'No, certes, brother,' quod this Troylus.
'And why?' – 'For that thow sholdest nevere spede.'   *succeed*
775 'Wostow that wel?' – 'Ye, that is out of drede,'
Quod Troylus, 'For al that evere ye konne:
She nyl to no swych wrecche [as I] be wonne.'

Quod Pandarus, 'Allas, what may this be,
That thow despered art thus causeles?   *unnecessarily*
780 What, lyveth not thi lady, bendicité?
How wostow so that thow art graceles?   *without favour*
Such yvel is not alwey boteles.   *hopeless*
Why, put not impossible thus thi cure,
Syn thyng to come is oft yn aventure.   *uncertain*

785 'I graunte wel that thow endurest wo
As sharp as doth he, Ticius, yn helle,
Whos stomak foughles tiren everemo,   *birds tear*
That highte volturis, as bokes telle.   *are named vultures*
But I may not endure that thow dwelle   *remain*
790 In so unskilful an opynyoun   *unreasonable*
That of thi wo is no curacioun.   *remedy*

'But ones nyltow, for thi coward herte,
And for thyn ire and folessh wilfulnesse,   *perversity*
For wantrust, tellen of thi sorwes smerte,   *distrust*
795 Ne to thyn owen help do bysynesse,   *concern yourself*

---

762 take pleasure in tearfully lamenting. 763 they are not concerned to find a
remedy. 777 *nyl: nyl not.* 779 *despered: desespered.* 786 *he: the.* 792 Not
once will you.

As m[u]che as speke a resoun more or l[e]sse,   *sentence*
But ly[est] as he that lest of nothyng recche –
What womman wolde love such a wrecche?

'What may she deme[n] other of thi deth,
800 If thou thus deye and she not whi it is,
But that for fere is yolden up thi breth,
For Grekes han byseged us, ywys?
Lord, which a thonk then shaltow han of this!   *what gratitude*
Thus wol she seyn, and al the toun atones,   *together*
805 "The wrecche is ded, the devel have his bones!"

'Thow mayst allone here wepe and crie and knele –
But love a woman that she wot it nought,
And she wole quyte [it] that thou shalt not fele: *repay*
Unknowe, unkyst, and lost, that is unsought.
810 What! many a man hath love ful dere y-bought
Twenty wynter that his lady wyste,
That nevere yet his lady mouth [he] kyste.

'What, shulde he therfore fallen in despeyr,
Or be recreaunte for his owene tene,
815 Or slen hymself, al be his lady feyr?   *even if*
Nay, nay, but evere yn oon be fressh and grene   *constantly*
To serven and love his dere hertes queene,
And thenk it is a guerdoun hire to serve,   *reward*
A thowsand fold more than he kan deserve.'

820 [And] of that word toke hede Troylus,
And thought anoon what folye he was inne;
And how that hym soth seyde Pandarus,
That forto slen hymself myght he not wynne,   *profit himself*
But bothe doon unmanhod and [a] synne,
825 And of his deth his lady nought to wyte: *blame*
For of his wo, God [woot, she] knoweth ful lyte.   *nothing*

And with that thought he gan ful sore syke,
And seyde, 'Allas, what is me best to do?'

796 *muche*: *meche*; *lesse*: *lasse*. 797 cares for nothing; *lyest*: *lyk*. 799 How else
can she interpret. 801 you have given up the ghost out of fear. 809 what is not
asked for. 811–2 Who knew his lady for twenty years without ever kissing; *he*:
yet. 814 a coward, to his own harm. 824 commit an action that was both
cowardly and sinful.

To whom Pandare answered, 'Yf the lyke,   *it suits you*
830 The best is that thow telle me al thi wo;
And have my trowthe, but thow it fynde so   *unless*
I be thi bote or that it be ful longe,   *healer, before*
To pieces do me drawe and sithen honge.'   *afterwards*

'Ye, so thow seyst,' quod Troylus tho, 'allas!
835 But God wot, it is not the rather so;
Ful hard were it to helpen yn this cas,   *situation*
For wel fynde I that Fortune is my fo;
Ne alle the men that riden konne or go   *walk*
May of here cruel whiel the harm withstonde,   *stand against*
840 For as here lyst she pleyeth with free and bonde.'

Quod Pandarus, 'Than blamestow Fortune
For thow art wroth, [ye], now at erst I se!   *first*
Wostow not wel that Fortune ys commune
To every maner wight yn som degree?
845 And yet thow hast this comfort, lo, pardé,
That as here joyes moten overgone,   *must pass away*
So mote hire sorwes passen everychone.

'For yf here whiel stynte any thyng to torne,   *ever stopped*
Thanne cessede she Fortune anoon to be.
850 Now, sith here whiel by no wey may sojourne,   *rest*
What wostow [i]f hire mutabilité   *changeableness*
Right as thiselven lyst wol don by the,
Or that she be not fer fro thyn he[l]pynge?
Paraunter thow hast cause forto synge.

855 'And therfore wostow wha[t] I the beseche?
Lat be thi wo and turnyng to the grounde;   *fainting*
For whoso lyst have helyng of his leche,   *doctor*
To hym byhoveth first unwre his wounde.   *uncover*
To Cerberus yn helle ay be I bounde:
860 Were it for my suster, al thi sorwe,
By my wil she sholde al be thyn tomorwe!

835 never the more so for that. 840 sports with freeman and slave. 843–4
every one experiences Fortune to some extent. 851 *if: of.* 852 Will bring about
exactly what you wish for yourself. 854 Perhaps you have reason to rejoice.
855 *what: whan,* 857 *helyng: helpyng.*

'Loke up, I seye, and telle me what she is,   *who*
Anoon that I may goon aboute thin nede.
Knowe ich here ought? For my love, telle me this;
865 Thenne wolde I hopen the rathere forto spede.'   *sooner*
Tho gan the veyne of Troylus to blede,
Fo[r] he was hit and wax al red for shame.   *blushed*
'Aha,' quod Pandare, 'here bygynneth game.'   *sport*

And with that word he gan hym forto shake,
870 And seyde, 'Thef, thow shalt here name telle.'   *Villain*
And tho gan sely Troylus forto quake,   *poor*
As though men sholde han lad hym [in]to helle,
And seyde, 'Allas, of al my wo the welle,   *source*
Than is my swete fo called Criseyde.'
875 And wel neygh with the word for fere he deyde.   *very nearly*

And whan that Pandare herd here name nevene,   *her named*
Lord, he was glad! and seyde, 'Frend so dere,
Now fare aright, for Joves name yn hevene,   *prosper well*
Love hath beset the wel; be of good chere,   *situated*
880 For of good name and wysdom and manere   *reputation*
She hath ynough, and ek of gentilesse –   *noble nature*
If she be fayr, thow wost thiself, I gesse.

'Ne nevere saw [I] a more bounteuous
Of here estat, ne a gladder, ne of speche   *rank*
885 A frendlioure, n[e] a more gracious
Forto do wel, ne lasse hadde nede to seche   *act*
What forto doon; and al this bet to eche,
In honoure, to as fer as she may strecche,
A kynges herte semeth by hires a wrecche.

[890 'And forthi loke of good comfort thow be;
For certeinly, the ferste poynt is this   *essential*
Of noble corage and wel ordeyne,   *heart, regulated*
A man to have pees with hymself, ywis;
So oghtist thow, for nought but good it is
895 To love wel, and in a worthy place;
The oughte not to clepe it hap but grace.]*

---

871 *gan: bigan.* 872 *hym: hymm.* 886–7 to take thought how to behave; and
to make all this still better. 888 In respect of honour, to the full extent of her
powers. 892–3 a noble-hearted and well conditioned man. 896 ought not to
call it (good) fortune.

'And also thenk, and therwith glade the,
That sith thy lady vertuous is al,   *wholly*
So folweth it that there is som pité
900 Amonges alle these othere in general;
And forthy se that thow yn special   *therefore*
Requere not that is ayen hire name,   *contrary to*
For vertue streccheth not hymself to shame.

'But wel is me that evere I was born,
905 That thou biset art yn so good a place;
For b[y] my trouthe, yn love I dorst have sworn
The sholde nevere [h]a[n] tyd so fayr a grace;   *befallen*
And wostow whi? For thow were woned to chace   *used, persecute*
At Love yn scorn, and for despit hym calle   *in scorn*
910 "Seynt Idyot, lord of these foles alle"!

'How ofte hastow mad thi nyce japes,   *foolish jests*
And seyd that Loves servantz everychone
Of nyceté ben verray Goddes apes;
And some wol[d]e mucche here mete allone,   *munch, food*
915 Lyggyng abedde, and [make] hem forto grone;
And som, thow seydest, hadde a blaunche fevere,   *white*
And preyedest God he sholde nevere kevere.   *recover*

'And som of hem toke on hem for the colde
More than ynough, so seydestow ful ofte;
920 And som han feyned ofte tyme, and tolde
How that they wake whan thei slepen softe;   *stayed awake*
And thus thei wolden han brought hemself alofte,
And natheles were under at the laste –
Thus seidestow, and japedest ful faste.

925 'Ye, seidestow [that], for the more part,
These loveres wolden speke in general,   *general terms*
And thought [that] it was a siker art
For faylyng, forto assay[e]n overal.
Now may I jape of the if that I shal;   *I felt like it*
930 But natheles, though that I sholde deye,
That thow art none of tho, that dorst I saye.

900 her other (virtues) together; 900, 901 **transposed**. 906 *by: be*. 913 In
their folly were truly God's jesters. 918 put on, against the chill. 922 have
exalted themselves. 923 finally cast down. 927–8 a sure guard against failure
to try everywhere.

'Now beet thi brest and seye to god of Love:
"Thi grace, lord, for now I me repente
If I mysspak, for now, myself, I love" –   *blasphemed*
935 Thus sey with al thyn hert yn good entente.'*   *sincerely*
Quod Troilus, 'A, lord, I me consente,
And pray to the my japes thow foryeve,
And I shal nevere more whil I leve.'   *live*

'Thow seyst wel,' quod Pandar[e], 'and now I hope
940 That thow the goddes wrath the hast al apesed;   *completely*
And sithen that thow hast wopen many a drope,   *since, wept*
And seyd swych thyng wherwith thi god is plesed,
Now wolde nevere God but thow were esed;   *given relief*
And thynk wel, she of whom rist al thi wo   *comes*
945 Hereafter may thi comfort be also.

'For thilke ground that bereth the wedys wykke
Bereth eke these holsome herbes a[s] ful ofte;
Next the foule netle, rough and thikke,
The rose waxeth swote and smothe and softe;   *grows (up)*
950 And nexst the valey is the hil alofte,   *closest to*
And nexst the derk nyght the glade morwe;
And also joye is nexst after sorwe.

'Now loke that atempré be thy brydel,   *controlled*
And for the beste ay suffre to the tyde –
955 Or elles alle oure labour is on ydel: *in vain*
He hasteth wel that wysly kan abyde.   *endure*
Be diligent and trewe, and ay wel hide;
Be lusty, fre, persevere yn thyn servyce,   *lively, gracious*
And al is wel – if thou werk yn this wyse.

960 'But he that parted is yn every place
Is nowher hool, as writen clerkes wyse.   *has no integrity*
What wonder is that such on have no grace?   *a person*
Ek wostow how it fareth on som service –
As plaunte a tre or herbe yn sondry wyse,   *diversely*
965 And on the morwe pulle it up as blyve!   *at once*
No wonder is thow[h] it mowe nevere thrive.*

---

938 never (offend) again as long as I live. 939 *Pandare: Pandarus.* 946 the
same soil that produces. 947 *as: al.* 954 always be patient until the time (is
ripe). 957 always conceal (your feelings). 960 divides (his affections) everywhere; *parted: departed.* 963 And you know how some men love.

'And sith that god of Love hath the bystowed
In place digne un[to] thi worthynesse –   *fitting to*
Stond fast, for to good port hastow rowed;
970 And of thyself, for any hevynesse,   *in spite of*
Hope alwey wel; for but if drerynesse   *despondency*
Or overhaste oure bothe labour shende,
I hope of this to make a good ende.

'And wostow whi I am the lasse afered   *less afraid*
975 Of this matere with my nece trete?
For this have I herd seyd of wyse y-lered: *learned men*
"Was nevere man ne woman yet bygete
That was unapt to suffren loves hete,
Celestial, or elles love of kynde" –
980 Forthi som grace I hope yn here [to] fynde.

'And forto speke of here in special,
Hire beauté to bythynke and hire youthe:
It sit hire nought to be celestial
A[s] yet, though that hire lyste bothe and kouthe;
985 But trewly, it sat here wel right nowthe   *at this time*
A worthy knyght to love and cherice –
And but she do, I holde it for a vice.

'Wherfore I am and wole be ay redy
To peyne me to do yow this servyse;   *try my hardest*
990 For bothe yow to plese thus hope I
Herafterward, for ye beth bothe wyse,   *discreet*
And konne it counseyl kepe yn such a wyse   *secret*
That no man shal of it the wiser be;
And so we may be gladed alle thre.

995 'For, b[y] my trowthe, I have right now of the
A good conceyt yn my wit, as I gesse,   *opinion*
And what [i]t is, I wol now that thow se:
I thenke, sith that Love of his goodnesse
Hath the converted out of wikkednesse,
1000 That thow shalt be the best post, I leve,   *support, believe*
Of al his lay, and most hise foos to greve.   *religion*

972 ruin all our efforts. 978–9 exempt from enduring the fire of love, whether
heavenly or in the way of nature. 982 Taking into account her. 983 is not
fitting for her. 984 she both wished for and was capable of (such love); *As*:
And. 995 *by*: *be*. 997 *it*: *that*.

'Ensample whi: se ye these wyse clerkes,
That erren aldermost ayen the lawe,
And ben converted from hire wykkede werkes,
1005 Thorugh grace of God that lyst hem to hym drawe,   *bring (back)*
Than arn thei folk that han most God yn awe,   *hold, in fear*
And strengest feythed ben, I understonde,
And konne an errour alderbest withstonde.'   *best of all*

Whanne Troylus had herd Pandare assentyd
1010 To ben his help yn lovyng of Criseyde,
Wex of his wo, as who seyth, untormentid,   *Became*
But hotter weex his love, and thus he seyde
With sobre chere, although his herte pleyde: *rejoiced*
'Now blysful Venus help, er that I sterve,   *die*
1015 Of the, Pandare, I may som thank deserve.

'But, dere frend, how shal myn wo ben lesse
Til this be don? And, good, eke telle me thisse:
How wyltow seyn of me and my destresse,   *speak*
Lest she be wroth (this drede I most, iwysse),
1020 Or nyl not heren or trowen how it ysse?   *things are*
Al this drede I, and ek for the manere   *convention*
Of the, here em, she nyl no swych thyng here.'

Quod Pandarus, 'Thou hast a ful grete care
Lest that the cherl wole falle out of the mone!
1025 Whi, Lord! I hate of the thi nyce fare.   *folly*
Whi, entremete of that thow hast to done!
For Goddes love, I bydde the a bone,
So lat me allone, and it shal be thi beste.'   *best for you*
'Whi, frend,' quod he, 'now do ri[g]ht as the leste.

1030 'But herke, Pandare, o word, for I nolde   *would not*
That thow in me wendest so gret folye,
That to my lady I desiren sholde
That toucheth harm or ony vilenye;   *dishonour*
For dredles me were levere dye
1035 Than she of me ought elles understode
But that that myght sownen ynto gode.'   *tend to*

1002 As a parallel case. 1003 most of all against religion. 1007 firmest in their
faith. 1008 able to combat heresy. 1022 She will not listen to such matters
from you who are her uncle. 1026 concern yourself with. 1029 *right: ritht.*
1031 think me so mad. 1034 assuredly, I would rather.

Tho lough this Pandare, and anoon answerde,   *Then laughed*
'And I thi borw? Fy, no wyght doth but so;
I rought nought though that she stode and herde
1040 How that thow seyst; but farewel, I wole go.
Adieu! Be glad! God spede us bothe two!
Yeve me this labour and this besynesse,   *task*
And of my sped be thyn al that swetnesse.'   *success*

[Tho] Troylus gan doun on knees to falle,
1045 And Pandare yn his armes hent faste,   *embraced*
And seyde, 'Now fy on the Grekes alle!
Yet, pardé, God shal helpe us at the laste;
And, dredles, yf that my lyf may laste,
And God toforn, lo, som of hem shal smerte –   *before*
1050 And yet me ofthynketh that this avaunt me asterte.

'Now, Pandare, I kan no more seye,
But thow wys, thow wost, thow mayst, thow art al!
My lyf, my deth, hool yn thyn hond I leye: *wholly*
Help now!' Quod he, 'Yis, b[y] my trouthe I shal.'
1055 'God yelde the, frend, and this yn special.'   *repay*
Quod Troylus, 'that thou me recomaunde   *commend*
To here that to the deth me may comaunde.'

This Pandarus, tho desirous to serve   *at that*
His fulle frend, thenne seyde yn this manere: *complete*
1060 'Farewel, and thenk I wole thi thank deserve,
Have here my trouthe, and that thou shalt wel here.'
And went his wey, thenkyng on this matere,
And how he [best] myght here beseche of grace,   *favour*
And fynde a tyme therto, and a place.

1065 For every wyght that hath an hows to founde
Ne renneth nought the werk forto bygynne   *hastens*
With rakel hond, but he wol byde a stounde,   *rash, time*
And send his hertes lyne out fro withinne
Alderfirst his purpos forto wynne: *accomplish*
1070 Al this Pandare yn his herte thoughte,
And caste his werk ful wysly or he wroughte.

1037 *answerde: answerede.* 1038 When I am your surety? 1039 I wouldn't care. 1044 *Tho: But; on: on his.* 1050 I am sorry that this boast escaped me. 1052 you have wisdom, knowledge, power. 1054 *by: be.* 1068 *lyne: lyue.* 1071 planned . . . before he set to work.

But Troilus lay tho no lengere down,
But up anoon upon his stede bay,   *at once*
And yn the feld he pleyde th[e] lyoun:
1075 Wo was that Grek that with hym mette that day!
And yn the town his manere tho forth ay
So goodly was, and gat hym so yn grace,   *gracious*
That eche hym lovede that loked on his face.

For he bycome the frendlyeste wyght,
1080 The gentileste, and ek the most fre,   *noblest, generous*
The thriftieste, and oon the beste knyght   *most admirable*
That yn his tyme was or myghte be;
Dede were his japes and his cruelté,   *Gone*
His heigh port, and his manere estraunge –
1085 And ech of tho gan for a vertu chaunge.*

Now late us stynte of Troylus a stounde,   *for now*
That fareth lyk a man that hurt is sore,
And is somdel of akynge of his wounde   *to some extent*
I-lyssed wel, but heled no del more,   *Relieved*
1090 And as an esy pacient the lore   *comfortable, skill*
Abit of hym that goth aboute his cure;   *Abides by*
And thus he drieth forth his aventure.

E[x]plicit liber Primus

1074 *the*: tho. 1076 behaviour from then on. 1077 gained such favour for
himself. 1084 lofty bearing and distant manner. 1086 stop (talking about).
1089 none the more. 1092 endures his fate.

BOOK TWO

[*Incipit prohemium secundi libri*]

Owt of these blake wawes forto sayle,
O wynd, O wynd, the weder gynneth clere:
For yn this see the bot hath swych travaylle,   *difficulty*
Of my co[nn]ynge that unnethe I it stere.
5 This see clepe I the tempestous matere   *call*
Of des[es]per that Troylus was inne –
But now of hope the kalendes bygynne.   *first day*

O lady myn, that called art Cleo,*
Thow be my sped fro this forth, and my muse,   *help*
10 To ryme wel this book til I have do;   *finished*
Me nedeth here noon [other] art to use.
Forwhi to every lovere I me excuse,
That of no sentement I this endite,
But out of Latyn in my tunge it write.

15 Wherfore I nel have neyther thank ne blame
Of al this werk, but pray yow mekely,
Disblameth me yf ony word be lame,   *Exonerate, awkward*
For as myn auctour seyde, so sey I.
Ek though I speke of love unfelyngly,   *insensitively*
20 No wonder is, for it no thyng of newe is:
A blynd man ne kan juggen wel yn hewys.   *colours*

Incipit prohemium secundi libri: Hic Incipit liber Secundus. 2 clear away the
clouds. 4 By my (unaided) skill I can hardly control it; *connynge: comynge.* 13
I am not composing this out of (my own) experience of love.

Ye knowe ek that in forme of speche is chaunge
Withinne a thousand yer, and wordes tho   *of that time*
That hadden prys now wonder nyce and straunge
25 Us thenketh hem, and yet they spak hem so,
And sped as wel in love as men now do;   *prospered*
Eke forto wynne love in sondry ages,   *different*
In sondry londes, sondry ben usages.   *customs*

And forthi yf it happe yn ony wyse
30 That here be ony lovere yn this place,   *present*
That herkeneth as the story wole devyse,   *hears, describe*
How Troylus com to hys lady grace,
And thenketh, 'So nold I not love purchace',
Or wondreth on his speche and his doyng,   *actions*
35 I not, but it is me no wonderynge;   *don't know*

For every wyght which that to Rome went
Halt not o path, or alwey o manere;
Ek yn som lond were al the game shent   *sport ruined*
If [that] thei ferd yn love as men don here: *behaved*
40 As thus, in open doyng or yn chere,
In vysitynge, in forme, or seyde hire sawes;   *manner*
Forthi men seyth, ech contre hath hise lawes.

Ek skarsly ben there in this place thre
That han yn love seyd lyk, and don yn al,
45 For to thi purpos this may lyken the,   *please*
And the right nought; yet al is seyd or shal.
Ek som men grave in tre, some in ston wal,   *carve, wood*
As it bitit; but syn I have begonne,   *chances*
Myn auctor shal I folwe if I konne. *

Explicit prohemium secundi libri

24-5 That were esteemed now seem to us extremely quaint and alien. 33 That's
not the way I would set about winning love. 37 Doesn't always keep to the
same route, or always (follow it in) the same way; *o: al o.* 40 in overt deeds or
behaviour. 41 (in the way they) made their speeches. 44 in all respects spoken
or acted alike.

Incipit liber Secundus

50 In May, that moder is of monethes glade,
   That fressh floures blewe and white and rede
   Ben quyke agayn, that wynter dede made,   *Come alive*
   And ful of bawme is fletynge every mede,
   Whan Phebus doth his bryghte bemes sprede
55 Right in the white Bole, so it bytydde,
   As I shal synge, on Mayes day the thridde,

   That Pandarus, for al his wyse speche,
   Felt ek his part of loves shotes kene,
   That koude he nevere so wel [of lovyng] preche,   *give advice*
60 It made his hewe a-day ful ofte grene;   *sickly*
   So shop it that hym felt that day a tene   *pang*
   In love, for which yn wo to bedde he went,
   And made er it was day ful many a went.

   The swalwe Proigne* with a sorwful lay,   *song*
65 Whan morwe com, gan make here weymentynge,   *lament*
   Whi she forshapen was – and evere lay   *transformed*
   Pandare abedde, half yn a slom[b]erynge,
   Til she [so neigh hym] made here cheterynge,
   How Tireux gan forth hire suster take,
70 That with the noyse of here he gan awake,

   And gan to calle and dresse hym up to ryse,
   Remembrynge hym his erand was to done
   From Troylus, and ek the gret emprise,   *enterprise*
   And cast and knew yn good plyt was the mone
75 To don viage, and tok [his] weye [ful] soone
   Unto his neces paleys ther bysyde: *close at hand*
   Now Janus, god of entre, thow hym gyde!

   When he was come unto his neces place:
   'Wher is my lady?' to hire folk seyde he;

53–5 every meadow is filled with sweet breezes, when the sun spreads its bright rays in the shining (sign of) Taurus. 58 share of . . . sharp arrows. 63 often tossed and turned. 68 *so neigh hym*: *hym so neigh.* 71 call (for his servant) and get ready to get up. 74–5 considered and recognised that the moon was favourably placed for achieving his undertaking. 77 god of doorways (and beginnings). 79 *to: unto.*

80 And they hym tolde, and he [forth yn] gan pace,
   And fond two othere ladyes sette, and she,   *seated*
   Withinne a paved parlour, and thei thre
   Herden a mayden reden hem the gest   *history*
   Of the sege of Thebes while hem leste.

85 Quod Pandarus, 'Madame, God yow see,   *protect*
   With yowre faire bok and al the companye!'
   'Ey, uncle myn, welcome ywys,' quod she;
   And up she ros and by the hond yn hye
   She tok hym fast and seyde, 'This nyght thrie –   *three times*
90 To good mot it turne – of yow I mette';   *may, dreamed*
   And with that word she doun on bench hym sette.

   'Ye, nece, ye shal fare wel the bet,
   If God wole, al this yer,' quod Pandarus;
   'But I am sory [that] I have yow let   *prevented*
95 To herken of youre book ye preysen thus.
   For Goddes love, what seith it? Telle it us:
   Is it of love? Som good ye me lere!'
   'Uncle,' quod she, 'youre maystresse is not here.'

   With that thei gonnen laughe, and she seyde,
100 'This romaunce is of Thebes that we rede;
    And we han herd how that kyng Layus deyde
    Thurgh Edyppus his sone, and al that dede;
    And here we stenten at these lettres rede,
    How the bisshop, as the bok kan telle –
105 Amphiorax – fil thurgh the ground to helle.'*   *fell*

    Quod Pandarus, 'Al this knowe I myselve,
    And al the assege of Thebes and al the care,   *suffering*
    For herof ben there maked bokes twelve –
    But lat be this and telle me how ye fare!
110 Do wey youre barbe and shewe youre face bare;
    Do wey youre book; rys up, and lat us daunce,
    And lat us don to May som observance.'   *homage*

---

80 *forth yn: yn forth.* 84 for as long as they took pleasure in it. 86 *With: With al.* 97 Give me some useful instruction. 101 *that: that the.* 102 all that happened (after that). 103 stopped reading at this rubricated heading. 110 Put aside your wimple.

'A, God forbede!' quod she, 'be ye mad?
Is that a wydewes lyf, so God you save?
115 By God, ye make me right sore adrad: *terrify me*
Ye ben so wylde, it semeth that ye rave.
It sat me wel bet ay in [a] cave
To bydde and rede on holy seyntes lyves:
Lat maydenes gon to daunce, and yonge wyves!'*

120 'As evere I thrive,' quod [this] Pandarus,
'Yet kowde I telle a thyng to don yow pleye.'
'Now, uncle dere,' quod she, 'tel it us,
For Goddes love – is thanne the assege aweye?
I am of Grekes so ferd that I deye.'
125 'Nay, nay,' quod he, 'as evere mot I thryve,
It is a thyng [wel bet than] such fyve.'

'Ye, holy God,' quod she, 'what thyng is that?
What? Bet than swych fyve? I, nay, iwys!
For al this world ne kan I reden what   *guess*
130 It sholde ben – som jape, I trowe, is this;
And but youreselven telle [us] what it is,
My wit is forto arede it al to lene: *solve, limited*
As help me God, I not not wha[t] ye mene!'   *don't know*

'And I youre bo[ru]gh, ne nevere shal, for me   *surety*
135 This thing be tolde to yow, as mote I thryve.'
'And why so, uncle myn? Why so?' quod she.
'By God,' quod he, 'that wole I telle as blyve;   *at once*
For proudder womman were there noon on lyve,
And ye it wyste, yn al the toun of Troye –   *If*
140 I jape nought, as evere have I joye.'

Tho gan she [wondren] more than byforn
A thousand fold, and doun hire eyen caste;
For nevere sith the tyme that she was born
To knowe thyng desired she so faste;
145 And with a syk she seyde hym at the laste,   *sigh*
'Now, uncle myn, I nel yow nowght displese,   *will*
Nor axen more that may do yow disese.'   *upset*

---

114 how a widow ought to live? 117–8 would be much more fitting for me
perpetually . . . to pray. 121 make you rejoice. 123 has the siege been lifted?
126 *wel bet than: is worth.* 133 *what: whan.* 134 *borugh: bourgh.* 141
wondren: jape.

So after this, with many wordes glade,
And frendly tales, and with mery chere,   *conversation*
150 Of this and that they pleyede, and gunnen wade   *ventured*
In many an unkouthe, glad, and depe matere,
As frendes don whanne thei ben met y-fere,   *together*
Til she gan axen hym how Ector ferde,
That was the townes wal and Grekes yerde.   *defence, scourge*

155 'Ful wel, I thanke God,' quod Pandarus,
'Save yn his arm he hath a litel wounde;
And ek his fressh brother Troylus,   *vigorous*
The wyse, worthi Ector the sec[o]unde,*
In whom that al vertu lyst abounde,   *pleases to*
160 As alle trowthe and al gentillesse,
Wysdom, honour, fredom, and worthinesse.'   *generosity*

'In good feyth, em,' quod she, 'that lyketh me   *uncle*
They faren wel – God save hem bothe two!
For trewly I hold it gret deynté,   *excellence*
165 A kynges sone in armes wel to do,
And ben of good condicions therto:
For gret power and moral vertu here
Is seelde y-seye in o persone y-fere.'

'In good feyth, that is soth,' quod Pandarus;
170 'But b[y] my trouthe, the kyng hath sones tweye –
That is to mene, Ector and Troylus –   *say*
That certaynly, though that I sholde deye,
They ben as voyde of vices, dar I seye,   *free*
As ony men that lyveth under the sonne:
175 Hire myght is wyde y-knowe, and what they konne.

'Of Ector nedeth it no more forto telle:
In al this world [th]er nys a bettre knyght
Than he, that is of worthinesse welle,   *source*
And he wel more vertu hath tha[n] myght –
180 This knoweth many a wys and worthi wyght.
The same prys of Troilus I seye;
God help me so, I knowe not swyche tweye!'   *two like them*

---

151 unfamiliar, entertaining and profound subject. 166 in addition to possess
noble qualities. 168 rarely seen together in the same person. 170 *by: be.* 175
their abilities. 177 *ther: ner.* 179 *than: that.* 181 I esteem Troilus equally
highly.

'Be God,' quod she, 'of Ector that is soth;
Of Troylus the same thing trowe I –
185 For dredles, men tellen that he doth   *certainly*
In armes day by day so worthily,
And bereth hym here at hom so gentilly   *graciously*
To every wight, that alle prys hath he   *praise*
Of hem that me were levest preysed be.'

190 'Ye sey right soth, ywys,' quod Pandarus;
'For yesterday whoso hadde with hym ben,
He myght have wondred upon Troylus –
For nevere yet so thikke a swarm of ben   *bees*
Ne fleygh, as Grekes gonne fro hym flen,   *flew, fled*
195 And thorough the feld in every wightes ere   *person's*
There nas no cry but: 'Troylus is there!'

'Now here, now there, he huntede hem so faste,
Ther nas but Grekes blood – and Troylus
Now h[y]m he hurte, and h[y]m alle down he caste;
200 Ay where he wente, it was arayed thus:
He was here deth, and lyf and sheld for us;
That al that day ther dorste noon withstonde,
Whil that he held his blody swerd yn honde.*

'Therto he is the frendlyest man   *In addition*
205 Of gret estat that evere I saw my lyve,   *high rank*
And wher hym lyst, best felawship kan
To suche as hym thenketh able forto thryve.'
And with that word tho Pandarus as blyve
He tok his leve and seyde, 'I wole go henne.'   *am leaving*
210 'Nay, blame have I, myn uncle,' quod she thenne.

'What eyleth yow to be thus wery soone,
And namelych of womm[e]n? Wol ye so?   *especially*
Nay, sitteth down; by God, I have to done
With yow to speke of wysdom er ye go.'
215 And every wight that was aboute hem two,

189 From those by whom I would most like to be praised. 195 *feld: fleld.* 199
this one . . . that one; *hym . . . hym: hem . . . hem.* 200 Wherever . . . it was
appointed that. 206-7 knows best how to be a companion to those; *wher: wher
that.* 211 to tire so quickly. 212 *wommen: womman.* 213-4 must have a
serious conversation.

That herd that, gan fer awey to stonde,   *withdrew*
Whil that they hadde al that hem liste yn honde.

Whan that here tale al brought was to an ende,
Of here estat, and of here governaunce,
220 Quod Pandarus, 'Now is [it] tyme I wende;
But yet I seye, aryseth and lat us daunce,
And cast youre wydwes habit to myschaunce!   *discard*
What lyst yow thus yow[r]self to disfigure,
Sith yow is tyd thus faire an aventure?'   *has befallen*

225 'A, wel bithought, for love of God,' quod she,
'Shal I not wete what ye mene of this?'   *know*
'No, [this] thyng axeth layser,' [tho] quod he,
'And eke me wolde muche greve, iwys,
If I it tolde, and ye it toke amys:
230 Yet were it bet my tonge forto stille   *stop*
Than sey a soth that were ayens youre wylle.

'For, nece, by the goddesse Mynerve,
And Juppiter, that maketh the thonder rynge,
And by the blysful Venus that I serve,
235 Ye be th[e] womman in this world lyvynge
(Withoute paramours) to my wytynge,   *knowledge*
That I best love and lothest am to greve:
And that ye wete wel yow[r]self, I leve.'   *am sure*

'Ywys, uncle,' quod she, 'grant mercy,
240 Youre frendship have I founden evere yet;   *always*
I am to no man holden, trewely,   *indebted*
So muche as yow, and have so litel quyt,   *repaid*
And with the grace of God, emforth my wit,
As yn my gilt I shal you nevere offende,   *Deliberately*
245 And yf I have er this, I wol amende.

'But, for the love of God, I yow beseche,
As ye ben he that I most love and tr[y]ste,
Lat be youre fre[mde] manere speche,   *distant*
And sey to me, youre nece, what yow lyste.'   *wish*

217 were occupied with all that they wished (to talk about). 219 her status (in Troy) and of the management of her affairs. 236 (with the exception of the lady I serve). 237 most unwilling to annoy. 243 within the limits of my understanding. 247 *tryste: truste.* 248 *fremde: frendly.*

250 And with that word here uncle anoon here k[y]ste,
    And seyde, 'Gladly, leve nece dere;
    Tak it for goud that I shal seye yow here.'

    With that she gan hire eyen down to caste,
    And Pandarus to koghe gan a lyte,
255 And seyde, 'Nece, lo, alwey, to the laste,   *in the end*
    Howso it be that som men hem delite
    With subtil art hire tales forto endite,
    Yet for al that, in here entencioun,
    Hire tale is al for som conclusioun   *purpose*

260 'And sith the ende is every tales strengthe,
    And this matere is so byhovely,   *respectable*
    What sholde I poynte or drawen it on lenghthe   *underline*
    To yow that ben my frend so feithfully?'
    And with that word he gan right inwardly   *intensely*
265 Byholden here, and loked on hire face,
    And seyde, 'On suche a mirour, good grace!'

    Thanne thoughte he thus: 'Yf I my tale endite
    Ought hard, or make a proces ony while,
    She shal no sav[o]ur han theryn but lite,   *pleasure*
270 And trowe I wold hire in my wyll bygile:
    For tendre wittes wenen al be wyle   *is trickery*
    There as they kan not pleynly understonde,   *Where, fully*
    Forthi here wit to serven wol I fonde.'

    And loked on here yn a besy wyse;   *attentively*
275 And she was war that he byheld here so,
    And seyde, 'Lord! so [faste] ye me avyse!
    Sey ye me nevere er now? What sey ye – no?'   *Saw*
    'Yes, yes,' quod he, 'and bet wole er I go!   *better*
    But b[y] my trowthe, I thought now yf ye   *was wondering*
280 Be fortunat, for now men shal it se.

    'For to every wight som goodly aventure   *fortune*
    Som tyme is shape, if he it kan receyven;   *devised*

---

250 *here: here he; kyste: keste.* 254 cleared his throat a little. 257 put together
what they have to say. 259 *tale: tales.* 260 *is: is of.* 268 drag it out to any
length. 269 *savour: savaur; lite: litel.* 270 deliberately deceive. 273 So I will
take care to adapt (my words) to her understanding. 276 look at me so fixedly.
279 *by: be.* 280 favoured by Fortune.

But yf that he wole take of it no cure,   *heed*
Whan tha[t] it cometh, but wylfully it wey[v]en,   *neglect*
285 Lo, neyther cas nor fortune hym deseyven,   *chance*
But right his verray slouthe and wrecchednesse –   *innate*
And swych [a] wyght is forto blame, I gesse.

'G[ood] aventure, O bele nece, have ye
Ful lightly founden if ye konne it take;   *easily*
290 And for the love of God, and ek of me,
Cache it anoon lest aventure slake.
What sholde I lengere proces of it make?
Yif me youre hond, for yn this world is noon   *Give*
(If that you lyst) a wyght so wel begon.   *placed*

295 'And sith I speke of good entencioun,
As I to yow have told wel heretoforn,   *earlier*
And love as wel youre honour and renoun
As creature yn al this world y-born,
By alle the othes that I have yow sworn,
300 And ye be wroth therfore and wene I lye,   *suppose*
Ne shal I nevere seen yow eft with eye.   *again*

'Beth nought agast, ne quaketh not: wherto?   *what for?*
Ne [chaung]eth not for fere so youre hewe!
For hardely the werste of this is do,   *truly*
305 And though my tale as now be to yow newe,
Yet trist alwey ye shal me fynde trewe;
And were it thyng that me thoughte unsittynge,   *improper*
To yow nold I no such tales brynge.'

'Now, [my] good em, for Goddes love, I prey,'   *uncle*
310 Quod she, 'com of, and telle me what it is;   *stop this*
For bothe I am agast what ye wole sey,
And ek me longeth it to wyte, ywys!   *know*
For whether it be wel or be amys,
Sey on, lat me not yn this fere dwelle.'
315 'So wol I don; now herkeneth – I shal yow telle:

'Now, nece myn, the kynges dere sone,
The good, wyse, worthi, fressh, and fre,

---

284 *that*: than; *weyven*: weylen. 291 opportunity passes. 299 *yow*: to yow.
303 *chaungeth*: quaketh. 317 virtuous, discreet, honourable, spirited, and
noble.

Which alwey forto do wel is his wone: *is accustomed*
The noble Troilus, so loveth the, _
320 That, bot ye helpe, it wole his bane be.   *death*
Lo, here is al – what sholde I more seye?
Doth what yow lyst to make hym lyve or deye.

'But yf thow late hym deye, I wole sterve: *die (too)*
Have here my trouthe, nece, I nel not lye[n];   *word*
325 Al sholde I with this knyf myn owene throte kerve.'
With that the teres brast out of his eyen,   *started*
And seyde, 'Yf that ye doon us bothe dyen,
Thus giltles, than have ye fysshed faire:
What mende ye, though that we both apeyre?

330 'Allas! he whiche that is my lord so dere,
That trewe man, that noble, gentil knyght,
That nought desireth but youre frendly chere,   *glance*
I se hym deye there he goth upright,   *on his feet*
And hasteth hym with al his fulle myght
335 Forto be slayn, yf Fortune wole assente;
Allas, that God yow swich a beauté sente!

'If it be so that ye so cruel be,
That of his deth yow lyst nought to recche,   *care*
That is so trewe and worthi as ye se,
340 No more than of a japere or a wrecche –   *trifler*
If it be swych, youre beauté may not strecche
To make amendes of so cruel a dede: *excuse*
Avysement is good byfore the nede.

'Wo worth the faire gemme vertules!   *Evil befall*
345 Wo worth that herbe also that doth no bote!   *healing*
Wo worth that beauté that is routheles!   *merciless*
Wo worth that wight that tret eche under fote!
And ye that ben of beauté crop and rote,
[If] therwithal in you there be no routhe,   *with it*
350 Than is it harm ye lyven, by my trouthe!

327 cause both our deaths. 328 Without (our) having deserved it. 329 What
good would it do you even if both of us perished. 343 It is good to take thought
before the necessity arises. 344 that lacks any special power. 348 beginning
and end. 349 If: And. 350 ye: that ye.

'And also thenk wel that this is no gaude;   *trick*
For me were levere thow and I and he   *I would prefer*
Were hanged, than I sholde be his baude –
As heyghe as men myghte on us alle y-se!
355 I am thyn em; the shame were to me
As wel as the, yf that I sholde assente,
Thorugh myn abet, that he thyn honour shente.   *help*

'Now understonde, for I yow nought requere
To bynde yow to hym thorugh no behest,   *promise*
360 But oonly that ye make hym bettre chere
Than ye han don er this, and more feste,
So that his lyf be saved at the leste:
This al and som, and playnly, oure entente;
God help me so, I nevere other mente!   *anything else*

365 'Lo, this request is not but skyle, ywys,   *reasonable*
Ne doute of reson, pardé, is there noon.
I sette the worste that ye dredden this: *put*
Men wolden wondren to se hym come or gon;
Therayenis answere I thus anoon,   *To that*
370 That every wyght, but he be f[oo]l of kynde,   *by nature*
Wol deme it love of fren[d]ship yn his mynde.

'[What!] who wole deme, though he se a man
To temple go, that he the ymages eteth?
Thenk ek how [wel and] wysly that he kan
375 Governe hymself, that he nothyng foryeteth,
That wher he cometh, he prys and thank hym geteth.   *wherever*
And ek therto, he shal come here so selde,   *seldom*
What fors were it though al the town behelde?

'Swych love of frendes regneth al this town,   *prevails in*
380 And wre yow yn that mantel everemo;   *hide yourself*
And, God so wys be my salvacioun,
As I have seyd, youre beste is to do so;
But alwey, good nece, to stynte his wo,   *end*

---

358 I am not asking you. 360 should look more favourably upon him. 361
and (make) more of a fuss (of him). 363 This is absolutely all we have in mind.
366 Nor, by God, are there any reasonable grounds for alarm. 370 fool: fel
('fierce'). 377 in addition to that. 378 would it matter. 381 as certainly as I
hope God will save me.

So lat youre daunger* sucred ben a lyte, *little*
385 That of his deth ye be nought to wyte.' *blame*

Criseyde, which that herd hym yn this wyse,
Thought, 'I shal fele what he meneth, ywys.' *find out*
'Now, em,' quod she, 'what wole ye devyse? *propose*
What is youre red I shal don of this?'
390 'That is wel seyd,' quod he, 'certayn, best is
That ye hym love ayen for his lovynge, *in return*
As love for love is skylful guerdonynge:'

'Thenk ek how elde wasteth every houre *ageing*
In eche of yow a partie of beauté;
395 And therfore, er [that] age the devoure, *consumes you*
Go love: for olde, ther wil no wight of the.
Lat this proverbe a lore unto yow be: *instruct you*
"To late y-war, quod Beauté, whan it paste" –
For Elde daunteth Daunger at the laste. *overcomes*

400 'The kynges fool is woned to cryen lowde, *accustomed*
Whan that hym thenketh a womman bereth here he[y]e:
"So longe mot ye lyve, and alle prowde,
Til crowes feet ben growen under youre eye,
And sende yow thanne a myrrour yn to prye, *pore*
405 In which ye may se youre face a-morwe." – *in the morning*
Nece, I bidde wisshe yow no more sorwe!'

With this he stente, and caste adown the hed, *paused*
And she bygan to brest a-wep anoon, *burst out crying*
And seyde, 'Allas! for wo why nere I ded? *am I not*
410 For of this world the feyth is al agon! *vanished*
Allas! what shulde straunge to me don, *a stranger*
Whan he that for my best frend y wende
[R]et me to love, and shold it me defende? *Counsels*

'Allas! I wold han trusted, douteles,
415 That yf that I thurgh myn disaventure *misfortune*
Had loved other hym or Achilles,* *either*
Ector, or ony mannes creature,
Ye nold han had no mercy ne mesure *restraint*

---

384 reserve be sweetened. 392 (a) reasonable reward. 396 once you are old, no one will desire you. 398 warned . . . it has vanished. 401 acts in a haughty manner; *heye: heighe*. 406 would not wish (on) you any greater. 413 *Ret: Bet*.

On me, but always had me in repreve.   *reproached me*
420 This false world, allas! who may it leve?   *trust in*

'What! is th[is] al the joye and al the feste?
Is this youre red? Is thys my blysful cas?
Is this the verray mede of youre behest?
Is al this peynted proces seyd, allas!
425 Right for this fyn? O lady myn, Pallas,*
Thow in this dredful cas for me purveye,
For so astonyed am I that I deye.'

With that she gan ful sorwfully to syke.   *sigh*
'Ay, may it be no bet?' quod Pandarus:
430 'By God, I shal no more come here this wyke,
And God toforn, that am mystrusted thus!   *before*
I se ful wel that ye sette lite of us,   *a low value on*
Or of oure deth; allas! I, woful wrecche!
Might he yet lyve, of me is nought to recche.   *worry about*

435 'O cruel god, O dispitous Marte!   *pitiless*
O Furyes thre of helle, on yow I crye!   *invoke*
So lat me nevere out of this hous departe
If that I mente harm or vylonye!
But sith I se my lord mot nedes dye,
440 And I with hym, here I me shryve and seye   *confess myself*
That wikkedly ye don us bothe deye.   *maliciously*

'But sith it lyketh yow that I be ded,
By Neptunus, that god is of the se,
Fro this forth shal I nevere eten bred,
445 Til I myn owen herte blod may se:
For certayn I wol deye as sone as he!'
And up he sterte and on his weye he raughte,
Til she agayn hym by the lappe caughte.

Criseyde, which that wel neigh starf for fere,
450 So as she was the ferfulleste wyght   *most timorous*
That myght be, and herde ek with here ere,

---

421 *this: that.* 423 that same reward you promised me? 424 deceitful pleading.
426 look after me in this frightening situation. 429 is this the best you can do?
438 *or: or ony.* 446 *certayn: certaynly.* 447 jumped and would have rushed on
his way. 448 pulled him back by the fold (of his garment); *agayn hym: hym
agayn.* 449 was almost dying of fright.

And saw the sorwful ernest of the knyght,   *sincerity*
And in his preyere eke saw noon unright,
And for the harm that myghte ek fallen more,
455 She gan to rewe and dradde hire wonder sore;   *be sorry*

And thoughte thus: 'Unhappes falle[n] thikke   *Misfortunes*
Alday for love, and in such manere cas,   *All the time*
As men ben cruel yn hemself, and wykke;   *innately*
And yf this man sle here hymself, allas!
460 In my presence, it wyl be no solas.   *comfort*
What men of hit wold deme I kan not seye: *How, interpret*
It nedeth me ful sleyly forto pleye.'

And with a sorwful syk she seyde thrie,   *thrice*
'A, Lord, what me is tyd a sory chaunce!   *has befallen*
465 For myn estat now lyth in jupartie,
And ek myn emes lyf lyth in balaunce;   *uncle's*
But natheles, with Goddes governaunce,
I shal don so, myn honour shal I kepe,
And ek his lyf' – and stynte forto wepe.   *stopped*

470 'Of harmes two, the lesse is forto chese;   *choose*
Yet have I levere maken hym good chere   *I would rather*
In honour than myn emes lyf to lese –
Ye seyn, ye nothyng elles me requere?'
'No, ywys,' quod he, 'myn owene nece dere.'
475 'Now wel,' quod she, 'and I wol don myn peyne:
I shal myn herte ayens my lust constreyne.   *inclinations, force*

'But that I nyl not holden hym yn honde,
Ne love a man ne kan I not, ne may,
Ayens my wil; but elles wol I fonde   *do my best*
480 (Myn honour sauf) plesen hym fro day to day.
Therto nold I nought onys have seyd nay,
But that I drede, as yn my fantasye: *imagination*
But cesseth cause, ay cesseth maladye.   *(once) ceases*

'And here I make a protestacioun,   *formal protest*
485 That yn this proces yf ye deppere go,   *further*

453 nothing blameworthy. 454 to prevent anything worse happening. 456
fallen: falles. 462 I must proceed very cautiously. 465 my position is now in
danger. 468 act in such a way. 477 give him false hopes. 481–2 I would never
once have denied him this, if my imaginings had not made me afraid.

That certaynly for no salvacioun
Of yow, though that ye sterve bothe two,
Though al the world on o day be my foo,
Ne shal I nevere of hym han other routhe.'
490 'I graunte wel,' quod Pandar[e], 'by my trouthe.'

'But may I trust wel therto,' quod he,
'That of this thyng that ye han hight me here,   *promised*
Ye wol it holden trewly unto me?'   *keep*
'Ye, doutles,' quod she, 'myn uncle dere.'
495 'Ne that I shal han cause in this matere,'
Quod he, 'to pleyne, or ofter yow to preche?'
'Why no, pardé, what nedeth more speche?'

Tho fillen thei yn othere tales glade,
Til at the laste, 'O good em,' quod she tho,
500 'For His love which that us bothe made,   *created*
Tel me how first ye wysten of his wo: *came to know*
Wot noon of hit but ye?' He seyde, 'No.'
'Kan he wel speke of love?' quod she, 'I preye,
Tell me, for I the bet me shal purveye.'   *prepare myself*

505 Tho Pandarus bygan forto smyle,
And seyde, 'By my trouthe, I shal yow telle.
This other day nought go ful long while,
Inwith the paleys gardyn by a welle,   *Within*
Gan he and I wel half a day to dwelle,
510 Right forto speken of an ordenaunce,   *plan*
How we the Grekes myghte disavaunce.   *repulse*

'Soone after that bygonne we to lepe,   *exercise*
And casten with oure dartes to and fro,   *throw*
Til at the laste he seyde he wolde slepe,
515 And on the gres adown he leyde hym tho;
And I therafter gan rome to and fro,   *stroll*
Til that I herd, as that I welk allone,   *walked*
How he bygan ful wofully to grone.

'Tho gan I stalke softly hym behynde,   *tiptoe*
520 And sikerly, the sothe forto seyne,

486–7 indeed, not even to save both of you from dying. 490 *Pandare: Pandarus.*
496 to reproach or more frequently lecture you. 498 Then they went on to
speak of other pleasing matters. 502 Doesn't anyone know about it? 504 I
shall prepare myself the better. 507 Not many days ago.

As I kan clepe ayen now to my mynde,   *recall*
Right thus to Love he gan hym forto pleyne:
He seyde, "Lord, have routhe on my peyne,
Al have I ben rebel yn myn entente,
525 Now, *mea culpa*, lord, I me repente.

' "O God, that at thi disposicioun
Ledest the fyn, by juste purveyaunce,
Of every wyght, my lowe confessioun
Accepte in gre, and sende me swych penaunce   *favourably*
530 As liketh the; but from desesperaunce,
That may my gost departe awey fro the,
Thow be my shield, for thy benignité.

' "For certes, lord, so sore hath she me wounded,
That stod in blak, wyth lokyng of here eyen,   *her gaze*
535 That to myn hertes [botme] it is i-sounded,
Thorugh which I wot that I mot nedes deyen;   *am bound to*
This is the worste, I dar me not bywryen,   *reveal*
And wel the hottere ben the gledes rede,   *embers*
That men h[e]m wrien with asshe[n] pale and dede."   *cover*

540 'With that he smot adown his hed anoon,   *cast*
And gan to motre, I not what, trewly;   *don't know*
And I awey with that stille gan to gon,   *stealthily*
And let therof as nothyng wyst hadde I,   *behaved*
And com ayen anoon, and stod hym by,   *returned*
545 And seyde, "Awake, ye slepen al to longe –
It semeth not that love doth yow longe,   *suffer*

' "That slepen so that no man may yow wake!
Who sey evere er this so dul a man?"   *lethargic*
"Ye, frend," quod he, "[do ye] yowre hedes ake
550 For love, and lat me lyven as I kan."
But though that he for wo was pale and wan,
Yet made he tho as fressh a contenaunce
As though he shulde have led the newe daunce.*

'This passede forth til now, this other day,   *went on*
555 It fel that I come romynge al allone

---

524 Even though ... will. 526-7 have the power to bring about the end, by
your true foresight. 531 separate my spirit. 532 protection, in your grace. 535
it went down to the depths of my heart. 539 *hem: hym.* 549 *do ye: ye do.*

Into a chaumbre, and fond how that he lay
Upon his bed; but man so sore grone
Ne herd I nevere, and what that was his mone
Ne wyst I nought, for as I was comynge
560 Al sodeynly he lefte his compleynynge.

'Of which I toke somwhat suspecioun,
And ner I com, and fond he wepte sore;   *closer*
And God so wys be my salvacioun,
As nevere of thyng ne hadde I routhe more;   *creature*
565 For neither with engyn ne with no lore,
Unethes myght I fro the deth hym kepe:
That yet fele I myn hert for hym wepe.   *even now*

'And God wot, nevere sith that I was born
Was I so bysy no man forto preche,   *concerned, lecture*
570 Ne nevere to wyght so depe was i-sworn,
Er he me tolde who myght ben his leche;   *heal him*
But now to yow rehersen al his speche,   *go over*
Or alle hise woful wordes forto sowne,   *utter*
Ne byd me not, but ye wol do me swone.   *faint*

575 'But forto save his lyf, and elles nought,
And to noon harm of yow, thus am I dreven;   *impelled*
And for the love of God, that hath us wrought,
Swych chere hym doth that he and I may lyven!   *go on living*
Now have I plat to yow myn herte shryven,   *frankly*
580 And syn ye wot that myn entent is clene,   *honourable*
Tak hede therof, for I noon yvel mene.

'And right good thryft, I pray to God, have ye, *fortune*
That han swych on y-caught withoute net;
And be ye wys as ye ben faire to se,
585 Wel yn the ryng than is the ruby set!
There were nevere two so wel i-met,
Whanne ye ben his al hool, as he is youre –
Ther myghty God yet graunte us se that oure!'   *May, time*

558–9 had no idea what he was lamenting. 565–6 my cunning and my learning
were hardly enough to preserve his life. 570 Nor did I ever have to swear so
many oaths to anyone. 575 and for no other reason. 578 go on living. 584 If
you have as much sense as beauty.

'Nay, therof spak I not, [ha ha!]' quod she;
590 'As helpe me God, ye shenden every del.'
'O, mercy, dere nece,' anoon quod he,
'What so I spak, I mente nought but wel,
By Mars, the god that helmed is of stel;
Now beth nought wroth, my blod, my nece dere.'
595 'Now [wel],' quod she, 'foryeven be it here.'

With this he tok his leve, and home he wente;
And, Lord! [so] he was glad and wel bygon!   *happy*
Criseyde aros, no lengere she ne stente,   *delayed*
But straught into hire closet went anoon,   *directly*
600 And sette here down as stille as ony ston,
And every word gan up and down to wynde,   *turn over*
That he hadde seyd, as it come here to mynde;

And was somdel astonyed yn here thought,   *daunted*
Right for the newe cas; but whanne that she   *novelty*
605 Was ful avised, tho fond she right nought
Of peril, why she ought aferd be.
For man may love, of possibilité,
A womman so his herte may to-breste,
And she nought love ayen but yf here leste.   *she pleased*

610 But as she sat allone and thoughte thus,
Ascry aros at skarmyssh al withoute,   *(An) uproar*
And men cryede in the strete, 'Se, Troylus
Hath right now put to flyght the Grekes route!'   *host*
With that gan al here meyné forto shoute: *household*
615 'A, go we se! Cast up the yates wyde!   *throw open*
For thurgh th[is] strete he mot to palays ryde;

'For other weye is ther to the yate noon
Of [D]ardanus,* ther [opy]n is the cheyne.' –
With that come he and al his folk anoon,
620 An esy pas rydynge yn routes tweyne,
Right as his happy day was, soth to seyne: *lucky*
For which, men say, may nought disturbed be
That shal bytyden of necessité.

---

590 you are spoiling everything. 595 *wel: wole* I. 605 Had considered the
matter fully. 607–8 it is possible that a man may break his heart through love
of a woman. 616 *this: that.* 618 *Dardanus: Gardanus; opyn: upon.* 620 Riding
at an amble in two companies. 623 must necessarily come about.

Th[i]s Troylus sat on his bay stede,
625 Al armed, save his hed, ful richely,
And wounded was his hors, and gan to blede,
On whiche he rod a pas ful softely;
But swych a knyghtly sight, trewely,
As was on hym was nought, withouten faile,
630 To loke on Mars that god is of batayle.

So lyk a man of armes and a knyght
He was to sen, fulfild of heigh prowesse;   *filled with*
For bothe he hadde a body and a myght
To don that thyng, as wel as hardynesse;   *perform*
635 And eke, to sen hym yn his gere hym dresse,
So fressh, so yong, so weldy semed he,   *powerful*
It was an hevene upon hym forto se.   *blissful*

His helm tohewe was yn twenty places,   *savagely hacked*
That by a tissew heng his bak byhynde;
640 His sheld to-dasshed was with swerdes and maces,
In which men myghte many an arwe fynde
That th[ir]lled hadde horn and nerf and rynde;
And ay the peple cryede, 'Here cometh oure joye,   *always*
And, nexst his brother, holdere up of Troye!'   *pillar*

645 For which he wex a litel red for shame,
Whan he the peple upon hym herde cryen,
That to biholde it was a noble game,
How sobrelyche he caste doun his eyen.   *modestly*
Cryseyde gan al his chere aspien,   *took note*
650 And let it so softe yn hire herte synke,
That to hiresel[f] she seyde, 'Who yaf me drynke?'

For of here owene thought she wex al red,
Remembrynge here right thus: 'Lo, this is he
Which that myn uncle swereth he mot be ded,
655 But I on hym have mercy and pité.'
And with that thought, for pure ashamed, she
Gan yn here hed to pulle, and that as faste,   *at once*
Whil he and al the peple forthby paste;*   *went by*

624 *This: Thus.* **639** hung behind him from a band of rich cloth. **640** badly dented. **642** pierced the horn, sinew, and hide (of the shield); *thrilled: thrilled.* **646** shout his praises. **651** a (love-)potion; *hireself: hireselven.*

And gan to casten and rollen up and down
660 Withinne here thought his excellent prowesse,
And his estat, and also his renoun,
His wit, [his] shap, and ek his gentillesse;
But most hire favour was for his distresse   *because*
Was al for here, and thought it was a routhe   *pitiful*
665 To slen swych on, yf that he mente trouthe.

Now myghte som envyous jangle thus:
'This was a sodeyn love – how myght it be
That she so lyghtly lovede Troylus   *easily*
Right for the firste syght, ye, parde?'
670 Now whoso seyth so, mot he nevere the!   *prosper*
For everythyng a gynnyng hath it nede
Er al be wrought, withouten ony drede.

For I sey nought that she so sodeynly
Yaf hym here love, but that she gan enclyne   *was disposed*
675 To lyke hym first (and I have told yow why);
And after that, his manhod and his pyne   *suffering*
Made love withinne hire [herte] forto myne,
For which, by proces and by good servi[s]e,
He gat here love, and in no sodeyn wyse.

680 And also blisful Venus, wel arayed,   *placed*
Sat in here sevenethe hows of hevene tho,
Disposed wel, and with aspectes payed,
To helpen sely Troilus of his wo* –   *the poor*
And soth to seyn, she nas not al a fo
685 To Troilus in his nativyté:
God wot that wel the sonner spedde he!

Now lat us stynte of Troylus a throwe,
That rideth forth, and late us tourne faste
Unto Criseyde that heng here hed ful lowe,
690 Ther as she sat allone, and gan to caste   *Where*
Whereon she wolde apoynt hire at the laste,   *decide*

659–60 consider and turn over in her mind. 665 such a person, if his intentions
were honourable. 666 malicious gossip chatter. 671–2 all things must of
necessity have a beginning before they are brought to completion. 678 *servise*:
service; in the course of time. 682 Auspiciously placed . . . favourable aspects.
684 wholly ill-disposed. 686 he prospered more quickly on account of that.
687 stop for a time. 688 return promptly.

If it so were hire em ne wolde cesse
For Troilus upon here forto presse.

And Lord, so she yn thought gan to argue
695 In this matere of which I have yow told,
And what to done best were, and what eschue,   *to avoid*
That plitede she ful ofte in many [a] folde;   *turned over*
Now was hire herte warm, now was it colde;
And what she thoughte, somwhat shal I write,
700 As to myn auctor lysteth forto endite.

She thought wel that Troylus persone
She knew by sight, and ek [his] gentillesse,
And thus she seyde: 'Al were it nought to done
To graunte hym love, yet, for his worthynesse,
705 It were honour, with pley and with gladnesse,   *joyfully*
In honesté with swych a lord to dele,
For myn estat, and also for his hele.

'Ek wel wot I my kynges sone is he;
And sith he hath to se me swych delit,
710 If I wolde uttirly his sight fle,
Paraunter he myght have me in dispit,
Thurgh which I mygh[t] stonde in worse plyt;   *situation*
Now were I wys me hate to purchace,   *get*
Withouten nede, there I may stonde in grace?

715 'In everythyng, I wot, there lith mesure;   *moderation*
For though a man forbede dronkenesse,
He nought forbet that every creature
Be drynklees for alwey, as I gesse;   *imagine*
Ek [sith I wot for me] is his distresse,
720 I ne ought not for that thyng hym despise,
Sith it is so he meneth in good wyse.

'[And] eke I knowe, of long tyme agon,
Hise thewes goode, and that he is not nyse;
Ne avaunter, certeyn, seyth men, is he non –   *boaster*
725 To wys is he to do so gret a [v]yse.   *commit, sin*

---

700 Following what my author is pleased to tell. 702 *his: by.* 707 my position
. . . his well-being. 711 He might perhaps bear me a grudge. 719 *sith I wot for
me: for me sith I wot; his: al his.* 721 his intentions are good. 723 virtues . . .
no fool; *he: she.* 725 *vyse: nyse.*

Ne als I nel hym nevere so cherishe,
That he may make avaunt, by juste cause,
He shal me nevere bynde in swich a clause.   *by, condition*

'Now set a cas: the hardest is, [y]wys,   *put, worst*
730 Men myghten deme that he loveth me: *suppose*
What dishonour were it unto me, this?
May I hym lette of that? Why nay, pardé!   *prevent*
I knowe also, and alday here and se,
Men loven wom[e]n al bysyde hire leve,
735 And whanne hem leste no more, lat hem byleve.   *leave off*

'I thenk ek how he able is to have
Of al this noble town the thryftiest   *most excellent*
To ben his love, so she here honour save –
For out and out he is the worthiest
740 (Save only Ector, which that is the best);
And yet his lyf al lyth now in my cure!   *power*
But swych is love, and ek myn aventure.

'Ne me to love, a wonder is it nought;
For wel wot I myself, so God me spede
745 (Al wolde I that noon wyste of this thought),
I am one the fairest, out of drede,   *certainly*
And goodlyest, whoso taketh hede
(And so men seyn), in al the town of Troye:
What wonder is though he of me have joye?

750 'I am myn owene woman, wel at ese
(I thank it God), as after myn estat,
Right [y]ong, and stond untyd in lusty lese,
Without jalousye or swych debat;   *argument*
Shal non hosbonde seyn to me: "Chekmat!"
755 (For either they ben ful of jalousye,
Or maisterful, or loven novellerye.)

'What shal I don? To what fyn lyve [I] thus?   *end*
Shal I not loven in cas yf that me l[e]st?   *I want to?*

---

726 behave so lovingly towards him. 734 quite without their permission;
women: a woman. 737 *this: this ilke.* 743 It isn't surprising that I should be
loved. 745 Although I wouldn't have anyone know. 749 *is: is it.* 750–1
comfortably situated . . . in accordance with my status. 752 free in a pleasant
pasture; *yong: thong.* 756 overbearing . . . fickle. 758 *lest: lyst.*

What, pardieux, I am not religious,   *a nun*
760 And though that I myn herte sette at reste   *fix*
Upon this knyght, that is the worthieste,
And kep alwey myn honour and my name,
By al right, it may do me no shame.'

But ryght as whanne the sonne shyneth bright,
765 In Marche, that chaungeth ofte tyme his face,
And that a cloud is put with wynd to flyght,
Which oversprat the sonne as for a space,   *covers*
A cloudy thought gan thorugh hire soule pace,
That overspradde here brighte thoughtes alle,
770 So that for fere almost she gan to falle.

That thought was this: 'Allas! syn I am fre,
Sholde I now love and put in jupartie   *doubt*
My sikernesse, and thrallen liberté?
Allas! how dorste I thenken that folye!   *entertain*
775 May I nought wel in other folk aspie
Hire dredful joye, here constreynt, and here peyne?
There loveth noon, that she nath weye to pleyne!   *cause*

'For love is yet the m[o]ste stormy lyf,
Right of hymself, that evere was bygonne;
780 For evere som mystrust or nyce stryf
Ther is in love, som cloud is over that sonne –
Therto we wrecched wommen nothyng konne,   *Against that*
Whan us is wo, but wepe and sitte and thynke;
Oure wreche is this, oure owene wo to drynke.   *misery*

785 'Also these wikkede tonges ben so prest   *prompt*
To speke us harm; ek men be so untrewe,
That right anoon as sesed is here lest,
So cesseth love – and forth to love a newe!
But harm i-don is don, whoso it rewe;   *regrets*
790 For though these men for love hem ferst to-rende,
Ful sharp bygynnynge breketh ofte at ende.

'How ofte tyme hath it knowe be,   *manifest*
The treson that to womm[e]n hath be do!

---

770 she almost swooned. 773 secure state and enslave my freedom. 778 *moste:
meste.* 779 From its own nature. 780 *stryf: stryft.* 787 their desire fails. 788
a: an. 790 tear themselves apart. 791 *at: at the.* 793 *wommen: womman.*

To what fyn is swych love, I kan not se,   *purpose*
795 Or wher bycomth it whenne it is [a]go –
Ther is no wyght that wot, I trowe so,
Wher it bycometh: lo! no wyght on it sporneth;   *stumbles*
That erst was nothyng, into nought it torneth.   *at first*

'How bysy, if I love, ek most I be
800 To plesen hem that jangle of love, and dremen,
And coye hem [that] they sey noon harm of me –   *cajole*
For though there be no cause, yet hem semen
Al be for harm that folk here frendes quemen;
And who may stoppe every wikked tunge –
805 Or sown of belles whanne that thei be runge?'

And after that, here thought bygan to clere,
And seyde, 'He which that nothyng undertaketh,
Nothyng ne acheveth, be hym loth or dere.'
And with another thought hire herte quaketh;   *a different*
810 Than slepeth hope, and after dred awaketh:
Now hot, now cold, but thus, bytwyxen tweye,
She rist here up, and went here forto pleye.

Adoun the steyre anoon right tho she wente
Into the gardeyn, with here neces thre,
815 And up and doun there made many a wente –   *took, turn*
Flexippe, she, Tharbe, and Antigone* –
To pleyen, that it joye was to se;
And othere of here wommen a gret rowte
Here fol[o]weden yn the gardeyn al abowte.

820 This [yerd] was large, and rayled all the aleyes,   *paths*
And shadwede with bowes blosmy and grene,
And benched newe, and sonded alle the weyes,   *sanded*
In which she walketh arm yn arm bytwene;
Til at the laste Antigone the shene   *fair*
825 Gan on a Troian song to synge clere,
That it an hevene was hire voys to here.   *heavenly*

---

795 what becomes of it when it has gone. 800 chatter and imagine things
about. 803 people do to please their friends. 804 *tunge: tungen.* 805 *runge:*
rungen. 808 whether it displeases or pleases him. 812 got up ... relax. 819
foloweden: foleweden. 820 *yerd: gardeyn.* 821 flowery and leafy boughs. 822
newly provided with benches (of earth and turf).

[*Cantus Antigone*]*

She seyde, 'O Love, to whom I have and shal
Ben humble subgit, trewe yn myn entente,   *subject, will*
As I best kan, to yow, lord, yeve ych al,   *give*
830 For everemore, myn herte[s] lust to rente;
For nevere yet thi grace no wyght sente
So blysful cause as me my lyf to lede
In al joye and sureté out of drede.   *security*

'Ye, blisful god, han me so wel beset   *placed*
835 In love, ywys, that al that bereth lyf   *living things*
Ymagynen ne kowde how to ben bet –
For, lord, withouten jalousye or stryf,
I love oon which [that] is most ententyf   *concerned*
To serven wel, unwery or unfeyned,
840 That evere was, and lest with harm distreyned.   *overcome*

'As he that is the welle of worthinesse,   *spring*
Of trouthe ground, myrour of goodlyhed,
[Of wit] Appollo, ston of s[iker]nesse,   *good faith*
Of vertu rote, of luf fyndere and hed,
845 Thurgh which is al sorwe fro me ded –
Iwys, I love hym best, so doth he me;
Now good thryft have he, wher[so] that he be!

'Whom sholde I thanke but yow, god of love,
Of al this blysse yn which to bathe I gynne?
850 And thonked be ye, lord, for that I love:
This is the right lyf that I am inne,
To flemen alle manere vice and synne;   *put to flight*
This doth me so to vertu forto entende,   *devote myself*
That day by day I yn my wil amende.   *consciously improve*

855 'And whoso seyth that forto love is vice,
Or thraldom, though he fele yn it distresse,   *servitude*
He outher is envyous or right nyce,
Or is unmyghty, for his shrewednesse,   *malice*

---

830 in payment for my heart's desire. 839 without fatigue or deceit. 842
foundation . . . beauty. 843 *Of wit: With*; *sikernesse: secrenesse*. 844 inventor
and source.

To loven; for swych maner folk, I gesse,
860 Defamen love as nothing of it knowe;
They speken, but they bente nevere his bowe.

'What, is the sonne wers, of kynde right,
Though that a man, for feblesse of his eyen,
May nought endure on it to se for bryght?
865 Or love the wers, though wrecches on it crien?   *complain*
No wele is worth that may no sorwe dryen.   *endure*
And forthi, he that hath an hed of verre,   *glass*
Fro cast of stones war hym in the werre!   *protect*

'But I, with al myn hert and al my myght,
870 As I have seyd, wole love unto my laste   *end*
My dere herte and al myn owene knyght,   *entirely*
In which myn herte [growen is] so faste   *firmly*
(And his in me) that it shal evere laste.
Al dredde I first to love hym to bygynne,
875 Now wote I wel there is no peril inne.'*

And of hire song right with that word she st[e]nte,
And therwithal: 'Now, nece,' quod Criseyde,   *at that*
'Who made this song [now] with so good entente?'   *will*
Antigone answerede anoon and seyde,
880 'Madame, iwys, the goodlyeste mayde
Of gret estat in al the town of Troye,
And led here lyf in most honour and joye.'

'Forsothe, so it semeth by hire song,'
Quod tho Criseyde, and gan therwith to syke,   *sigh*
885 And seyde, 'Lord, is there such blysse among
These lovers, as they konne faire endite?'
'Ye, wys,' quod fressh Antigone the white,
'For alle the folk that han or ben on lyve
Ne konne wel the blysse of love dyscrive.

890 'But wene ye that every wrecche wot   *do you suppose?*
The parfit blysse of love? Whi nay, ywys!
They wenen al be love yf oon be hoot;   *any part, hot*

862-3 to blame, through its own nature, even if. 864 cannot bear to gaze at it
because of its brilliance? 866 No good thing is worth having. 872 *growen is: is
growen.* 874 Even though I was at first afraid. 876 *stente: stynte.* 886 they are
able to describe so attractively? 890 every churl has experienced.

Do wey, do wey, they wot nothyng of this!
Men moste axe of seyntes if it is   *demand*
895 Aught faire yn hevene (whi? for they konne telle),
And axen of fendes is it f[o]ul yn helle.'   *devils*

Criseyde unto that purpos nought answerede,   *argument*
But seyde, 'Ywys, it wole be nyght as faste.'   *very soon*
But every word which that she of here herde,
900 She gan to prenten yn here herte faste,
And ay gan love hire lasse forto agaste   *terrify*
Than it dide erst, and synken yn hire herte,
That she wa[x] somwhat able to converte.

The dayes honour, and the hevenes [eye],
905 The nyghtes fo – al this clepe I the sonne –   *call*
Gan westren faste and downward forto wrye,
As he that hadde his dayes cours y-ronne;
And white thynges wexen dymme and donne   *dark*
For lak of lyght, and sterres forto appere,
910 That she and here folk in went y-fere.   *together*

So whan it liked hire to gon to reste,
And voyded were they that voyden oughte,
She seyde that to slepe wel hire leste.   *much wished*
Hire wommen soone til hire bed here broughte.
915 Whan al was hust, thanne lay she stille and thoughte   *quiet*
Of alle this thyng the manere and the wyse:
Reherce it nedeth nought, for ye ben wyse.

A nyghtyngale upon a cedre grene,*
Upon the chambre wal there as she lay,
920 Ful loude sang ayen the mone shene,   *in the moonlight*
Paraunter, yn his bryddes wyse, a lay   *song*
Of love, that made hire herte fressh and gay.
That herkened she so longe yn good entente,   *attentively*
That at the laste the dede slep hire hente.   *took (hold of)*

925 And as she slep, anoon right tho here mette   *dreamed*
How that an egle, fethered whit as bon,

---

900 firmly to impress upon her heart. 903 became to some extent ready to
change her mind; *wax: was*. 904 *eye: heighe*. 906 move west and hide below
(the horizon). 912 all those were dismissed who ought to be. 917 It's not
necessary to repeat it.

Under hire brest his longe clawes sette,
And out hire herte he rente, and that anoon,   *tore*
And dide his herte into hire brest to goon –   *caused*
930 Of which she nought agros, ne nothing smerte –
[And] forth he fleygh with herte left for herte.*

Now late here slepe, and we oure tales holde   *keep to*
Of Troylus, that is to palays ryden
Fro the skarmuch of the whiche I tolde,
935 And yn his chambre sit, and hath abyden   *waited*
Til two or thre of his messages yeden   *messengers went*
For Pandarus, and sought hym ful faste,
Til they hym founde, and brought hym at the last.

This Pandarus come lepyng in at ones,   *rushing*
940 And seide thus: 'Who hath ben wel y-bete
Today with swerdes and with slyng-stones,
But Troylus, that hath caught hym now an hete?'   *fever*
And gan to jape, and seyde, 'Lord, so ye swete!
But rys, and late us soupe and go to reste.'
945 And he answered hym, 'Do we as the leste.'   *you wish*

With al the haste goodly that they myghte,   *decently*
They spedde hem fro [the] souper unto bedde;
And every wyght out at the dore hym dyghte,   *went*
And wher hym lyst upon his wey he spedde.
950 But Troilus, [that] thoughte his herte bledde
For wo til that he herde som tydynge,
He seyde, 'Frend, shal I now wepe or synge?'

Quod Pandarus, 'Ly stille and late [me] slepe;
And don thyn hod – thi nedes sped be;   *call it a day*
955 [And] chese if thow wolt synge or daunce or lepe!
At short wordes, thow shalt trowe me.   *have faith in*
Sire, my nece wole do wel by the,
And love the best, by God and by my trouthe,
But la[k] of pursuyte make it in [thi] slouthe.

960 'For thus ferforth I have thi werk bygonne,
Fro day to day, til this day by the morwe,

---

930 was not frightened, nor in the least hurt. 931 *And: But.* 949 went quickly
to wherever he wished to be. 953 *me: us.* 959 Unless your slothful nature
makes you fail to persevere; *lak: lat.* 960 to such an extent.

Here love of frendship have I to the wonne,
And also hath she leyd hire feyth to borwe;   *pledged*
Algate a fot is hameled of thi sorwe!'
965 What sholde I lengere sermon of it holde?
As ye han herd byfore, al he hym tolde.

But right as floures, thorugh the colde of nyght
Y-closed, stoupen on hire stalk[es] lowe,
Redressen hem ayen the sonne bryght,   *Recover*
970 And spreden on hire kynde cours by rowe,
Right so gan tho his eyghen up to throwe   *turn*
This Troylus, and seyde, 'O Venus dere,
Thi myght, thi grace, y-her[i]ed be it here!'   *worshipped*

And to Pandar[e] he held up bothe his hondes,
975 And seyde, 'Lord, al thyn be that I have!
For I am hol – al brosten ben my bonde[s];   *broken*
A thousand Tro[yes] whoso that me yave,   *gave*
Eche after other, God so wys me save,
Ne myght me so gladen; lo, myn herte,
980 It spredeth so for joye, it wole to-sterte!   *burst*

'But, Lord, how shal I don? How shal I lyven?
Whanne shal I nexst my dere herte se?
How shal this longe tyme awey ben y-dreven   *got through*
Til that thow be ayen at here fro me?
985 Thow mayst answere, "Abyd, abyd" – but he   *Be patient*
That hangeth by the nekke, soth to seyne,
In grete disese abydeth for the peyne.'   *torment, remains*

'Al esily now, for the love of Marte,'
Quod Pandarus, 'for every thyng hath tyme.
990 So long abyd til that the nyght departe;
For also syker as thow lyst here by me,
And God toforn, I wole be there at pryme;   *before, 9 a.m.*
And forthi, werk somwhat as I shal seye,   *therefore*
Or on som other wyght this charge leye.   *person*

---

964 At least one foot has been lamed. 965 go on about it at more length. 967
of: of the. 970 open, as is natural to them, one after the other. 974 *Pandare*:
Pandarus. 976 *bondes*: *bonden.* 977 *Troyes*: *Troians.* 979 Could not give me
such joy. 987 *disese*: *dishese.* 991 as surely as you are lying.

995 'For, pardé, God wot I have evere y[i]t   *at all times*
    Ben redy the to serve, and to this nyght   *until*
    Have I nought fayned, but emforth my wit   *according to*
    Don al thi lust, and shal with al my myght.
    Do now as I shal seye and [fare] aryght;   *prosper*
1000 And if thow nylt, wyte al thiself thy care: *blame*
    On me ys nought ylong thyn yvel fare!

    'I wot [wel] that thow wysere art than I
    A thousand fold, but yf I were a[s] thow,
    God helpe me so, as I wolde outrely,   *directly*
1005 [Right] of myn owene hond write here right now
    A lettre, in which I wolde here telle how
    I ferd amys, and here beseche of routhe: *suffered*
    Now help thiself, and leve it not for slouthe.   *put if off*

    'And I mynself wil therwith to here gon;
1010 And whanne thow wost that I am with here there,
    Worth [thow] upon a courser right anon –   *Get*
    Ye, hardyly, [right] yn thi beste gere;   *clothes*
    And ryd forth by the place as nought ne were,   *casually*
    And thow shalt fynde us, yf I may, sittynge
1015 At som wyndowe ynto the strete lokynge.

    'And yf the lyke, than maystow us saluwe,   *greet*
    And upon me make thi contenaunce;
    But by thi lyf, be war and faste eschuwe
    To taryen ought – God shilde us fro myschaunce!
1020 Ride forth thi wey and hold thy governaunce;   *self-control*
    And we shal speke of the somwhat, I trowe,
    [W]han thow art goon, to do thyne eeres glowe!   *burn*

    'Towchyng thi lettre, thow art wys ynowh: *As regards*
    I wot thow nylt it digneliche endite,   *pompously*
1025 And make it with thise argumentz towh,   *difficult*
    Ne scryvenyssh or craftyly thow it wryte;
    Beblotte it with thi teeres eke a lyte,
    And yf thow write a goodly word al softe,   *tenderly*
    Though it be good, reherce it not to ofte.   *repeat*

---

995 *yit: yet.* 998 Accomplished everything you wished. 999 *fare: do.* 1001
Your lack of success will not be my fault. 1017 look directly at me. 1018–9
resolutely avoid hanging about . . . protect us from failure. 1022 *Whan: Than.*
1023 *thow: that thow.* 1026 Nor like a professional scribe.

1030 'For though the best harpour upon lyve   *alive*
     Wolde on the best souned joly harpe   *toned*
     That evere was, with all hise fyngres fyve
     Touche ay o streng, or ay o werbul harpe,   *flourish*
     Were hise nayles poynted nevere so sharpe,
1035 It shulde make every wyght to dulle   *grow weary*
     To here his gle, and of hise strokes fulle.

     'Ne jompre ek no discordaunt thing y-fere,   *confuse*
     As thus: to usen termes of phisyk   *medicine*
     In loves termes; hold [of] thi matere
1040 The forme alwey, and do that it be lyk;
     For if a peyntour wolde peynte a pyk   *pike*
     With asses feet, and hede it as an ape,
     It cordeth nou[g]ht – so [n]ere it but a jape!'   *agrees*

     This counseyl liked wel unto Troylus;
1045 But, as a dredful lovere, he seyde this: *timorous*
     'Allas, my dere brother Pandarus,
     I am ashamed forto write, ywys,
     Lest of myn innocence I seyde amys,
     Or that she nolde [it] for despit receyve: *scorn*
1050 Thanne were I ded; there myght it nothing weyve.'

     To that Pandare answered, 'Yf the l[e]st,
     Do that I seye, and lat me therwith gon;
     For by [that Lord] that formede est and west,   *created*
     I hope of it to brynge answere anoon
1055 [Ryght] of here hond – and yf that thow nylt non,
     Lat be, and sory mot he ben his lyve,
     Ayens thi lust that helpeth the to thryve.'

     Quod Troylus, 'Depardieux, I assente:
     Syn that the lyst, I wyl aryse and wryte;
1060 And blysful God I pray with good entente,
     The viage, an[d] the lettre I shal endite,   *undertaking*
     So spede it; and thow, Mynerva the white,*   *prosper*

1031 *souned: sounded.* 1036 music . . . resounding. 1039 *of: up.* 1040 see that
it agrees. 1042 give it the head of. 1043 *nought: noutht; nere: were.* 1050
would be no way of avoiding it. 1051 *lest: lyst.* 1053 *that Lord: hym.* 1056–7
may he be sorry for the rest of his life, who helps you to prosper against your
will.

Yef thow me wit my lettre to devyse' –   *contrive*
And set hym down, and wrot ryght yn this wyse:

1065 Fyrst he gan [hire] his right lady calle,   *true*
His hertes lyf, his lust, his sorwes lec[h]e,   *healer*
His blysse, and ek this[e] othere termes alle,
That yn such cas alle these loveres seche;   *seek out*
And yn ful humble wyse, as in his speche,
1070 He gan hym recomaunde unto here grace –
To telle al how, it axeth muche space.

And after [this], ful lo[w]ely he here prayede   *humbly*
To be nought wroth though he of his folye
So hardy was to hire to write, and seyde   *bold*
1075 That love it made, or elles moste he dye;
And pitously gan mercy forto crye.
And after that he seyde (and ley ful loude)   *lied*
Hymself was lytel worth, and lesse he koude.

And that she wolde han his konnyng excused,   *skill*
1080 That litel was – and ek he dredde hire so,
And his unworthynesse he ay acused;
And after that than gan he telle his wo
(But that was endeles, withouten ho),   *infinite, end*
And seyde he wolde yn trouthe alwey hym holde;   *keep*
1085 And radde it over, and gan the lettre folde.*

And with his salty teres gan he bathe
The ruby yn his signet, and it sette
Upon the wex delyverlyche and rathe;   *nimbly, quickly*
Therwith a thousand tymes er he lette,   *stopped*
1090 He cussed tho the lettre that he shette,   *kissed, sealed*
And seyde, 'Lettre, a blysful destené
The shapen is: my lady shal the se.'

This Pandar[e] tok the lettre and that by-tyme   *promptly*
A-morwe, and to his neces paleys sterte;   *hurried*
1095 And faste he swor that i[t] was passed pryme,
And gan to jape, and seyde, 'Y-wys, myn herte
So fressh it is, although it so[re] smerte,

1071 To give the details in full would take up. 1072 *lowely*: *louely*. 1092 Is contrived for you. 1093 *Pandare*: *Pandarus*. 1095 *it*: *is*. 1097 is very painful.

I may not slepe nevere a Mayes morwe;
I have a jolly wo, a lusty sorwe.'

1100 Criseyde, whan that she here uncle herde,
With dredful herte, and desirous to here
The cause of his comynge, thus answerde:
'Now by youre feyth, myn uncle,' quod she, 'dere,
What maner wyndes gydeth yow now here?   *blow*
1105 Tel us youre joly wo and youre penaunce: *suffering*
How ferforth be ye put in Loves daunce?'   *advanced*

'By God,' quod he, 'I hop[p]e alwey byhynde!'
And she to-laughe, it thought here herte brest.
Quod Pandarus, 'Lok alwey [that] ye fynde
1110 Game in myn hod; but herkeneth, yf yow leste:
There is right now y-come into towne a geste,   *visitor*
A Griek espie, and telleth newe thynges,   *brings news*
For which I come to telle yow newe tidynges.*

'Into the gardyn go we and ye shal here
1115 Al prevely of this a long sermon.'   *discourse*
With that they wente arm in arm y-fere
Into the gardeyn from the chaumbre doun.
And whan that he so fer was that the soun
Of that they spoke no man here myghte,
1120 He seyde here thus (and out the lettre plighte):   *plucked*

'Lo, he that is al holly youres fre,   *freely*
Hym recomaundeth lowly to youre grace,
And sent you this lettre here by me:
Aviseth you on it, whan ye han space,
1125 And of som goodly answere yow purchace,
Or helpe me God, so pleynly forto seyne,   *to speak*
He may not longe lyven for his peyne.'

Ful dredfully tho gan she stonde stille,
And tok it nought, but al here humble chere
1130 Gan forto chaung[e], and seyde, 'Scryt ne bille,
For love of God, that toucheth this matere,

1099 cheerful grief, a lively sorrow. 1102 *answerde: answerede.* 1107 always
bring up the rear. 1108 laughed so much, it seemed to her. 1109–10 you laugh
at me. 1113 *I: I am.* 1124 Consider it . . . leisure. 1125 provide yourself with.
1130 Nothing in writing.

Ne bryng me noon; and also, uncle dere,
To myn estat have more reward, I preye,   *consideration*
Than to his lust – what sholde I more seye?

1135 'And loketh now yf this be resonable,
And letteth nought for favour ne for slouthe   *hold back*
To sey a soth; now were it covenable   *proper*
To myn estat, by God and by youre trouthe,
To taken it, or to han of hym routhe,
1140 In harmyng of myself, or yn repreve?   *reproach*
Ber it ayeyn, for hym that ye on leve!'

This Pandarus gan on here forto stare,
And seyde, 'Now is this the grettest wonder
That evere I sey! Lat be this nyce fare.
1145 To deth mot I be smet with thonder   *struck down*
If for the cité whiche that stondeth yonder,
Wold I a lettre unto yow brynge or take
To harm of yow! What lyst yow thus to make?

'But thus ye faren, wel nyh al and some:
1150 That he that most desireth yow to serve,
Of hym ye recche lest wher he bycome,
And whether that he lyve or elles sterve.
But for al that that evere I may deserve,
Refuse it nought,' quod he, and hent here faste,   *held*
1155 And in here bosom the lettre doun he thraste,

And seyde here, 'Now cast it away [a]noon,
That folk may sen and gaueren o[n] us tweye.'   *stare at*
Quod she, 'I kan abyde til they be gon',
And gan to smyle, and seyde, 'Em, I preye,
1160 Swych answere as yow lyst yow[r]self purveye,   *provide*
For trewely I wole no lettre write.'
'N[o]? Thanne wole I,' quod he, 'so ye endite.'

Therwith she lough, and seyde, 'Go we dyne;'
And he gan at hymself to jape faste,

1141 Take it back, for (the sake of that God) that you believe in. 1144 Give up
this foolish behaviour. 1148 Why do you choose to take it in this way? 1149
But nearly all of you behave in this way. 1151 You care least what happens to
him. 1156 *anoon*: or *noon*. 1157 *on*: or. 1162 As long as you compose it (for
me).

1165 And seyde, 'Nece, I have so gret a pyne
     For love that every other day I faste – '
     And gan hise beste japes forth to caste,
     And made here so to laughe [at] his folye
     That she for laughter wende forto dye.'

1170 And whanne that she was comen into halle:
     'Now em,' quod she, 'we wole go dyne anoon;'
     And gan som of hire women to hire calle,
     And streygh[t] into here chaumbre gan she gon;
     But of hire bysynesse[s] this was on   *concerns*
1175 (Amonges othere thynges, out of drede),
     Ful prevyly this lettre forto rede.   *secretly*

     Avysed word by word yn every lyne,
     And fond no lak – she thoughte he koude good!
     And up it putte, and went hire yn to dyne.
1180 But Pandarus, that yn a study stood,
     Or he was war, she took [hym] by the hood,   *Before*
     And seyde, 'Ye were caught er [that] ye wyste!'   *knew it*
     'I vouche sauf,' quod he: 'do what yow lyste.'   *grant it*

     Tho wesshen they, and sette hem doun, and ete;
1185 And after noone ful sleyly Pandarus
     Gan drawe hym to the wyndowe nexst the strete,   *Moved over*
     And seyde, 'Nece, who hath arayed thus   *done up*
     The yonder hous, that stont afornyeyn us?'   *facing*
     'Which hous?' quod she, and gan forto byholde,
1190 And knew it wel, and whos it was hym tolde;

     And fillen forth yn speche of thynges smale,
     And seten yn the wyndowe bothe tweye.
     Whan Pandarus sawe tyme to his tale,
     And saw wel that here folk weren aweye: *had left*
1195 'Now, nece myn, tel on,' quod he, 'I seye:
     How liketh yow the lettre that ye wot?
     Kan he theron? For, b[y] my trouthe, I not.'

     Therwith al rosy hewed [tho] wax she,
     And gan to humme, and seyde, 'So I trowe.'

1168 *at*: *of.* 1169 thought she would. 1178 no flaw . . . he had good sense.
1191 of trivial matters. 1193 saw the right moment for what he had to say.
1197 Is he good at such things . . . really don't know; *by*: *be.*

1200 'Aquyte hym wel, for Goddes love,' quod he;   *Repay*
     'Myself to medes wole the lettre sowe.'
     And held hise honde[s] up, and sat on knowe:
     'Now, goode nece, be it nevere so lyte,
     Yif me the labour it to sowe and plyte.'   *fold*

1205 'Ye, for I kan so write,' quod she tho,
     'And ek I not what I sholde to hym seye.'   *yet*
     'Nay, nece,' quod Pandare, 'sey not so:
     Yet at the leste thanketh hym, I preye,
     Of his good wil, and doth hym not to deye.   *cause*
1210 Now, for the love of me, my nece dere,
     Refuseth not at this tyme my preyere!'

     'Depardieux,' quod she, 'God leve al be wel:
     God helpe me so, this is the firste lettre
     That evere I wrote, ye, al or ony del.'   *part*
1215 And into a closet forto avyse here bettre   *private room*
     She wente allone, and gan hire herte unfettre
     Out of Disdayns prison but a lyte,*   *little*
     And sette here doun, and gan a lettre write.

     Of which to telle in short is myn entente
1220 Th'effect – as fer as I kan understonde.   *sense*
     She thonked hym of al that he wel mente   *sincerely*
     Towardes hire – but holden hym in honde   *deceive*
     She wolde nought, ne make hireself bonde
     In love, but as his suster, hym to plese,
1225 She wolde [ay] fayn, to don his herte an ese.   *gladly (be)*

     She shette it, and to Pandarus gan gon,   *sealed*
     There as he sat and loked into [the] strete,
     And doun she sette here by hym on a ston
     Of jaspre, upon a quysshon gold y-bete,   *embroidered*
1230 And seyde, 'As wysly helpe me God the grete,
     I nevere dide a thing with more peyne   *anguish*
     Than write this, to whiche ye me constreyne!'

     And tok it hym; he thonked here and seyde,
     'God wot, of thing ful ofte loth bygonne   *unwillingly*
1235 Cometh ende good; and nece myn, Criseyde,

1201 As a reward, I will personally sew. 1202 went on his knees. 1212 Indeed
. . . God grant. 1227 *the: a.* 1230 As surely as I hope that.

That ye to hym of hard now be y-wonne   *with difficulty*
Oughte he be glad, by God and yonder sonne:
Forwhi men seyth, "Impressiones lyghte
Ful lyghtly ben ay redy to the flyghte".

1240 'But ye han pleyed [the] tyrant neigh to longe,   *almost*
And hard was it youre herte forto grave;   *engrave*
Now stynte that ye no lengere on it honge
(Al wolde ye the forme of daunger save);
But hasteth yow to don hym joye have –
1245 For trusteth wel, to longe [y-]don hardnesse
Causeth despit ful often, for distresse.'   *anger*

And right as [they] declamed this matere,   *debated*
Lo, Troylus, right at the stretes ende,
Come rydyng with his tenthe some y-fere,   *ten others*
1250 Al softly, and thederwardes gan bende
There as they sete, as was his wey to wende
To palays-ward; and Pandar[e] hym aspyde
And seyde, 'Nece, y-se who cometh here ryde!

'O fle not yn – he seyth us, I suppose –   *am sure*
1255 Lest he may thynke that ye hym eschuwe.'   *are avoiding*
'Nay, nay,' quod she, and waxe as red as rose.
With that he gan hire humbly to saluwe,
With dredful chere, and ofte his hewes muwe;   *timid*
And up his look debonairly he caste,   *modestly*
1260 And bekked on Pandare, and forth [he] paste.   *nodded*

God wot yf he sat on his hors aright,   *properly*
Or goodly was beseyn, that ilke day!   *in appearance*
God wot whe[r] he was lyk a manly knyght!   *whether*
What sholde I drecche, or telle of his aray?   *spin it out*
1265 Criseyde, which that all these thynges say,   *saw*
To telle yn short, hire lyked al y-fere:
His persone, his aray, his look, his chere,

1238–9 easily taken are likely to disappear just as quickly. 1242 don't persist
in (this attitude) any longer. 1243 Even though you wish to keep up the
appearance of reserve. 1245 hard-heartedness persisted in for too long. 1247
they: he. 1250–1 moved towards where they were sitting. 1252 *Pandare*:
Pandarus. 1256 *rose*: the rose. 1258 he changed colour. 1266 absolutely
everything.

His goodly manere, and his gentillesse,
So wel that nevere sith that she was born
1270 Ne hadde she swych routhe of his distresse;
And how so she hath hard ben here byforn,   *even though*
To God hope I she hath now caught a thorn,
She shal not pulle it out this nexst wyke:
God sende mo swich thornes on to pyke!*

1275 Pandare, which that stod hire faste by,   *close at hand*
Felt iren hot, and he bygan to smyte,   *strike*
And seyde, 'Nece, I pray yow hertely,
Telle me that I shal axen yow a lyte:
A womman that were of his deth to wyte,   *to blame for*
1280 Withouten his gilt, but for hire lakked routhe,
Were it wel don?' Quod she, 'Nay, by my trouthe!'

'God help me so,' quod he, 'ye sey me soth;
Ye felen wel youreself that I not lye.
Lo, yend he ritt!' ['Ye,'] quod she, 'so he doth.'
1285 'Wel,' quod Pandare, 'as I have told yow thrye: *thrice*
Lat be youre nice shame and youre folye,   *ridiculous*
And spek with hym in esyng of his herte;
Lat niceté not do yow bothe smerte.'

But thereon was to heven and to done:
1290 Considered all thyng, it may not be;
And whi? For shame, and it were ek to soone
To graunten hym so gret a liberté.
For playnly hire entent, as seyde she,
Was forto love hym unwist, if she myghte,   *unknown*
1295 And guerdone hym with nothyng but with sighte.   *reward*

But Pandarus thoughte, 'It shal not be so,
Yf that I may, this nyce opinioun   *attitude*
Shal not be holde fully yeres two.'
What sholde I make of this a long sermoun?
1300 He moste assente on that conclusioun
As for the tyme; and whanne that it was eve,
And al was wel, he ros and toke his leve.

1270 *routhe: a routhe.* 1274 other thorns like it to pick out. 1278 Give me a
short answer to. 1284 See, there he rides! 1288 Don't allow foolish scruples to
cause you both pain. 1289 a great deal of hard work remained to be done.
1300 agree to that decision.

And on his way ful faste homward he spedde,
And right for joye he felte his herte daunce;
1305 And Troylus he fond alone abedde,
That lay, as doth these loveres, yn a traunce,
Bytwixen hope and derk desesperaunce.   *despair*
But Pandarus, right at his in comynge,
He song, as who seyth, 'Sumwhat I brynge!'

1310 And seyde, 'Who is in his bed so soone
Y-buryed thus?' 'It am I, frend,' quod he.
'Who, Troylus? Nay, helpe me so the mo[o]ne,'
Quo[d] Pandarus, 'thow shalt ryse and se
A charme that was sent right now to the,
1315 The which kan helen the of thyn accesse,   *fever*
Yf thow do forthwith al thi besynesse.'

'Ye, thorough the myght of God,' quod Troylus.
And Pandarus gan hym the lettre take,   *gave*
And seyde, 'Pardé, God hath holpen us:
1320 Have here a lyght and loke on al this blake.'   *writing*
But ofte gan the herte glade and quake
Of Troylus whil that he gan it rede,
So as the wordes yaf hym hope or drede.

But fynally he tok al for the beste
1325 That she hym wrot, for sumwhat he byheld   *had written*
On which hym thoughte he myghte his herte reste,
Al covered she the wordes under sheld.
Thus to the more worthi part he held,   *profitable*
That, what for hope and Pandarus byhest,   *promise*
1330 His grete wo foryede he at the leste.   *put aside*

But as we may alday oureselven se,   *all the time*
Thorugh more wode and col, the more fyr –
Right so encres of hope, of what it be,   *increase*
Therwith ful ofte encresseth ek desir;*
1335 Or as an ok cometh of a litel spir,   *shoot*
So thorugh this lettre which that she hym sente
Encressen gan desir, of which he brente.

1321 became (now) glad, (now) fearful. 1325 he found something in what he
read. 1327 Even if she concealed the (meaning of her) words. 1333 from
whatever source.

Wherfore I seye alwey that day and nyght
This Troylus gan to desiren more
1340 Than he dede erst, thurgh hope, and dide his myght
To pressen on, as by Pandarus lore,   *instruction*
And writen to hire of his sorwes sore,
Fro day to day – he let it not refreyde,   *grow cool*
That by Pandare he wrot somwhat or seyde;

1345 And dide also his othere observaunces
That to a lovere longeth yn this cas;
And after that these dees turnede on chaunces,
So was he outher glad or seyde, 'Allas!'
And held after his gistes ay his pas;
1350 A[nd] after swych answeres as he hadde,
So were hise dayes sory outher glade.   *or*

But to Pandar[e] alwey was his recours,
And pytously gan ay til hym to pleyne,
And hym bysoughte of red and som socours;   *advice, help*
1355 And Pandarus, that sey his wod peyne,   *saw, frenzied*
Wex wel neigh ded for r[o]uthe, soth to seyne,
And bysily with al his herte caste
Som of his wo to slen, and that as faste;

And seyde, 'Lord, and frend, and brother dere:
1360 God wot that thi disese doth me wo!   *pain*
But woltow stynten al this woful chere,
And by my trouthe, or it be dayes two,
And God toforn, yet shal I shape it so,
That thou shalt come into a certayn place   *appointed*
1365 There as thow mayst thiself hire preye of grace.   *Where*

'And certaynly – I not yf thow it wost,
But tho that ben expert yn love it seye –
It is oon of the thynges that furthereth most
A man, to have a leyser forto preye,   *opportunity*
1370 And syker place, his wo forto bywreye: *secure, reveal*
For yn good herte it mot som routhe impresse
To here and se the gilt[l]es in distresse.

1340 in the beginning. 1345 performed . . . rites. 1346 are proper in these
circumstances. 1347 according to how these dice fell. 1349 controlled his
speed by his throws. 1350 *And: As.* 1352 *Pandare: Pandarus.* 1358 bring to
an end, and immediately. 1360 *disese: dishese.* 1368 is of most help to.

    'Paraunter thenkestow: "Though it be so
    That Kynde wolde don here to bygynne   *Nature*
1375 To han a manere routhe upon my wo,   *some degree of*
    Seyth Daunger, 'Nay, thow shalt me nevere wynne'.
    So reuleth here hir[e her]tes gost withinne,   *spirit*
    That though she bende, yet she stant on rote.
    [W]hat in effect is this unto my bote?"   *remedy*

1380 'Thenk here ayens: whan that the sturdy ok,   *however*
    On which men hakketh ofte for the nones,   *some time*
    Receyved hath the happy fallyng strok,
    The grete sweigh doth it come al at onys,   *momentum*
    As doth these rokkes, or these myl-stones –
1385 For swyfter cours cometh thyng that is of wighte,   *heavy*
    Whan it descendeth, than don thynges lyghte.

    'And ried that boweth doun for every blast,   *reed*
    Ful lightly, cesse wynd, it wol[e] aryse:
    But so nyl not an ok whan it is cast   *felled*
1390 (It nedeth me nought the longe to forbyse).
    Men shal rejoyssen of a gret emprise   *undertaking*
    Acheved wel, and stant withouten doute,
    Al han men ben the lengere theraboute.   *Even though*

    'But Troylus, yet telle me, yf the l[e]ste,
1395 A thing now which that I shal axen the:
    Which is thi brother that thou lovest best,
    As yn thi verray hertes prevyté?'
    'I-wys, my brother Deyphebus,'* quod he.
    'Now,' quod Pandare, 'er owres twyes twelve,
1400 He shal the ese, unwyst of it hymselve.

    'Now lat me allone, and werken as I may,'
    Quod he – and to Deiphebus wente he tho,
    Which hadde his lord and gret frend ben ay
    (Save Troylus, no man he loved so).
1405 To telle in short, withouten wordes mo:

1373 Possibly you think. 1378 firmly rooted. 1379 *What*: *That*. 1382 lucky
stroke that brings it down. 1383 *it*: *it to*. 1388 *wole*: *wold*. 1390 teach by
proverbs. 1392 brought to a successful and lasting conclusion. 1394 *leste*:
lyste. 1399 before a day (has gone by). 1400 give you relief, without knowing
that he has done so. 1401 to do things my own way.

Quod Pandarus, 'I pray yow that ye be
Frend to a cause whiche that toucheth me.'   *concerns*

'Yis, pardé,' quod Deiphebus, 'wel thow wost,
In al that evere I may, and God tofor[e],
1410 Al nere it but for man I love most   *Excepting only*
(My brother Troylus) – but sey wherfore
It is, for sith that day that I was bore,
I na[s], ne nevere mo to ben I th[y]nke,
Ayeyns a thyng that myght the forthynke.'

1415 Pandare gan hym thonke and to hym seyde,
'Lo, sire, I have a lady yn this town,
That is my nece, and called is Criseyde,
Which som men wolden do oppressioun,   *persecute*
And wrongfully have hire possessioun;   *what is hers*
1420 Wherfor I of youre lordship yow byseche,
To ben oure frend, withoute more speche.'

Deiphebus hym answerede, 'O, is not this,
That thow spekest of to me so straungely,   *formally*
Criseyda, my frend?' He seyde, 'Yis.'
1425 'Thanne nedeth,' quod Deiphebus, 'hardely,   *indeed*
No more to speke, for trusteth wel that I
Wol be hire chaumpioun with spore and yerde;
I rought nought though alle here foos it herde!*

'But telle me, thow that wost alle this matere,
1430 How I myght best avaylen.' 'Now, lat se:'   *help*
Quod Pandarus, 'yf ye, my lord so dere,
Wolden as now don this honour to me,   *at this time*
To prayen here tomorwe, lo, that she
Come unto yow, here pleyntes to devyse –
1435 Hire adversaries wolde of hit agryse.   *take fright*

'And yf I more dorste prey yow as now,
And chargen yow to have so gret travayle,   *trouble*
To han som of youre bretheren here with yow,
That myghten to here cause bet avayle,   *further help*

1409 I can ever do, I swear to God; *tofore*: toforn. 1413 *thynke*: thenke.
1414 Opposed to anything that might displease you. 1420 implore your
protection. 1427 spur and stave. 1428 would not care if. 1434 set out her
grievances. 1436 ask you another favour.

1440 Than wot I wel she myght nevere fayle
     Forto be holpen – what at youre instaunce,
     What with here othere frendes governaunce.'   *guidance*

     Deiphebus, wh[ic]h that comen was of kynde
     To al honour and bounté to consente,
1445 Answered, 'It shal be don; and I kan fynde
     Yet grettere help to this yn myn entente.   *mind*
     What wolt thow seyn yf I for Eleyne sente
     To speke of this? I trowe it be the beste –
     For she may ledyn Parys as here leste.   *govern*

1450 'Of Ector, which that is my lord, my brother,
     It nedeth nought to prey hym frend to be,
     For I have herd hym, o tyme [and ek] other,
     Speke of Criseyde swich honour that he   *so highly of*
     May seyn no bet, swych hap to hym hath she.   *favour*
1455 It nedeth nought his helpes forto crave: *beg*
     He shal be swych right as we wole hym have.   *exactly*

     'Spek thow thiself also to Troylus
     On myn byhalve, and pray hym with us dyne.'
     'Sire, al this shal be don,' quod Pandarus,
1460 And toke his leve; and nevere wolde he fyne,   *pause*
     But to his neces hous as streyt as lyne
     He com, and fond here fro the mete aryse,
     And sette hym down, and spak right in this wyse.

     He seyde, 'O veray God, so have I ronne!
1465 Lo, nece, se ye nought how I swete?
     I not whether ye me the more thank konne –
     Be [ye] nought war how false Polyphete*
     Is now abowte eftsoones forto plete,
     And bryng on yow advocacies newe?'   *accusations*
1470 'I? No,' quod she, and chaunged al here hewe.

     'What is he more aboute, me to drecche   *harass*
     And don me wrong? What shal I do, allas?

───

1441–2 helped both by your urging and by. 1443 was naturally disposed;
which: *wheh*. 1444 To agree to anything that was honourable and good. 1451
It is unnecessary. 1452 *and ek*: *ek and*. 1462 she had got up from table. 1466
will be the more grateful to me for it. 1467 Don't you know. 1468 prepared
immediately to go to law.

Yet of hymself nothyng nold I recche   *care*
Nere it for Antenor and Eneas,   *If it were not*
1475 That ben his frendys yn swych manere cas.*
But for the love of God, myn uncle dere,
No fors of that – late hym have al y-fere: *matter for*

Withouten that, I have ynowh for us.'
'Nay,' quod Pandare, 'it shal nothyng be so,
1480 For I have ben right now at Deiphebus,
At Ector, and myne othere lordes mo,   *more of*
And shortly made eche of hem his fo,
That, by my thryft, he shal it nevere wynne,
For ought he kan, whan that so he bygynne.'

1485 And as they casten what was best to done,   *pondered*
Deiphebus of his owene curtasye   *innate*
Com hire to preye yn his propre persone,   *own*
To holde hym on the morwe companye
At dyner; which she wolde not denye,
1490 But good[ly] gan to his preyere obeye.   *graciously*
He thonked hire, and wente upon his weye.

Whanne this was don, this Pandare up anoon
(To tellen in short), and forth gan forto wende
To Troilus, as stille as ony ston,
1495 And al this thing he tolde hym, word and ende,
And how that he Deiph[e]bus gan to blende,   *deceive*
And seyde hym, 'Now is tyme, if that thow konne,
To bere the wel tomorwe, and al is wonne.

'Now spek, now prey, now pitously compleyne –
1500 Lat not for nice shame or drede or slouthe!   *foolish*
Somtyme a man mot telle his owene peyne;
Bileve it, and she shal han on the routhe;
Thow shalt be saved, by thi feyth, in trouthe.
But wel wot I [th]ow art now yn drede,
1505 And what it is, I ley I kan arede.   *bet, guess*

'Thow thinkest now: "How sholde I don al this?
For b[y] my cheres mosten folk aspye   *looks*

1475 business of this kind. 1477 let him take it all. 1484 anything he is able to
do. 1492 at once got up. 1497 have the power. 1498 conduct yourself. 1500
Don't refrain. 1501 himself speak of. 1504 *thow: yow.* 1507 *by: be.*

That for hire love is that I fare amys;   *suffer*
[Yet] hadde I levere unwyst for sorwe dye."
1510 Now thenk not so, for thou dost gret folye,
For right now have I founden o manere
Of sleyghte forto coveren al thi chere.

'Thow shalt gon over nyght, and that b[y]lyve,   *speedily*
Unto Deiphebus hous, as the to pleye –
1515 Thi maladye awey the bet to dryve
(Forwhy thou semest syk, soth forto seye).
And after that, doun in thi bed the leye,
And sey thow mayst no lengere up endure;   *bear to be up*
And lye right there, and byde thyn aventure.   *await, fortune*

1520 'Sey that thi fever is wont the forto take
The same tyme, and lasten til amorwe;   *the next day*
And lat se now how wel thow kanst it make –   *convincing*
For pardé, syk is he that is in sorwe.
Go now, farewel – and Venus here to borwe,   *as a pledge*
1525 I hope and thow this purpos holde ferme,   *if*
Thi grace she shal there fully conferme.'

Quod Troylus, 'Ywys, thow nedeles
Counseylest me that syklyche I me feyne,
For I am syk yn ernest, douteles,
1530 So that wel neygh I sterve for the peyne.'   *am dying*
Quod Pandarus, 'Thow shalt the bet[t]re pleyne, *complain*
And hast [the] lasse nede to countrefete,
For hym men demen hot that men seen swete.

'Lo, holde the at thi tryste clos, and I
1535 Shal wel the der unto thi bowe dryve.'
Therwith he tok his leve softely,
And Troylus to palays went blyve;   *quickly*
So glad ne was he nevere yn al his lyve,
And to Pandarus reed gan all assente,   *advice, wholly*
1540 And to Deiphebus hous at nyght he wente.

1509 would rather, without it being known; *Yet: That.* 1511–12 a cunning way
of hiding (the reason for) your appearance. 1514 amuse yourself. 1516 Because
you really do look ill. 1527–8 You really don't need to advise me to pretend to
be ill. 1533 suppose to be … sweat. 1534 keep yourself hidden at your
hunting station.

What nedeth yow to tellen al the chere   *welcome*
That Deiphebus unto his brother made;
Or his accesse, or syklyche manere –   *fever*
How men gan hym with clothes forto lade   *blankets, load*
1545 Whanne he was leyd, and how men wolde hym glade?   *cheer up*
But al for nought; he held forth ay the wyse
That ye han herd Pandare er this devyse.

But certeyn is, er Troylus hym leyde,
Deiphebus had hym prayed over-nyght   *that night*
1550 To ben a frend and helpyng to Criseyde –
God wot that he it grauntede anoon right,   *at once*
To ben here fulle frend with al his myght.
(But swych a nede was to prey hym thenne,
As forto bydde a wo[od] man forto renne!)   *mad, run*

1555 The morwen com, and neyhen gan the tyme   *approach*
Of mel-tid that the faire queene Eleyne   *dinner*
Shapt here to ben, an owre after the pryme,   *Intended*
With Deiphebus, to whom she nold not feyne.
But as his suster, homly, [soth] to seyne,   *informally*
1560 She com to dyner yn here playn entente –
But God and Pandare wyst what al this mente!

Come ek Criseyde, al innocent of this,
Antigone, hire sister Tarbe also;
But fle we now prolixité best is,
1565 For love of God, and late us faste go
Right to the effect, withoute tales mo,   *point*
Whi al this folk assembled in this place –
And late us of here saluynges pace.

Gret honour dide hem Deiphebus, certeyn,
1570 And fedde hem wel with al that myghte like;   *please*
But evere more, 'Allas!' was his refreyn,
'My goode brother, Troylus, the syke,
Lyth yet!' And therwithal he gan to syke;
And after that he peyned hym to glade
1575 Hem as he myghte, and chere good he made.

1546 he kept on behaving in exactly the way. 1554 *wood man: womman.*
1559 *soth: for.* 1560 unsuspectingly. 1564 it is best for us . . . to avoid long-
windedness. 1568 pass over their greetings. 1573 Is still ill in bed. 1574-5
took all the trouble he could to cheer them up.

Compleyned ek Eleyne of his sykenesse
So feythfully that pité was to here;　　　　　　　　*sincerely*
And every wight gan waxen for accesse
A leche anoon and seyde, 'In this manere　　　　*This is how*
1580　Men curen folk'; 'This charme I wole yow lere'.　*teach*
But there sat oon, al lyst here nought to teche,
That thought: 'Best cowde I yet ben his leche.'

After compleynt, hym gonnen thei to preyse,
As folk don yet whan som wyght hath bygonne
1585　To preyse a man, and [up] with prys hym reyse　*exalt*
A thousand fold yet hyer than the sonne:
'He is, he kan, that fewe lordes konne . . .'
And Pandarus, of that [they] wolde afferme,　　*maintain*
He not forgat here preysyng to conferme.

1590　Herde al this thyng Criseyde wel ynowh,
And every word gan [for]to notefye,　　　　　*take note of*
For whiche, with sobre chere, here herte lowh –　*grave*
For who is that ne wold here glorifye,
To mowen swych a knyght [don] lyve or dye?
1595　But al passe I, lyst ye to longe dwelle;
For for o fyn is al that evere I telle.　　　　　*one purpose*

The tyme come fro dyner forto ryse,
And as hem oughte, aryse everychon,　　　　　*got up*
And gonne a while of this and that devyse;　　*converse*
1600　But Pandarus brak al this speche anoon,　　*interrupted*
And seide to Deiphebus, 'Wole ye gon,　　　*proceed*
If youre wille be, as I yow preyde,
To speke here of the nedes of Criseyde?'

Eleyne, whiche that by the hond here held,
1605　To[k] first the tale, and seyde, 'Go we blyve';
And goodly on Criseyde she byheld,
And seyde, 'Joves lat hym nevere thryve
That doth yow harm, and bryng hym soone of lyve,　*to die*
And yeve me sorwe but he shal it rewe,
1610　If that I may, and alle folk be trewe.'

1578-9 acted like a doctor for the fever. 1581 care to give instruction. 1582 I
know best how to cure him; *cowde: cowede.* 1587 has abilities. 1588 *they: he.*
1594 have the power to cause. 1595 I pass over all that for fear of keeping you
too long. 1605 Was the first to speak.

'Tell [th]ow thi neces cas,' quod Deiphebus   *Explain*
To Pandarus, 'for thow kanst best it telle.'
'My lordys and my ladyes, it stant thus:
What sholde I lengere,' quod he, 'do yow dwelle?'
1615 He rong hem [out] a proces lyk a belle   *accusation*
Upon here fo, that highte Poliphete,
So heynous that men myghte on it spete.   *hateful, spit*

Answer[d]e of this eche worse of hem than other,
And Poliphete they gonnen thus to waryen: *curse*
1620 'Anhonged be swych on, were he my brother!'   *Hanged*
'And so he shal, for [it] ne may not varyen!'
What sholde I lengere yn this tale taryen?
Pleynly al at ones they here hyghten
To ben hire helpe in al that evere they myghten.   *all ways*

1625 Spak than Eleyne, and seyde, 'Pandarus,
Woot ought my lord my brother this matere –
I mene Ector? Or wot it Troylus?'
He seyde, 'Ye, but wole ye now [me] here?
Me thenketh this: sith that Troylus is here,   *since*
1630 It were good, if that ye wolde assente,
She tolde hereself hym al this er she wente.

'For he wole have the more here grief at herte
Bycause, lo, that she a lady ys;
And, by youre leve, I wole but right yn sterte
1635 And [do] yow wete, and that anoon, ywys,
If that he slepe, or wole ought here of this.'
And yn he lepte, and seyde hym in his ere,
'God have thi soule, i-brought have I the bere!'   *bier*

To smylen of this gan tho Troylus,
1640 And Pandarus, withoute rekenynge,
Out wente anoon to Eleyne and Deiphebus,
And seyde hem, 'So there be no taryinge,
Ne more pres, he wole wel that ye brynge   *crowding*
Criseyda, my lady, that is here;
1645 And as he may endure, he wole here.   *for as long as*

1611 *thow*: yow. 1614 cause you delay. 1618 Responded to. 1621 cannot be
altered; *it*: he. 1623 Unreservedly . . . promised. 1632 feel . . . more intensely.
1634 just look in. 1635 let you know. 1640 (further) consideration.

    'But wel ye wot, the chaumbre is but lite,   *only small*
    And fewe folk lightly may make it warm;   *easily*
    Now loke ye – for I wole have no wytè   *no blame*
    To bryng yn pres that myghte don [hym] harm,
1650 Or hym disesen, for my bettre arm –
    Wher it be bet she byde til eftson[i]s?
    Now loke ye, that knoweth what to don is.

    'I sey for me, best is, as I kan knowe,   *for my part*
    That no wight yn ne wente but ye tweye,   *nobody*
1655 But it were I, for I kan yn a throwe
    Reherce here cas unlyk that she kan seye;
    And after this, she may hym ones preye
    To ben good lord, yn short, and take here leve:
    This may not mechel of his ese hym reve.

1660 'And ek, for she is straunge he wole forbere   *set aside*
    His ese, which that he thar nought for yow;   *need*
    Ek other thing, that touche[th] not to here,
    He wole [yow] telle – I wot it wel, right now –
    That secret is, and for the townes prow.'   *advantage*
1665 And they, that nothing knewe of his entent,
    Withoute more to Troilus yn they went.

    Eleyne, in al here good[ly softe] wyse,
    Gan hym saluwe, and womanly to pleye,   *tease*
    And seyde, 'Ywis, ye moste alweyes aryse;   *nevertheless*
1670 Now, fa[i]re brother, beth al hool, I preye!'   *get well*
    And gan here arm right over his sholder leye,
    And hym with al here wit to recomforte;
    As she best kowde, she gan hym [to] disporte.   *cheer up*

    So after this quod she, 'We yow byse[k]e,   *beg*
1675 My dere brother Deiphebus and I,
    For love of God (and so doth Pandare eke)
    To ben good lord and frend right hertely   *sincerely*
    Unto Criseyde, which that certeynly

1650 discomfort . . . right arm; *disesen: dishesen.* 1651 Whether it would be better for her to wait until later; *eftsonis: eftsones.* 1652 is acceptable. 1655 Unless . . . short time. 1656 Set out her business differently from the way she would. 1658 (her) protector. 1659 cause him great discomfort. 1662 isn't relevant; *toucheth: toucher.* 1663 *yow: me.* 1665 *his: this.* 1667 *goodly softe: goode softly.* 1674 *byseke: byseche.*

Receyveth wrong – as wot wel here Pandare,
1680 That kan here cas wel bet tha[n] I declare.'   *set out*

This Pandarus gan newe his tunge affyle,   *make sharp*
And al here cas reherce, and that anoon.   *go over*
Whan it was seyd, soone after in a while,
Quod Troylus, 'As sone as I may gon,   *walk*
1685 I wole right fayn with al my myght ben oon
(Have God my trouthe) here cause to susteyne.'   *support*
'Good thryft have ye,' quod Eleyne the queene.   *fortune*

Quod Pandarus, 'And it youre wille be,
That she may take here leve, er that she go?'
1690 'O, elles God forbede [it,' tho] quod he,
'If that she vouchesaf forto do so.'   *condescend*
And with that word quod Troilus, 'Ye two,
Deiphebus and my suster leef and dere,   *esteemed*
To yow have I to speke of o matere,   *a particular*

1695 'To ben avysed by youre red the bettre.'   *counsel*
And fond, as hap was, at his beddes hed,   *it chanced*
The copye of a tretes and a lettre   *document*
That Ector hade hym sent to axen red
If swych a man was worthi to ben ded –
1700 Woot I nought who, but in a grysly wyse   *grim manner*
He preyede hem anoon on it avyse.   *to look*

Deiphebus gan this lettre to unfolde
In ernest gret – so dede Eleyne the queene;
And, romynge outward, fast it g[onne] byholde,   *closely*
1705 Downward a steyre, into an herber grene,   *garden*
This ilke thing thei redden hem bytwene;
And largely the mountaunce of an owre,   *fully, space*
Thei gon on it to rede and to powre.   *scrutinize*

Now late hem rede, and turne we anoon
1710 To Pandarus, that gan ful faste prye
That al was wel, and out he gan to gon
Into the grete chambre, and that yn hye,   *in haste*
And seyde, 'God save al this companye!

1680 *than: that.* 1703 very earnestly. 1704 strolling out (of the room) . . .
closely; *gonne: gan,* 1710 very quickly ascertained.

    Come, nece myn, my lady queene Eleyne
1715 Abydeth yow, and ek my lordes tweyne.   *Awaits*

    'Rys, take with yow yowre nece Antigone,
    Or whom yow lyst – or no fors: hardyly,
    The lasse pres the bet – come forth with me,
    And loke that ye thonke humbely
1720 Hem alle thre; and whan ye may goodly   *reasonably*
    Youre tyme y-se, taketh of hem youre leve,
    Lest we to longe his reste hym [by]reve.'   *deprive*

    Al in[n]ocent of Pandarus entente,   *intention*
    Quod tho Criseyde, 'Go we, uncle dere.'
1725 And arm in arm inward with hym she wente,   *inside*
    Avysed wel here wordes and here chere;
    And Pandarus yn ernestful manere
    Seyde, 'Alle folk, for Goddes love, I preye,
    Stynteth right here, and softely yow pleye.

1730 'Avise[th] yow what folk ben here withinne,   *Consider*
    And yn what plit oon is, God hym amende!'
    And inward thus, 'Ful softely bygynne:
    Nece, I conjure, and heighly yow defende,
    On his byhalve which that us alle sowle sende,
1735 And in the vertue of corounes tweyne,
    Sle nought this man, that hath for yow this peyne.*

    'Fy on the devel! Thenk which on he is,
    And in what plyt he lith; come of anoon!   *hurry up*
    Thenk al swych taried tid but lost it nys –   *time*
1740 That wole ye bothe seyn whan ye ben on.   *united*
    Secundelich, ther yet devyneth noon   *guesses*
    Upon yow two – come of now, yf ye konne: *About*
    Whil folk is blent, lo, al the tyme is wonne.

    'In titeryng and pursuyte and delayes,
1745 The folk devyne at waggynge of a stre;
    And though ye wolden han after merye dayes,

1717 no matter: indeed. 1718 less of a crowd the better. 1723 *innocent*:
incocent. 1729 Stop just here, and amuse yourselves quietly. 1731 what a state
. . . make him well. 1733 implore (you) . . . strictly forbid. 1737 what kind of
a person. 1739 *al: that al*. 1743 deceived . . . all the advantage is yours. 1744
Through hesitation, persistence. 1745 People guess (what is going on) from the
waving of a straw. 1746 would later wish for joy.

Than dar ye nought – and why? For she and she
Spak swych a word; thus loked he and he!
Las tyme y-lost! I dar not with yow dele;
1750 Com of, therfore, and bryngeth hym to hele.'*   *health*

But now to yow, ye lovers that ben here,
Was Troylus nought in a kankedort,*   *dilemma*
That lay and myghte whysprynge of hem here,
And thought, 'O Lord, ryght now renneth my sort
1755 Fully to dye or han anoon comfort';   *Completely*
And was the firste tyme he shulde here preye
Of love – O myghti God, what shal [he] seye?

Explicit Secundus liber

1747 this woman or that. 1749 Alas . . . have to do with you. 1754 fate is
being decided. 1757 *he: I.*

BOOK THREE

Incipit prohemium Tercii libri

O blysful light, of whiche the bemes clere*
Adorneth al the thridde hevene faire;
O sonnes lyef, O Joves doughter dere,*   *beloved*
Plesaunce of love, O goodly debonaire,   *most gracious*
5 In gentil hertes ay redy to repaire;   *dwell*
O verray cause of hele and of gladnesse –
I-heried be thi myght and thin goodnesse.   *Extolled*

In hevene and helle, in erthe and salte se,
Is felt thi myght, [i]f that I w[el] descerne;   *perceive*
10 As man, bryd, beste, fissh, herbe, and grene tre
The fel[e] in tymes with vapour eterne.
God loveth, and to love wol nough[t] werne;   *refuse*
And in this wor[l]d no lyves creature   *living*
Withouten love is worth or may endure.   *has value*

15 Ye Joves first to thilke affectes* glade,
Thorugh whiche that thinges lyven alle and be,
Comeveden, and amoreux h[y]m made
On mortal thyng, and as yow lyst ay ye
Yeve hym in love ese or adversité,   *Grant*
20 And in a thousand formes* doun h[y]m sente   *shapes*
For love in erthe, and whom yow lyste, he hente.   *embraced*

9 *if: of; wel: wole.* 11 Experience at (due) times your eternal influence; *fele:
feld.* 15–17 You first prompted Jove to those joyful desires as a result of which
all things are given life and being; 17, 20 *hym: hem.*

Ye fierse Mars apeysen of his ire,   *appease, anger*
And as yow lyste, ye maken hertes digne: *worthy*
Algates hem that ye wole sette afyre,   *At any rate*
25 Thei dreden shame, and vices thei resigne;   *give up*
Ye do hem corteys be, fresch and benigne;   *gracious*
And hye or lowe, after a wyght entendeth,   *just as*
The joyes that he hath, youre myght it sendeth.*

Ye holden regne and hous in unité;
30 Ye sothfast cause of frendship ben also;
Ye knowe al thilke covered qualité
Of thing[es], which that folk on wondren so,
Whan they kan not construe how it may jo   *explain*
She loveth hym, or whi he loveth here:
35 As whi this fissh and nought that cometh to were.*

Ye folk a lawe han set in universe   *established*
(And this knowe I by hem that loveres be)
That whoso stryveth with yow hath the w[e]rse.
Now, lady bryght, for thi benignité,
40 At reverence of hem that serven the,   *In*
Whos clerk I am, so techeth me devyse   *scribe, describe*
Som joye of that is felt in thi servyce.   *(part of the)*

Ye in my nakede herte sentement
Inhelde, and do me shewe of thi swetnesse.
45 Caliope,* thi voys be now present,
For now is nede – sestow not my destresse,
How I mot telle anon right the gladnesse
Of Troylus, to Venus heriynge?   *praise*
To which [gladnesse], who nede hath, God hym brynge!*

Explicit prohemium Tercii libri

22 *ire: iire.* 29 kingdom and household. 31 hidden essence. 33 cannot
understand how it can happen [that]. 35 is trapped. 36 *universe; universite.*
38 *werse: worse.* 42 *thi: this.* 43–4 Pour into my empty heart the capacity to
feel. 46–7 can't you see how daunted I am at having, right now, to narrate.

Incipit liber Tercius

50 Lay al this mene while Troylus,
   Recordynge his lesson in this manere: *Going over*
   'Mafey,' thought he, 'thus wole I sey, and thus;
   Thus wole I pleyne unto my lady dere;
   That word is good, and this shal be my chere;   *comfort*
55 This nyl I not foryeten in no wyse' –
   God leve hym werke as he [k]an devyse!

   And Lord, so his herte gan to quappe,   *thump*
   Herynge here come, and short forto syke!   *pant*
   And Pandarus, that lad here by the lappe,
60 Com ner, and gan [in] at the curtyn pyke,   *peeped*
   And seyde, 'God do bote on alle syke!   *relieve*
   Se who is here yow comen to visite:
   Lo, here is she that is youre deth to wyte.'   *blame (for)*

   Therwith it semed as he wepte almost.
65 'A ha,' quod Troylus so rufully,   *piteously*
   'Wher me be wo, O myghty God, [th]ow woost –   *If I am*
   Who is al there? I se nought, trewely.'
   'Sire,' quod Criseyde, 'it is Pandare and I.'
   'Ye, swete herte? Allas, I may nought ryse,
70 To knele, and do yow honour in some wyse' –

   And dressede hym upward, and she right tho
   Gan bothe here hondes softe upon hym leye.
   'O, for the love of God, do ye not so
   To me,' quod she, 'I, what is this to seye?
75 Sire, come am I to yow for causes tweye:
   First, yow to thonke, and of youre [lordshipe] eke
   Continuance I wolde yow bese[k]e.'

   This Troilus, that herde his lady preye
   Of lordship hym, wax neyther quyk ne ded,*   *alive*
80 Ne myght a word for shame to it seye,
   Although men sholde smyte of his hed;   *cut off*
   But Lord, so he wex sodeynlyche red!

52 By my faith . . . I will say (first) this, (then) that. 55 I won't forget this (one)
on any account. 56 God grant that he may act as he plans to; *kan: gan.* 66
thow: yow. 76 your protection; *lordshipe: mercy.* 77 *beseke: beseche.*

And sire, his lesson that [he] wende konne,
To preyen hire, is thurgh his wit y-ronne.

85 Cryseyde al this aspiede wel ynowh,   *perceived*
For she was wys, and lovede hym nevere the lasse,   *had sense*
Al nere he malapert, or made it towh,
Or was to bold to synge a fol a masse.   *flatter*
But whan his shame gan somwhat to passe,
90 His resones, as I may my rymes holde,   *What he said*
I yow wole telle, as techen bokes olde.

In chaunged voys, right for his verrey drede,
Which voys ek quooke, and therto his manere   *shook*
Goodly abayst, and now his hewes rede,   *humbled*
95 Now pale, unto Criseyde his lady dere,
With look doun cast and humble yolden chere,
Lo, the alderfirst word that hym asterte
Was twyes: 'Mercy, mercy, swete herte!'

And stynte awhil[e], and whan h[e] myghte out-brynge,
100 The nexte word was: 'God wot that I have,
As feythfully as [I] have had konnynge,
Ben yowres, also God my sowle save,
And shal til that I, woful wyght, be grave;   *buried*
And though I dar ne kan unto yow pleyne,
105 Iwys, I suffre nought the lasse peyne.

'Thus muche as now, O wommanlyche wyf,
I may out-brynge, and yf this yow displese,
That shal I wreke upon myn owne lyf   *avenge*
Right sone, I trowe – and don youre herte an ese,
110 If with my deth youre herte [I] may apese;
But syn that ye han herd me somwhat seye,   *a little*
Now recche I nevere how sone that I deye.'   *care*

Therwith his manly sorwe to byholde,
It myght han mad an herte of ston to rewe;   *feel pity*
115 And Pandare wep as he to watre wolde,
And poked evere his nece newe and newe,

83–4 he thought he had learnt, to ask her favour, has passed out of his mind.
87 Although he was not presumptuous or overbearing. 90 within the limits of
my rhyming skill. 96 submissive countenance. 97 very first . . . escaped. 99
paused . . . recovered speech; *awhile: awhily; he: ho.* 114 *to: forto.* 115 as if he
would turn to water. 116 went on nudging . . . again and again.

And seyde, 'Wo bygon ben hertes trewe!   *Afflicted*
For love of God, make of this thyng an ende,
Or sle us bothe at ones er that ye wende.'

120 'I, what?' quod she, 'By God and by my trowthe,
I not nought what ye wille that I shal seye.'   *don't know*
'"I, what?"!' quod he: 'That ye han on hym routhe,
For Goddes love, and doth hym nought to deye!'
'Now thanne thus,' quod she, 'I wolde hym preye
125 To telle me the fyn o[f] his entente –
Yet wyst I nevere wel what that he mente.'   *clearly*

'What that I mene, O swete herte dere?'
Quod Troylus, 'O goodly fresshe fre!
That with the stremes of youre eyen clere   *beams, bright*
130 Ye wolde som tyme frendly on me se,   *look*
And thanne agreen that I may ben he,
Withoute braunch of vice yn ony wyse,   *part*
In trowthe alwey to don yow my servyse,

'As to my lady right, and chief resort,   *true*
135 With al my wit and al my deligence;
And [I] to han, right as yow lyst, comfort,   *receive*
Under yowre yerde, egal to myn offence –   *correction*
As deth, if that I breke youre defen[c]e;
And that ye d[e]igne me so muche honoure,   *grant*
140 Me to comaunden ought yn any owre;

'And I to ben yowre verray, humble, trewe,
Secret, and yn myn paynes pacient,
And evere mo desire fresshly newe
To serven, and ben ay i-lyke diligent,   *equally*
145 And with good herte al holly youre talent
Receyven wel, how sore that me smerte –
Lo, 'this mene I, myn owene swete herte!'

Quod Pandarus, 'Lo, here an hard request,
A[nd] resonable, [a] lady forto werne!
150 Now, nece myn, by natal Joves feste,

125 exactly what he has in mind; *of: on.* 128 fair, young, noble (lady). 138 infringe anything you prohibit; *defence: defende.* 140 anything at any time. 145–6 Accept graciously all your wishes, however much it pains me. 148–9 a request difficult to grant and reasonable for a lady to refuse! 150 feast of Jove's birth.

Were I a god ye sholde sterve as yerne,   *die at once*
That heren wel that this man wole nothyng yerne   *desires*
But youre honour, and sen hym almost sterve,
And ben so loth to suffren hym yow serve.'   *allow*

155 With that she gan hire eyen on hym caste
Ful esyly and ful debonairly,   *gently, modestly*
Avysyng here, and hied not to faste   *hastened*
With nevere a word, but seyde hym softely:
'Myn honour sauf, I wol wel trewely,   *assured*
160 [And] in swych forme as he gan now devyse,   *set out*
Receyven hym fully to my servyce,

'Bysechyng hym for Goddes love that he
Wolde in honour of trouthe and gentilesse,
As I wel mene, eke mene wel to me,
165 And myn honour with wit and besynesse   *diligence*
Ay kepe; and yf I may don hym gladnesse,
Fro hen[ne]sforth, i-wys, I nyl not feyne: *hesitate*
Now beth al hol; no lengere ye ne pleyne.

'But nathelees, this warne I yow,' quod she,
170 'A kynges sone although ye be, iwys,
Ye shul no more have soverayn[e]té   *lordship*
Of me in love than right in that cas is;   *proper*
Ne I nyl forbere, yf that ye don amys,   *refrain*
To wrathen yow; and whil that ye me serve,   *anger*
175 Cherycen yow right after ye deserve.

'And shortly, my dere herte and al my knyght,
B[e]th glad and draweth yow to lustynesse,
And I shal trewely with al my myght
Youre bittre tornen al [in]to swetnesse,
180 If I be she that may [y]ow do gladnesse;
For every wo ye shal recovere a blysse.'
And hym in armes toke, and gan hym kysse.

Fil Pandarus on knees, and up his eyen   *Fell*
To hevene threw, and held hise hondes hye;   *raised*
185 'Inmortal god,' quod he, 'that mayst nought dyen,

153 almost at the point of death. 160 *And: But.* 164 my intentions are sincere.
168 completely healed. 175 Show you favour. 177 incline to cheerfulness;
Beth: Buth. 180 *yow: now.* 181 In place of.

Cupide I mene, of this mayst glorifie;*
And Venus, thow mayst make melodie;
Withouten hond, me semeth that in the towne,
For this merveyle ich here eche belle sowne.

190 'But ho, no more now of this matere,   *stop*
Forwhi this folk wole comen up anoon   *Because*
That han the lettre red – lo, I hem here!
But I conjure the, Criseyde, and on,   *urge*
And two, thow Troylus, whan thow mayst gon,
195 That at myn hows ye ben at myn warnynge,
For I ful wel shal shape youre comynge;   *contrive*

'And eseth there youre hertes right ynough,
And lat se which of yow shal bere the belle
To speke of love aright' – therwith he lough –   *at which*
200 'For there have ye a layser forto telle.'
Quod Troylus, 'How longe shal Y dwelle   *wait*
Er this be don?' Quod he, 'Whan thow mayst ryse,
This thing shal be right as I yow devyse.'

With that Eleyne and also Deiphebus
205 Tho comen upward, right at the steyres ende;   *to the top*
And, Lord, so thanne gan grone Troylus
His brother and his suster forto bl[e]nde!   *deceive*
Quod Pandarus, 'It is tyme that we wende;   *left*
Tak, nece myn, youre leve at alle thre,
210 And late hem speke, and cometh forth with me.'

She toke here leve at hem ful thryftyly,   *courteously*
As she wel koude, and they here reverence   *honour*
Unto the fulle here deden hardely,   *fully*
And wonder wel spaken in here absence
215 Of here in preysyng of here excellence,
Hire governaunce, hire wit, and here manere   *bearing*
Commendeden it joye was to here.

Now late here wende unto here owne place,   *go (back)*
And torne we to Troylus aye[y]n,
220 That gan ful lyghtly of the lettre passe

186 have cause to boast. 188 Without being pulled by. 193–4 both of you.
195 when I tell you. 198 take the lead. 200 you will have time to talk (about
it). 207 *blende: blynde.* 220 very rapidly disposed of.

That Deiphebus hadde yn the gardeyn seyn;   *seen*
And of Eleyne and hym he wolde f[e]yn
Delyvered ben, and seyde that hym l[e]ste
To slepe, and after tales have reste.   *talking*

225 Eleyne hym kyste, and tok here leve blyve;
Deiphebus ek, and hom wente every wyght;
And Pandarus, as faste as he may dryve,
To Troylus tho com as lyne right,
And on a paillet al that glade nyght   *mattress*
230 By Troylus he lay with mery chere
To tale, and wel was hem thei were y-fere.   *converse*

Whan every wyght was voyded but they two,   *had left*
And alle the dores were faste y-shette,
To telle in short, withoute wordes mo,
235 This Pandarus, withouten ony lette,   *delay*
Up ros, and on his beddes side hym sette,
And gan to speke in a sobre wyse   *serious*
To Troylus, as I shal yow devyse.

'Myn alderlevest lord and brother dere,   *most beloved*
240 God wot, and thow, that it sat me [so] sore   *so pained me*
When I the saw so langwysshyng to-yere   *this year*
For love, of which thi wo wax alwey more,   *grew*
That I with al my myght and al my lore   *knowledge*
Have evere sethen do my bysynesse   *since, utmost*
245 To brynge the to joye out of distresse;

'And have it brought to swich plit as thow wost,   *point*
So that thorugh me thow stondest now in weye
To fare wel – I sey it for no bost,
And wostow whi? For shame it is to seye:
250 For the have I a game bygonne to pleye
Which that I nevere don shal eft for other,
Although he were a thousand fold my brother.

'That is to seye, for the am I becomen,   *for your sake*
Bytwene game and ernest, swych a mene   *go-between*
255 As maken wommen unto men to comen.—
Al sey I nought, thow wost wel what I mene;

222 *feyn: fayn.* 223 *leste: lyste.* 247–8 are now likely to prosper. 251 do again
for anyone else.

For the have I my nece of vices clene
So fully mad thi gentilesse triste,
That al shal ben right as thiselve lyste.   *exactly, want*

260 'But God, that alle wot, take I to wytnesse
That nevere I this for coveytise wroughte,
But oonly forto abrygge that destresse   *lessen*
For which wel nygh thow deydest, as me thoughte.
But, gode brother, do now as the oughte,
265 For Goddes love, and kep hire out of blame
(Syn thow art wys) and save alwey here name.

'For wel thow wost, the name as yet of here
Among the peple, as who seyth, [h]alwed is;   *venerated*
For that man is unbore, dar I swere,   *not born*
270 That evere wyste [that] she dide amys.   *wrong*
But wo is me that I, that cause al this,
May thenken that she is my nece dere,
And I here em, and traytour eke y-fere!   *all at once*

'And were it wyst that I through myn engyn   *contrivance*
275 Hadde in my nece i-put this fantasye   *inclination*
To do thi lust and holly to be thyn –
Why, al the world upon it wolde crye,
And seye that I the worste trecherye
Dide yn this cas that evere was bygone,
280 And she forlost – and thow ryght nought [y-]wonne!

'Wherfore, er I [wole] ferther go a pas,   *step*
Yet eft I the byseche and fully seye   *implore, stress*
That preveté go with us in this cas –   *secrecy*
That is to seye, that thow us nevere wreye;   *betray*
285 And be nought wroth though I the ofte preye
To holden secre swych an heigh matere,   *important*
For skylful is, thow wost wel, my preyere.

'And thenk what wo ther hath bytyd er this,
For makynge of avauntes, as men rede;
290 And what myschaunce in this world yet is,   *misfortune*

257 who is wholly virtuous. 261 did this through desire for money. 266 always
preserve her reputation. 280 utterly ruined – and you no real victor! 287 you
know well that what I am asking is reasonable. 289 Through boasting (of
success in love).

Fro day to day, right for that wykkede dede.
For whiche these wise clerkes that ben dede   *now dead*
Han evere yet proverbed to us yonge,
That firste vertu is to kepe tonge.   *silent*

295 'And nere it that I wilne as now t'abregge
Diffusioun of speche, I koude almost
A thousand olde storyes the alegge   *cite*
Of wommen lost thorugh fals and foles bost:
Proverbes kanst thyselve ynowe and wost   *plenty of*
300 Ayens that vice forto ben a labbe,   *gossip*
Al seyde men soth as often as the[y] gabbe.   *talk nonsense*

'O tonge, allas, so often here byforn   *in the past*
Hastow made many a lady bright of hewe
Sey: "Welaway the day that I was born!"   *Accursed be*
305 And manye a maydes sorwes forto newe.   *renew*
And, for the more part, al is untrewe
That men of yelpe, and it were brought to preve:
Of kyn[d] noon avaunt[our] is to leve.

'Avauntoure and a lyere is al on,   *one and the same*
310 A[s] thus: I pose a womman graunte me   *put the case*
Here love, and seyth that other wole she non,
And I am sworn to holde it secre –
And after I go telle [it] two or thre.
Iwys, I am avauntour at the leste,
315 And a lyere, for I breke myn heste.   *promise*

'Now loke thanne yf they be nought to blame,
Swych maner folk – what shal I clepe hem? what? –   *call*
That hem avaunte of wommen, and by name,
That nevere yet byhight hem this ne that,
320 Ne knewe hem no more than myn olde hat!
No wonder is, so God me sende hele,   *well-being*
Though womm[e]n drede with us men to dele.

293 taught us in proverbs when we were young. 295–6 wish at this time to cut
short all wordiness. 304 *Sey: Seyd.* 307 men boast about, if it were put to the
test. 308 From (his own) nature, no boaster is to be believed; *kynd: kyng;
avauntour: avauntures.* 319 promised them anything at all. 322 fear to have
(close) dealings with; *wommen: womman.*

'I sey this not for no mystrust of yow,
Ne for no wyse men, but for foles nice,
325 And for the harm that in the world is now,
As wel for foly ofte as for malice;*   *much*
For wel wot I in wys folk that vice   *discreet*
No womma[n] drat, if she be wel avised,   *fears*
For wyse ben by foles [harm] chastised.

330 'But now to purpos, leve brother dere;   *the point*
Have al this thing that I have seyd in mynde,
And kep the clos, and be now of good chere,   *it hidden*
For at thi day thow shalt me trewe fynde.
I shal thi proces sette yn swych a kynde,   *suit*
335 And God toforn, that it shal the suffice;   *satisfy*
For it shal ben right as thow wolt devyse.

'For wel I wot thow menest [wel], pardé;
Therfore I dar this fully undertake.
Thow wost eke what thi lady graunted the;
340 And day is set thi chartres up to make.
Have now good nyght; I ma[y] no lengere wake;   *stay awake*
And byd for me, syn thow art now yn blysse,   *pray*
That God me sende deth or soone lysse.'   *relief*

Who myghte telle half the joye and feste   *pleasure*
345 Whiche that the sowle of Troylus tho felte,
Herynge th'ef[fect] of Pandarus byheste?   *substance, promise*
His olde wo that made his [herte] swelte,   *faint*
Gan tho for joye wasten and to-melte;
And alle the richnesse of his sikes sore   *abundance*
350 At ones fledde; he felte of hem no more.

But right so [as] these holtes and these hay[i]s,
That han in wynter ded ben and dreye,   *withered*
Revesten hem in grene when that May is,
Whan every lusti lyketh best to pleye,   *sport*
355 Right in that selve wyse, soth forto seye,   *same*
Wax sodeynlyche his herte ful of joye,
That gladder was there nevere man yn Troye.

328 *womman: wommat.* 329 are schooled by. 340 draw up the contract
between you. 341 *may: make.* 346 *th'effect: the feyth.* 347 *herte: sorwe.* 348
dwindle and melt to nothing. 351 woods and hedges; *hayis: hayes.* 353 Clothe
themselves once more.

And gan his lok on Pandarus up caste,   *gaze, turn up*
Ful sobrely and frendly forto se,
360 And seyde, 'Frend, in Ap[e]ril the laste –
As wel thow wost, if it remembreth the –
How neigh the deth for wo thow founde me,   *close to*
And how thow dedest al thi bysynesse
To knowe of me the cause of my distresse.

365 'Thow wost how longe I it forbar to seye   *declined*
To the, that art the man that I best triste;   *trust*
And peril was it noon to the bywreye,   *disclose*
That wyst I wel; but telle me, yf the lyste,
Sith I so loth was that thiselfe it wyste,
370 How dorst I mo tellen of this matere,   *any others*
That quake now and no wyght may us here?

'But natheles, by that God I the swere,
That as hym lyst may al this world gouverne –
And, yf I lye, Achilles with his spere   *(may)*
375 Myn herte cleve, al were my lyf eterne,
As I am mortal, yf I late or yerne   *ever*
Wolde it bywreye, or dorste, or sholde konne,   *be able to*
For al the good that God made under sonne –

'That rather deye I wolde and determyne,
380 As thenketh me now, stokked yn presoun,   *fettered*
In wrecchednesse, in filthe, and yn vermine,
Ca[y]tif to cruel Kyng Agamenoun:*   *Prisoner*
And this yn alle the temples of this town,
Upon the goddes alle, I wole the swere
385 Tomorwe day, if that it lyketh [the] here.

'And that thow hast so meche don for me   *much*
That I ne may it nevere more deserve,
This knowe I wel, al myghte I now for the
A thowsand tymes in a morwen sterve;   *die*
390 I kan no more, but that I the wole serve   *can (say)*
Right as thi [scl]ave, whider so thow wende,
For everemore, unto my lyves ende.

---

363 tried so hard. 366 *I: I to.* 375 split, even if I were immortal. 379 come to
my end. 382 *Caytif: Castif.* 385 at dawn tomorrow. 391 *sclave* altered to
knave.

'But here with al myn herte I the byseche,
That nevere in me thow deme swych folye   *suppose*
395 As I shal seyn: me thowghte by thi speche
That this which thow me dost for companye,   *as a friend*
I sholde wene it were a baudery –   *act of a bawd*
I am nought [wood], al yf I lewed be;   *ignorant*
It is not so, that wote I well, pardé!

400 'But he that goth for gold or for richesse
On swych message, calle hym what the lyst;   *you please*
And this that thow dost, calle it gentilesse,
Compassioun, and felawship, and tryst –   *friendship*
Departe it so, for wyde where is wyst
405 How that there is dyversité requered
Bytwyxen thynges lyk, as I have lered.   *been taught*

'And that thow knowe I thenke nought, ne wene,   *imagine*
That this servise a shame be, or jape –
I have my faire suster Polixene,
410 Cassandre,* Eleyne, or ony of the frape,   *company*
Be she nevere so faire or wel i-shape,   *formed*
Tel [me] which thow wylt of everychone
To han for thyne, and late me thanne allone!

'But syn that thow hast don me this servyce,
415 My lyf to save, and for noon hope of mede,   *gain*
So, for the love of God, this grete emprise   *undertaking*
Parforme it out, for now is most nede.   *Carry*
For hygh and low, withouten ony drede,
I wol alwey thyne hestes alle kepe;   *commands*
420 Have now good nyght, and late us bothe slepe!'

Thus held hym eche with other wel apayed,   *satisfied*
That al the world ne myght it bet amende;   *improve*
And on the morwe, whan thei were arayed,   *dressed*
Eche to his owen nedes gan entende.   *attend*
425 But Troylus, thou[gh] as the fyr he brende   *burned*
For sharp desir of hope and of plesaunce,
He not forgat his gode governaunce.   *self-control*

---

398 *mad* (?) written above *yf.* 404–6 Make this distinction, because it is
everywhere acknowledged, that discrimination is necessary between things (that
look) alike. 407 so that you may know. 413 let me get on with it. 425 *though:*
thouhte.

But in hymself with manhod gan restreyne
Eche rakel dede and eche unbrydled chere,
430 That alle tho that lyven, soth to seyne,
Ne sholde han wyst, by word or by manere,
What that he mente, as towchyng this matere: *in respect of*
From every wyght as fer as is the clowde
He was – so well dissimulen he kowde. *feign*

435 And al the while whiche that I yow devyse, *tell you of*
This was hys lyf: with al his fulle myght
By day he was in Martes highe servyse –
This is to seyn, in armes as a knyght;
And for the more part, the longe nyght *greater*
440 He lay and thoughte how that he myght serve
His lady best, he[re] thank forto deserve. *gratitude*

Nyl I nought swere, although he lay softe, *I won't*
That in his thought he nas sumwhat disesed, *uneasy*
Ne that he tornede on his pylwes ofte,
445 And wolde of that hym myssed han ben sesed.
But yn swych cas m[a]n is nought alwey y-plesed
(For ought I wot) no more than was he:
That kan I deme of possibilité. *suppose likely*

But certeyn is, to purpos forto go,
450 That in this while, as wreten is in geste, *chronicle*
He say his lady somtyme, [and] also
She with hym spak whan that she dorste and leste; *wished (to)*
And by hire bothe avys, as was the beste, *joint decision*
Apoynteden full warly in this nede,
455 So as they dorste, how they wolden procede.

But it was spoken in so short a wyse, *so briefly*
In swych [awayt] alwey, and in swych fere, *so guardedly*
Lest ony wyght dyvynen or devyse *guess, imagine*
Wolde of hem two, or to it leye an eere,
460 That al this world so lef to h[e]m ne were

---

429 hasty action and uncontrolled expression. 436 to the full extent of his
powers. 443 *disesed: dishesed.* 445 would have liked to have been put in
possession of what he lacked. 446 *man: men.* 453 *as: as it.* 454 Determined
very cautiously. 460 would not have been so dear to them; *hem: hym.*

As that Cupido wolde hem grace sende
To make of here speche aryght a[n] ende.

But thilke lytel that they spake or wroughte,   *what, did*
His wyse gost tok ay of al swych hede,   *spirit*
465 It semed here he wyste what she thoughte   *to her*
Withouten word, so that it was no nede   *being told*
To bidde hym ought to done or ought forbede;   *tell*
For which she thoughte that love, al come it late,*   *even if*
Of alle joye hadde opned here the yate.

470 And shortly of this proces forto pace,
So wel his werk and wordes he bysette,   *employed*
That he so ful stod in his lady grace,   *completely*
That twenty thousand tymes, or she lette,   *before, stopped*
She thonked God she evere with hym mette.
475 So koude he hym governe in swych servyse,
That al the world ne myght it bet devyse.

Forwhi she fond hym so dyscret in al,   *Because*
So secret, and of swych obeysaunce,
That wel she felte he was to hire a wal
480 Of stel, and sheld from every dysplesaunce;   *trouble*
That to ben in his good governaunce,
So wys he was, she nas no more afered –
I mene as fer as oughte ben requered.   *expected*

And Pandarus to quyke alwey the fyr,   *kindle*
485 Was evere ylyk prest and dyligent;   *prompt*
To ese his frend was set al his desir:
He shof ay on, he to and fro was sent,   *pressed*
He lettres bar whan Troylus was absent,
That nevere man, as in his frendes nede,
490 Ne bar hym bet than he, withouten drede.

But now, paraunter, som man wene wolde
That every word, or sonde, or lok, or chere   *message*
Of Troylus that I rehersen sholde,   *relate*
In al this while unto his lady dere –
495 I trowe it were a long thing forto here,

462 bring an end to (the need for) further speech. 476 improve upon it. 490
Conducted himself. 491 would perhaps expect. 495 would take a long time.

Or of what wyght that stont in swych disjoynte,
Hise wordes alle, or every lok, to poynte.

Forsothe, I have not herd it don er this,   *in the past*
In storye noon, ne no man here, I wene!
500 And though I wold, I koude not, iwys:
For there was som epistel hem bytwene
That wolde, as seyth myn auctor, wel contene *take up*
Neigh half this bok, of which hym lyst not write –
How sholde I thanne a lyne of it endite?*   *write down*

505 But to the grete effect: than sey I thus, *main point*
That stondyng in concord and in quiete,
This ilke two, Criseide and Troylus,
As I have told, and in this tyme swete –
Save only often myght thei not mete,
510 Ne layser have hire speches to fulf[e]lle –
That it befel right as I shal yow telle.

That Pandarus, that evere dide his myght
Right for the fyn that I shal speke of here, *to the end*
As forto brynge to his hous som nyght
515 His faire nece and Troylus y-fere,
[W]hereas at leyser al this heigh matere
Towchyng here love were at the fulle upbounde,
Hadde out of doute a tyme to it founde.

For he with gret deliberacioun
520 Hadde everything that here[to] myghte avaylle *be useful*
Forncast and put in execucioun,
And neither laft for cost ne for travayle; *spared, labour*
Come yf hem lest, hem sholde nothing fayle –
And forto ben in ought espied there,   *at all*
525 That, wyst he wel, an inpossible were.

Dredles it clere was in the wynd
From every pye and every lette-game;

496–7 Or to describe in detail all the words or expressions of anyone in the
same straits. 510 Nor have the opportunity to talk at length to one another;
fulfelle: fulfille. 516 *Whereas: Thereas.* 517 Relating to . . . arranged in every
detail. 521 Foreseen and carried out. 523 If they wished to come, they would
lack nothing. 526–7 Certainly, it was clear to the windward of every magpie
and spoil-sport.

Now al is wel, for al the world is blynd
In this matere, bothe fremed and tame   *wild*
530 This tymber is al redy up to frame;   *set up*
Us lakketh nought but that we weten wolde   *know*
A certeyn houre in whiche she comen sholde.   *definite time*

And Troylus, that al this purvyaunce   *preparation*
Knew at the fulle, and waytede on it ay,
535 Hadde hereupon ek made gret ordenaunce,   *arrangements*
And founde his cause, and therto his aray,   *excuse*
Yf that he were myssed, nyght or day,
Ther while he was abowte this servyse,
That he was gon to don his sacrifice,

540 And most at swych a temple alone wake,   *keep vigil*
Answered of Appollo forto be,
And first to sen the holy laurer quake,   *laurel*
Er that Apollo spak out of the tre
To telle hym next whan Grekes sholden fle –   *be defeated*
545 And for[thy] lette hym no man, God forbede,   *hinder*
But prey Apollo helpen in this nede.*

Now is there but litel more forto done,
But Pandare up, and shortely forto seyne,   *rose*
Right soone upon the chaungyng of the moone,
550 Whan lyghtles is the world a nyght or tweyne,   *dark, two*
And that the walkene shop hym forto reyne,
He straught amorwe unto his nece wente
(Ye han wel herd the fyn of his entente).

Whanne he was come, he gan anoon to pleye
555 As he was woned, and of hymself to jape;   *accustomed*
And fynally he swor and gan here seye,
By this and that, she shold hym not escape,
Ne lengere don hym after here to gape;
But certeynly she moste, by here leve,   *permission*
560 Come soupen in his hous with hym at eve.

At whiche she lough, and gan here faste excuse,
And seyde, 'It rayneth – lo, how shal I gon?'
'Lat be,' quod he, '[ne] stond not thus to muse;

538 During that time.   551 the heavens got ready to rain.   552 directly next
morning.   563 don't keep thinking it over.

This mot be don! Ye shal be there anoon.'
565 So, at the laste herof they felle at oon   agreed
(Or elles, softe he swor here in here ere,   quietly
He nolde nevere come there she were).

Soone after this, to hym she gan to rowne,   whisper
And asked hym yf Troylus were there.
570 He swor here nay, for he was out of towne,
And seyde, 'Nece, I pose that he were –   supposing
Yow dorste have nevere the more fere;
For rathere than men myght h[y]m ther aspie,
Me were levere a thousand fold to dye.'   I would prefer

575 Nought lyst myn auctour fully to declare
What that she thought whan that he seyde so
(That Troylus was out of towne y-fare),
As yf he seyde there[of] soth or no;*
But that, withouten awayte, with hym to go   delay
580 She graunted hym, sith he hire that bisoughte,
And as his nece obeyed as here oughte.

But natheles yet gan she hym byseche,
Although with hym to gon it was no fere,   (reason to)
Forto be war of gosylyche peple speche,   geese-like
585 That dremen thynges whiche that nevere were,
And wel avyse hym whom he brought there;
And seyde hym, 'Em, syn I most on yow triste,
Loke al be wel, and do now as yow lyste.'

He swor 'Yis', by stokkes and by stones,   on every idol
590 And by the goddes that in hevene dwelle,
Or elles were hym levere, soule and bones,   preferable
With Pluto kyng as depe ben yn helle
As Ta[n]talus – what sholde I more telle?*
Whan al was wel, he ros and toke his leve;   settled
595 And she to souper com whan it was eve,

With a certayn of here owene men,   (number)
And with here faire nece Antigone,
And othere of here wommen nyne or ten;

---

573 *hym*: hem. 575–6 My author isn't concerned to describe her thoughts in detail. 577 had left the city. 580 since he asked her to do that. 586 consider carefully. 595 *to*: unto the.

But who was glad now – who, as trowe ye,
600 But Troylus, that stod and myght it se
Thurghout a lytel wyndowe in a st[e]we,
Ther he byshet syn mydnyght was [in] mewe,   *cooped up*

Unwist of every wight but of Pandare?*
But to the poynt: now whanne she was y-come,
605 With alle joye and alle frendes fare,
Here em anoon in armes hath here nome,   *embraced her*
And after to the souper, alle and some,
Whan tyme was, ful softe they h[e]m sette –   *comfortably*
God wot, ther was no deynté forto fette!   *lacking*

610 And after souper gonnen they to ryse,
At ese wel, with hertes fressh and glade,
And wel was hym that koude best [de]vyse   *contrive*
To like here, or laughen that here made.   *please*
He song, she pleyde, he told tales of Wade;*
615 But at the laste, as every thing hath ende,
She tok here leve, and nedes wolde wende.   *of necessity*

But O Fortune, executrice of wyerdes!
O influen[c]es of thise hevenes hye! –   *(planetary)*
Soth is that under God ye ben oure hierdes,   *controllers*
620 Though to us bestez ben the causes wrie.   *hidden*
This mene I [now] for she gan homward hye,   *hurry*
But execut was al byside here leve
The goddes wyl, for which she moste bleve.   *remain*

The bente mone with hire hornes pale,
625 Saturne, and Jove in Cancro joyned were,*
That swych a rayn from hevene gan avale,   *pour down*
That every maner womman that was there
Hadde of that smoky reyn a verray fere;   *real fear*
At which Pandare tho lough and seyde thenne:
630 'Now were it tyme a lady to go henne!

601 small heated room; *stewe: stuwe.* 603 Without the knowledge of anyone
but Pandarus. 605 and in the most friendly way. 608 *hem: hym.* 612 *devyse:
avyse.* 616 *wolde: she wolde.* 617 who carries out (our) destinies; *destine*
written above *wyerdes.* 618 *influences: influentes.* 622 quite without her
permission. 630 a fine time for.

'But, goode nece, yf I myght evere plese
Yow any thing, thanne prey [ich] yow,' quod he,
'To don myn herte as now so gret an ese   *comfort*
As forto dwelle here al this nyght with me –
635 Forwhi this is yowre owene hous, pardé   *Because*
For b[y] my trouthe, I sey it for no game,   *seriously*
To wende now it were to me a shame.'   *go*

Criseyde, whiche that kowde as muche good
As half a world, tok hede of his preyere;
640 And syn it ron, and al was on a flod,
She thoughte, 'As good chep may I dwellen here,   *profitably*
And graunte [it] gladly with a frendes chere,
And have a thank, as grucche and thanne abyde –
For hom to gon, it may nought wel betyde.

645 'I wole,' quod she, 'myn uncle lef and d[er]e,   *grant*
Syn that yow lyst, it skile is to be so;   *is reasonable*
I am right glad with yow to dwellen here –
I seyde but a-game I wolde go.'
'Iwys, graunt mercy, nece,' quod he tho,
650 'Were it a-game or no, soth forto telle,
Now am I glad, syn that yow lyst to dwelle.'

Thus al is wel; but tho bygan aright
The newe joye, and al the feste agayn.   *conviviality*
But Pandarus, yf goodly hadde he myght,
655 He wolde han hyed here to bedde fayn,   *hurried*
And seyde, 'Lord, this is an huge rayn!   *monstrous*
This were a weder forto slepen inne;
And that I rede us soone to bygynne.

'And, nece, wot ye where I wol yow leye,
660 For that shul not lyggen fer asonder,   *apart*
And for ye neither shullen, dar I seye,
Heren noyse of reynes nor of thond[er]?
By God, right in my litel closet yonder;

---

636 *by: be.* 638–9 knew as well as most people what was right. 640 went on
raining. 642 friendly face. 643 grumble and still have to stay. 644 is out of
the question. 645 *dere: drede.* 648 was only joking when I said. 654 could
have managed it politely. 657 the sort of weather to sleep through. 658 advise
. . . start doing. 659 intend to put you. 662 *thonder: thondre.*

And I wole in that o[ut]er hous allone
665 Be wardeyn of youre wommen everychone.   *guardian*

'And in this myddel chaumbre that ye se
Shul youre wommen slepen wel and softe;   *comfortably*
And there I seyde, shal youreselve be –   *where*
And yf ye liggen wel tonyght, come ofte,
670 And careth not what weder is on lofte.   *above*
The wyn anon, and whan so that yow leste,   *now*
So go we slepe; I trowe it be the beste.'

Ther nys no more, but hereafter soone,
The voydé dronke, and travers drawe anoon,
675 Gan every wight that hadde nought to done
More in that place out of that chaumber gon;
And everemo so sternelych it ron,   *fiercely, rained*
And blew therwith so wonderlyche loude,
That wel neigh no man heren other koude.

680 Tho Pandarus, here em, right as hym oughte,
With women swych as were hire most aboute,
Ful glad unto hire beddes side here broughte,
And toke his leve, and gan ful lowe lowte,   *bowed*
And seyde, 'Here [at] this closet dore withoute,
685 Right overthwart, youre wommen lyggen alle,   *opposite*
That whom yow lyste of hem, ye may here calle.'

So whanne that she was yn the closet leyd,
And alle here wommen forth by ordenaunce   *as arranged*
A-bedde weren, there as I have seyd,
690 There was no more to s[kipp]en nor to traunce,
But boden go to bedde with myschaunce,   *told, a curse*
If ony wight was sterynge onywhere,   *moving (about)*
And late hem slepe that a-bedde were!

But Pandarus, that wel koude eche a del   *part*
695 The olde daunce, and every poynt therinne,
Whan that he sey that al[le] thyng was wel,
He thought he wolde on his werk bygynne,

---

664 *outer: other.* 669 sleep comfortably. 674 nightcap . . . curtain. 681 closest
to her. 684 *at: in.* 686 whichever of them you want. 690 prancing or tramping
about; *skippen: speken.* 695 sport of love . . . detail of it.

And gan the stewe dore al softe unpynne,
And stille as ston, withouten lenger lette,   *delay*
700 By Troylus adown right he hym sette.

And shortly to the poynt ryght forto gon:
Of alle this werk he told hym word and ende,   *business*
And seyde, 'Make the redy ryght anoon,
[For] thow shalt into hevene blysse wende.'
705 'Now blisful Venus, thow me grace sende,'
Quod Troylus, 'for nevere yet no nede
Hadde ich er now, ne halvendel the drede.'

Quod Pandarus, 'Ne drede the nevere a del,   *bit*
For it shal ben right as thow wylt desire:
710 So thrive I, this nyght shal I make it wel,
Or casten al the growel in the fyre.'
'Yit, blisful Venus, this nyght thow me enspire,'
Quod Troylus, 'as wys as I the serve,   *truly*
And evere bet and bet shal til I sterve.   *better, die*

715 'And yf I hadde, O Venus ful of m[y]rthe,   *bliss*
Aspectes badde of Mars or of Saturne,
Or thow comb[u]st or let were [in] my byrthe,
Thi fader prey al thilke harm disturne   *ward off*
Of grace, and that I glad ayen may turne,
720 For love of hym thow lovedest yn the shawe   *wood*
(I mene Adoon, that with the bor was slawe).*

'[O,] Jove ek, for the love of faire Europe,
The whiche in forme of bole away thow fette,   *bull, abducted*
Now help! O Mars, thow with thi blody cope,
725 For love of Cipres, thow me nought ne lette!
O Phebus, thenk whan Dane hereselven shette
Under the bark, and laurer wax for drede,*   *turned into a*
Yet for here love, O help now at this nede!   *crisis*

'Mercurye, for the love of Hierse ek,
730 For which Pallas was with Aglawros wroth,*
Now help! And ek Diane, I the bysek   *implore*

---

698 quietly unfasten. 706–7 never before did I have such need (of it), nor was
half as afraid. 715 *myrthe: murthe.* 716 Evil influences (at my nativity). 717
your influence was obscured (through closeness to the sun) or hindered; *com-
bust: combest.* 725 don't hinder me.

That this viage be not to the loth.
O fatal sustren, which er ony cloth   *sisters*
Me shapen was, my destené me sponne,
735 So help[eth] to this werk that is bygonne.'

Quod Pandarus, 'Thow wrecched mouses herte,
Art thow agast so that she wole the byte?
Whi, do on this furred cloke above thi sherte,   *put*
And folewe me, for I wol han the wyte;   *take the blame*
740 But byde, and late me go byfore a lyte.'   *wait, little*
And with that word he gan undo a trappe,   *trap-door*
And Troylus he brough[t] in by the lappe.

The sterne wynd so lowde gan to route   *roar*
That no wight other noyse myghte here;
745 And they that lay at the dore without,   *outside*
Ful sikerly thei slepten al i-fere;   *soundly*
And Pandarus with a ful sobre chere,   *serious*
Goth to the dore anoon wit[h]owten lette,
There as they laye, and softely it shette.   *closed*

750 And as he come ayenward prevely,   *quietly back*
His nece awook and asked: 'Who goth there?'
'My dere nece,' quod he, 'it am I –
Ne wondreth not, ne haveth of it no fere.'   *be alarmed*
And ner he com and seyde here yn here ere: *closer*
755 'No word, for love of God, I yow byseche!
Lat no wight rysen and heren of oure speche.'   *stir*

'What! Which weye be ye comen, benedicité?'   *bless us*
Quod she – 'And how [thus] unwyst of us alle?'
'Here at this secre trappe dore,' quod he.
760 Quod tho Criseyde, 'Lat me som wyght calle!'
'I! God forbede that it sholde falle,'   *happen*
Quod Pandarus, 'that ye swych foly wroughte –
They myght deme thyng they nevere [er] thoughte.

'It is nought good a slepyng hound to wake,
765 Ne yeve a wyght a cause to devyne.

---

732 enterprise does not displease you. 737 *agast: agarst.* 742 fold (of his cloak). 758 without any of us hearing you. 762 such a foolish thing; *Quod: Quod tho.* 763 imagine things that had never entered their heads before. 765 give anyone reason to be suspicious.

Youre wommen slepen alle, I undertake,   *assure you*
So that for hem the hous men myghte myne,
And slepen wolen til the sonne shyne;
And whanne my tale al brought is to an ende,
770 Unwist, right as I cam, so wole I wende.

'Now, nece myn, ye shul wel understonde,'
Quod he, 'so as ye wommen demen alle,   *agree*
That forto holde in love a man in honde,
And hym here lef and dere herte calle,   *darling*
775 And maken hym an howve above a calle   *hoodwink*
(I mene, as love another in this while):   *all this time*
She doth hireself a shame and hym [a] gyle.   *deceit*

'Now, wherby that I telle yow al this?   *why do I*
Ye wot yourself as wel as ony wyght   *anyone*
780 How that youre love [al] fully graunted is
To Troylus, the worthieste knyght
On of this world, and therto trouthe plyght,   *in addition*
That, but it were on hym along, ye nolde
Hym nevere falsen while ye lyven sholde.   *be false to*

785 'Now stant it thus, that sith I fro yow wente,
This Troylus, right platly forto seyn,   *bluntly*
Is thurgh a goter by a prevy wente
Into my chaumbre come in al this reyn,
Unwyst of every manere wyght, certeyn,
790 Save of myself, as wysly have I joye,
And by that feith I shal Pryam of Troye.   *(owe to)*

'And he is come in swich peyne and distresse
That but he be al fully wod by this,   *mad*
He sodeynly mot falle into wodnesse,
795 But yf God helpe – and cause whi is this: *Unless*
He seyth hym told is of a frend of his
How that ye loven sholde on that hatte Horaste,*   *is called*
For sorwe of whiche this nyght shal ben his laste.'

___

767 as far as they are concerned . . . tunnel under. 770 in exactly the way. 773 keep putting off. 776 *while: mene while.* 780 *al: that.* 781-2 One of the noblest knights. 783 if it depended only on. 785 it has come about. 787 a gutter . . . secret passage. 790 certainly as I hope to. 798 *shal: shalt.*

Criseyde, which that alle these thynges herde,
800 Gan sodeynly aboute here herte colde,   *Felt a sudden chill*
And with a syk she sorwfully answerede: *sigh*
'Allas! I wende whoso tales tol[d]e,
My dere herte wolde me [n]ot holde
So lyghtly fals. Allas! conseytes wronge,   *opinions*
805 What harm they don! for now lyve I to longe.

'Horaste, allas! – and falsen Troylus?   *deceive*
I knowe hym not – God helpe me so,' quod she.
'Allas! what wykked spirit told hym thus?   *malicious*
Now certes, em, tomor[w]e, yf I hym se,
810 I shal therof as fully excuse me
As evere dide womman, yf he lyke' –   *wishes (it)*
And with that word she gan ful sore syke.

'O [God],' quod she, 'so worldly selynesse,   *happiness*
Which clerkes callen fals felicité,   *learned men*
815 Y-medled is with many a bitternesse!   *Mingled*
Ful angwysshous than is, God wot,' quod she,
'Condicioun of veyn prosperité: *hollow*
For o[u]ther joyes comen nough[t] y-fere,   *either, at once*
Or elles no wight hath hem alwey here.

820 'O brotel wele of mannes joye unstable!
With what wyght so thow be, or how thow pleye,   *operate*
Outher he wot that thow, joye, art muable,   *changeable*
O[r] wot it not – it mot ben on of tweye.   *(the) two*
Now yf he wot it not, how may he seye
825 That he hath verray joye and selynesse,   *true*
That is of ignoraunce ay in derknesse?

'Now yf he wot that joye is transitorie –
As every joye of worldly thyng mot fle –   *pass away*
Than every tyme he [that] hath in memorie,
830 The drede of lesyng maketh hym that he   *loss*
May in no parfit selynesse be;
And yf to lese his joye he set a myte,
Than semeth it that joye is worth but lyte.*   *little*

---

802 would have thought that; *tolde: tolle*. 803–4 not so readily have thought
me unfaithful; *not: uot*. 819 possesses them for ever on this earth. 820 fragile
prosperity. 823 *Or: Other he.* 832 cares in the least about losing.

'Wherfore I wole deffyne in this manere: *conclude*
835 That trewely, for ought I kan espie,   *see*
Ther is no verray wele in this world here.
But O thow wykked serpent jalousye,   *malicious*
Thow mysbeleved, envyous folye: *untrustworthy*
Whi hastow mad Troylus to me untriste,   *distrustful*
840 That nevere yet agylte hym that I wyste?'

Quod Pandarus: 'Thus fallen is this cas.'
'Whi, uncle myn,' quod she, 'who tolde [hym] this?
Whi doth myn dere herte thus, allas?'
'Ye wote, ye, nece myn,' quod he, 'what is;
845 I hope al shal be wel that is amys,
For ye may quenche al this yf that yow leste –
And doth right so, for I holde it the beste.'   *consider*

'So shal I do tomorwe, ywys,' quod she,
'And God toforn, so that it shal suffise.'   *satisfy (him)*
850 'Tomorwe? Allas, that were a fayre!' quod he;   *fine thing*
'Nay, nay, it may not stonden yn this wyse!   *like this*
For, nece myn, thus writen clerkes wyse,
That "Peril is with drecchyng yn i-drawe" –
Nay, swych abodes be nought worth an hawe.   *putting off*

855 'Nece, al thing hath tyme, I dar avowe;   *swear*
For whan a chaumber a-fyr is, or an halle,
More nede is it sodeynly to rescowe
Than to dispute, and axe amonges alle
How this candele in the straw is falle.
860 A, benedicité! for al among that fare
The harm is don, and farewel feldfare!   *all is up!*

'And, nece myn – [ne] take it not [a]gref –   *wrongly*
If that ye suffre hym al nyght in this wo,   *(to remain)*
God help me so, ye hadde hym nevere lef
865 (That dar I seyn, now there is but we two).
But wel I wot ye wole not do so;
Ye ben to wys to do so gret folye,   *commit*
To putte his lyf al nyght in jupartie.'   *danger*

836 no true prosperity. 840 consciously did him wrong. 841 This is how things
stand. 842 *hym: yow.* 843 behaves in this way. 853 Danger is attracted by
delay. 857 promptly to salvage. 858 question all present. 860 while all that is
going on. 864 can never have loved him.

'Hadde [I] hym nevere lef? By God, I wene   *believe*
870 [Ye] hadde nevere thing so lief!' quod she.
'Now by my thryft,' quod he, 'that shal be sene,
For syn ye make this ensample of me,
If I al nyght wolde hym in sorwe se,
For al the tresour yn the town of Troye,
875 I bidde God I nevere mot have joye.

'Now loke thanne, yf ye that ben his love   *consider*
Shul putte al nyght his lyf in jupartie   *danger*
For thing of nought, now, by that God above,   *trivial*
Nought only this delay cometh of folye,
880 But of malis, if that I shal nought lye.
What! platly, and ye suffre hym in distresse,   *bluntly*
Ye neyther bounté don ne gentilesse.'

Quod tho Criseyde: 'Wole ye don o thing,   *(just) one*
And ye therwith shal stynte al his disese?
885 Have here, and bereth hym this blewe ryng,   *take*
For there is nothing myght hym bettre plese,
Save I myself, ne [more] his herte apese;   *set at rest*
And sey my dere herte that his sorwe
Is causeles – that shal ben sene tomorwe.'   *unfounded*

890 'A ryng?' quod he. 'Ye, haselwodes shaken!*
Ye, nece myn, that ryng moste han a ston
That myghte a dede man alyve maken,
And swych a ryng I trowe that ye have non.
Discrecioun out of youre hed is gon –   *Good sense*
895 That fele I now,' quod he, 'and that is routhe;
O tyme y-lost, wel maystow cursen slouthe!   *wasted*

'Wot ye not wel that noble and heigh corage   *exalted*
Ne sorweth not – ne stenteth ek – for lyte?
But yf a fol were in a jalous rage,
900 I nold not sette at his sorwe a myte,   *value*
But feffe hym with a fewe wordes white

---

869 *I: ye.* 870 loved anyone as much; *Ye: I.* 871 upon my word. 872 since you are bringing me into it. 882 You behave neither kindly nor graciously. 884 bring all this suffering to an end. 887 *more: bettre.* 890 a pointless thing to do! 891 would have to have (in it). 898 Does not become sorrowful – or cease to be so – for a trivial cause. 901 bestow a few specious words upon him.

Another day, whan that I myght hym fynde –
But this thing stont al in another kynde.

'This is so gentil and so tender of herte,
905 That with his deth he wole his sorwes wreke –   *avenge*
For trusteth wel, how sore that hym smerte,
He wole to yow no jalouse wordes speke;
And forthi, nece, er that his herte breke,
[S]o speke youreself to him of this matere,
910 For with o word ye may his herte stere.   *one, direct*

'Now have I told what peril he is inne,
And his comyng unwyst is to every wyght;
Ne, pardé, harm may there be non, ne synne –   *Nor*
I wol myself be with yow al this nyght.
915 Ye knowe ek how he is youre owne knyght,
And that by right ye moste upon hym triste,
And I al prest to fecche hym whan yow liste.'   *ready*

This accident so petous was to here,
And ek so lyk a soth at pryme face,   *first glance*
920 And Troylus hire knyght to hire so dere,
His prevé comyng, and the siker place,
That though that she dide hym as thanne a grace,
Considered alle thinges as they stode,
No wonder is, syn she dide al for gode.   *the best*

925 Cryseyde answered: 'As wysly God at reste   *to*
My sowle brynge, as me is for hym wo!   *I am grieved*
And em, ywys, fayn wolde I do the beste,   *gladly*
Yf that I hadde grace forto do so.
But whether that ye dwelle or for hym go,   *stay*
930 I am, til God me bettre mynde sende,   *clearer*
A[t] dulcarnon, right at my wittes ende.'

Quod Pandarus, 'Ye, nece, wol ye here?
Dulcarnon called is "Flemyng of wrecches"* –
It semeth hard, for wrecches wol not lere,   *study*
935 For verray slouthe and othere wilful t[e]cches

---

903 is essentially different. 909 *So: To.* 918 What had happened was made to
sound so pitiful. 931 Totally at a loss. 933 the defeat of miserable (school)boys.
935 innate laziness . . . deliberate faults; *tecches: tacches.*

This seyd by h[e]m that [ben] not worth two f[e]cches;   *beans*
But ye ben wys, and that we han on honde
Nis neither hard ne skylful to withstonde.'   *reasonable*

'Thanne, em,' quod she, 'doth herof as yow lyst;   *act in this*
940 But er he come I wil up first aryse,
And, for the love of God, syn al my trist
Is on yow two, and ye ben bothe wyse,
So wyrcheth now in so discret a wyse   *act*
That I honour may have and he plesaunce –
945 For I am here al yn youre governaunce.'   *under, control*

'That is wel seyd,' quod he, 'my nece dere –
[Ther good] thryft on that wyse gentil herte!
But liggeth stille, and taketh hym ryght here;   *receive*
It nedeth not no ferthere for hym sterte.   *rush off*
950 And eche of yow ese otheres sorwes smerte,   *pain*
For love of God; and, Venus, I the herye,   *praise*
For soone hope I we shulle ben alle merye.'

This Troylus ful sone on knes hym sette
Full sobrely, ryght by here beddes hede,
955 And yn his beste wyse his lady grette;
But Lord, so she wax sodeynlych red!
Ne though men sholden smyten of here hed,
She kowde nought a word aryght out-brynge
So sodeynly, for his sodeyn comynge.   *Immediately*

960 But Pandarus, that so wel koude fele   *feel sympathy*
In every thyng, to pleye anoon bygan,
And seyde, 'Nece, se how this lord kan knele!
Now, for youre trouthe, seth this gentil man!' –   *look at*
And with that word he for a quysshon ran,   *cushion*
965 And seyde, 'Kneleth now, whil that yow l[e]ste;   *for as long as you please*
There God youre hertes brynge soone at reste!'   *May*

Kan I not seyn, for she bad hym not ryse,   *since*
If sorwe it put out of here remembraunce,   *mind*
Or elles yf she toke it in the wyse
970 Of dueté, as for his observaunce;   *act of homage*

936 *hem: hym; ben: is; fecches: facches.* 947 May good fortune come upon;
Ther good: That. 957 even at the cost of losing her head. 958 utter a single
word clearly. 962 knows how to. 965 for as long as you please; *leste: lyste.*

But wel fynde I she dide hym this pleasaunce,
That she hym kyste, although she siked sore,   *sighed*
And bad hym sytte adown withowten more.   *(delay)*

Quod Pandarus: 'Now wol ye wel bygynne;
975 Now doth hym sitte – now gode nece dere! –   *make*
Upon youre beddes side [al] there withinne,
That eche of yow the bet may other here.'   *better*
And with that word he drow hym to the f[e]re,
And tok a lyght, and fond his contenaunce
980 As forto loken upon an old romaunce.

Criseyde, that was Troylus lady right,   *true*
And cler stod on a grounde of sykernesse,
Al thoughte she, here servaunt and hire knyght   *Even if*
Ne sholde of right noon untrouthe in here gesse,
985 Yet natheles, considered his distresse,
And that love is in cause of swych folye,   *madness*
Thus to hym spak she of his jelousye:

'Lo, herte myn, as wolde the excellence
Of Love, ayeyns the which that no man may –
990 Ne oughte ek, goudly – make resistence,   *reasonably*
And ek bycause I felte wel and say   *saw*
Youre grete trouthe and servyse every day,
And that yowre herte al myn was, soth to seyne:
This drof me first to rewe upon yowre peyne.

995 'And youre goodnesse have I founden alwey y[i]t,
Of whiche, my dere herte and al my knyght,   *wholly*
I thonke it yow as fer as I have wit,
Al kan I nought as muche as it were right;
And I emforthe my konnynge and my myght,
1000 Have, and ay shal, how sore that me smerte,   *it pains me*
Ben to yow trewe and hol with al myn herte;   *entire*

'And dredles, that shal be founde at preve.
But, herte myn, what al this is to seyn   *signifies*

---

974 you are making a good start. 978 moved over to the fire; *fere: fyre.* 979 took up the attitude. 982 stood out in bright colours against a background of truth. 984 by right suppose any falseness in her. 985 taking into account. 995 *yit: yet.* 999 to the limits of my understanding and strength. 1002 if put to the test.

Shal wel be told, so that ye yow not greve,
1005 Though I to yow right on yow[r]self compleyne.
For therwith mene I fynally the peyne,
That halt youre herte and myn in hevynesse,   *holds, sorrow*
Fully to slen, and every wrong redresse.   *end, right*

'My goode love, not I for whi, ne how,
1010 That jalousye, allas, that wikkede wyvere,   *serpent*
Thus causeles is cropen into yow –
The harm of which I wolde fayn delyvere.   *destroy*
Allas! that he, al hool, or of hym slyvere,   *fragment*
Shuld have his refuyt in so digne a place:
1015 Ther Jove soone out of youre herte hym race!

'But O thow Jove, O auctor of nature –   *creator*
Is this an honour to thi deité,   *godhead*
That folk ungiltyf suffren here injure,   *innocent*
And who that gyltyf is, al quyt goth he?   *quite free*
1020 O were it leful that I pleyne of the,   *lawful*
That undeserved suffrest jalousie,
[Of] that I wolde [up]on the pleyne and crye!

'Ek al my wo is this, that folk now usen
To seyn right thus: "Ye, jalousye is love!"
1025 And wolde a busshel venym al excusen
For that o greyn of love is on it sho[v]e.   *a single, put*
But that wot heighe God that sit above,
If it be liker love or hate or grame –
And after that it oughte to bere his name.

1030 'But certeyn is, som manere jalousye
Is excusable more than som, iwys;   *some (others)*
As whanne cause is, and some swych fantasye   *imaginings*
With pité so wel repressed is
That it unnethe doth or seyth amys,   *hardly*
1035 But goodly drynketh up al his distresse –   *swallows*
And that excuse I for the gentilesse.

1009 don't know why. 1011 has without reason crept. 1014 refuge in so
noble. 1015 May Jove quickly tear him out. 1021 allow jealousy when it has
not been deserved. 1022 Of: And. 1023 are now accustomed. 1026 *shove:*
shone. 1028 closer to . . . anger. 1036 nobility (of his behaviour).

'And some so ful of furye is and despit   *resentment*
That it sourmounteth his repressioun;
But, herte myn, ye be not in that plyt,   *state*
1040 That thanke I God, for whiche yowre passioun
I wol not calle it but illusioun,
Of habundaunce of love and bysy cure,   *anxious care*
That doth youre herte this disese endure,   *distress*

'Of which I am right sory, but not wroth;
1045 But for my devoir and youre hertes reste,   *sake*
Wherso yow lyste, by ordal or by oth,*
By sort, or in what wyse so yow l[e]ste,   *casting lots*
For love of God, lat preve it for the beste;
And yf that I be gyltyf, do me deye!
1050 Allas, what myght I more do or seye?'

With that a fewe bryghte terys newe   *fresh*
Out of here eyen fille, and thus she seyde: *fell*
'Now God thow wost, in thought ne dede untrewe
To Troylus was nevere yet Criseyde.'
1055 With that here hed into the bed down she leyde,
And with the shete it wreygh, and sighed sore,   *covered*
And held here pes; not o word spak she more.

But now help God to quenchen al this sorwe! –   *blot out*
So hope I that he shal, for he best may;
1060 For I have seyn of [a] ful mysty morwe   *morning*
Folwen ful ofte a merye someres day,
And after wynter folweth grene May.
Men sen alday, and reden ek in storyes,   *constantly*
That after sharpe shoures ben victories.   *attacks*

1065 This Troylus, whan he here wordes herde,
Have ye no care, hym lyst not to slepe;
For it thoughte hym no strokes of [a] yerde
To here or sen Criseyde his lady wepe.
But wel he felte aboute his herte crepe,
1070 For every teere which that Criseyde asterte,
The crampe of deth, to streyne hym by the herte.

1038 overcomes his power to repress it. 1043 *disese: dishese.* 1047 *leste: lyste.*
1049 have me killed. 1066 You needn't worry that he felt like sleeping. 1067
it seemed to him worse than a mere beating. 1070 escaped from. 1071 constrict
him about.

And in his mynde he gan the tyme ac[o]rse
That he cam there, and that he was born;
For now is wykke i-turned unto worse   *bad*
1075 And al the labour he hath don byforn,
He wend it lost; he thoughte he nas but lorn.   *supposed*
'O Pandarus,' thoughte he, 'allas! thi wyle   *cunning*
Serveth of nought, so welawey the while!'

And therwithal he heng adown the hed,
1080 And fil on knes, and sorwfully he sighte.   *sighed*
What myght he seyn? He felte he nas but ded –
For wroth was she that shulde his sorwes lyghte.   *lighten*
But natheles, whanne that he speken myghte,
Than seyde he thus: 'God wot that of this game,
1085 Whan al is wyst, than am I not to blame.'

Therwith the sorwe so his herte shette,   *shut up*
That from his eighen fil there not a tere;   *eyes*
And every spirit his vigour yn knette,   *contracted*
So they astoned and oppressed were.
1090 The felyng of his sorwe, or of his fere,   *All sense*
Or of ought elles, fled was out of towne –
And doun he fel al sodeynly aswowne.*   *in a faint*

This was no litel sorwe forto se;
But al was hust, and Pandare up as faste: *still*
1095 'O nece, pes, or we be lost,' quod he,
'B[e]th nought agast!' – but certeyn, at the laste,
For this or that, he hym into bedde caste,
And seyde, 'O thef, is this a mannes herte?'   *wretch*
And of he rente al to his bare sherte.   *tore*

1100 And seyde, 'Nece, but ye helpe us now,
Allas, yowre owne Troylus is lorn!'   *done for*
'Iwys, so wolde I, and I wiste how,   *if I knew*
Ful fayn,' quod she, 'allas that I was born!'   *Very gladly*
'Ye, nece, wole ye pulle out the thorn   *do you want to*
1105 That stiketh in his herte?' quod Pandare:
'Sey "Al foryeve", and stynt is al this fare.'

1072 *acorse: acurse.* 1078 Has achieved nothing, alas the day! 1084 all that
has happened here. 1085 comes to light. 1089 So stupefied and crushed were
they. 1091 of anything else, had quite vanished. 1096–7 truly, in the end, one
way and another; *Beth: Buth.* 1106 all this upset will be over.

'Ye, that to me,' quod she, 'ful levere were
Than al the good the sonne aboute goth.'
And therwithal she swor hym in his ere: *at that*
1110 'Iwis, my dere herte, I am nought wroth;
Have here my trouthe, and many another oth;
Now spek to me, for it am I Cryseyde.'
But al for nought; yet myght he no[t] abreyde.

Therwith his pows and pawmes of his hondes   *pulse*
1115 They gan to frote, and wete his temples tweyne;   *rub*
And forto delyveren hym from bittre bondes,
She ofte hym kyste; and, shortly for to seyne,
Hym to revoken she dide at hire peyne.
And at the laste, he gan his breth to drawe,
1120 And of his swough sone after that a-dawe.   *swoon, awake*

And bet gan mynde and reson to hym take;   *better*
But wonder sore he was abayst, iwys,   *ashamed*
And with a syk, whan he gan bet awake,
He seyde, 'O mercy, God, what thing is this?'
1125 'Whi do ye with yowreselven thus amys?'
Quod tho Criseyde; 'Is this a mannes game?   *behaviour*
What, Troylus, wol ye do thus for shame?'

And therwithal here arm over hym she leyde,
And al foryaf, and ofte tyme hym k[e]ste.   *forgave*
1130 He thonked here, and to hyr spak and seyde
As fil to purpos for his hertes reste;   *was needed*
And she to that answered hym as hir l[e]ste,
And with hire goodly wordes hym disporte   *cheered up*
She gan, and ofte his sorwes to comforte.

1135 Quod Pandarus, 'For ought I kan espyen,   *see*
This lyght nor I ne serven here of nought;
Lyght is not good for syke folkes eyen!
And for the love of God, syn ye be brought
In thus good plit, lat now non hevy thought   *state*
1140 Ben hangynge in the hertes of yow tweye' –   *Remain*
And bar the candele to the chimeney.   *fireplace*

1107–8 would be much dearer than (to possess) all the wealth on earth. 1113
could not yet recover his senses. 1118 did her utmost to revive him. 1124 what
has happened? 1125 behave yourself so badly? 1129 *keste: kyste.* 1132 *leste:
lyste.* 1136 (Neither) . . . are doing any good here.

Soone after this, though it no nede were,
Whan she swych othes as hire lyste devyse   *think up*
Hadde of hym take, here thought tho no fere,   *danger*
1145 Ne cause ek non to bidde hym thennes ryse.
Yet lesse thing than othes may suffise
In many a cas; for every wyght, I gesse,
That loveth wel, meneth but gentilesse.   *intends*

But in effect she wolde wite anoon
1150 Of what man, and ek where, and also why,
He jelous was, syn there was cause non;
And ek the signe that he tok it by,   *evidence*
She bad hym that to telle here bysily;   *straight away*
Or elles, certeyn, she bar hym on honde,   *accused him*
1155 That this was don of malys, hire to fonde.   *test*

Withouten more, shortly forto seyne,
He moste obeye unto hys lady heste;   *command*
And for the lasse harm, he moste feyne.
He seyde here, whanne she was at swych a feste,
1160 She myght on hym han loked, at the leste –
Not I not what, al dere ynow a rysshe,
As he that nedes moste a cause fysshe.

And she answered, 'Swete, al were it so,   *even if*
What harm was that, syn I noon yvel mene?   *nothing wrong*
1165 For by that God that bought us bothe two,   *redeemed*
In alle thynge is myn entente clene.   *pure*
Swych argumentz [ne] ben not worth a bene:
Wol ye the chyldyssh jalous contrefete?   *imitate*
Now were [it] worthy that ye were y-bete.'

1170 Tho Troylus gan sorwfully to syke
(Lest she be wroth, hym thoughte his herte deyde),
And seyde, 'Allas, upon my sorwes syke   *sick*
Have mercy, swete herte myn Cryseyde!
And yf that in tho wordes that I seyde
1175 Be ony wrong, I wol no more trespace: *not sin again*
Doth what yow lyst, I am al in youre grace.'

1142 was not necessary. 1149 wanted to know at once. 1161–2 I don't know
what (else) – none of it worth a rush, as from one who had to fish about for a
reason (for his jealousy). 1168 *jalous: jalousye.* 1169 you deserve to be beaten.
1171 For fear of her anger.

And she answered, 'Of gilt mysericorde;   *sin, mercy*
That is to seyn, that I foryeve al this;
And everemore on this nyght yow recorde,   *remember*
1180 And beth wel war ye do no more amys!'   *sin no more*
'Nay, dere herte myn,' quod he, 'iwys.'
'And now,' quod she, 'that I have do yow smerte,
Foryeve it me, myn owene swete herte.'

This Troilus, with blysse of that supprised,
1185 Put al in Godes hond, as he that mente
Nothyng but wel, and sodeynly avysed,   *determined*
He here in armes faste to hym hente.   *pulled*
And Pandarus, with a ful good entente,
Leyd hym to slepe and seyde, 'Yf ye ben wyse,
1190 Swowneth not now, lest more folk aryse!'   *wake up*

What myght or may the sely larke seye,   *innocent*
Whan that the sparhauk hath it in his fote?   *claw*
I kan no more, but of this ilke tweye –
To whom this tale s[ucre] be or sot –
1195 Though that I tarye a yer, somtyme I mot
After myn auctor tellen here gladnesse,
As wel as I have told here hevynesse.   *sorrows*

Criseyde, which that felte here thus i-take,   *seized*
As writen clerkes in here bokes olde,
1200 Right as an aspes lef she gan to quake,   *aspen*
Whan she hym felte here in [his] armes folde.
But Troylus, al hool of cares colde,
Gan thanken [tho] the blysful goddes sevene:
Thus sondry peynes bryngen folk to hevene.   *varied*

1205 This Troylus yn armes gan here streyne,   *crush*
And seyde, 'O swete, as evere mot I gon,
Now be ye kaught, now is there but we tweyne –   *trapped*
Now yeldeth yow, for other bote is noon.'
To that Criseyde answered thus anoon:
1210 'Ne hadde I er now, my swete herte dere,
Ben yolden, ywys, I were now not here!'

1182 have caused you pain. 1194 Whether what I say will be sweet or bitter;
sucre: sour. 1202 quite cured of (his) bitter sorrows. 1208 surrender, for there
is no other remedy. 1210–11 If I had not before this time . . . surrendered.

O soth is seyd, that heled forto be   *it is truly*
As of a fevere, or othere gret syknesse,
Men moste drynke (as men may often se)
1215 Ful bittre drynk; and forto han gladnesse,   *potion*
Men drynken often peyne and gret distresse –
I mene it here as for this aventure,
That thourgh a peyne is founden al his cure.

And now swetnesse semeth the more swet,
1220 That bitternesse assayed was byforn;   *experienced*
For out of wo in blysse now they flete   *float*
(Non swych they felten sith that they were born).
Now is this bet than bothe two be lorn –
For love of God, take every womman hede
1225 To werken thus, yf it come to the nede!   *act in this way*

Criseyde, al quyt from every drede and tene,   *free, affliction*
As she that just cause hadde hym to tryste,
Made hym swych feste it joye was to sene,
Whan she his trowthe and clene entent wyste;
1230 And as abowte a tre, with many a twyste,
Bytrent and wrythe the soote wodebynde,   *Entwines, twists*
Gan eche of hem in armes other wynde.   *embrace*

And as the newe abaysshed nyghtyngale,
That stynteth first whan she gynneth to synge,
1235 Whan that she hereth any herde tale,   *shepherd speak*
Or in the hegges ony wight sterynge,
And after syker doth here voys out rynge –   *confidently*
Right so Criseyd, whan here drede st[e]nte,
Opened here herte and tolde hym here entente.

1240 And right as he that seth his deth is shapen,   *determined*
And deye mot, in ou[gh]t that he may g[e]sse,
And sodeynly rescous doth hym escapen,   *rescue*
And from his deth is brought in sykernesse,   *to safety*
For al this wor[l]d, in swych present gladnesse
1245 Was Troylus, and hath his lady swete:
With worse hap God lat us nevere mete!   *fortune*

1217 I apply it here to this situation. 1228 Showed him such affection. 1233–4
nightingale, just frightened, that stops at the beginning of her song. 1236
anything moving. 1238 fear ceased; *stente: stynte.* 1241 is bound to die, as far
as he can tell; *gesse: gysse.*

Here armes smale, he[re] streyght bak and softe,   *slender*
Here sydes longe, fleysshly, smothe, and white,
He gan to stroke, and good thryft bad ful ofte
1250 Here snowyssh throte, here brestes rounde and lyte;   *small*
Thus in this [hevene] he gan hym [to] delyte,
And therwithal a thowsand tyme here kyste,   *in addition*
That what to done for joye unnethe he wyste.   *hardly knew*

Thanne seyde he thus: 'O Love, O Charité,
1255 Thi moder ek, Citherea the swete,
After thiself next heried be she –
Venus mene I, the wel-willy planete! –   *beneficent*
And next the, Imeneus, I the grete,
For nevere man was to yow goddes holde   *indebted*
1260 As I, which ye han brought fro cares colde.

'Benyngne Love, thow holy bond of thynges: *Gracious*
Whoso wole grace, and lyst the nought honouren,
Lo, his desir wole fle withouten wynges –   *(try to) fly*
For no[l]destow of bounté hem socouren
1265 That serven best and most alwey labouren,
Yet were al lost, that dar I wel seye certes,
But yf thi grace passed oure desertes.*

'And for thow me, that lest kowde deserve   *since*
Of hem that nombred be [un]to thi grace,
1270 Hast holpen, there I lykly was to sterve,   *die*
And me bistowed in so heygh a place
That thilke boundes may no blysse passe –   *its limits*
I kan no more, but laude and reverence   *praise, worship*
Be to thy bounté and thin excellence!'   *goodness*

1275 And therwithal Criseyde anoon he kyste,   *at that*
Of which, certeyn, she felte no disese,   *discomfort*
And thus seyde he: 'Now wolde God, I wyste,
Myn herte swete, how I yow myghte plese!
What man,' quod he, 'was evere thus at ese

1249 often invoked blessings upon. 1256 may she next be praised. 1262
Whoever desires grace, but does not deign to worship you. 1264 if you would
not, in your goodness, give them help. 1265 diligently toil. 1267 If your grace
did not surpass our merits. 1269 are counted among your grace's servants.
1276 *disese: dishese.*

1280 As I, on whiche the faireste and the beste
     That evere I say deyneth here herte reste.   *saw*

     'Here may men se that mercy passeth ryght –
     The experience of that is felt in me
     That am unworthi to so swete a wyght
1285 But herte myn, of youre benyngnité,   *grace*
     So thenk thowgh that I unworthi be,
     Yet mot I nede amenden in som wyse,
     Right thourgh the vertu of yowre heyghe servyce.   *power*

     'And for the love of God, my lady dere,
1290 Syn God hath wrought me for I shal yow serve –   *created*
     As thus I mene, that ye wole be my stere,   *guide*
     To do me lyve yf that yow lyste, or sterve –
     So techeth me how that I ma[y] deserve
     Youre thank, so [that I] thurgh myn ignoraunce
1295 Ne do no thing that yow be displesaunce.

     'But certes, fressh, wommanliche wyf,
     This dar I seye: that trouthe and diligence –
     That shal ye fynde in me al my lyf;
     Ne I wole, certeyn, breken youre defence;
1300 And yf I do, present or in absence,
     For love of God, lat sle me with the dede,   *at once*
     If that it lyke to youre womanhede.'   *womanly nature*

     'Iwys,' quod she, 'myne owne hertes lyst,   *pleasure*
     My ground of ese, and al myn herte dere,
1305 Graunt mercy, for on that is al my trist;   *Great thanks*
     But late us falle aweye fro this matere,   *move*
     For it suffiseth this that seyd is here,   *is enough*
     And at o word, withouten repentaunce
     Welcome my knyght, my pes, my suffisaunce.'

1310 Of here delyt or joyes oon the leste   *least one of*
     Were impossible to my wyt to seye –
     But juggeth ye that han ben at the feste

1281 condescends to. 1282 goes beyond justice. 1287 must of necessity
improve. 1290 *for: for that.* 1292 make me live or die according to your
pleasure. 1299 infringe any prohibition of yours. 1304 The basis of my joy,
and entirely. 1309 (the source of) my tranquillity and contentment. 1312
yourselves taken part in the celebration.

Of swych gladnesse, yf that hem lyste pleye.   *felt happy*
I kan no more but thus [thise] ilke tweye   *pair*
1315 That nyght, betwexen dred and sikernesse,
Felten in love the grete worthynesse.*   *security*

O blysful nyght of hem so longe y-sought,   *desired*
How blithe unto hem bothe [two] thow were!   *joyful*
Why ne hadde I swych on with my soule y-bought,
1320 Ye, or the leeste joye that was there?
Awey, thow fowle daun[g]er and thow fere,
And lat hem in this hevene blyss[e] dwelle,
That is so heygh that al ne kan I telle.   *exalted*

But soth is though I kan not telle al,   *everything*
1325 As kan myn auctor of his excellence,
Yet have I seyd, and God toforn, and shal   *given*
In every thyng al hoolly his sentence;
And yf that I, at loves reverence,   *to, honour*
Have ony word in-eched for the beste,   *added*
1330 Doth therwithal right as yow[r]selven leste.

For myne wordes, here and every part,
I speke hem alle under correccioun
Of yow that felyng han in loves art,   *sensitivity*
And putte it al yn youre discrecioun
1335 To encrese or maken dyminucioun   *amplify, condense*
Of my langage – and that I yow byseche;
But now to purpos of my rather speche.   *earlier*

Thise ilke two, that ben in armes laft,   *remained*
So loth to hem asondry go [it] were,   *separate*
1340 That eche from other wenden ben byraft –   *deprived*
Or elles, lo, this was here most fere: *greatest*
That al this thyng but nyce dremes [w]ere;   *empty*
For which ful ofte eche of hem seyde, 'O swete,
Clippe ich yow thus, or elles I it mete?'

1345 [And] lord, so he gan gladly on here se,   *how, look*
That nevere his lok ne blente from here face,   *moved*

1316 Experienced the supreme excellence of love. 1319–20 bought . . . such a
(night) or even the smallest delight that. 1321 *daunger: daunder.* 1322 *blysse:*
blyssyd. 1327 The whole of his meaning at every point. 1330 Treat it exactly
as pleases you. 1339 *it: ne.* 1342 *were: nere.* 1344 Am I really holding you, or
do I dream it?

And seyde, 'O dere herte may it be
That it be soth that ye ben in this place?'   *you are really*
'Ye, herte myn, God thank I of his grace,'
1350 Quod tho Criseyde, and therwithal hym kyste,
That where his spirit was for joye he nyste.   *didn't know*

This Troylus ful ofte here eighen two
Gan forto kysse and seyde, 'O eyen clere:
It were ye that wroughte me swych wo,   *caused*
1355 Ye humble nettes of my lady dere;   *snares*
Though there be mercy wreten yn youre chere,
God wot the text ful hard is, soth, to fynde –   *small print*
How koude ye withowten bond me bynde?'

Therwith he gan here faste in armes take,
1360 And wel an hundred tymes gan he syke,   *sigh*
Nought swych sorwful sykes as men make
For wo, or elles whanne that folk ben syke,   *sick*
But esy sykes, swyche as ben to lyke,
That shewed his affeccion withinne;
1365 Of swich sikes koude he nought blynne.   *leave off*

Sone after this they speke of sondry thynges
As fil to purpos of this aventure,   *were relevant*
And pleyinge entrechaungeden here rynges,   *exchanged*
Of which I kan nough[t] tellen no scripture;
1370 But wel I wot a broche, gold [and] asure,
In whiche a ruby set was lyk an hert   *heart-shaped*
Criseyde hym yaf, and stak it on his sherte.*

Lord, trowe ye a coveytous or a wrecche
That blameth love and holt of it despit,   *scorns*
1375 That of the pens that he kan mok[r]e and k[r]ecche,
Was evere yet y-yeve hym swych delyt   *granted*
As ys in love, in oo poynt, in som plyt?
Nay, douteles, for also God me save,
So parfit joye may no nygard have.   *Such*

1351 So that . . . couldn't tell. 1363 comfortable sighs, such as are pleasant.
1366 various matters. 1369 I don't know what was engraved on them. 1370
and: of. 1372 gave and pinned. 1373 do you believe a miser or a churl. 1375
coins that he can heap up and scrape together. 1377 in a single detail, in any
situation.

1380 They wole sey, 'Yis!' – but lord, so they lye!
Tho bysy wrecches ful of wo and drede!
They callen love a woodnesse or folye;
But it shal falle hem as I shal yow rede: *happen, tell*
They shul forgo the white and eke the rede,*
1385 And leve in wo – there God yeve hem myschaunce,   *live*
And every lovere yn his trouthe avaunce.   *further*

As wolde God that wrecches that dispise   *Would to*
Servyse of love hadde eerys also longe
As hadde Myda, ful of coveytise;
1390 And therto drenken hadde as hoot and stronge
As Crassus dide for his affectis wronge,*   *wrong*
To techen hem that they ben in the vice,
And loveres nought, although they holde hem nyce.

This ilke two of whom that I yow seye,
1395 Whan that here hertes wel assured were,   *confident*
Tho gonne thei to speke and to pleye,
And ek reherce how and whanne and where   *go over*
They knewe h[e]m first and every wo and feere
That passed was – but al swych hevynesse
1400 (I thanke it God) was tourned to gladnesse.

And evere more whan that hem fille to speke   *chanced*
Of ony thing of swych a tyme agon,   *past*
With kyssyng alle that tale sholde breke   *interrupt*
And fallen in a newe joye anoon,
1405 And dede al here myght, syn they were oon,   *united*
Forto recoveren blysse and ben at e[y]se,
And passed woo with joye countrepeyse.

Reson wil not that I speke of s[l]ep,
For it accordeth nough[t] to my matere   *agrees*
1410 (God wot they toke of that ful lytel kepe),   *heed*
But lest this nyght that was to hem so dere
Ne sholde in veyn escape in no manere,
It was byset in joye and bysynesse
Of al that sowneth into gentilesse.   *tends to*

1380 *so: so that.* 1382 one kind of madness or another. 1384 will have to give
up. 1391 unnatural desires. 1398 *hem: hym.* 1407 balance former sorrow.
1408 It is not reasonable to expect that; *slep: shep.* 1412 slip by unprofitably.
1413 employed in active joy.

1415 But whanne the kok, comune astrologer,   *general*
     Gan on his brest to bete and after crowe,   *then*
     And Lucifer, the dayes messager,
     Gan forto ryse and out here bemes throw,
     And afterward ros, to hym that kowde it know,   *recognize*
1420 Fortuna Maior* – that anoon Criseyde,
     With herte sore to Troylus thus seyde:

     'Myn hertes lyf, my tryst and my plesaunce,
     That I was born, allas, what me is wo,
     That day of us mot make desseveraunce –   *part us*
1425 For tyme it is to ryse and hens to go,
     Or ellys I am lost for eueremo.   *ruined*
     O nyght, allas, whi nyltow over us hove,
     As longe as whanne Almena lay by Jove?*

     'O blake nyght, as folk in bokes rede,
1430 That shapen art by God this world to hide   *created*
     At certeyn tymes with thi derke wede,   *fixed, mantle*
     That under that men myghte in reste abyde –
     Wel oughte bestes pleyne, and folk the chide,
     That there as day with labour wolde us breste,   *break*
1435 That thow thus flest, and deynest us nought reste.

     'Thow dost, allas, to shortly thyn office,
     Thow rakel nyght – there God, makere of Kynde,   *hasty*
     The for thyn hast and thyn unkynde vice   *unnatural*
     So faste ay to oure hemyspere bynde,
1440 That nevere more under the ground thow wynde!   *move*
     For now, for thow so hyest out of Troye,   *hasten*
     Have I forgon thus hastely my joye.'

     This Troyles, that with tho wordes felte,
     As thoughte hym tho, for pitous distresse   *then*
1445 The blody teerys from his herte melte,
     As he that nevere yet swych hevynesse
     Assayed hadde, out of so gret gladnesse,   *Experienced*
     Gan therwithal Criseyde his lady dere,
     In armes streyne, and seyde in this manere: *press*

1416 *crowe: to crowe.* 1423 how grieved I am. 1427 why won't you remain
over us. 1433 people reproach you. 1435 fly away, and do not care to give us
rest. 1436 perform ... your duties too quickly. 1437 may God, creator of
Nature.

1450 'O cruel day, accusour of the joye   *betrayer*
    That nyght and love han stole and faste y-wryen,   *hidden*
    Acursed be thy comyng into Troye,
    For every bore hath oon of thi bryght eyen!   *tiny hole*
    Envyous day, what lyst the so to spyen?
1455 What hastow lost? Why sekestow this place? –   *seek out*
    Ther God thi lyght so quenche for his grace!   *May*

    'Allas, what han these loveres the agilt?
    Dispitous day, thyn be the pyne of helle!   *Cruel*
    For many a lovere hastow shent and wilt –   *destroyed*
1460 Thi pouryng in wol nowhere late hem dwelle.
    What proferestow thi light here forto selle?
    Go selle it hem that smale selys graven –   *engrave*
    We wol the nought; us nedeth no day haven.'   *day (light)*

    And ek the sonne, Tytan,* gan he chyde,   *rail against*
1465 And seyde, 'O fol, wel may men the dispise,
    That hast the dawyng al nyght by thi syde   *dawn*
    And suffrest here so soone up fro the ryse   *allows*
    Forto disesen loveres yn this wyse.   *distress*
    What, hold youre bed ther – thow and ek thi morwe!   *keep*
1470 I bidde God so yeve yow bothe sorwe.'*

    Therwith ful sore he sight and thus he seyde: *sighed*
    'My lady right, and of my wele or wo,
    The welle and rote, O goodly myn, Criseyde,   *source*
    And shal I ryse, allas, and shal I go?   *must*
1475 Now fele I that myn herte mot atwo,   *split*
    For how sholde I an houre my lyf save,
    Syn that with yow is al the lyf I have?

    'What shal I don? for certes I not how,
    Ne whanne, allas, I shal the tyme se
1480 That yn this plit I may be eft with yow;
    And of my lyf, God wot how that shal be,
    Syn that desir ryght now so brenneth me   *consumes*
    That I am ded anoon, but I retorne: *unless*
    How shold I longe, allas, fro yow sojourne?

1457 how have ... offended you? 1460 gazing in allows them no peace
anywhere. 1461 are you offering ... for sale? 1464 *he: he to.* 1480 I may be
with you again under these (same) circumstances. 1484 continue to live away
from you.

1485 'But natheles, myn owene lady bryght,
     [Yet] were it so that I wist outrely   *absolutely*
     That I youre humble servaunt and youre knyght,
     Were in youre herte set so fermely
     As ye in myn – the whiche thyng, trewely,
1490 Me levere were than these wor[l]des tweyne –
     Yet sholde I bet endure al my peyne.'   *Then*

     To that Cryseyde answered right anoon,
     And with a syk she seyde, 'O herte dere,
     The game, ywys, so forferth now is gon
1495 That first shal Phebus falle fro his spere,   *orbit*
     And every egle ben the dowves fere,   *companion*
     And every roche out of his place sterte –   *jump*
     Er Tro[y]les out of Criseydes herte.

     'Ye be so depe inwith myn herte grave,
1500 That though I wold it turne out of my thought,
     As wysly verray God my soule save,
     To dyen in the peyne, I kowde nowght;   *under torture*
     And for the love of God that us hath wrought,
     Lat yn youre brayn noon other fantasye   *imagining*
1505 So crepe that it cause me to dye.

     'A[nd] that ye me wolde han as faste in mynde   *firmly*
     As I have yow, that wold I yow byseche;
     And yf I wyste sothly that to fynde,
     God myght not a poynt my joyes eche,   *increase*
1510 But herte myn, withoute more speche,
     Beth to me trewe, or elles were it routhe,   *otherwise*
     For I am thyn, by God and by my trouthe.

     'Beth glad forthi and lyve in sykernesse –   *security*
     Thus seyde I nevere er this, ne shal to mo;
1515 And yf to yow it were a gret gladnesse
     To turne ayen soone afte[r] that ye go,   *come back*
     As fayn wolde I as ye it were so,
     As wysly God myn herte brynge at reste' –
     And hym in armes toke and ofte keste.

1490 I would rather have than (possess). 1494 Truly, things have by now gone
so far. 1499 engraved within. 1506 *And: At.* 1508 was certain of finding that.

1520 Agayns his wil, syn it mot nedes be,
    This Troylus up ros and faste hym cledde;   *dressed*
    And in his armes tok his lady fre
    An hundred tyme, and on his wey hym spedde;
    And with swych wordes as his herte bledde,
1525 He seyde, 'Farewel, my [dere herte] swete:
    There God us graunte sound and soone to mete.'   *safely*

    To which no word for sorwe she answerde,
    So sore gan his partyng here destreyne;   *afflict*
    And Troylus unto his palays ferde,   *went*
1530 As wo bygon as she was, soth to seyne;
    So hard hym wrong of sharp desir the peyne   *tormented*
    Forto ben eft there he was in plesaunce   *To return*
    That it may nevere out of his remembraunce.

    Retorned to his real palais soone,   *royal*
1535 He softe into his bedde gan forto slynke,
    To slepe longe as he was woned to done: *usually did*
    But al for nought – he may wel lygge and wynke,
    But slep ne may there in his herte synke,
    Thenkynge how she for whom desir hym brende   *inflamed*
1540 A thousand fold was worth more than he wende.

    And in his thought gan up and doun to wynde
    Hi[r]e wordes alle and every contenaunce,
    And fermely impressen yn hi[s]e mynde
    The leste poynt that to hym was plesaunce;
1545 And verraylyche of thilke remembraunce   *this same*
    Desir al new hym brende, and lust to brede   *grow*
    Gan more than erst, and yet toke he noon hede.   *before*

    Criseyde also, right in the same wyse,
    Of Troylus gan in here herte shette   *kept close*
1550 His worthinesse, his lust, his dedes wyse,
    His gentilesse – and how she with hym mette;
    Thonkynge love he so wel here bysette,   *bestowed*
    Desiryng eft to have here herte dere   *again*
    In swych a plyt she dorst make hym chere.

1525 *my: myn; dere herte: herte and dere.* 1527 *answerde: answerede.* 1537
indeed lie down and shut his eyes. 1540 *had imagined.* 1541 *turned over and
over.* 1542 *each one of her expressions; Hire: Hise.* 1543 *hise: hire.* 1544
smallest detail. 1554 *Under such circumstances.*

1555 Pandare, amorwe which that comen was
Unto his nece and gan hire fayre grete,
Seyde, 'Al this nyght so reynede it, allas,
That al my drede is that ye, nece swete,
Han litel layser had to s[l]epe and mete;   *dream*
1560 Al nyght,' quod he, 'hath reyn so do me wake,
That som of us, I trowe, here hedes ake.'

And ner he come and seyde, 'How stont it now,   *are things*
This murye morwe? – nece, how kan ye fare?'   *bright*
Criseyde answerede, 'Nevere the bet [for] yow,
1565 Fox that ye ben, God yeve youre herte care!
God helpe me so ye cause[d] al this fare.   *business*
Trow I,' quod she, 'for alle youre wordes whyte,
[O!] whoso seth yow, knoweth yow ful lite!'   *(only) sees*

With that she gan here face forto wrye   *cover*
1570 With the shete, and wax for shame al red;
And Pandarus gan under forto prye,   *peer*
And seyde, 'Nece, yf that I shal ben ded,   *must die*
Have here a swerd and smyte of myn hed!'
With that his arm al sodeynly he thriste   *thrust*
1575 Under here nekke, and at the laste here k[i]ste.

I passe al that which chargeth nought to seye,
What! God foryaf his deth an[d] she also
Foryaf, and with here uncle gan to pleye,   *joke*
For other cause was ther noon but so.
1580 But of this thing right to the effect to go,
Whan tyme was, hom til here hous she wente,
And Pandarus hath fully his entente.

Now torne we ayen to Troylus,
That resteles ful longe a-bedde lay,
1585 And prevely sente after Pandarus
To hym to come in al the haste he may;
He come anoon – nought onys seyde he nay,   *did he refuse*
And Troylus ful sobrely he grette,   *greeted*
And doun upon his beddes syde hym sette.

1555 who had come in the morning. 1558 *nece: my nece.* 1559 *slepe: shepe.*
1560 kept me awake. 1566 *caused: causes.* 1567 plausible speech. 1568
knoweth: he knoweth. 1575 *kiste: keste.* 1576 which does not need to be said.
1578 *to: forto.* 1582 achieved his object. 1584 sleepless in bed.

1590 This Troylus, with al the affeccioun   *warmth*
     Of frendes love that herte may devyse,
     To Pandarus on knees fil adown,
     And er that he wolde out of the place aryse,
     He gan hym thonken in his beste wyse
1595 A hondred sithe, and gan the tyme bl[e]sse,   *times*
     That he was born to brynge hym fro distresse.

     He seyde, 'O frend of frendes the alderbeste
     That evere was, the sothe forto telle,
     Thow hast in hevene y-brought my soule at reste
1600 Fro Flegiton, the fery flood of helle;*
     That though I myght a thousand tymes selle
     Upon a day my lyf in thy servise,
     I[t] myght nought a mot in that suffise.   *scrap*

     'The sonne, whiche that al the worlde may se,
1605 Saw nevere yet, my lyf that dar I leye,   *wager*
     So inly feyr and goodly as is she,   *innately*
     Whos I am al, and shal, til that I deye;
     And that I thus am heres, dar I seye,
     That thanked be the heigh worthynesse
1610 Of love, and ek thy kynde bysynesse.   *diligence*

     'Thus hastow me no lytel thyng y-yeve: *given*
     For which to the obliged be for ay   *pledged*
     My lyf – and why? for thorugh thyn help I leve,   *live*
     For elles ded hadde I be many a day.'
1615 And with that word doun in his bed he lay,
     And Pandarus ful sobrely hym herde,
     Til al was seyd, and thanne he [thus] answerde:

     'My dere frend, yf I have don for the
     In ony cas, God wot, it is me lief;   *dear to*
1620 And am as glad as man may of it be,
     God help me so, but tak it not agrief
     That I shal seyn: be war of [this] myschief,   *misfortune*
     That, there as thow now brought art into blysse,
     That thow thiself ne cause it nought to mysse.   *go wrong*

1625 'For of Fortunes sharp adversité   *bitter hostility*
     The worste kynde of infortune is this:

1595 *blesse: blysse.* 1617 *thus: hym.* 1621 *don't be annoyed.* 1622 *this: of.*

A man to have be in prosperité,
And it remembren whan it passed is.
Thow art wys ynowh – forthi do nought amys!
1630 Be not to rakel, though thou sitte warme,
For if thow be, certeyn, it wol the harme.

'Thow art at ese and holde the wel therinne,
For also seur as red is every fire,
As gret a craft is kep wel as wynne;
1635 Bridle alwey wel thi speche and thi desir –
For worldly joye halt not but by a wir.
That preveth wel – it brest alday so ofte;
Forthi nede is to werke with it softe.'   *gently*

Quod Troylus, 'I hope, and God toforn,
1640 My dere frend, that I shal so me bere
That in my gilt ther shal nothing be lorn,
Ne I nyl not rakle as forto greven here.
It nedeth not this matere ofte [s]tere –   *turn over*
For wistow myn herte wel, Pandare,
1645 God wot, of this thow woldest litel care.'   *worry about*

Tho gan he telle hym of his glade nyght,
And wherof first his herte dredde, and how,   *of what*
And seyde, 'Frend, as I am trewe knyght,
And by that feyth I shal to God and yow,   *must (owe)*
1650 I hadde it nevere half so hote as now;   *felt*
And ay the more that desir me biteth
To love here best, the more it me delyteth.

'I not myself not wisly what it is,   *certainly*
But now I fele a newe qualité,   *capacity*
1655 Ye, al another [than] I dede er this.'
Pandare answerede and seyde thus: that 'he
That onys may in hevene blysse be,
He feleth other weyes, dar I leye,
Than thilke tyme he first herd of it seye.'

1630 are comfortably placed. 1632 take care to stay that way. 1634 skill is
(demanded) in keeping (what you have won) as in winning (it). 1637 every day
it breaks. 1640 conduct myself. 1641 through my fault. 1642 act so rashly as
to give her pain. 1655 *than: er.* 1658 experiences (things) differently.

1660 This is o word for al: this Troylus   *To sum it up*
    Was nevere ful to speke of this matere,   *weary of*
    And forto preyse unto Pandarus
    The bounté of his right lady dere;
    And Pandarus to thanke and maken c[h]ere –   *encourage*
1665 This tale was ay span newe to bygynne,   *brand new*
    Til that the nyght departed hem atwynne.

    Soone after this, for that Fortune it wolde,
    I-comen was the blysful tyme swete,
    That Troylus was warned that he shulde,
1670 Ther he was erst, Criseyde his lady mete;   *Where*
    For which he felt his herte in joye flete,   *float*
    And feythfully gan all the goddes herye –   *praise*
    And lat se now yf that he kan be merye!

    And holden was the forme and al the wyse   *kept, manner*
1675 Of here comynge, and of his also,
    As it was erst – whych nedeth nought devyse –
    But playnly to the effect right forto go:
    In joye and seurté Pandarus hem two
    A-bedde brought whan that hem bothe leste,   *wished (it)*
1680 And [thus] thei ben in quyete and yn reste.

    Nought nedeth it to yow, syn they ben met,
    To aske at me yf that they blythe were,
    For yf it erst was wel, tho was it bet
    A thousand fold – this nedeth not enquere.
1685 Agon was every sorwe and every fere,   *Departed*
    And bothe, ywys, they hadde and so they wende,   *thought*
    As muche joye as herte may comp[r]ende.   *grasp*

    This is no litel thyng of forto seye;
    This passeth every wyt forto devyse;
1690 For eche of hem gan otheres lust obeye –
    Felicité,* which that these clerkes wyse
    Commenden so, ne may not here suffice.
    This joye may not y-wrete ben with inke;   *written*
    This passeth al that herte may byth[i]nke.   *imagine*

1664 *chere: clere.* 1666 separated them. 1673 knows how to be. 1684 it is not
necessary to ask. 1687 *comprende: complende.* 1688 trivial matter to speak of.
1689 goes beyond all human intelligence to describe. 1692 Rate so highly is (a
word) not adequate here. 1694 *bythinke: bythenke.*

1695 But cruel day, so welawey the stounde,   *time*
       Gan forto aproche, as they by sy[g]nes knewe;
       For which hem thoughte felen dethes wounde –
       So wo was hem that changen gan here hewe,   *colour*
       And day they gonnen to dispise al newe,   *afresh*
1700 Callyng it traytou[r], envyous, and worse,
       And bitterly the dayes light they curse.

       Quod Troylus, '[Allas!] now am I war   *I realize*
       That Piros and tho swyfte stedes thre
       Which that drawen forth the sonnes char   *chariot*
1705 Han gon som by-path in despit of me;
       That maketh it so soone day to be –
       And for the sonne hym hasteth thus to ryse,
       Ne shal I nevere don h[ym] sacrifice.'*

       But nedes day departe moste hem soone,
1710 And whanne here speche don was and here chere,
       They twynne anoon as they were woned to done,   *separate*
       And setten tyme of metyng eft y-fere;   *fixed*
       And many a nyght they wrought yn this manere.
       And thus Fortune a tyme ladde in joye   *led*
1715 Criseyde and ek this kynges sone of Troye.

       In suffisaunce, in blisse, and in syngynges,   *fulfilment*
       This Troylus gan al his lyf to lede:
       He spendeth, justeth, maketh festeyynges,   *festivities*
       He yeveth frely ofte, and chaungeth wede;   *spends*
1720 And held [aboute hym] alwey, out of drede,
       A world of folk, as kam hym wel of kynde –   *multitude*
       The fresshest and the beste he koude fynde;   *liveliest*

       That swych a voys was of hym and [a] stevene
       Thoroughout the world, of honour and largesse,   *generosity*
1725 That it rong up into the yate of hevene;
       And as in love he was yn swych gladnesse,
       That in his herte he demede, as I gesse,   *judged*
       That there nys lovere yn this world at ese
       So wel as he – and thus gan love hym plese.   *gratify*

1700 *traytour: traytous.* 1705 taken some short cut. 1708 *hym: here.* 1710
glances (of love). 1718 *maketh: and maketh; festeyynges: festeynynges.* 1720
aboute hym: hym aboute. 1723 such (good) things were said about him.

1730 The goodlihede or beauté which that Kynde   *excellence*
     In ony other lady hadde y-set
     Kan not the mountaunce of a knot unbynde   *extent*
     Aboute his herte of al Criseydes net;
     He was so narwe y-ma[s]ked and y-knet,
1735 That it undon on any manere syde,
     That nyl not ben, for ought that may betyde.

     And by the hond ful ofte he wolde take
     This Pandarus, and into gardeyn lede,
     And swych a feste and swych a proces make
1740 Hym of Criseyde, and of here womanhede,
     And of here beauté that, withouten drede,
     It was an hevene his wordes forto here;   *heavenly*
     And thanne he wolde synge in this manere:

                 [*Canticus Troili*]

     'Love, that of erthe and se hath governaunce;
1745 Love, that his heste[s] hath in hevene hye;   *commands*
     Love, that with an holsom alliaunce   *beneficial*
     Halt peples joyned, as h[y]m lyst h[e]m gye;   *control*
     Love, that knetteth lawe of companye,
     And couples doth in vertu forto dwelle:
1750 Bynd this acord that I have told and telle.

     'That that the world with feyth, which that is stable,
     Dyverseth so his stoundes concordynge;
     That elementes that ben so discordable   *discordant*
     Holden a bond perpetuely durynge;   *everlasting*
1755 That Phebus mot his rosy day forth brynge,   *dawn*
     And that the mone hath lordship over the nyghtes:
     Al this doth Love – ay heryed be his myghtes.   *power*

     'That that the se, that gredy is to flowen,
     Constreyne to a certeyn ende so
1760 His flodes that f[iers]ly they ne growen   *swell*
     To drenchen erthe and al for everemo –   *drown*

1734 tightly enmeshed and tied up. 1736 anything that may happen. 1739
speak so joyfully and at such length about. 1747 *hym*: hem; *hem*: hym. 1748
draws together social custom. 1750 harmony of which I spoke, and will speak
again. 1752 gives such variety to its harmonious seasons. 1759 So forces within
fixed limits. 1760 *fiersly*: freshly.

And yf that Love ought late his bridel go,
Al that now loveth asonder sholde lepe,   *fly apart*
And al were lost that Love halt now to-hepe.   *together*

1765 'So wolde God, that auctor is of Kynde,
That with his bond Love of his vertu liste   *would deign*
To cerc[l]en hertes alle and faste bynde,   *encompass*
That from his bond no wight the weye out wyste;   *would know*
And hertes colde, hem wolde I that he twyste   *torment*
1770 To make hem love, and that hem lest ay rewe
On hertes sore, and kep hem that ben trewe.'   *protect*

In alle nedes for the townes werre
He was, and ay, the firste in armes dight;   *arrayed*
And certaynly, but if that bokes erre,   *lie*
1775 Save Ector, most y-drad of ony wight;   *feared*
And this encres of hardinesse and myght   *increase*
Cam hym of love, his ladyes thank to wynne,
That altered his spirit so withinne.

In tyme of trewe, on haukynge wolde [he] ryde,   *truce*
1780 Or elles hunten bore, bere or lyoun –
The smale bestes leet he gon bysyde;
And whan that he come rydyng into town,
Ful ofte his lady from hire wyndow down,
As fresch as fawkon come[n] out of muwe,   *pen*
1785 Ful redy was hym goodly to saluwe.   *graciously*

And most of love and vertu was his speche,
And in despit hadde alle wrecchednesse;
And douteles, no nede was hym byseche   *implore*
To honouren hem that hadde worthynesse,
1790 And esen hem that weren in distresse;   *comfort*
And glad was he yf any wyght wel ferde,   *prospered*
That lovere was, whan he it wyste or herde.

For soth to seyn, he lost held every wyght   *considered*
But yf he were in Loves heyghe servyse   *Unless*
1795 (I mene folk that oughte it ben of right).   *by*

1762 at all relaxed his control.1767 cerclen: cerchen. 1769 twyste: it wyste.
1770 they always incline to pity. 1772 At all times of crisis . . . war. 1781 he
allowed to escape. 1784 comen: cometh. 1787 ignoble behaviour.

And over al this, so wel koude he devyse   *speak*
Of sentement, and in so unkow[th] wyse   *feeling*
Al his aray, that every lovere thoughte
That al was wel what so he seyde or wroughte.   *did*

1800 And though that he be come of blod royal,
Lyst hym of pride at no wyght forto chase;   *harass*
Benygne he was to ech yn general,   *everyone*
For which he gat hym thank in every place.   *won*
Thus wold Love, y-heryed be his grace,
1805 That Pride, Envye, Ire, and Avaryce*
He gan to fle – and every other vice.   *avoid*

Thow lady bryght, the doughter to Dyone,*
Thy blynde and wynged sone ek, Daun Cupide,   *Lord*
Ye sustren nyne ek, that by Elycone,*   *sisters*
1810 I[n] hil Parnaso lysten forto abyde,
That ye thus fer han deyned me to gyde –
I kan no more, but syn that ye wol wende,
Ye heryed ben for ay withouten ende.   *perpetually*

Thourgh yow have I seyd fully in my song
1815 Th'effect and joye of Troylus servyce,
Al be that there were som disese among.*
As to myn auctor listeth to devyse.
My thridde book now ende ich in this wys;
And Troylus in lust and in quiete   *pleasure*
1820 Is with Criseyde, his owne herte swete.

[*Explicit liber Tercius*]

1797–8 novel a way did he dress. 1810 delight in making their dwelling. 1812
will now leave (me). 1816 this was mixed with some distress; *disese: dishese.*
Explicit liber Tercius now set after IV.28.

BOOK FOUR

[Incipit prohemium quarti libri]

But al to litel, weylawey the whyle,   *alas the day*
Lasteth swych joye – y-thonked be Fortune,
That semeth trewest whan she wole bygyle,
And kan to foles so here song entune,   *intone*
5 That she hem hent and blent – traytour comune!
And whan a wyght is from here whiel y-throwe, *cast from*
Than laugheth she, and maketh here the mowe. *grimaces*

From Troylus she gan here brighte face
Awey to writhe, and tok of hym noon hede, *turn*
10 But caste hym clene out of his lady grace,
And on here whiel she sette up Diomede:
For which ry[g]ht now myn herte gynneth blede,
And now my penne, allas, with which I write,
Quaketh for drede of that I mot endite.

15 For how Criseyde Troylus forsook –
Or at the leste how that she was unkynde –
Mot hennesforth ben matere of my book, *(the) subject*
As writen folk thorugh which it is in mynde.
Allas, that they shulde evere cause fynde
20 To speke here harm – and yf they on here lye,
Ywys, hemself sholde han the vilonye.* *bear, shame*

---

3 intends to deceive. 4 *kan: kand.* 5 catches and blinds, traitress to all. 12 *ryght: rytht.* 14 what I have to tell. 16 lacking in proper feeling. 18 who have caused (the story) to be remembered.

O ye Herynes, nyghtes doughtren thre,
That endeles compleyne[n] evere in pyne:
Megera, Alete and ek Thesyphone;
25 Thow cruel Mars ek, fader to Quyryne,*
This ilke ferthe book me helpeth fyne,   *complete*
So that the losse of lyf and love y-fere   *together*
Of Troylus be fully shewed here.*

Explicit [prohemium quarti libri]

Incipit Quartus liber

Liggynge yn ost, as I have seyd er this,   *Encamped*
30 The Grekys stronge aboute Troye town,
Byfel that whanne that Phebus shynyng is   *It happened*
Upon the brest of Hercules Lyoun,*
That Ector, with [ful] many a bold baroun,
Caste on a day with Grekes forto fighte   *Decided*
35 (As he was woned to greve hem what he myghte).

Not I how longe or short it was bytwene   *I don't know*
This purpos and that day they fighte mente;
But on a day, wel armed, bryght and shene,   *glittering*
Ector and many a worthi wight out wente,
40 With spere [i]n hond and bygge bowes bente;
And in the berd, withoute lenge[r] lette,
Here fomen in the feld anoon hem mette.   *at once*

The longe day, with speres faste y-grounde,   *sharply*
With arwes, dartes, swerdes, maces fele,   *many*
45 They fyghte and bryngen hors and man to grounde,
And with here axes out the braynes quelle;   *dash*
But in the last shour, soth forto telle,
The folk of Troye hemselven so mysledden   *misconducted*
That with the worse at nyght homward they fledden.

23 incessantly . . . in torment; *compleynen: compleynes.* **After 28** *prohemium quarti libri: liber Tercius.* **35** Since it was his custom to do them all the harm he could. **37** (Making) this plan, and the day they had determined to fight. **40** *in: on.* **41** face to face, without more delay.

50 At whiche day was taken Antenor,
    Maugre Polydamas or Monesteo;
    Santippe, Sarpedon, Polynestor,
    Polyte, or eke the Troian daun Rupheo,   *? even*
    And othere lasse folk as Phebuseo* –
55 So that for harm that day the folk of Troye
    Dredden to lese a gret part of here joye.   *Feared*

    Of Pryamus was yeve, at Grekes requeste,   *granted*
    A tyme of trewe, and tho thei gonne trete   *negotiate*
    Here prisoneres to chaungen, most and leste,
60 And for the surplus yeve sommes grete.
    This thing anoon was kouth in every strete,   *common knowledge*
    Bothe in th'assege, in towne, and everywhere,   *besiegers*
    And with the firste it cam to Calkas ere.

    Whan Calkas knew this tretys sholde holde,
65 In consistorie among the Grekes soone   *council*
    He gan in thrynge forth with lordes olde,
    And sette hym there as he was woned to done,   *usually did*
    And with a chaunged face hem bad a bone,   *asked a favour*
    For love of God to don that reverence   *pay, respect*
70 To stynte noyse and yeve hym audyence.   *be quiet*

    Thanne seyde he thus: 'Lo, lordes myne, I was
    Troian, as it is knowen, out of drede;   *without doubt*
    And if that yow remembre, I am Calkas,
    That alderfirst yaf comfort to youre nede,   *gave*
75 And told wel how that ye sholden spede –   *succeed*
    For dredles, thorugh yow shal in a stounde   *shortly*
    Ben Troye y-brend and bete doun to grounde.   *burned, rased*

    'And in what forme, or for what manere wyse,
    This town to shende and al youre lust to acheve,
80 Ye han er this wel herd [me yow] devyse:
    This knowe ye my lordes, as I leve,   *believe*
    And for the Grekes were[n] me so leve,   *dear to*
    I com myself in my propre persone,   *own*
    To teche in this how yow was best to done,   *instruct*

---

59 exchange, whatever their status. 60 pay great ransom for the rest. 63 one of the first to hear of it was Calchas. 66 pushed his way in. 69 *don: don hym.* 79 destroy . . . wishes. 80 *me yow: it me.* 82 *weren: weres.* 84 what was your best course of action.

85 'Havynge unto my tresour ne my rente   *income*
   Right no resport, to respect of youre ese;
   Thus al my good I loste and to yow wente,
   Wenyng in this you lordes forto plese.   *Supposing*
   But al that losse ne doth me no disese –
90 I vouchesaf, as wysly have I joye,   *(would) agree*
   For you to lese al that I have in Troye.   *lose*

   'Save of a doughter that I lafte, allas!   *abandoned*
   Slepynge at hom, whanne out of Troye I sterte.   *went hastily*
   O sterne and cruwel fader that I was!
95 How myght I have yn that so hard an herte?
   Allas, I ne hadde y-brought here in here sherte! *shift*
   For sorwe of which I wol not lyve tomorwe,   *another day*
   But yf ye lordes rewe upon my sorwe.

   'For by that cause I say no tyme er now   *saw*
100 Here to delyvere, I holden have my pes;   *free*
   But now or nevere, yf that it lyke yow,
   I may here have right sone, douteles.
   O help and grace among al this pres: *throng*
   Rewe on this olde caytyf in destresse,   *wretch*
105 Syn I for yow have al this hevynesse!   *sorrow*

   'Ye have now kaught and fetered in preson   *captured*
   Troians ynowe – and yf youre wille[s] be,   *plenty of*
   My chy[l]d with on may have redempcion;
   Now for the love of God, and of bounté,
110 On of so fele, allas, so yeve hym me!   *grant to*
   What nede were it this preyere forto werne   *refuse*
   Syn ye shul bothe han folk and town as yerne?

   'On peril of my lyf, I shal not lye:
   Appollo hath me told it feythfully;
115 I have ek founden it by astronomye,   *astrology*
   By sort, and by augurye ek trewely,
   I dar wel seye the tyme is faste by   *close*
   That fir and flaumbe on al the toun shal sprede,
   And thus shal Troye turnen [to] asshen dede.

---

86 no regard compared with your advantage. 89 *disese: dishese.* 108 her
deliverance. 109 out of the goodness of your hearts. 110 One out of so many.
112 very soon now. 116 By the casting of lots and from the flight of birds.
119 *to: in.*

120 'For certeyn, Phebus and Neptamus bothe,
    That ma[ke]den the walles of the toun,   *built*
    Ben with the folk of Troye alwey so wrothe   *angered*
    That thei wole brynge it to confusioun,   *destruction*
    Right in despit of kyng Lameadoun;*
125 Bycause he nolde payen hem here hire,   *wages*
    The town of Troye shal ben set on fire.'*

    Tellyng his tale alwey this olde greye,   *grey (beard)*
    Humble in speche and yn his lokynge eke,
    The salte terys from his eyen tw[e]ye
130 Ful faste ronnen doun by eyther cheke.   *each*
    So longe he gan of socour hem byse[k]e,
    That forto helen hym of his sorwes sore
    They yaf hym Antenor withoute more.

    But who was glad ynowh but Calkas tho?   *at that time*
135 And of this thing ful sone hise nedes leyde
    On hem that sholden for the tretis go,
    And hem for Antenor ful ofte preyde   *begged*
    To bryng h[o]m kyng Toas* and Criseyde –
    And whan Pryam his save-gard sente,   *safe-conduct*
140 The ambassiatours to Troye streyght thei wente.

    The cause y-told of here comynge, the olde
    Pryam the kyng ful soone in general
    Let here-upon his parlement to holde,
    Of which the effect rehersen yow I shal: *outcome, tell*
145 Th'embassadours ben answered for fynal,   *in the end*
    Th'eschaunge of prisoners and al this nede
    Hem lyketh wel, and forth in they procede.

    This Troylus was present in the place,
    Whan axed was for Antenor Criseyde,
150 For which ful soone chaungen gan his face,
    As he that with tho wordes wel neygh deyde;
    But natheles he no word to it seyde
    Lest men sholde his affeccioun espye –

131 implored their support; *byseke: byseche.* 133 granted . . . at once. 135–6
promptly entrusted his needs in this matter to those who must negotiate the
treaty. 138 *hom: hem.* 141 (Once) the reason for their coming was declared.
143 Immediately convoked. 147 went in together. 151 Like one nearly slain by
that debate.

With mannes herte he gan his sorwes drye.   *endure*

155 And ful of angwyssh and of grysly drede,   *fearful*
     Abod what lordes wolde unto it seye;
     And yf they wolde graunte – as God forbede! –
     Th'eschaunge of here, than thought he thynges tweye:
     First, how to save here honour, and what weye
160 He myghte best th'eschaunge of here withstonde:
     Ful faste he cast how al this myghte stonde.

     Love hym made al prest to don hire byde,
     And rather dye than she sholde go;
     But Resoun seyde hym on that other syde: *hand*
165 'Withoute assent of here do not so,
     Lest for thi werk she wolde be thi fo   *actions*
     And seyn that thorugh thi medlyng is [y-]blowe
     Yowre bothere love, there it was erst unknowe.'*   *previously*

     For which he gan deliberen for the beste,   *decide*
170 That though the lordes wolde that she wente,
     He wolde late hem graunte what hem leste,
     And telle his lady fyrst what that they mente;   *intended*
     And whanne that she hadde seyd hym here entente,
     Therafter wolde he werken also blyve,
175 Though al the world ayen it wolde stryve.   *contend*

     Ector, which that wel the Grekis herde,
     For Antenor how they wolde han Criseyde,
     Gan it withstonde, and sobrely answerde,   *oppose, gravely*
     'Sires, she nys no presoner,' he seyde;
180 'I not on yow who [that] this charge leyde,
     But on my part ye may eftsone hym telle   *at once*
     We usen here no wommen forto selle.'

     The noyse of peple up stirte thanne at onys,   *started*
     As breme as blase of straw y-set [o]n fyre –   *fierce*
185 For infortune it wolde, for the nonys,   *indeed*
     They sholde hire confusion desire.

---

156 Waited (to see). **161** He considered intently how all this might be achieved. **162** very ready to make her stay. **163** *go: gon.* **167–8** interference the love between you both is made public. **174** He would immediately act in accordance with that. **178** *answerde: answerede.* **180** I don't know who gave you this commission. **182** are not accustomed . . . to barter. **184** *on: in.* **186** wish for their own destruction.

'Ector,' quod they, 'what gost may yow enspire,
This womman thus to shilde and don us lese   *protect, lose*
Daun Antenor – a wrong wey now ye chese –   *choose*

190 'That is so wys and ek so bold baroun –
And we han nede [of] folk, as men may se.
He is ek on the grettest of this town –
O Ector lat tho fantasyes be!
O kyng Pryam,' quod they, 'thus seggen we:
195 That al oure voys i[s] to forgon Criseyde' –
And to delyveren Antenor they preyde.   *free*

O Juvenal, lord, trewe is thi senten[c]e: *decree*
That lite[l] weten folk what is to yerne,
That they ne fynde yn here desir offence;   *harm*
200 For cloud of errour lat hem not descerne   *allows*
What best is* – and, lo, here ensample as yerne:
This folk desiren now delyveraunce   *(the) freeing*
Of Antenor, that brought hem to myschaunce.*   *disaster*

For after he was traytour to the town   *subsequently*
205 Of Troye – allas they quyt hym out to rathe.
O nyce world, lo, thi dyscrescion!
Criseyde, which that nevere dede hem skathe   *harm*
Shal now no lengere in here blysse bathe;
But Antenor, he shal come hom to towne,
210 And she shal out – thus seyden here and howne.

For which was delibered by parlement,   *decided*
For Antenor to yelden up Criseyde
And it pronuncede by the precident   *decreed*
(Althey that Ector 'nay' ful ofte preyde);
215 And fynaly, what wyght that it withseyde,
It was for nought: it moste ben, and sholde,
For substaunce of the parlement it wolde.   *(the) majority*

Departed out of parlement echone,
This Troylus, withoute wordes mo,

187 (evil) spirit. 191 *of: to.* 192 one of the most powerful (men); *town: stown.*
193 give up such delusions. 194 this is our opinion. 195 our unanimous
judgment; *is: it.* 197 *sentence: sentente.* 198 do people know what is desirable;
litel: liten. 201 an instance ready (to hand); *here: here an.* 205 ransomed him
too quickly. 206 foolish ... discernment. 210 high and low. 214 *preyde:
preyede.* 215 whoever might oppose it. 218 When everyone had left.

220 Unto his chaumbre spede hym faste allone,   *hastened*
   But yf it were a man of his or two –   *Except only for*
   The whiche he bad out faste forto go,
   Bycause he wolde slepe, as he seyde;
   And hastely upon his bed hym leyde.

225 And as yn wynter leves ben byraft,   *stripped*
   Eche after other til the tre be bare,
   So that ther nys but bark and braunche y-laft,
   Lyth Troylus byraft of eche welfare,
   I-bounde in the blake bark of care,   *Confined within*
230 Disposed wod out of his wit to breyde:
   So sore hym sat the chaungynge of Criseyde.

   He rist hym up and every dore he shette   *rose, closed*
   (And wyndowe ek), and tho this sorweful man
   Upon his beddes side adoun hym sette,
235 Ful lyk a ded ymage, pale and wan,
   And in his brest the hepede wo bygan   *accumulated*
   Out brest, and he to werkyn in this wyse   *broke, act*
   In his woodnesse, as I shal yow devyse.   *madness*

   Ryght as the wylde bole bygynneth sprynge,
240 Now here, now there, i-darted to the herte,   *pierced*
   And of his deth roreth yn compleynynge: *(imminent)*
   Righ[t] so gan he aboute the chaumbre sterte,   *rush*
   Smytyng his brest ay with his festes smerte;
   His hed to the wal, his body to the grounde,
245 Ful ofte he swapte, himself to confounde.*

   His eyen two, for pité of his herte,
   Out stremeden as swyfte welles tweye;   *rushing springs*
   The heyghe sobbes of his sorwes smerte
   His speche hym rafte – unnethes myght he seye:
250 'O deth, allas, whi nyltow do me deye?   *won't you*
   Acursed be the day which that nature
   Shop me to ben a lyves creature.'   *Formed, living*

   But after, whan the furye and the rage
   Whiche that his herte twyste and faste threste,

---

228 Lies ... deprived of every comfort. 230 In a state to go violently mad.
231 bitterly did he feel. 243 constantly and violently with his fists. 245 dashed
... destroy. 249 took away ... hardly. 254 wrung ... oppressed.

255 By lengthe of tyme somwhat gan asswage,
Upon his bed he leyde hym down to reste;
But tho bygonne his terys more outbreste,   *start out*
That wonder is the body may suffise   *endure*
To half this wo which that I yow devyse.

260 Thanne seyde he thus: 'Fortune, allas the while!
What have I don? What have I thus agilt?   *offended*
How myghtestow, for reuthe, me bygyle?
Is ther no grace, and shal I thus be spilt?
Shal thus Criseyde awey for that thow wylt?   *wish (it)*
265 Allas, how maystow yn thin herte fynde
To ben to me thus cruel and unkynde.

'Have I the nought honoured al my lyve
(As thow wel wost) above the goddes alle?
Why wiltow me fro joye thus depryve?
270 O Troylus, what may men the now calle
But wrecche of wrecches, out of honour falle
Into myserie – yn which I wol bywayle
Criseyde, allas, til that the breth me fayle?

'Allas, Fortune, yf that my lyf yn joye
275 Displesed hadde unto thy foule envye,
Why ne haddestow my fader, kyng of Troye,
Byraft the lyf, o[r] don my bretheren deye,   *Deprived of*
Or slayn myself, that thus compleyne and crye:
I, combre-world, that may of nothing serve,
280 But evere dye and nevere fully sterve.

'If that Criseyde allone were me laft,
Nought rought I wh[i]der thow woldest me stere;
And here, allas, than hastow me byraft.
But everemore, lo, this is thi manere,
285 To reve a wyght that most is to hym dere,   *deprive*
To preve yn that thi g[e]reful violence: *changeable*
Thus am I lost, there helpeth no defence.

'O verray lord of Love! O god, allas!
That knowest best myn herte and al my thought,

262 for pity('s sake) destroy me. 263 must I be brought to ruin in this way?
277 *or: on.* 279 burden to the. 280 always be on the point of death, but never
completely die. 282 I would not care where you might take me; *whider: wheder.*

290 What shal my sorwful lyf don in this cas,   *situation*
Yf I forgo that I so dere have bought?   *give up*
Syn ye Cryseyde and me han fully brought
Into youre grace, and bothe oure hertes seled,
How may ye suffre, allas, it be repele[d]?

295 'What [shal I] don? I shal, whil I may dure
On lyve in torment and yn cruwel peyne,   *Alive*
This infortune or this disaventure   *evil chance*
Al[one] as I was born, ywys, compleyne;
Ne nevere wyl I seen it shyne or reyne;
300 But ende I wil as Edippe yn derknesse
My sorwful lyf, and dyen in dystresse.*

'O [wery] gost that errest to and fro,   *wanders*
Why nyltow fle out of the wofulleste
Body that evere myght on grounde go!
305 O soule lurkynge in this wo, unneste;
Fle forth out of myn herte and lat it breste,
And folwe alwey Criseyde, thi lady dere;
Thi righte place is now no lengere here.   *proper home*

'O wofulle eyen two, syn youre desport   *delight*
310 Was al to seen Criseydes eyen bryght,   *wholly*
What shal ye don but for my discomfort,
Stonde[n] for nought and wepen out youre sight,
Syn she is queynt that wont was yow to lyght?   *put out*
In veyn fro this forth have I eyen tweye   *this (time) on*
315 Y-formed, syn youre vertu is aweye.   *power*

'O my Criseyde, O lady sovereyne
Of this woful soule that thus crieth,
Who shal now yeven comfort to [my] peyne?
Allas, no wight! – but when myn herte dyeth,
320 My spirit, which that unto yow so hyeth,   *hastens*
Receyve in gre, for that shal ay yow serve;
Forthi no fors is though the body sterve.

'O ye loveres, that hey[g]he upon the whiel

---

293 joined together. 294 *repeled: repeles.* 295 *shal I: I may.* 298 *Alone: Allas.*
302 *wery: verray.* 304 walk on earth. 305 leave the nest. 312 Be useless;
Stonden: Stondeth. 314 this time on; *tweye: tweyne.* 318 *my: the.* 321 Be
pleased to accept. 322 So that the death of the body is of no consequence.

Ben set of Fortune, yn good aventure: *plight*
325 God leve that ye fynde ay love of stel,   *grant*
And longe mot youre lyf yn joye endure!*   *may*
But whanne ye comen b[y] my sepulture,   *tomb*
Remembreth that youre felawe resteth there –
For I loved ek, though I unworthi were.   *too*

330 'O olde, unholsom, and mys[ly]ved man –
Calkas I mene – allas, what eyleth the
To ben a Grek, syn thou art born Troian?
O Calkas, which that wilt my bane be,   *cause my death*
In cursed tyme was thow born for me!
335 As wolde blysful Jove for his joye   *If only*
That I the hadde where as I wolde in Troye!'

A thousand sykes, hottere than the glede,
Out of his brest eche after other wente,   *proceeded*
Meddle[d] with pleyntes newe his wo to fede,   *Mingled*
340 For which his woful terys nevere stente;   *ceased*
And shortly: so his peynes hym to-rente,
And wex so mat, that joye nor penaunce   *misery*
He feleth noon, but lyth forth in a traunce.

Pandare, whiche that in the parlement
345 Hadde herd what every burgeys and lord seyde,
And how ful graunted was, by on assent,   *unanimously*
For Antenor to yelden so Criseyde,
Gan wel neygh wod out of his wit to breyde,   *run*
So that for wo he nyste what he mente,   *intended*
350 But yn a res to Troylus he wente.   *hastily*

A certeyn knyght that for the tyme kepte   *guarded*
The chaumbre dore undede it hym anoon,
And Pandare, that ful tendreliche wepte,
Into the derke chaumbre, as stille as ston,
355 Toward the bed gan softely to gon,
So confus that he nyst what to seye: *bewildered*
For verray wo his wit was neigh aweye.*   *absolute*

---

327 *by: be.* 330 corrupt and sinful; *myslyved: mysbyleved* ('faithless'). 331–2
what possessed you to become a. 337 sighs . . . embers. 339 *Meddled: Meddles.*
341 torments tore him to pieces. 343 goes on lying in a swoon. 354 *as: as ony.*
357 sense had almost left him.

And with his chere and lokyng al to-torn   *dishevelled*
For sorwe of this, and with his armes folden.
360 He stod this woful Troylus byforn,
And on his pitous face he gan byholden;
But lord, so often gan his herte colde[n],   *grow chill*
Seyng his frend in wo, whos hevynesse   *sadness*
His herte slow[h] as thought hym, for distresse.   *killed*

365 This woful wight, this Troylus that felte   *sensed*
His frend Pandare y-comen hym to se,
Gan as the snow ayen the sonne melte,   *in the face of*
For w[h]ych this sorwful Pandare, of pyté
Gan forto wepe as tendrelyche as he;
370 And specheles thus ben this[e] ilke tweye,   *same*
That neyther myghte o word for sorwe seye.   *a (single)*

But at the laste this woful Troylus,
Ney ded for smert, gan bresten out to rore,   *Almost, pain*
And with a sorwful noyse he seyde thus
375 (Among his sobbes and his sikes sore):
'Lo, Pandare, I am ded withouten more;   *already*
Hastow nought herd at parlement,' he seyde,
'For Antenor how lost is my Criseyde?'

This Pandarus, ful dede and pale of hewe,   *deathly*
380 Ful pytously answerede, and seyde, 'Yis:
As wysly were it fals as it is trewe,   *If only*
That I have herd and wot al how it is.
O mercy, God, who wolde have trowed this?   *believed*
Who wolde have wend that yn so lytel a throwe
385 Fortune oure joye wolde han overthrowe?

'For yn this world there is no creature,
As to my dom, that evere saw ruyne
Straungere than this, thorugh cas or aventure.
But who may al eschewe, or al devyne?   *avert, foresee*
390 Swych is this world; forthi I thus defyne: *conclude*
Ne trust no wyght to fynden in Fortune
Ay propreté – hi[re] yeftes ben comune.*   *promiscuous*

---

368 *whych: wyych.* 384 imagined that in so short a time. 387–8 a more
unexpected catastrophe than this. 391–2 Let no one expect ever to have
personal rights over Fortune; *hire: his.*

'But tel me this, whi thou art now so mad   *out of control*
To sorwen thus? Why listow in this wyse,   *do you lie*
395 Syn thi desir al holly hastow had,   *completely*
So that by right it oughte ynow suffise?   *satisfy*
But I, that nevere felte in my servyse
A frendly chere, or lokyng of an eye,   *glance*
Lat me thus wepe an[d] wayle til I dye.

400 'And over al this, as thow wel wost thiselve,   *beyond*
This town is ful of ladyes al aboute;   *around*
And to my dom fairere than swych twelve
As evere she was, shal I fynde yn som route,   *company*
Ye, oone or two, withouten any doute.
405 Forthi be glad, myn owen dere brother:
Yf she be lost, we shul recovere another.

'What! God forbede alwey that eche plesaunce
In o thyng were and [in] noon other wyght:
If oon kan synge, another kan wel daunce;
410 Yf this be goodly, she is glad and lyght,   *lively*
And this is fayr, and that kan good aright.
Ech for his vertu holden is for dere,
Bothe heronere and faukon of ryvere.

'And ek as writ Zauzis that was ful wys:
415 "The newe love out cacheth ofte the olde";   *drives*
And upon newe cas lyth newe avys.
Thenk ek thi [lif] to save thow art holde;   *bound*
Swych fyr by proces shal of kynde colde:
For syn it is but casuel plesaunce,   *accidental*
420 Som cas shal putte it out of remembraunce.   *accident*

'For also seur as day cometh after nyght,   *as certainly*
The newe love, labour, or other wo,
Or ellys selde seynge of a wyght,   *infrequent sight*
Don olde affections al over go.   *Cause, pass away*
425 And for thi part thow shalt have one of tho
To abrigge with thi bittre peynes smerte;   *shorten*
Absence of here shal dryve here out of herte.'

---

402 to my judgment more beautiful than. 408 Was confined to one person and no other. 412 is esteemed for its (particular) excellence. 413 falcon for hunting herons, and for hunting waterfowl. 416 a fresh situation demands fresh consideration. 417 lif: self. 418 cool in the course of nature.

(This[e] wordes seyde he for the nones alle,
To helpe his frend, lest he for sorwe deyde;
430 For douteles to don his sorwe to falle   *certainly, lessen*
He rought not what unthryf[t] [that] he seyde.)
But Troylus, that neigh for sorwe deyde,
Tok litel hed of al that evere he mente –   *said*
Oon eere it herde, at the other out it wente.*

435 But at the laste he answered and seyde, 'Frend,
This lechecraft, or heled thus to be,   *medicine*
Were wel sittyng, if that I were a fende,   *suitable*
To tra[y]sen here that trewe is unto me.   *betray*
I pray God lat this consayl nevere the!   *prosper*
440 But do me rathere anoon sterve right here,
Er I thus do as thow me woldest lere.   *teach*

'She that I serve, ywys, what so thow seye,
To whom myn her[t] enhabyt is by right,   *? devoted*
Shal han me holly heres til that I deye,
445 For Pandarus, syn I have trouthe here hight,   *sworn*
I wol not ben untrewe for no wyght;
But as here man I wole ay lyve and sterve,
And nevere other creature serve.

'And there thow seyst thow shalt as faire fynde
450 As she – lat be, make no comparyson
To creature y-formed here by Kynde.   *Nature*
O leve Pandare, in conclusion,
I wol not be of thyn opynyon
Towchyng al this; for whiche I the byseche,   *Regarding*
455 So hold thi pes: thow sleste me with thi speche.   *kill*

'Thow biddest me I sholde love another   *tell*
Al fresshly newe, and lat Criseyde go.
It lith not in my power, leve brother;   *lies, dear*
And though I myght, I wil not do so.
460 But kanstow pleyen raket to and fro,
Netle in, dokke out – now this, now that, Pandare?
Now fowle falle here that for thi wo hath care.

428 purely on the spur of the moment. 431 didn't care what nonsense he
talked. 435 *Frend: A frend.* 438 *traysen: trassen.* 438, 439 in reverse order.
439 *God: to God.* 440 die on the spot at once. 445 *syn: syn that.* 461 dock
leaf. 462 evil befall the lady.

'Thow farest ek by me, thow Pandarus,
As he that, whan a wyght is wo bygon,   *sorrowful*
465 He cometh to hym a pas, and seyth right thus: *quickly*
"Thenk not on smert, and thow shalt fele noon."
Thow most me first transmuwen in a ston,   *change into*
And reve me my passions alle,   *take away*
Er thow so lightly do my wo to falle.

470 'The deth may wel out of my brest departe
The lyf, so longe may this sorwe myne;   *(under)mine*
But fro my sowle shal Criseyde[s] darte
Out nevere mo, but downe with Proserpyne*
Whan I am ded, I wol go wone in pyne;   *dwell*
475 And ther I wol eternally compleyne
My wo, and how that twynned be we tweyne.   *parted*

'Thow hast here mad an argument for fyn,   *to establish*
How that it sholde a lasse peyne be
Creseyde to forgon, for she was myn,
480 And leve[d] in ese and yn felicité.
Whi gabbestow, that seydest thus to me,
That "Hym is wors that is fro wele y-throwe,   *prosperity*
Than he hadde erst non of that wele knowe"?   *first*

'But tel me now syn that the thenketh so lyght   *easy*
485 To chaungen so in love ay to and fro,
Whi hastow not don bysyly thi myght
To chaungen here that doth the al thi wo?
Why neltow lete here fro thyn herte go?   *won't you*
Why nyltow love another lady swete
490 That may thin herte setten in quyete?   *at rest*

'If thow hast had in love ay yet myschaunce,
And kanst it not out of thyn herte dryve,
I, that levede yn lust and in plesaunce   *delight*
With here as muche as creature on lyve,
495 How sholde I that foryete, and that so blyve?   *promptly*
O where hastow ben hid so longe in muwe,   *cooped up*
That kanst so wel and formely arguwe?   *correctly*

---

463 are acting towards me. 470 may indeed cause to leave. 481 do you talk
(this) nonsense, when you (earlier) said. 486 earnestly tried your hardest. 491
always until now.

'Nay, [nay,] God wot, nought worth is al thi red,   *advice*
For which for what that evere may byfalle,
500 Withouten wordes mo I wol be ded.
O Deth, that endere art of sorwes alle,
Com now syn I so ofte after the calle;
For sely is that deth, soth forto seyne,   *blessed*
That ofte y-cleped, cometh and endeth peyne.

505 'Wel wot I whil my lyf was in quyete,
Er thow me slowe, I wolde have yeven h[i]re;
But now thi comynge is to me so swete,
That in this world I nothing so desire.
O Deth, syn with this sorwe I am a-fyre,
510 Thou other do me anoon yn teris drenche,   *either, drown*
Or with thi colde strok myn hete quenche.

'Syn that thow sleest so fele in sondry wyse
Ayens hire wil, unpreyed, day and nyght,
Do me at my requeste this service:
515 Delyvere now the world, so dostow right,
Of me that am the wofulleste wyght
That evere was – for tyme is that I sterve,
Syn in this world of right nought may I serve.'

This Troylus in teris gan distille,
520 As licour of a lambyc ful faste;   *retort*
And Pandarus gan holde his tunge stille,
And to the ground his eyen doun he caste;
And natheles, thus thought he at the laste:
'What! pardé, rather than my felawe deye,
525 Yet shal I somwhat more unto [hym] seye.'

And seyd, 'Frend, syn thow hast swych distresse,
And syn thow list myn argumentz [to] blame,
Why nylt thiself helpen don redresse   *set right*
And with thy manhod letten al this grame?
530 [G]o ravysshe here – ne kanstow not, for shame!   *abduct*
And other lat here out of towne fare

506 I would have paid a ransom so that you should not kill me; *hire: here.* 510
yn: yn this. 512 so many in different ways. 513 without being asked. 515 you
will perform a good action. 517 it is time for me to die. 525 *hym: it.* 529
manfully prevent all this harm (from coming about). 530 *Go: To.* 531 either
allow her to leave the city.

Or hold here stille, and lef thi nyce fare. *folly*

'Artow in Troye, and hast noon hardiment *boldness*
To take a womman which that loveth the,
535 And wolde hereselven be of thyn assent?* *agree with you*
Now is not this a nyce vanyté? *idleness*
Rys up anoon and lat this wepynge be,
And kyth thow art a man, for yn this owre *show*
I wil be ded, or she shal bleven oure.' *still be ours*

540 To this answerede hym Troylus ful softe,
And seyde, 'Pardé, leve brother dere,
Al this have I myself yet thought ful ofte,
And more thyng than thow devysest here. *speak of*
But whi [this] thyng is laft thow shalt wel here;
545 And whan thow me hast yeve an audience,
Therafter mayst thow telle all thi sentence.

'F[yr]st, syn thow wost this town hath al this werre
For ravysshyng of womman so [b]y myght,
It sholde not be suffred me to erre, *transgress*
550 As it stant now, ne don so gret unright:
I sholde han also blame of every wyght,
My fadres graunt yf that I so withstode: *decree*
Syn she is chaunged for the townes goode.

'I have ek thought, so it were here assent, *if she agreed*
555 To aske hire at my fader of his grace;
Thanne thenk I this were here accusement,
Syn wel I wot I may here not purchace: *obtain*
For syn my fader in so heigh a place
As parlement hath here eschaunge enseled, *ratified*
560 He nyl for me his lettre be repeled. *decree*

'Yet drede I most here herte to pertourbe *make anxious*
With violence, yf I do swych a game; *play*
For yf I wolde it openly distourbe,
It most ben disclaundre to here name. *reproach*
565 And me were levere ded than here defame –
As nold God, but yf I sholde have
Here honour levere than my lyf to save.

544 course of action has been rejected. 545 heard what I have to say. 546
what you have in mind. 547 *Fyrst: Fryst.* 548 *by: my.* 550 commit such a
great offence. 566–7 God prevent that I should not hold her honour dearer than.

'Thus am I lost, for ought that I kan se;
For certeyn is, syn that I am here knyght,
570 I moste here honour levere han than me
In every cas, as lovere oughte of right.
Thus am I with desir and reson twyght: *tormented*
Desir forto distourben here me redeth,
And reson nyl not – so myn herte dredeth.'

575 Thus wepynge that he koude nevere cesse,   *stop*
He seyde, 'Allas, how shal I, wrecche, fare?
For wel fele I alwey my love encresse,   *increase*
And hope is lasse and lasse alwey, Pandare;   *diminishes*
Encressen ek the causes of my care.
580 So welawey, whi nyl myn herte breste?
For as in love ther is but litel reste.'

Pandare answerede, 'Frend, thow mayst for me
Don as the list, but hadde ich it [so] hote,
And thyn estat, she sholde go with me,   *status*
585 Though al this town criede on this thyng by note:
I nold sette at al that noyse a grote!   *value*
For when men han wel cried, than wol they rowne –
A wonder last but nyne nyght nevere yn towne.   *more than*

'Devyne not in reson ay so depe,
590 Ne curteysly, but help thiself anoon;*   *politely*
Bet is that othere than thiself wepe,   *It is better*
And namly, syn ye two ben al oon,   *especially*
Rys up, for by myn hed she shal not gon;
And rathere be in blame a lite y-founde,
595 Than sterve here as a gnat, withowte wounde.

'It is no shame to yow, ne no vice,
Here to witholden that the loveth most: *keep back*
Paraunter she myght holden the for nyce   *consider*
To late here go thus unto the Grekes ost.
600 Thenk ek Fortune – as wel thiselven wost –

---

573 counsels me to upset her. 576 what will happen to me, miserable creature.
582 as far as I am concerned. 583 if I felt so passionately; *so: for*. 585 against
it in unison. 587 have shouted enough they will speak softly. 589 Don't keep
arguing it out in your mind at such length. 594 found slightly at fault; *lite: litel*
(also 603).

Helpeth hardy man to his emprise *undertaking*
And weyveth wrecches for here cowardise. *abandons*

'And though thi lady wolde a lite here greve, *feel angry*
Thow shalt thi pes ful wel hereafter make;
605 But as for me, certayn, I kan not leve *believe*
That she wolde it as now for yvel take.
Whi sholde thanne of fered thyn herte quake? *through fear*
Thenk ek how Parys hath, that is thi brother,
A love – and whi shaltow not have another?

610 'And Troylus, o thyng I dar the swere,
That if Criseyde, whiche that is thi lef, *beloved*
Now love[th] the as wel as thow dost here,
God helpe me so, she nyl not take a-gref *be upset*
They thou do bote anoon in this myschef;
615 And yf she wilneth fro yow forto passe,
Thanne is she fals – so love here wel the lasse!

'Forthi tak herte and thenk right as a k[ny]ght:
Thourgh love is broken alday every lawe.* *all the time*
Ky[t]h now sumwhat thi corage and thi myght;
620 Have mercy on thiself for ony awe.
Lat not this wrecched wo thin herte gnawe,
But manly set the world on sixe and sevene – *in an uproar*
And yf thow deye a martir, go to hevene!

'I wol myself be with the at this nede, *crisis*
625 Theygh ich and al my kyn upon a sto[u]nde
Shulle in a strete as dogges liggen dede,
Thourgh-girt with many a wyd and blody wounde;* *Run through*
In every cas I wol a frend be founde.
And yf the lyst here sterven as a wrecche,
630 Adieu – the devel spede hym that recche!'

This Troylus gan with tho wordes to quyken, *revive*
And seyde, 'Frend, graunt mercy, ich assente.
But certaynly thow mayst not me so pryken, *spur me on*
Ne peyne noon ne may me so tormente,

---

606 be displeased. 614 do something to help yourself. 617 *knyght: kynght.*
619 *Kyth: Kygh.* 620 whatever the danger. 625 Even though I and all my
kinsfolk at the same time. 629 to die miserably. 630 prosper him who cares
for you.

635 That for no cas it is not myn entente,
     At short wordes, though I deyen sholde,
     To ravysshen hire, but yf hereself it wolde.'

     'Why so mene I,' quod Pandarus, 'al this day.
     But tel me thanne, hastow here w[i]l assayed,
640 That sorwest thus?' – and he answered 'Nay'.
     'Wherof artow,' quod Pandare, 'than amayed,   *alarmed about*
     That nost not that she wol ben evele apayed,   *displeased*
     To ravysshen here, syn thow hast not ben there –
     But if that Jove told it yn thin eere?   *Unless*

645 'Forthi rys up, as nought ne were, anoon,
     And wassh thi face, and to the kyng thow wende,
     Or he may wondren whider thow art gon.
     Thow most with wysdom hym and othere blende,
     Or upon cas he may after the sende
650 Er thow be war; and shortly, brother dere,
     Be glad, and lat me werke in this matere.

     'For I shal shappe it so, [that] sikerly   *contrive*
     Thow shalt this nyght som tyme, in som manere,
     Com speke with thi lady prevely,
655 And by here wordes ek a[s] by here chere
     Thow shalt ful sone aparceyve and wel here   *realise*
     Al here entente, and yn this cas the beste;
     And fare now wel, for in this poynt I reste.'

     The swyfte Fame,* whiche that false thynges
660 Egal reporteth lyk the thynges trewe,   *As fully as*
     Was thoroughout Troye y-fled with preste wynges   *rapid*
     Fro man to man and made this tale of newe,
     How Calkas doughter with here brighte hewe,
     At parlement, withoute wordes more,   *further debate*
665 I-graunted was yn chaunge of Antenore.

     The whiche tale anoon right as Criseyde   *as soon as*
     Had herd, she that of here fader roughte,   *cared for*
     As in this cas right nought, ne whanne he deyde,

---

637 unless she consented. 639 found out what she wants; *wil: wel.* 645 as if
all were well. 648 carefully . . . deceive. 655 *as: and.* 657 Everything that is in
her mind, and what is best (to do) in this situation. 662 kept telling the story
afresh.

Ful bysily to Juppiter bysoughte
670 Yeve h[e]m myschaunce that this tretis broughte;
But shortly, lest this[e] tales soth were,   *rumours*
She dorste at no wyght asken it, for fere,

As she that hadde here herte and al here mynde
On Troylus y-set so wonder faste,
675 That al the world ne koude here love unbynde,
Ne Troylus out of here herte caste:
She wol ben his whil that here lyf may laste.
And thus she brenneth bothe in love and drede,
[So] that she nyste what was best to rede.

680 But as men sen in towne and al aboute
That wommen usen frendes to visite,   *are accustomed*
So to Criseyde of wommen come a rowte,
For pitous joye and wenden here delite,
And with here tales – dere ynowh a myte –
685 These wommen, whiche that yn the cité dwelle,
Thei sette hem doun, and seyde as I shal telle.

Quod first that oone, 'I am glad, trewely,
Bycause of yow, that shal youre fader se.'
Another answered, 'Iwys, so am not I:
690 For al to litel hath she with us be.'
Quod the thridde, 'I hope, ywys, that she
Shal brynge us the pes on every side,
That, whanne she gooth, almyghti God here gyde.'

Tho wo[r]des and tho wommanyssh thyng[i]s,   *concerns*
695 She herd hem ryght as though she then[ne]s were;   *elsewhere*
For, God it wot, here herte on other thing is,
Although the body sat among hem there.
Here adverten[c]e is alwey ellyswhere,   *attention*
For Troylus ful faste here herte soughte,
700 Withouten word, alwey on hym she thoughte.

This[e] wommen, that wenden here to plese,
Aboute nought gonne alle here tales spende;

---

669 earnestly implored. 670 *hem: hym.* 679 what advice was best to follow.
683 expected to give her pleasure. 684 overpriced at. 688 On your account,
who; *that: that ye.* 694 *thyngis: thynges.* 698 *advertence: advertente.* 702
Expended all their words in vain.

Swych vanité ne kan don he[re] non ese,   *empty talk*
As she that al this mene while brende
705 Of other passion than that they wende,   *supposed*
So that she felte almost here herte deye,
For wo and wery of that companye.

[For which no lenger myghte she restreyne
Hir teeris, so they gonnen up to welle,   *gush*
710 That yaven signes of the bittre peyne   *made obvious*
In which hir spirit was, and moste dwelle,
Remembryng hir fro heven into which helle
She fallen was, syn she forgoth the syghte
Of Troilus – and sorwfully she sighte.]*   *sighed*

715 And thilke foles sittynge here aboute
Wende that she wepte and syked sore
Bycause that [she] sholde out of that route
Departe, and nevere pleye with hem more.   *socialize*
And they that hadde y-knowen here of yore,
720 Seygh here so wepe, and thoughte it kyndenesse,
And eche of hem wepte eke for here distresse.

And bisily they gonnen here comforten
Of thing, God wot, on which she litel thoughte,
And with here tales wenden here disporten;
725 And to be glad they often here bysoughte.   *cheerful*
But swich an ese therwith they here wroughte
Right as a man is esed forto fele,
For ache of hed, to clawen hym on his hele.

But after al this nyce vanyté
730 They tok here leve; and hom they wenten alle.
Crysede, ful of sorwful pité,
Into here chaumbre up wente out of the halle,
And on here bed she gan for ded to falle,   *as if dead*
In purpos nevere thennes forto ryse;   *Intending*
735 And thus she wroughte, as I shal yow devyse.   *relate*

Here ownded heer, that sonnyssh was of hewe,   *wavy*
She rente, and ek here fyngres longe and smale   *slender*

---

703 *here*: hem. 704 time was consumed. 717 their company. 720 natural affection. 724 And thought to cheer her up with their conversation. 726–8 by doing this they gave her the kind of relief that a man with a headache feels if his heel is scratched. 736 in colour like the sun.

Sho wrong ful ofte, and bad God on here rewe,   *take pity*
And with the deth to don bote on here bale.
740 Here hewe whilom bryght, that tho was pale,   *once*
Bar witnes of here wo and [here] constreynte;   *distress*
And thus she spak, sobbynge in here compleynte.   *as she made*

'Alas,' quod she, 'out of this regioun
I, woful wrecche and infortuned wight,   *ill-fated*
745 And born in corsed constellacioun,
Mot gon and thus departen fro my knyght.
Wo worth, allas, that ilke dayes lyght   *Evil befall*
On which I saw hym first with eyen tweyne,
That causeth me – and I hym – al this peyne.'

750 Therwith the terys from here eighen two
Doun fille as shour in Aperill swythe;   *as fast*
Here white brest she bet and for the wo
After the deth she cried a thousand sithe,
Syn he that wont here wo was forto lythe,   *alleviate*
755 She mot forgon – for which disaventure   *give up*
She held hereself a forlost creature.   *ruined*

She seyde, 'How shal he do, and I also?
How sholde I lyve yf [that] I from hym twynne?   *part*
O dere herte ek, that I love so,
760 Who shal that sorwe sleen that ye ben inne?
O Calkas, fader, thyn be al this synne!
O moder myn that cleped were Argyve,*
Wo worth that day that thow me bere on lyve!

'To what fyn sholde I lyve and sorwen thus?   *purpose*
765 How sholde a fyssh withoute water dure?   *survive*
What is Criseyde worth from Troylus?
How sholde a plaunte or lyves creature   *living*
Lyve withoute his kynde noriture?   *natural food*
For which ful ofte a byword here I seye,   *proverb*
770 That "Roteles mot grene sone deye."

'I shal don thus: syn neyther swerd ne darte
Dar I noon handle for the cruwelté,

739 relieve her suffering. 745 under an accursed. 760 bring to an end. 763 gave birth to me. 765 *a: I a.* 770 The green plant that is without roots must. 772 suffering it would cause.

That ilke day that I from hym departe,
If sorwe of that nyl not my bane be,
775 Than shal no mete or drynk come in me
Til I my soule out of my brest unshethe,   *draw*
And thus myselven wil I do to dethe.

'And Troylus, my clothes everychone
Shul blake ben yn tokenynge, herte swete,
780 That I am as out of this world agon,
That wont was yow to setten in quiete;   *at rest*
And of myn ordre ay til deth me mete,
The observaunce evere yn youre absence
Shal sorwe ben, compleynte and abstinence.

785 'Myn herte and ek the woful gost therinne   *spirit*
Biquethe I with youre spirit to compleyne
Eternally – for they shul nevere twynne;
For though in erthe twynned be we tweyne,
Yet in the feld of pité,* out of peyne.   *torment*
790 That hight Elysos, shul we ben y-fere,   *united*
As Orpheus and Erudice his fere.

'Thus, herte myn, for Antenor, allas,
I soone shal be chaunged, as I wene.
But how shul ye don yn this sorwful cas?
795 How shal youre tendre herte this sustene?   *bear*
But, herte myn, foryet this sorwe and tene,
And me also – for sothly forto seye,
So ye wel fare, I recche not to deye.'   *As long as*

How myght it evere y-red be or y-songe,   *read (aloud)*
800 The pleynte that she made in here distresse?
I not; but as for me, my litel tonge,   *cannot tell*
If I discreven wolde here hevynesse,
It sholde make here sorwe seme lesse
Than that i[t] was, and chyldisshly deface
805 Here heyghe compleynte – and therfore I it pace.   *lofty*

Pandare which that sent was from Troylus
Unto Criseyde, as ye han herd devyse,   *tell*

---

774 will not kill me. 780 as one who has taken leave of this world. 782–3
while you are absent, the rites of my (religious) order will be. 801 my limited
(command of) language. 804 distort and make (seem) childish; *it: is.*

That for the beste it was accorded thus,   *decided upon*
And he ful glad to don hym that service –
810 Unto Criseyde in a ful secre wyse,
Ther as she lay in torment and in rage,   *violent grief*
Come here to telle al holly his message.   *in full*

And fond that she hereselven gan to trete   *speak*
Ful pitously, for with here salte terys
815 Here brest, here face, y-bathed was ful wete;
The myghty tresses of here sonnyssh herys   *hair*
Unbroyden hangen al aboute here eris,   *Loose*
Which yaf hym verray signal of ma[rti]re   *suffering*
Of deth, which that here herte gan desire.

820 When she hym saw she gan for sorwe anoon
Here tery face atwixe here armes hyde;
For which this Pandare is so wo bygon,
That in the hous he myghte unnethe abyde,
As he that felte pyté on every syde:
825 For yf Criseyde hadde erst compleyned sore,   *before that*
Tho gan she pleyne a thousand tymes more.

And in here aspre pleynt than she seyde: *bitter*
'Pandare, first of joyes mo than two
Was cause causynge unto me, Criseyde,
830 That now transmuwed ben in cruel wo.   *are changed*
Wher shal I seye to yow welcome or no,
That alderferst me brough[t] into servise   *first of all*
Of love, allas, that endeth in this wyse?

'Endeth thanne love in wo? Ye, [o]r men lieth;
835 And alle worldly blysse, as thenketh me.
The ende of blisse ay sorwe it occupieth;
And who that troweth not that it so be,
Lat hym upon me, woful wrecche, y-se,   *look*
That myself hate and ay my birthe acc[o]rse,
840 Felynge alwey fro w[ikke] I go to worse.   *bad*

'Whoso me seth, he seth sorwe al at onys: *sees*
Peyne, torment, pleynt, wo and distresse.

---

818 *martire: matere.* 821 tear-stained . . . between. 823 could hardly bear to
remain. 829 the primary cause. 831 Am I to make you. 834 *or: er.* 836 In the
end joy is always replaced by. 839 *accorse: accurse.* 840 *wikke: wo.*

Out of my woful body harm ther non is,   *Outside*
As angwyssh, langour, cruel bitternesse,   *affliction*
845 Anoy, smert, drede, fury and ek sikenesse.   *Vexation*
    I trow, iwys, from hevene teris reyne
    For pité of myn aspre and cruwel peyne.'   *harsh*

'And thow my suster, ful of discomfort,'
Quod Pandarus, 'what thenkestow to do?
850 Whi ne hastow to thiselven som resport?
    Wh[i] woltow thus thiselve [allas,] fordo?   *destroy*
    Lef al this we[r]k, and take now hede to   *Give up*
    That I shal seyn, and herkene of good entente   *carefully*
    This which by me thi Troylus the sente.'

855 Torned here tho Criseyde, a wo makynge
    So gret that it a deth was forto se.
    'Allas,' quod she, 'what wordes may ye brynge?
    What wold my dere [herte] seyn to me,
    Which that I drede nevere mo to se?
860 Wol ye have pleynte or terys er I wende?   *Do you want*
    I have ynowe, yf he therafter sende!'

She was right swych to sen in hire visage   *appearance*
As is that wight that men on bere bynde;   *bier*
Here face, lyk [of] paradys the ymage,
865 Was al i-chaunged in another kynde.
    The pleye, the laughtre, men was wont to fynde
    In here, and ek here joyes everychone,
    Ben fled – and thus lith now Criseyde allone.

Aboute here eyen two a purpre ryng
870 Bytrent, in sothfast tokenynge of here peyne,   *Encircles*
    That to byholde it was a dedly thing;
    For which Pandare myght not restreyne
    The terys from hise eyen forto reyne.
    But natheles, as he best myght, he seyde
875 From Troylus this[e] wordes to Criseyde:

'Lo nece, I trowe ye han herd al how   *in full detail*
The kyng, with othere lordes, for the beste,
Hath mad eschaunge of Antenor and yow,

849 do you imagine you are doing? **850** Why don't you have some regard for yourself. **864** *of: a.* **865** entirely transformed. **866** lively behaviour.

That cause is of this sorwe and this unreste. *disquiet*
880 But how this cas doth Troylus moleste, *torment*
That may non erthely mannes tonge seye;
For verray wo his wit is al awey. *pure, has fled*

'For which we han so sorwed, he and I,
That into litel bothe it hadde us slawe:
885 But thurgh my conseyl this day fynally,
He somwhat is fro wepyng now withdrawe;
It semeth me that he desireth fawe *eagerly*
With yow to ben al nyght forto devyse
Remede in this, yf ther were any wyse.

890 'This short and pleyn, th'effect of my message,
As ferforth as my wit may comprehende: *far*
For ye that ben of torment in swych rage
May to no long prologe as now entende;
And herupon ye may an answere hym sende.
895 And for the love of God, my nece dere,
So lef this wo er Troylus be here.' *give up*

'Gret is my wo,' quod she, and sighed sore,
As she that felt dedly sharpe distresse,
'But yet to me his sorwe is muche more,
900 That loveth hym bet than he hymself, I gesse.
Allas, for me hath he swych hevynesse?
Kan he for me so pitously compleyne?
Iwis, his sorwe doubleth al my peyne.

'Grevous to me, God wot, is forto twynne,'
905 Quod she, 'but yet it hardere is to me
To sen that sorwe whiche that he is inne,
For wel wot I it wole my bane be,
And deye I wole in certayn,' tho quod she;
'And bidde hym come er deth, that thus me t[h]reteth,
910 Dryf out the gost which in myn herte beteth.' *spirit*

This[e] wordes seyd, she on here armes two
Fil gruf, and gan to wepe pitously. *face downwards*

884 it has very nearly caused both our deaths. 886 has to some extent stopped weeping. 889 if any such could be found. 890 In brief and in full, this is the substance of. 893 to: as to. 894 And concerning this matter. 900 better . . . suppose. 910 beteth: he beteth.

Quod Pandarus, 'Allas, whi do ye so,
Syn ye wel wot the tyme is faste by   *close at hand*
915 That he shal come? Arys up hastely
That he yow not bywopen thus ne fynde –   *in tears*
But ye wol han hym wod out of his mynde.

'For wist he that ye ferde in this manere,   *were acting*
He wolde hymselve sle; and yf I wend
920 To han this fare, he sholde not come here
For al the good that Pryam may despende.
For to what fyn he wolde anoon pretende,   *end, aim*
That know I wel, and forthi yet I seye,
So lef this sorwe or platly he wole deye.   *certainly*

925 'And shappeth yow his sorwe forto abregge,
And nought encresse, leve nece swete;
B[e]th rather to hym [cause] of flat than egge,*
And with som wysdom ye his sorwes bete.   *cure*
What helpeth it to wepen ful a strete,
930 Or though ye bothe in salte teris dre[ynt]e?   *drowned*
Bet is a tyme of cure ay than of pleynte.

'I mene thus: whan I hym here brynge,
Syn ye ben wyse and bothe of on assent,
So shappeth how distourbe this goynge,
935 Or come ayen soone after ye be went –   *return*
Wommen ben wyse in short avysement –
And lat sen now how youre wit shal avayle,   *serve*
And what that I may helpe, it shal not fayle.'

'Go,' quod Criseyde, 'and uncle, trewely,
940 I shal don al my myght me to restreyne   *my utmost*
From wepyng in his sight, and bysily   *diligently*
Hym forto glade I shal don al my peyne,
And in myn herte seken every veyne;   *search, corner*
If to this sor ther may be founden salve,   *wound*
945 It shal not lakken, certain, on myn halve.'

---

917 Unless you want him to go completely mad. 919–20 if I thought that this
would have come about. 921 wealth ... disburse. 925 find a means of
lessening. 927 of healing rather than wounding (afresh); *Beth: Buth.* 930
dreynte: drenche. 934 prevent ... departure. 936 grasp (what is to be done)
very quickly. 945 not be wanting, certainly, for anything I can do.

Goth Pandarus, and Troylus he soughte,
Til in a temple he fond hym allone,
As he that of his lyf no lenger rowhte;   *cared*
But to the petouse goddes everychone
950 Ful tendrely he preyde and made his mone,   *pitifully*
To don hym sone out of this world to pace,   *let*
For wel he thou[g]hte ther was noon other grace.

And shortly, al the sothe forto seye,
He was so fallen in despeyr that day,*
955 That outrely he shop hym forto deye.
For right thus was his argument alwey:
He seyde he nas but lorn, waylawey: *lost*
'For al that cometh, comth by necessité:
Thus to be lorn, it is my destyné.

960 'For certaynly, this wot I wel,' he seyde,
'That forsight of dyvyne purveyaunce
Hath seyn alwey me to forgon Criseyde,
Syn God seth every thing, out of doutaunce,   *(fore)sees*
And hem desponeth, thourgh his ordenaunce,
965 In here merites sothly forto be,
As they shul comen by predestiné.

'But natheles, allas, whom shal I leve?   *believe*
For ther ben clerkes grete many on,   *scholars*
That destyné thorugh argumentz preve;   *prove*
970 And som men seyn that nedly ther is noon,
But that fre choys is yeven us everychon.   *given (to)*
O welawey! so sley arn clerkes olde   *cunning*
That I not whose opynyon I may holde.   *don't know*

'For so[m] men seyn, yf God seth al byforn –
975 And God may not deceyved ben, pardé –
Than mot it falle, they men hadde it swo[rn],
That purveyaunce hath seighen byfore to be.

952 nothing else that could help him. 955 absolutely prepared himself for
death. 958 everything that happens. 961-2 That God in his providence has
foreseen from all eternity that I would lose Criseyde. 964-6 And through his
(divine) plan disposes them to be exactly as they are foreordained, according to
their merits. 970 nothing comes about through necessity. 972 ancient philoso-
phers. 974 sees everything in advance. 976-7 Then whatever providence has
foreseen will come about must do so, even though men had sworn (the
contrary).

Wherfor I seye that from eterne yf He   *eternity*
Hath wyst byforn oure thought ek as oure dede,   *in advance*
980 We have no fre choys, as these clerkes rede.   *instruct*

'For other thought, nor other dede also,
Myght nevere be, but swych as purveyaunce,
Which may not ben deceyved nevere mo,
Hath feled biforn, withouten ignoraunce.
985 For yf there myghte ben a variaunce
To writhen out fro Goddes purveyinge,
There nere no prescience of thyng comynge.

'But it were rathere an opynyon
Uncerteyn, and no stedefast forseynge;   *firm*
990 And certes, that were an abusion,   *a nonsense*
That God shuld han no parfit cler witynge
More than we men that han doutous wenynge:
But swych an errour upon God to gesse   *ignorance, impute*
Were fals and foul and corsed wykkednesse.   *perversity*

995 'Ek this is an opynyon of some
That han here top ful heighe and smothe y-shore:
They seyn right thus: that thyng is not to come
For that the prescience hath seyghen byfore
That it shal come; but they seyn that therfore   *because*
1000 That it shal come, therfore the purveyaunce
Wot it byforn, withouten ignoraunce.   *beforehand*

'And in this manere this necessité
Retorneth in his part contrarie agayn;
For nedfully byhoveth it not to be
1005 That thilke thinges fallen in certayn
That ben purveyed; but nedely, as they seyn,   *of necessity*

981–7 For no alternative thought or action could ever exist unless providence, which can never at any time be mistaken, had certainly perceived it beforehand. Because if there could be an alternative, (a way) to wriggle out of what God had foreseen, there could be no (sure) foreknowledge of events to come. 991–2 no absolutely clear knowledge beyond that of us men who can only guess uncertainly. 996 the tops of their heads tonsured. 998–9 Because (divine) foreknowledge has seen in advance that it must happen. 1002–6 in this way it is the other side of the matter that is governed by necessity; for it is not that particular events necessarily and inevitably come about because they are foreseen.

Byhoveth it that thinges whiche that falle,   *It is needful*
That they in certayn ben purveyed alle.   *inevitably*

'I mene as though I laboured me in this
1010 To enqueren which thyng cause of which thyng be:
As wheyther that the prescience of God is
The certayn cause of the necessité
Of thinges that to comen ben, pardé;
Or yf necessité of thing comynge
1015 Be cause certeyn of the purveyinge.   *foreknowledge*

'But now ne enforce I me nought in shewynge
How the ordre of causes stant; but wel wot I,
That it byhoveth that the byfallyng
Of thinges wyst byforn certeynly
1020 Be necessarie, al seme it not therby
That prescience put fallyng necessa[ir]e
To thing to come, al falle it foule or fayre.   *whether*

'For if ther sit a man yond on a see,
Than by necessité byhoveth it
1025 That, certes, thin opynyon soth be
That wenest or conje[c]test that he sit;
And ferther over now ayenward yit,
Lo, right so it is of the part contrarie,   *opposite side*
As thus – now herkene, for I wol not tarie: *linger*

1030 'I seye that yf opynion of the
Be soth, for that he sit, than seye I this:
That he mot sitten by necessité;
And thus necessité in eyther is.   *on both sides*
For yn hym nede of syttyng is, ywys,
1035 And [in the] nede of soth; and thus, forsothe,
T[h]er mot necessité ben in yow bothe.

'But thou maist seyn the man sit not therfore
That thyn opynyon of his sittyng soth is;

1009 I intend to take pains in this (matter). 1012–13 of the inevitability of
future events. 1016–7 I will not at this time strive to demonstrate the sequence
of causation. 1020–2 even though it does not appear from that that foreknowledge makes inevitable the occurrence of future events; *necessaire: necessarie.*
1023 sits on a seat over there. 1026 Who assumes or supposes that he is sitting
(there); *conjectest: conjestest.* 1027 in addition on the other hand. 1034–5 he
is necesssarily sitting, and your opinion is necessarily true. 1037 does not sit
because.

But rather for the man sit ther byfore,
1040 Therfore is thyn opynyon soth, ywys.
And I seye, though the cause of soth of this
Comth of his sittyng, yet necessité   *from*
Is entrechaunged bothe in hym and the.   *shared*

'Thus [i]n this same wyse, out of doutaunce,   *certainly*
1045 I may wel make, as it semeth me,
My resonynge of Goddes pourveyaunce
And of the thinges that to comen be;
By which reson men may wel y-se
That thilke thinges that in erthe falle,
1050 That by necessité they comen alle.

'For although that, for thyng shal come, ywys,
Therfore it is purveyed certaynly
(Nough[t] that it comth for it purveyed is),
Yet natheles byhoveth it nedfully
1055 That thing to come be purveyed, trewely;
Or elles thinges that purvey[e]d be,
That thei bytiden by necessité.   *happen*

'And this suffiseth right ynow, certeyn,
Forto destroye oure fre choys every del.   *bit*
1060 But now is this abusion to seyn,   *falsification*
That fallynge of the thinges temporel
Is cause of Godes prescience eternel.
Now trewely, that is a fals sentence,   *judgment*
That thing to come sholde cause his prescience.

1065 'What myght I wene, and ich hadde swych a thought,
But that God purveyed thyng that is to come
For that it is to come, and ellis nought?   *otherwise*
So myght I wene that thinges alle and some
That whylom ben byfalle and overcome,

1039 because the man is already seated. 1044 *in: on.* 1045–6 I may, I think, safely draw conclusions about. 1048 From which arguments. 1052 It is on that account. 1058 And this is quite enough, indeed. 1061 the coming about of transitory events. 1065 could I suppose if I thought in this way. 1068–71 that the totality of events that have happened and occurred in the past was the reason for that supreme providence that foresees everything (to come) without (possibility of) error.

1070 Ben cause of thilke sovereyn purveyaunce
     That forwot al withouten ignoraunce.

     'And over al this, yet sey I more therto,
     [That] right a[s] whan I wot ther is a thing,
     Iwys, that thing mot nedefully be so;
1075 Ek right so, whan I wot a thyng comynge,
     So mot it come; and thus the byfallyng
     Of thinges that ben wyst byfore that tyde,   *their time*
     They mowe not ben eschewed on no syde.'*   *averted*

     Thanne seyde he thus: 'Almyghty Jove in trone,   *throne*
1080 That wost of alle thinge the sothfastnesse,
     Rewe on my sorwe [and] do me deye sone,   *let*
     Or bryng Criseyde and me fro this distresse.'
     And whil he was in al this hevynesse,   *dejection*
     Disputynge with hymself in this matere,   *on this topic*
1085 Come Pandare [in], and seyde as ye may here.*

     'Almyghti God,' quod Pandarus, 'in trone,
     I! who seygh evere a wys man faren so?   *behave*
     Whi, Troylus what thenkestow to done?
     Hastow swych lust to ben thyn owen fo?   *a desire*
1090 What, pardé, yet is not Criseyde ago!
     Why lust the so thynself fordon for drede,
     That in thyn hed thyn eyghen semen dede?   *So that, look*

     'Hastow not lyved many a yer byfore
     Withouten here, and ferd ful wel at ese?
1095 Artow for here and for noon other bor[e]?
     Hath Kynde the wrought al oonly here to plese?
     Lat be, and thenk right thus in [thi] disese: *distress*
     That in the des right as there fallen chaunces,   *dicing*
     Right so in love there come and gon plesaunces.   *delights*

1100 'And yet this is a wonder most of alle,
     Whi thow thus sorwest, syn thow nost not yet,
     Touchyng here goynge, how that it shal falle,   *turn out*

1072 beyond all this, I go on to add. 1073 know that something exists. 1075
In just the same way. 1081 *and: or.* 1090 Criseyde hasn't gone yet. 1091 Why
do you take such pleasure in killing yourself through fear? 1094 been very
comfortable. 1095 *bore: born.* 1096 Nature created you solely for her pleasure?
1101 still don't know.

Ne yf she kan heresel[f] distorben it.
[Th]ow hast not yet assayed al here wit.
1105 A man may al by-tyme his nekke bede
Whan it shal of, and sorwen at the nede.

'Forthi take hede of that that I shal seye:
I have with here y-spoke and longe y-be,   *stayed*
So as accorded was bytwyxe us tweye.
1110 And evere mo me thenketh thus, that she   *all the time*
Hath somwhat in here hertes preveté,   *inmost heart*
Wherwith she kan, yf I shal right arede,   *interpret*
Distorbe al this of which thow art in drede.   *Prevent*

'For w[h]ych my counseyl is, whan it is nyght
1115 Thow to here go and make of this an ende;
And blissyd Juno* thourgh here grete myght
Shal as I hope here grace unto us sende.
Myn herte seyth: "Certeyn she shal not wende";   *tells (me)*
And forthi putte thyn herte a whyle in reste,
1120 And hold thi purpos, for it is the beste.'*

This Troylus answerede and sight sore:
'Thow seyst right wel, and I wil do right so.'
And what hym lyste, he seyde unto it more.
And whan that it was tyme forto go,
1125 Ful prevely hymself, withouten mo,   *further (delay)*
Unto here com as he was wont to done,   *came*
And how thei wroughte, I shal yow telle sone.

Soth it is whanne they gonne first to mete,
So gan the peynes here hertes forto twyste,   *wring*
1130 That neyther of hem other myght grete,
But hem in armes tok and after kyste.
The lasse wofulle of hem bothe nyste
Wher that he was, ne myght o word outbrynge,   *utter*
As I seyde erst, for wo and for sobbynge.

1135 Tho woful teris that they leten falle
As bittre weren out of teris kynde,
For peyne, as is ligne aloes or galle: *aloe*

1103 *hereself:* hereselven. 1104 put her intelligence fully to the test; *Thow:* Yow.
1105 soon enough offer his neck (to the executioner). 1106 must (come) off.
1114 *whych:* swych. 1121 sighed bitterly. 1136 contrary to the nature of.

So bittre teris weep nought, as I fynde,   *wept*
The woful Myrra thou[rgh] the bark and rynde;*
1140 That in this world ther nys so hard an herte
That nolde han rewed on hire peynes smerte.   *taken pity*

But whanne here woful wery gostes tweyne
Retorned ben ther as hem oughte dwelle,
And that somwhat to wayken gan the peyne   *grow less*
1145 By lenthe of pleynte, and ebben gan the welle   *spring*
Of here teris, and the herte unswelle,
With broken voys, al hoors for[sh]right, Criseyde
To Troylus thise ilke wordes seyde:

'O Jove, I deye, and mercy I be[se]che!
1150 Help, Troylus!' and therwithal here face
Upon his brest she leyde, and lost speche –
Here woful spirit from his propre place,
Righ[t] with the word, alwey [o] poynt to pace.
And thus she lith with hewes pale and grene,   *lies*
1155 That whilom fresch and fairest was to sene.

This Troylus, that on here gan byholde,
Clepynge here name – and she lay as for ded,   *Calling*
Withouten answere, and felte here lymes colde,
Here eyen throwen upward to here hed.   *in*
1160 This sorwful man kan now noon other red,
But ofte tyme here colde mouth he kyste:
Wher hym was wo, God and hymself it wyste!   *Whether*

He rist hym up, and long streyght he hyre leyde;
For signe of lyf, for ought he kan or may,
1165 Kan he noon fynde in no thing on Criseyde,   *no respect*
For which his song f[u]l ofte is 'weylaway'.
But whan he sawgh that specheles she lay,
With sorwful voys, and herte of blysse al bare,
He seyde how she was fro thi world y-fare.

1170 So after that he longe hadde here compleyned,
His honde[s] wrong, and seyde that was to seye,   *what*

1139 *thourgh:* thought. 1147 made hoarse and worn out by shrieking; *for-
shright: for bright.* 1153 ready to fly away; *o: up.* 1160 can think of nothing
else to do. 1163 laid her out full length. 1166 *ful, is: fyl, his.* 1168 wholly
deprived of. 1169 that she had died.

And with his teris salte here brest by-reyned,   *showered*
He gan tho teris wypen of ful dreye,
And pitously gan for the soule preye,
1175 And seyde, 'O lord, that set art in thy trone,
Rewe ek on me, for I shal folwe here sone!'

She cold was and withouten sentement,   *feeling*
For [ought he] wot, for breth ne felte he noon;
And this was hym a preignant argument   *convincing*
1180 That she was forth out of this world a-gon;   *departed*
And whan he seygh ther was noon other won,
He gan here lymes dresse in swych manere   *arrange*
As men don hem that shul be leyd on bere.

And after this with sterne and cruwel herte,
1185 H[is] swerd anoon out of his shethe he twyghte,   *plucked*
Hymself to slen, how sore that hym smerte,
So that his sowle here sow[l]e folwen myghte,
There as the dom of Mynos wolde it dyghte;*
Syn Love and cruwel Fortune it ne wolde
1190 That in this world he lenger lyven sholde.

Thanne seyde he thus, fulfilled of heigh desdayn: *full of*
'O cruwel Jove, and thow Fortune adverse,   *hostile*
This al and som, that falsly have [ye] slayn
Criseyde, and syn ye may do me no werse,
1195 Fy on youre myght and werkes so diverse!   *variable*
Thus cowardly ye shul me nevere wynne;   *overcome*
Ther shal no deth me fro my lady twynne.   *separate*

'For I this world, syn ye han slayn here thus,
Wol lete, and folowe here spirit lowe or hye;   *forsake*
1200 Shal nevere lovere seyn that Troylus
Dar not for fere with his lady dye;
For certeyn, I wole bere here companye!
But syn ye wol not suffren us [lyven here]   *allow*
Yet suffreth that oure soules ben y-fere.   *together*

1205 'And thow, cité, whiche that I leve in wo,
And thow, Pryam, and bretheren al y-fere,

1178 *ought he: I.* 1181 nothing else for it. 1185 *His: He.* 1186 however
painful it might be. 1188 To the place to which Mynos would assign it. 1189
would not consent. 1193 is the whole of it. 1203 *lyven here: y-fere.*

And thow, my moder, farewel, for I go;
And Attropos, make redy thow my bere.
And thow Criseyde, O swete herte dere,
1210 Receyve now my spirit,' wold he seye,
With swerd at herte, al redy forto deye.*

But as God wolde, of swough therwith she abreyde,
And gan to syke and 'Troylus' she cride,
And he answerde, 'Lady myn, Cryseyde;
1215 Lyve ye yet?' and let his swerd doun glide.   *slip*
'Ye, herte myn, that thanked be Cupide,'
Quod she, and therwithal she sore syghte,
And he bygan to glade here as he myghte:

Tok here in armes two, and kyst here ofte,
1220 And here to glade he dide al his entente;
For which here gost, that flekered ay on lofte,
Into here woful herte ayen it wente.   *returned*
But at the laste, as that here eyen glente
Asyde, anoon she gan his swerd aspye,
1225 As it lay bare, and gan for fere crie.   *unsheathed*

And asked hym whi he hadde it out drawe;
And Troylus anoon the cause tolde,
And how hymself therwith he wolde have slawe;   *killed*
For which Criseyde upon hym gan byholde,
1230 And gan hym in here armes faste folde,
And seyde, 'O mercy, God, lo, swych a dede!   *what*
Allas, how neigh we were bothe dede!

'Thanne yf I ne hadde spoken, as grace was,
Ye wolden han slay[n] yourreself anoon?' quod she.
1235 'Ye, douteles'; and she answerede, 'Allas,
For by that ilke lord that mad me,
I nolde a forlong wey on lyve han be
After youre deth, to han be crowned quene
Of al the londz the sonne on shyneth shene.   *brightly*

1240 'But with this selve swerd whiche that here is,

1207 *for: for now.* 1212 at that she suddenly came out of her swoon. 1216
may Cupid be thanked for it. 1218 cheer her up as best he could. 1221 was all
this time fluttering above (them). 1223-4 glanced to one side. 1237 would not
have lived more than a few minutes. 1238 not even to have been.

Myselve I wolde have slayn,' quod she tho.
'But ho, for we han right ynow of this,
And late us rise and streyght to bedde go.
And ther lat us speken of oure wo –
1245 For by the morter which that I se brenne,   *lamp*
Knowe I right wel that day is not fer henne.'   *away*

Whanne they were in here bed in armes folde,
Nought was yt lyk the nyghtes here-byforn;
For pitously eche gan other byholde,
1250 As thei that hadden al here blisse y-lorn,
Bywaylyng ay the day that they were born.   *all the time*
Til at the last this sorwful wyght Criseyde,
To Troylus these ilke wordes seyde: *very*

'Lo, herte myn, wel wot ye this,' quod she,
1255 'That yf a wyght alwey his wo compleyne,
And seketh nought how holpen forto be,   *helped*
It [n]is but folye and encres of peyne;
And syn that here assembled be we tweyne,
To fynde bote of wo that we be inne,
1260 It were al tyme sone to bygynne.

'I am a womman, as ful wel ye wot,
And as I am avised sodeynly,
So wole I telle yow whil it is hot:
Me thenketh thus: that neyther ye ne I
1265 Ought half this wo to make skilfully;
For there is art ynow forto redresse
That yet is mys, and slen this hevynesse.   *put an end to*

'Soth is, the wo [the] whiche that we ben inne,
For ought I wot, for nothyng elles is
1270 But for the cause that we sholden twynne;
Considered al, ther is no more amys.
But what is thanne a remede unto this,
But that we shape us sone forto mete?
This al and som, my dere herte swete.

1242 let us stop, for we have (spoken) quite enough about. 1260 is high time
to start. 1262 have sudden intuitions. 1265 Have any reason to make. 1266
are plenty of ways to set right. 1269–70 solely on account of the fact that we
must part. 1273 contrive things so that. 1274 is the long and short of it.

1275 'Now that I shal wel bryngen it aboute
       To come ayen, soone after that I go,
       Therof am I no manere thyng in doute;   *not in the least*
       For dredles, withinne a wowke or two,   *week*
       I shal ben here – and that it may be so,
1280 By alle right and in a wordes fewe,
       I shal yow wel an hep of weyes shewe.   *host*

       'For which I wo[l] not make long sermon,   *speech*
       For tyme y-lost wol not recovered be;
       But I wol gon to my conclusyon,
1285 And to the beste, in ought that I kan se.
       And, for the love of God, foryeve it me,
       If I speke ought ayen youre hertes reste;   *peace of mind*
       For trewely, I speke it for the beste.

       'Makynge alwey a protestacion
1290 That now these wordes whiche that I shal seye,
       Nys but to shewe yow my mocion   *desire*
       To fynde unto oure helpe the beste weye;
       And taketh it non other wyse, I preye.
       For yn effect what so ye me comaunde,
1295 That wol I don, for that is no demaunde.

       'Now herkeneth this: ye han wel understonde
       My goynge graunted is by parlement
       So ferforth that it may not be withstonde   *completely*
       For al this world, as by my juggement;   *in my opinion*
1300 And syn ther helpeth noon avisement
       To letten it – lat it passe out of mynde,   *prevent*
       And lat us shape a bettre wey to fynde.   *contrive*

       'The sothe is that the twynnynge of us tweyne   *separation*
       Wol us disese and cruwellyche anoye;
1305 But hym byhoveth somtyme han a peyne
       That serveth love, yf that he wol have joye.
       And syn I shal no ferthere out of Troye
       Than I may ryde ayen on half a morwe,   *back, morning*
       It ought the lasse causen us to sorwe.

1282 *wol: wot.* 1285 best (solution) as far as. 1295 there is no question about
that. 1296 *ye: for ye.* 1300 no amount of thought. 1304 distress . . . afflict;
disese: dishese. 1305 it is needful for him.

1310 'So as I shal not so ben hid in muwe,   *cooped up*
That day by day, myn owene herte dere –
Syn ye wel wot that it is now a truwe –   *(time of) truce*
Ye shul ful wel al myn estat y-here.
And er that truwe is don, I shal ben here:
1315 And thanne have ye bothe Antenor y-wonne
And me also – beth glad now yf ye konne!

'And thenk right thus: "Criseyde is now agon;
But what! – she shal come hastely ayen."   *very soon*
And whanne, allas? – By God, lo righ[t] anoon,
1320 Er dayes ten, this dar I saufly seyn.
And thanne at erst shal we ben so fayn,
So as we shulle togederes evere dwelle,
That al this world ne myghte oure blysse telle.

'I se that ofte tyme ther as we ben now,   *(even) as*
1325 That for the beste, oure conseyl forto hide,   *secret, keep*
Ye speke not with me – nor I with yow –
In fourtenyght, ne se yow go ne ryde.
May ye not ten dayes thanne abyde,   *wait*
For myn honour yn swych [an] aventure?
1330 Iwys, ye mowen ellys lite endure!

'Ye knowe ek how that al my kyn is here,
But yf that onlyche it my fader be,
And ek myn othere thinges alle y-fere;
And namelyche my dere herte, ye,   *in particular*
1335 Whom that I nolde leven forto se   *give up seeing*
For al this world, as wyd as it hath space –
Or elles se ich neve[re] Joves face!

'Whi trowe ye my fader yn this wyse
Coveyteth so to se me, but for drede   *Is so anxious*
1340 Lest yn this town that folkes me dispise
Bycause of hym, for his unhappy dede?*   *ill-fated*
What wot my fader what lyf that I lede?
For, and he wyste in Troy how wel I fare   *if*
Us nedede for my wendyng nought to care.

1313 hear a full account of how I am getting on.   1321 for the first time (since
our parting).   1329 To (preserve) my honour under these circumstances.   1330
lite: litel.   1344 We would not have to worry about my going away.

1345 'Ye sen that every day ek, more and more,   *speak*
    Men trete of pees, and it supposed is
    That men the queene Eleyne shal restore,
    And Grekes us restore that is mys.*   *lacking*
    So though there nere comfort noon but this,
1350 That men purposen pes on every syde,   *intend*
    Ye may the bettre at ese of herte abyde.

    'For yf that it be pes, myn herte dere,
    The nature of the pes mot nedes dryve
    That men moste entrecomunen y-fere,
1355 And to and fro ek ryde and gon as blyve   *quickly*
    Alday, as thikke as ben flen from an hyve,   *bees, fly*
    And every wyght han liberté to bleve   *stay*
    Wher as hym lyst the bet, wit[h]outen leve.

    'And though so be that pes ther may be noon,
1360 Yet hider, though there nevere pes ne were,
    I moste come – for wh[i]der sholde I gon,
    Or how, myschaunce, sholde I dwellen there   *alas*
    Among tho men of armes evere in fere?
    For which, as wysly God my soule rede,
1365 I kan not sen wherof ye sholden drede.   *why*

    'Have here another wey, if it so be   *reason*
    That al this thing ne may yow not suffice:
    My fader as ye k[n]owen wel, pardé,
    Is old, and elde is ful of coveytise;*   *old age*
1370 And I right now have founden al the gyse,   *means*
    Withoute net, wherwith I shal hym hente;   *entrap*
    And herkeneth how, if that ye wole assente.

    'Lo, Troylus, men seyn that hard it is
    The wolf ful and the wether hol to have: *sheep*
1375 This is to seyn, that men ful ofte, ywys,
    Mote spenden part, the remenaunt forto save;   *rest*
    For ay with gold men may the herte grave   *impress*
    Of hym that set is upon coveitise;
    And how I mene, I shal it yow devyse.

1353 of necessity bring it about. 1354 have dealings with each other. 1358
Wherever he prefers, without (asking) permission. 1359 even if it should
happen. 1361 *whider: wheder.* 1364 as certainly as God may guide. 1373
hard: ful hard.

1380 'The moble which that I have yn this town
Unto my fader shal I take, and seye,
That right for trust and for savacio[w]n — safe-keeping
It sent is from a frend of his or tweye,
The wh[i]che frendes ferventlyche hym preye
1385 To sende after more, and that in hye, — promptly
Whil that this town stant thus in jupartie. — danger

'And that shal ben an huge quantité –
Thus shal I seyn – but lest it folk asspi[d]e, — perceived
This may be sent by no wyght but by me;
1390 I shal ek shewen hym, yf pes bytyde, — come about
What frendes [that] ich have on every syde
Toward the court, to don the wrathe pace — cause
Of Priamus, and don hym stonde in grace.

'So [w]hat for o thyng and for other, swete,
1395 I shal hym so enchaunten with my sawes, — what I say
That right in hevene his sowle is, shal he mete, — imagine
For al Appollo, or his clerkes lawes,
Or calkullynge, avayleth nought thre hawes;
Desir of gold shal so his soule bl[e]nde,
1400 That as ne lyst I shal wel make an ende.

'And yf he wolde ought by hys sort it preve,
If that I lye, in certayn I shal fonde — try
Distorben hym and plukke hym by the sleve,
Makynge his sort, and beren hym on honde,
1405 He hath not wel the goddes understonde
(For goddes speken in amphibologies, — ambiguously
And for a soth they tellen twenty lyes). — a single

'"Eke drede fond first goddes, I suppose" – — created
Thus shal I seyn – and that [h]is cowarde herte
1410 Made hym amys the goddes text to glose, — interpret
Whan he, for fered, out of his Delphos sterte. — rushed
And but I make hym soone to converte, — change

1380 moveable property. 1384 *whiche: wheche.* 1393 bring him into favour.
1394 *what: that; o: other o.* 1397 scholarly rules; *or: and or.* 1398 calcula-
tion(s) are not worth. 1399 *blende: blynde.* 1401 wishes at all to test by the
casting of lots. 1404 deceive him (into thinking). 1411 through being afraid.

And don my red withinne a day or tweye,
I wol to yow oblige me to deye.'*

1415 (And trewelyche, as wreten wel I fynde,
That al this thyng was seyd of good entente;   *sincerely*
And that here herte trewe was and kynde
Towardes hym – and spak right as she mente;
And that she starf for wo neigh whan she wente,
1420 And was in purpos evere to be trewe:
Thus writen they that of here werkes knewe.)   *actions*

This Troylus with herte and eerys spradde   *wide open*
Herde al this thyng devysen to and fro,   *discuss*
And verraylich hym semed that he hadde
1425 The same wit – but yet to late he[r] go   *opinion*
His herte mysforyaf [hym] evere mo.   *misgave*
But fynally he gan his herte wrest   *compel*
To trusten here, and tok it for the beste.

For which the grete furye of his penaunce   *anguish*
1430 Was queynt with hope; and therwith hem bitwene   *assuaged*
Bygan for joye the amorouse daunce.
And as the briddes whan the sonne is she[ne]
Deliten in here song yn leves grene,
Right so the wordes that they spake y-fere
1435 Deliten hem, and made hire hertes clere.   *brightened*

But nath[e]les, the wendyng of Criseyde,
For al this world may nought out of his mynde;
For whiche ful ofte he pitously here preyde
That of here heste he myght here trewe fynde,   *promise*
1440 And seyde here, 'Certes, yf ye be unkynde,   *cruel*
And but ye come at day set into Troye,   *appointed*
Ne shal I nevere have hele, honour, ne joye.   *well-being*

'For also soth as sonne uprist on morwe,   *rises*
And God so wisly thow me, woful wrecche,
1445 To reste brynge out of this cruwel sorwe,
I wol myselven sle yf that ye drecche.   *delay*

1413 carry out my plan. 1419 almost died of grief. 1420 always intended.
1423 the ins and outs of this matter discussed. 1437 Cannot be forgotten for
any consideration. 1445 peace of mind.

But of my deth though litel be to recche,
Yet er that ye me cause so to smerte,
Dwelle rathere here, myn owene swete herte.

1450 'For trewely, myn owene lady dere,
Tho sleyghtes yet that I have herd yow stere
Ful shaply ben to fayllen alle y-fere.   *likely*
For thus men seyn: "That oon thenketh the bere,
But al another thenketh h[i]s ledere."
1455 Youre sire is wys, and seyd is out of drede: *father*
"Men may the wyse at-renne but not a[t]-rede."

'It is ful hard to halten unespied
Byfore a crepul, for he kan the craft;   *cripple, knack*
Youre fader is in sleyghte as Argus eyed* –   *cunning*
1460 For al be that his moeble is hym byraft,
His olde sleyghte is yet so with hym laft,
Ye shal not blende hym for youre womanhede,
Ne feyne aright – and that is al my drede.

'I not yf pes shal evere mo bytyde,   *come about*
1465 But pes or no, for ernest ne for game,
I wot, syn Calkas on the Grekes syde
Hath ones ben, and lost so foule his name,   *reputation*
He dar no more come here ayen for shame;
For which that weye – for ought I kan espye –   *discern*
1470 To trusten to, nys but a fantasye.   *delusion*

'Ye shal ek sen yowre fader shal yow glose   *cajole*
To ben a wyf, and as he kan wel preche,
He shal som Grek so pre[i]se and wel alose,   *extol*
That ravysshen he shal yow with his speche,   *enchant*
1475 Or do yow don by force as he shal teche;   *make*
And Troylus, of whom he nyl han routhe,
Shal causeles so sterven in his trouthe.   *innocently*

'And over al this, youre fader shal despise
Us alle, and seyn this cité nys but lorn,

1447 although my death would be of little consequence. 1448 cause me such pain. 1451 tricks ... propose. 1453–4 The bear thinks one thing, but his master thinks something very different. 1456 surpass in running but not in counselling. 1457 to limp without being found out. 1458 *kan: kan on.* 1460 goods ... taken away. 1461 cunning ... left. 1462 feminine nature. 1463 lie successfully.

1480 And that th'assege nevere shal aryse,
　　　Forwhy the Grekes han it alle sworn,　　　　　　　*Because*
　　　Til we be slayn and doun oure walles torn:
　　　Al thus he shal you with his wordes fere,　　　　　　*terrify*
　　　That ay drede I that ye wol bleve there.　　　　　　*remain*

1485 'Ye shul ek sen so mani a lusty knyght　　　　　　*dashing*
　　　Among the Grekes, ful of worthynesse,
　　　And eche of hem with herte, wit, and myght,
　　　To plesen yow don al his besynesse,　　　　　　*utmost*
　　　That ye shul dullen of the rudenesse　　　　*grow weary*
1490 Of us sely Troians, but yf routhe　　　　　　　*simple*
　　　Remorde yow, or vertue of youre trouthe.

　　　'And this to me so grevous is to th[y]nke,
　　　That fro my brest it wole my soule rende;　　　　　*tear*
　　　Ne dredles in me ther may not synke
1495 A good opynyoun, yf that ye wende;
　　　Forwhy youre faderes sleyghte wole us shende.　　　*ruin*
　　　And yf ye gon, as I have told yow yore,　　　*long since*
　　　So thenk I am but ded, withoute more.

　　　'For which with humble, trewe and pitous herte,
1500 A thousand tymes mercy I yow preye;
　　　So rewe[th] on myn aspre peynes smerte,
　　　And doth somwhat as that I shal yow seye,　　　　　*act*
　　　And lat us stele away bytwext us tweye;
　　　And thenk that folye is, whan man may chese,　　　*choose*
1505 For accident [h]is substaunce ay to lese.

　　　'I mene this: that syn we mowe er day　　　　　　*may*
　　　Wel stele away and ben togedre so,　　　　　　*thus*
　　　What nede were it to putten in assay,　　　　　*hazard*
　　　In cas ye sholde to youre fader go,　　　*Supposing*
1510 If that ye myghte come ayen or no?
　　　Thus mene I: that it were a gret folye
　　　To putte that sikernesse in jupartie.　　　*assured state*

1480 the siege will never be lifted. 1490-1 unless compassion or the power of
your pledged faith should move you. 1492 *thynke: thenke.* 1494-5 Nor
certainly could (my mind) entertain an optimistic thought. 1501 take pity on
my bitter, sharp torments; *reweth: rewes.* 1505 to go on losing what is essential
for what is not.

'And vulgar[l]y to speken of substaunce: *about money*
Of tresour may we bothe with us lede   *take away*
1515 Ynowh to lyve in honour and plesaunce
Til into tyme that we shul ben dede;   *that time*
And thus we may eschewen al this drede: *escape*
For everych other wey ye kan recorde,   *call up*
Myn herte, ywys, may not therwith acorde.   *agree*

1520 'And hardely, ne dredeth no poverte,
For I have kyn and frendes elleswhere,
That though we comen in oure bare sherte,
Us sholde neyther lakke gold ne gere,   *possessions*
But ben honoured while we dwelten there.
1525 And go we anoon – for as yn myn entente,
This is the beste, yf that ye wole assente.'

Criseyde with a syk right in this wyse
Answered: 'Ywys, my dere herte trewe,
We may wel stele away as ye devyse,   *suggest*
1530 And fynde swyche unthryfty weyes newe;
But afterward ful sore it wole us rewe.
And helpe me God so at my most nede,
As causeles ye suffren al this drede.   *unreasonably*

'For thilke day that I for cherysshynge   *favour*
1535 Or drede of fader, or of other wight,
Or for estat, delit, or for weddynge,   *status, pleasure*
Be fals to yow, my Troylus, my knyght,
Saturnus doughter, Juno, thorugh here myght,
As wod as Athamante do me dwelle   *crazed*
1540 Eternaly in Stix, the put of helle.*   *pit*

'And this on every god celestial
I swere it yow, and ek on eche goddesse,
On every nymphe and deité infernal,
On satiry and fawny more and lesse,
1545 That halve goddes ben of wildernesse;   *demi-gods*
And Attropos my thred of lyf thow breste,   *snap*
If I be fals – now trowe me yf thow leste!   *wish*

1525 to my way of thinking. 1527 sighing, in just these words. 1530 unprofit-
able courses. 1531 we would bitterly regret it. 1532 As God may help me in
my hour of greatest need. 1544 satyrs and fauns, great and small.

'And thow Symoys,* that as an arwe clere   *shining*
Thorugh Troye ay rennest downward to the see
1550 Bere wittenesse of this word that seyd is here:
That thilke day that ich untrewe be   *That same*
To Troylus, myn owen herte free,   *noble*
That thow retorne bakward to thi welle,   *source*
And I with body and soule synke in helle.

1555 'But that ye speke alwey thus forto go
And leten alle youre frendes – God forbede   *abandon*
For ony womman that ye sholden so!
And namly syn Troye hath now swych nede
Of help; and ek of o thyng taketh hede:
1560 If this were wist, my lyf lay in balaunce,
And your honour – God shilde us fro myschaunce.

'And yf so be that pes herafter take –   *come about*
As alday happeth after anger game –
Why, lord, the sorwe and wo ye wolden make,
1565 That ye ne dorste come ayen for shame!
And er that ye juparten so youre name,   *endanger*
B[eth] nought to hasty in this hote fare –
For hasty man ne wanteth nevere care.

'What trowe ye that the peple ek al about
1570 Wolde of it seye? It is ful lyght to arede:
They wolden seye – and swere it out of doute –
That love ne drof yow nought to don this dede,
But lust voluptuous, and coward drede.
Thus were al lost, ywys, myn herte dere,
1575 Yowre honour which that now shyneth so clere.

'And also thenketh on myn honesté,
That floureth yet – how foule it sholde it shende!
And with what filthe it spotted sholde be,
If in this forme I sholde with yow wende.
1580 Ne though I lyvede unto the worldes ende,   *Even if*
My name sholde I nevere ayenward wynne;   *recover*
Thus were I lost, and that were routhe and synne.*

1555 go on insisting in this way. 1561 protect from misfortune. 1563 constantly joy comes after distress. 1567 fiery behaviour; *Beth: But.* 1569 *al: of al.*
1570 very easy to guess. 1572 it wasn't love that impelled you. 1576 take
thought for my good name. 1577 be put to shame.

'And forthi sle with reson al this hete;
Men seyn: "The suffraunt overcometh", pardé;
1585 Ek: "Whoso wole han leef, he leef mote lete" –
Thus maketh vertue of necessité.
B[e] pacient and thenk that lord is he   *master*
Of Fortune ay, that nought wol of here recche; *care about*
And she ne daunteth no wight but a wrecche.   *discourages*

1590 'And trusteth this: that certes, herte swete,
Er Phebus suster, Lucyna the shene,
The Leon passe out of this Ariete,*
I wol ben here withouten ony wene.   *doubt*
I mene, as helpe me Juno, hevenes queene,
1595 The tenthe day, but yf that deth me assayle,   *unless*
I wol yow sen withouten ony fayle.'

'And now, so this be soth,' quod Troylus,   *if*
'I shal wel suffre unto the tenthe day,   *endure*
Syn that I se that nede it mot be thus.
1600 But for the love of God, yf it be may,
So lat us stele pryvely away;   *secretly*
For evere in oon, as for to lyve in reste,   *always*
Myn herte seyth it wole ben the beste.'

'O mercy God, what lyf is this?' quod she   *state*
1605 'Allas, ye sle me thus for verray tene.
I se wel now that ye mystrusten me,
For by youre wordes it is wel i-sene.   *very obvious*
Now for the love of Cynthe[a] the shene,
Mystrust me not thus causeles, for routhe;   *pity's sake*
1610 Syn to be trewe I have yow plyght my trouthe.

'And thenketh wel that som tyme it is wit   *good sense*
To spende a tyme, a tyme forto wynne;
Ne, pardé, lorn am I nought fro yow yet,   *lost to*
Though that we ben a day or two atwynne.
1615 Dryf out the fantasies yow withinne,
And trusteth me, and leveth ek youre sorwe,
Or, her[e] my trouthe, I wol not lyve til morwe.

1583 so quench all this fire. 1584 patient man wins through. 1585 Whoever
wishes to win a desired object, must give it up (for a time). 1587 *Be: By.* 1591
the Sun's sister, the bright Moon. 1605 pure vexation. 1608 *Cynthea: Cynthes.*
1617 take my word (for it).

'For if ye wiste how sore it doth me smerte,
Ye wolde cesse of this – for God thow wost,
1620 The pure spirit wepeth in myn herte
To se yow wepen that I love most,
And that I mot gon to the Grekes ost.
Ye, nere it that I wist remedie   *if I didn't know*
To come ayeyn, right here I wolde dye.

1625 'But certes, I am not so nyce a wyght   *simple-minded*
That I ne kan ymagynen a weye
To come ayen that day that I have hight,
For who may holde [a] thing that wole away?   *keep confined*
My fader nought, for al his queynte pley.
1630 And by my thryft, my wendyng out of Troye   *on my word*
Another day shal torne us alle to joye.

'Forthy with al myn herte I yow bese[k]e,
Yf that yow lyst don ough[t] for my preyere,
And for the love which that I love yow eke,
1635 That er that I departe fro yow here,
That of [so] good [a] comfort and a chere   *countenance*
I may you sen, that [ye] may brynge at reste
Myn herte which that is o poyn[t] to breste.

'And over al this, I pray yow,' quod she tho,
1640 'Myn owen hertes sothfast suffisaunce,   *true*
Syn I am thyn al hool withouten mo,
That whil that I am a[b]sent, no plesaunce
Of othere do me fro youre remembraunce –
For I am evere agast, forwhi men rede   *terrified*
1645 That love is thing ay ful of bysy drede.   *constant*

'For yn this world ther lyveth lady noon,
If that ye were untrewe (as God defende),
That so bytraysed were or wo-bygon
As I, that al trouthe in yow entende.   *perceive*
1650 And douteles, yf that ych other wende,

1629 cunning practices. 1630–1 my departure . . . will later turn into happiness
for us both. 1632 *beseke: beseche.* 1633 If you choose to do at all as I ask you.
1636 *so: the; a comfort: of comfort.* 1641 absolutely completely. 1642–3 no
delight in anyone else will banish me from your memory; *absent: assent.* 1643
do: do ye. 1650 if I supposed anything else (to be true).

I nere but ded; and er ye cause fynde,
For Goddes love so beth me not unkynde.'

To this answerede Troylus and seyde,
'Now God to whom ther nys no cause y-wrye,   *hidden*
1655 Me glade, as wys I nevere unto Criseyde,   *surely, towards*
Syn thilke day I saw here first with eye,
Was fals, ne nevere shal til that I dye.
At short wordes, wel ye may me leve;
I kan no more, it shal be founde at preve.'

1660 'Graunt mercy, good myn, ywys,' quod she,   *treasure*
'And blysful Venus lat me nevere sterve
Er I may stonde of plesaunce in degre   *(a) state*
To quyte hym wel that so wel kan deserve;   *repay*
And whil that my wit wol me conserve,   *preserve*
1665 I shal so don, so trewe I have yow founde,
That ay honour to meward shal rebounde.   *back to me*

'For trusteth wel, that youre estat royal,
Ne veyn delit, nor oonly worthinesse
Of yow in werre or torney marcial,   *tournament*
1670 Ne pompe, aray, nobley, or ek richesse,
Ne made me to rewe on youre distresse;
But moral vertue grounded upon trouthe –
That was the cause I first hadde on yow routhe.

'Ek gentil herte and manhod that ye hadde,   *noble*
1675 And that ye hadde, as me thoughte, in despit
Every thing that souned into badde,   *tended*
As rudenesse and pepelyssh appetit,
And that yowre reson brydled youre delit:
This made, aboven every creature,
1680 That I was youre, and shal whil I may dure.   *survive*

'And this may lengthe of yeres not fordo,   *destroy*
Ne remuable Fortune deface;   *changeable*
But Juppiter, that of his myght may do   *make*
The sorwful to be glad, so yeve us grace,
1685 Er nyghtes ten to meten in this place,

1670 splendour, display, high rank. 1675 seemed to me to hold in contempt.
1677 Such as churlish behaviour and vulgar desires.

So that it may youre herte and myn suffice;
And fare now wel, for tyme is that ye ryse.'

And after that they longe y-pleyned hadde,
And ofte i-kyst and streyght in armes folde,   *tightly*
1690 The day gan ryse, and Troylus hym cladde,
And rowfullych his lady gan byholde,
As he that felte dethes cares colde.   *chill*
And to hi[re] grace he gan hym recomaunde;
Wher hym was wo, this holde I no demaunde.

1695 For mannes hed ymagynen ne kan,
N'entendement considere, ne tonge telle,   *understanding*
This[e] cruwel peynes of this sorwful man,
That passen every torment doun in helle.
For [whan] he saugh that she ne myghte dwelle,
1700 Which that his soule out of his herte rente,
Withouten more out of the chaumbre he wente.   *Immediately*

Explicit liber Quartus

1687 *fare: fareth.* 1693 *hire: his.* 1694 There is to me no question that he was
sorrowful.

BOOK FIVE

Incipit liber Quintus

Approchen gan the fatal destyné
That Joves hath in disposicioun,   *(his) power*
And to yow angry Parcas, sustren thre,
Comytted to don execucioun;*   *put into effect*
5 For which Criseyde moste out of the toun,
And Troylus shal dwelle forth yn pyne
Til Lathesis his threed no lengere twyne.

The gold-tressed Phebus heighe on lofte   *above*
Thries hadde al with his bemes cle[n]e
10 The snowes molte, and Zephirus as ofte
Y-brought ayen the tendre leves grene,
Syn that the sone of Ecuba the queene
Bygan to love here first, for whom his sorwe
Was al that she departe sholde o morwe.*   *next morning*

15 Ful redy was at pryme Dyomede,   *9 a. m.*
Criseyde unto the Grekes ost forto lede,
For sorwe of which she felte here herte blede,
As she that nyst what was best to rede.
And trewely, as men in bokes rede,
20 Men wyst nevere womman han the care,
Ne was so loth out of town to fare.   *journey*

---

6 must continue to live in torment. 9 *clene: clere.* 18 didn't know the best
course to follow.

This Troylus, withouten red or lore,
As man that hath his joyes ek forlore,   *wholly lost*
Was waytynge on his lady everemore,
25 As she that was the sothfast crop and more
Of al his lust or joyes here byfore.
But Troylus, farewel now al thi joye:
For shaltow nevere sen here eft in Troye!   *again*

Soth is that whil he bod in this manere,   *waited*
30 He gan his wo ful manly forto hyde,
That wel unethe it sene was in his chere;   *visible*
But at the yate there she sholde out ryde
With certeyn folk he hovede here t'abyde,   *remained*
So wo-bygon (al wolde he nought hym pleyne),
35 That on his hors unnethe he sat for peyne.   *hardly*

For ire he quok, so gan his herte gnawe,
Whan Diomede on hors gan hym dresse,   *mount*
And seyde unto hymself this ilke sawe:
'Allas,' quod he, 'thus foul a wrecchednesse,   *misery*
40 Why suffre ich it? Whi nyl ich it redresse?   *right*
Were it not bet at onys forto dye
Than everemore in langour thus to drye?

'Whi nyl I make at onys ryche and pore   *one and all*
To have ynowh to done er that she go?
45 Why nyl I brynge al Troye upon a rore?   *into confusion*
Why nyl I slen this Diomede also?
Why nyl I rathere with a man or two
Stele here away? Whi wole I this endure?
Whi nyl I helpen to myn owene cure?'

50 But whi he nolde don so fel a dede,   *violent*
That shal I seyn, and why hym lyst it spare:
He hadde in herte alweys a manere drede,   *kind of*
Lest that Cryseyde, yn rumour of this fare,
Sholde han ben slayn – lo this was al his care,
55 And elles, certeyn, as I seyde yore
He hadde it don withouten wordes more.

22 counsel . . . instruction. 25 true beginning and end. 36 He trembled with
rage, with such anguish at heart; *ire: Iire.* 38 these same words. 40 *nyl ich: nyl
ich do.* 42 endure such distress. 44 their hands full. 51 why he was ready to
abandon (the idea). 53 in such a violent disturbance.

Criseyde, whan she redy was to ryde,
Ful sorwfully she sight and seyde 'allas';
But forth she mot for ought that may bytyde,   *has to go*
60 And forth she rit ful sorwfully a pas.
Ther nys non other remedye yn this cas;   *situation*
What wonder is [though that] here sore smerte,
Whan she forgoth here owene swete herte.

This Troylus, yn wyse of curtasie,   *courtly style*
65 With hauk on hond and with an huge route
Of knyghtes, rod and dide here companye,   *kept*
Passynge al the valey fer withoute,
And ferthere wolde han ryden out of doute
Ful fayn, and wo was hym to gon so sone:
70 But torne he moste, and it was ek to done.

And right with that was Antenor i-come
Out of the Grekes ost, and every wyght
Was of it glad and seyde he was welcome
And Troylus, al nere his herte lyght,
75 He peynede hym with al his fulle myght   *strove*
Hym to withholde of wepynge at the leste: *keep from*
And Antenor he kyste and made feste.

And therwithal he moste his leve take
And caste his eye upon here pitously,
80 And ner he rod his cause forto make,
To take here by the hond al sobrely;   *gravely*
And, lord! so she gan wepen tendrely,
And he ful softe and sleyghly gan here seye,   *secretly*
'Now hold yowre day, and doth me not to deye.'

85 With that his courser torned he aboute   *steed*
With face pale, and unto Diomede
No word he spak, ne non of al his route;
Of which the sone of Tydeus* toke hede,   *note*
As he that koude more than the crede   *basics*
90 In swych a craft, and by the reyne here hente;   *took*
And Troylus to Troye homward he went.

60 rides at a walking pace; *rit*: *right*. 62 she endured bitter pain; *though that*:
that though. 63 is giving up. 67 Continuing far beyond the (?) ramparts. 70
had to be done. 74 even though his heart was heavy. 77 made a fuss of. 80
rode closer to achieve his purpose. 85 *he*: *he al*.

This Diomede, that ladde here by the bridel,
Whan that he saw the folk of Troye aweye,　　　*were gone*
Thoughte, 'Al my labour shal not ben on ydel,　　　*wasted*
95　If that I may, for somwhat shal I seye;
For at the worste it may yet shorte oure weye.
I have herd seyd ek tymes twyes twelve:
"He is a fool that wole foryete hymselve."'

But natheles this thoughte he wel ynowh,
100　That 'certaynly I am aboute nought,
If that I speke of love or make it tough:
For douteles, yf she have in here thought
Hym that I gesse, he may not ben y-brough[t]
So sone awey – but I shal fynde a mene
105　That she shal not as yet wete what I mene.'　　　*intend*

This Diomede, as he that koude his good,
Whan this was don gan fallen forth in speche
Of this and that, and asked whi she stood
In swych desese, and gan here ek byseche　　　*distress*
110　That yf that he encrese myghte or eche　　　*add to*
With ony thing here ese, that she sholde
Comaunde it hym, and seyde he don it wolde.

For trewely he swor here as a knyght,
That there nas thing with whiche he myght here plese,
115　That he nolde don his peyne and al his myght
To don it, for to don here herte an ese;　　　*perform*
And preyde here, she wolde here sorwe apese,
And seyde, 'Ywys, we Grekes kon have joye　　　*take*
To honouren yow, as wel as folk of Troye.'　　　*In*

120　He seyde ek thus: 'I wot yow thenketh straunge　　　*added*
(No wonder is, for it is to yow newe)
Th' aqueyntaunce of these Troians to chaunge
For folk of Grece, that ye nevere knewe.
But wolde nevere God but [if] as trewe
125　A Grek ye shulde among us alle fynde
As ony Troian is, and ek as kynde.

95 If I have anything to do with it. 99 he realised clearly enough. 100 will get
nowhere. 101 push too hard. 104 So quickly out of it . . . a way. 106 knew
what was to his advantage. 107 began to talk. 115 take the utmost pains.
124–5 may God never permit that you should not find a Greek as faithful.

'An[d] by the cause I swor yow right, lo, now,
To ben youre frend and helply to my myght,   *helpful*
And for that more acqueyntaunce ek of yow
130 Have ich had than another straungere wight,
So fro this forth I pray yow, day and nyght,
Comaundeth me, how sore that me smerte,   *it pains me*
To don al that may like to youre herte;

'And that ye me wolde as youre brother trete,
135 And take not my frendship in despit;   *scorn*
And though youre sorwes be for thinges grete
(Not I not whi) – but out of more respit,
Myn herte hath forto amenden it gret delit:
And yf I may youre harmes not redresse,   *put right*
140 I am right sory for youre hevynesse.

'And though ye Troians with us Grekes wrothe
Han many a day be, alwey yet, pardé,
O god of Love in soth we serven bothe;
And for the love of God, my lady fre,
145 Whomso ye hate, as beth not wroth with me:
For trewely ther kan no wight yow serve,
That half so loth yowre wraththe wolde deserve.

'And nere it that we ben so neigh the tente
Of Calkas, which that sen us bothe may
150 I wolde of this yow telle al myn entente;   *mind*
But this enseled til another day.   *shut up*
Yeve me youre hond: I am, and shal ben ay,
God help me so, whil that my lyf may dure,   *last*
Youre owene above[n] every creature.

155 'Thus seyde I nevere er now to womman born –
For God myn herte as wysly glade so,
I lovede nevere womman here byforn
As paramours, ne nevere shal no mo.   *Passionately*
And for the love of God, beth not my fo;
160 Al kan I not to yow, my lady dere,
Compleyne aryght, for I am yet to lere.   *have, learn*

---

130 any other unfamiliar person. 137 without more delay. 142 for all this
time. 146–7 there is no one capable of being your servant (in love) who would
be half as unwilling to. 148 if we were not (now) so close to. 160 Even if I
don't know how.

'And wondreth not, myn owen lady bryght,
Though that I speke of love to you thus blyve;   *promptly*
For I have herd [er] this of many a wyght
165 Hath loved thyng he nevere saugh his lyve.   *in all his*
Ek I am not of power forto stryve   *contend*
Ayens the god of Love, but hym obeye
I wole alwey, and mercy I yow preye.

'Ther ben so worthi knyghtes in this place,   *such*
170 And ye so feyr, that everich of hem alle
Wol peynen hym to stonden in youre grace,
But myght me so fair a grace falle,
That ye me for youre servaunt wolde calle,
So lowly ne so trewely you serve   *humbly*
175 Nil noon of hem, as I shal, til I sterve.'

Criseide unto that purpos lite answerde,
As she that was with sorwe oppressed so
That in effect she nought his tales herde
But her[e] and there – now here a word or two.
180 Hire thoughte here sorwful hert brast atwo –
For whan she gan here fader fer aspye,
Wel neigh doun on here hors she gan to sye.   *sink from*

But natheles she thonked Diomede
Of al his travayle and his goode chere,   *For, pains*
185 And that hym lyst his frendship here to bede;   *offer*
And she accepteth it in good manere,
And wold do fayn that is hym lef and dere;
And trusten hym she wolde, and wel she myghte
(As seyde she), and from hire hors she alighte.

190 Here fader hath here in his armes nome,   *taken*
And tweynty tyme he kyste his doughter swete,
And seyde, 'O, dere doughter myn, welcome.'
She seyde ek she was fayn with hym to mete,
And stod forth mewet, mylde, and mansuete.
195 But here I leve here with here fader dwelle,
And forth I wole of Troylus yow telle.

---

164 er: of. **171** exert himself. **174** you: you to. **176** lite: litel; answerde:
answerede. **178** in fact she didn't hear what he was saying. **181** caught sight of
her father from a distance. **194** silent, gentle, and submissive.

To Troye is come this woful Troylus,
In sorwe aboven alle sorwes smerte,
With felon lok and [face] dispitous.
200 Tho sodeynly doun from his hors he sterte,   *leaped*
And thorugh his paleys with a swollen herte
To chambre he went – of no thing toke he hede,
Ne noon to hym dar speke a word, for drede.

And there his sorwes that he spared hadde
205 He yaf an yssue large, and 'Deth' he cride;
And in his throwes frenetyk and madde   *spasms*
He cursed Jove, Appollo, and ek Cupide;
He cursed Ceres, Bacus, and Cipryde;*
His burthe, hymself, his fate and ek nature,
210 And, save his lady, every creature.   *living thing*

To bedde he goth and w[alwi]th there and torneth   *tosses*
In furye, as doth he, Ixion in helle;*
And in this wyse he neigh til day sojourneth.   *goes on*
But tho bygan a lyte his herte unswelle
215 Thorugh teris which that gonnen up to welle,
And pitously he cride upon Criseyde,
And to hymself right thus he spak and seyde:

'Wher is myn owene lady lief and dere?
Where is here white brest, wher is it, where?
220 Where ben here armes an[d] here eyen clere,
That yesternyght this tyme with me were?
Now may I wepe allone many a tere,
And graspe aboute I may, but in this place,
Save a pilwe, I fynde nought t'enbrace.

225 'How shal I do? Whan shal she come ayen?   *What*
I not, allas! Whi let ich here to go?   *have no idea*
As wolde God ich hadde as tho be sleyn!
O herte myn Criseyde, O swete fo!
O lady myn that I love and no mo,   *exclusively*
230 To whom for evermo myn herte I dowe,   *dedicate*
Se how I deye – ye nyl me not rescowe!

198 beyond all (other) bitter sorrows. 199 fierce . . . angry. 204 had held back.
205 gave full expression to. 211 *walwith: weyleth.* 214 emotions subside; *lyte:*
lytel. 227 If only God had granted that I had then.

'Who seeth yow now my right lode sterre?   *pole star*
Who sit right now or stant in yowre presence?
Who kan conforten now youre hertes werre?   *strife*
235 Now I am gon, whom yeve ye audience?
Who speketh for me right now in myn absence?
Allas, no wight, and that is al my care,
For wel wot I, as yvele as I ye fare.

'How shulde I thus ten dayes ful endure,   *whole*
240 Whan I the firste nyght have al this tene?   *anguish*
How shal she don ek, sorwful creature?
For tendresse how shal she [ek] sustene
Swich wo for me? O pitous, pale and grene
Shal ben youre fresshe womanlych face
245 For langour, er ye torne into this place.'

And whan he fill in ony slomerynges,   *dozed at all*
Anoon byg[y]nne he sholde forto grone,
And dremen of the dredfulleste thinges
That myghte ben – as mete he were allone   *dream*
250 In place horrible, makynge ay his moone,   *complaint*
Or meten that he was amonges alle
His enemys, and in here hondes falle.

And therwithal his body sholde sterte,   *convulse*
And with the stert al sodeynlych awake,
255 And swich a tremor fele aboute his herte,
That of the feer his body sholde quake;
And therwithal he sholde a noyse make,   *cry out*
And seme as though he sholde falle depe
From heighe alofte, and than he wolde wepe,

260 And rewen on hymself so pytously,   *sorrow for*
That wonder was to here his fantasye.
Another tyme he sholde myghtily
Conforte hymself, and seine it was folye,   *say*
So causeles swych drede forto drye,   *endure*
265 And eft bygynne his aspre sorwes newe,
That every man myghte on his sorwes rewe.   *pity*

235 whom do you receive (into your presence). 238 you are suffering as much
as I am. 242 How may her delicate nature likewise endure; *ek: this.* 245
affliction . . . return here. 247 *bygynne: bygonne.* 249 *he: as he.* 265 recomm-
ence afresh his bitter grief.

Who koude telle aright or ful discryve   *adequately*
His wo, his pleynte, his langour and his peyne?
Nought al the men that han or ben on lyve:
270 Thow, redere, mayst thyself ful wel devyne   *suppose*
That swych a wo my wit kan not defyne.   *describe*
On ydel forto write it sholde I swynke,
Whan that my wit is wery it to th[y]nke.

On hevene yet the sterres were sene,   *visible*
275 Although ful pale y-woxen was the moone;   *grown*
And whiten gan the orisonte shene   *bright horizon*
Al estward, as it wonted is to done;   *accustomed*
And Phebus with his rosy carte sone
Gan after that to dresse hym up to fare,
280 Whan Troylus hath sent after Pandare.

This Pandare, that of al the day biforn
Ne myght have comen Troylus to se,   *Was not able*
Although he on his hed it hadde i-sworn –
For with the kyng Pryam al day was he,
285 So that it lay not in his liberté
Nowher to gon – but on the morwe he wente
To Troylus, whan that he for hym sente.*

For in hys herte he koude wel dyvyne   *imagine*
That Troilus al nyght for sorwe wook,   *lay awake*
290 And that he wolde telle hym of his peyne –
This knew he wel ynough withoute book;   *prompting*
For which to chaumbre streyght the wey he took,
And Troylus tho sobrelyche he grette,
And on the bed ful soone he gan hym sette.

295 'My Pandarus,' quod Troylus, 'the sorwe
Which that I drye, I may not longe endure.   *suffer*
I trowe I shal not lyve til tomorwe;
For which I wolde alwey, on aventure,
To the devysen of my sepulture   *tomb*
300 The forme – and of my moeble thow dispone
Right as the semeth best is forto done.

269 ever have lived or are (still) alive. 272 In vain would I labour to set it
down. 273 exhausted by thinking about it; *thynke: thenke.* 279 prepare for his
journey. 285–6 he was not free to go anywhere (else). 298–9 for fear (of that),
describe to you. 300 dispose of my (moveable) goods.

'But of the fyr and flaumbe funeral
In whiche my body brenne shal to glede,   *embers*
And of the feste and pleyes palestral
305 At my vigile, I pray the take good hede   *wake*
That al be wel, and offre Mars my stede,
My swerd, myn helm and, leve brother dere,
My sheld to Pallas yef, that shyneth clere.   *give*

'The poudre in which myn herte y-brend shal torne,
310 That prey I the thow take and it conserve   *keep*
In a vessel that men clepeth an urne   *is called*
Of gold, and to my lady that I serve,
For love of whom thus pitously I sterve,
So yeve it here, and do me this plesaunce,
315 To preyen here kepe it for a remembraunce.*

'For wel I fele by my maladye,
And by my dremes now and yore ago,   *of long*
Al certeynly that I mot nedes dye:
The owle ek, which that hatte Escaphilo,*   *is called*
320 Hath after me shright alle this[e] nyghtes two.   *shrieked*
And, god Mercurye,* of me now, woful wrecche,
The soule gide, and whan the lyst, it fecche.'   *you wish*

Pandare answerede, and seyde, 'Troylus,
My dere frend, as I have told the yore,
325 That it is folye forto sorwen thus,
And causeles, for which I kan nomore.
But whoso wole not trowen rede ne lore,
I kan not seen in hym no remedye,
But late hym worthe with his fantasye!   *remain*

330 'But Troylus, I pray the telle me now,
If that thow trowe er this that ony wyght
Hath loved paramours as wel as thow?
Ye, God wot! and fro many a worthi knyght
Hath his lady gon a fourtenyght,
335 And he not yet made halvendel the fare.
What nede is the to maken al this care?

---

304 athletic games. 315 *kepe*: to kepe. 327 whoever will not accept advice or
instruction. 332 passionately as much. 335 half as much fuss (as you).

'Syn day by day thow mayst thiselven see
That from his love, or elles from his wyf,
A man mot twynnen of necessité –   *part*
340 Ye, though he love here as his owene lyf;
Yet nyl he with hymself thus maken stryf.
For wel thow wost, my leve brother dere,
That alwey frendes may not ben y-fere.

'How don this folk that seen here loves wedded
345 By frendes myght, as it bytyt ful ofte,
And sen hem in here spouses bed y-bedded?
God wot, they take it wysly, faire and softe,
Forwhy good hope halt up here herte olofte,   *holds, high*
And for they kan a tyme of sorwe endure,   *period*
350 As tyme hem hurt, a tyme doth hem cure.

'So sholdestow endure and late slyde   *slip by*
The tyme, and fond to ben glad and lyght;
Ten dayes nys so longe not t'abyde,
And syn she the to come hath byhyght,   *promised*
355 She nyl here hestes breken for no wight.   *promises*
For drede the not that she nyl fynden weye
To come ayen – my lyf that dorst I leye!

'Thy swevenes ek and [al] swich fantasye   *dreams*
Dryf out and lat hem faren to myschaunce,
360 For thei proceden of thi malencolye –   *grow out*
That doth the fele in slep al this penaunce.   *experience*
A straw for alle swevenes signifiaunce!
God helpe me so, I counte hem not a bene: *value*
Ther wot no man aright what dremes mene.   *exactly*

365 'For prestes of the temple tellen this:
That dremes ben the revelacions
Of goddes, and as wel they telle, ywys,
That they ben infernals illusions;
And leches seyn that of complexions

---

343 not remain together all the time. 344 people (behave). 345 compulsion . . .
happens. 347 sensibly, graciously and quietly. 350 at one season they experienced pain, at another they found the remedy. 352 strive . . . cheerful. 355 *nyl*:
nyl not. 359 come to a bad end. 369 physicians . . . bodily humours; *seyn*:
seynt.

370 Proceden thei, or fast, or glotonye:
     Who wot in soth thus what they signifie?   *then*

     'Ek othere seyn that thorough impressions,
     As yf a wight hath faste a thing in mynde,
     That thereof cometh swich avysions;   *visions*
375 And othere seyn, as they in bokes fynde,
     That after tymes of the yer by kynde,   *naturally*
     Men dreme, and that th'effect goth by the mone –   *follows*
     But lef no drem, for it is nought to done.*   *believe*

     'Wel worth of dremes ay these olde wyves,
380 And treweliche ek augurye of this fowel[y]s –
     For fere of which men wenen lese here lyves,
     As ravenes qualm, or shrykyng of these owlys.   *croaking*
     To trowen on it bothe fals and foule is.
     Allas, allas, so noble a creature
385 As is a man sha[l] drede swiche ordure!   *rubbish*

     'For which with al myn herte I the beseche
     Unto thiself that al this thou foryeve,   *give up*
     And rys up now withoute more speche,
     And lat us caste how forth may best be dreve
390 This tyme, and ek how fresshly we may leve
     Whan that she cometh, the which shal be righ[t] sone:
     God help me so, the beste is thus to done.

     'Rys, lat us speke of lusti lyf in Troye
     That we han lad, and forth the tyme dryve;
395 And ek of tyme comynge us rejoye,
     That bryngen shal oure blysse now so blyve;   *soon*
     And langour of these twyes dayes fyve
     We shal therwith so fo[r]yete or oppresse   *repress*
     That [wel] unnethe it don shal us duresse.

400 'This town is ful of lordes al aboute,
     And trewes lasten al this mene while:
     Go we pleye us in som lusti rowte   *cheerful company*
     To Sarpedon,* not hens but a myle.   *from here*

379 Dreams are always very suitable for old women. 380 *fowelys: foweles.*
381 think they will die. 385 *shal: shad.* 389 consider . . . passed. 390 joyfully
. . . live. 392 this is the best course of action. 395 rejoice in (thoughts of) the
future. 398 *or: oure.* 399 it will hardly at all distress us. 401 the truce
continues for the time being.

And thus thou shalt the tyme wel bygile,   *while away*
405 And dryve it forth unto that blisful morwe,   *pass*
That thow here se that cause is of thi sorwe.

'Now rys, my dere brother Troylus,
For certes it noon honour is to the
To wepe, and in thi bed to jowken thus;   *lurk*
410 For trewely of o thing thow trust to me:
If thow thus ligge a day or two or thre,
The folk wol wene that thou for cowardyse
The feynest syk, and that thow dar not ryse.'*

This Troylus answered, 'O brother dere,
415 This knowen folk that han y-suffred peyne,
That though he wepe and make sorwful chere,
That feleth harm and smert yn every veyne,
No wonder is; and though I evere pleyne,   *constantly*
Or alwey wepe, I am no thing to blame,
420 Syn I have lost the cause of al my game.   *joy*

'But syn of fyn force I mot aryse,
I shal aryse as soone as evere I may,
And God to whom myn herte I sacrefise
So sende us hastely the tenthe day;
425 For was there nevere foule so fayn of May
As I shal ben whan that she cometh in Troye
That cause is of my torment and my joye.

'But whider is thi red,' quod Troylus,
'That we may pley us best in al this town?'
430 'By God my conseyl [is], 'quod Pandarus,
'To ryde and pley us with kyng Sarpedoun.'
So longe of this thei speken up and doun,
Til Troylus gan at the laste assente   *finally*
To ryse, and forth to Sarpedoun they wente.

435 This Sarpedoun, as he that honourable
Was evere his lyve, and ful of heigh prowesse,
With al that myghte y-served ben on table,
That deynté was, al cost it gret richesse,   *even if*

410 you can believe what I say on this point. 413 You pretend to be. 418 It
isn't surprising. 421 sheer necessity. 425 bird as glad. 428 where would you
advise (us to go). 432 in every way.

He fedde hem day by day, that swich noblesse,
440 As seyden bothe the meste and the leste,
Was nevere er that day wyst at ony feste.   *found*

For in this world ther is noon instrument
Delicious, thorugh wynd or touche o[f] corde,
As fer as ony wyght hath evere y-went,
445 That tonge telle or herte may recorde,   *remember*
That a[t] that feste it nas wel herd accorde;
Ne of ladyes ek so fayr a companye
On daunce, er tho, was nevere y-seyn with eye.

But what avayleth this to Troylus
450 That for his sorwe nothing of it roughte?   *cared for*
For evere in oon his herte pitous   *all the time*
Ful bysily Criseyde his lady soughte;
On here was evere al that his herte thoughte:
Now this, now that, so faste ymagynynge,
455 That glade, ywys, kan hym no festeynge.   *gladden*

These ladyes ek that at this feste ben,
Syn that he saw his lady was aweye,
It was his sorwe upon hem forto sen,   *look*
Or forto here on instrumentz so pleye,
460 For she that of his herte bereth the keye
Was absent – lo, this was his fantasye:
That no wight sholde make melodye.   *ought to*

Nor ther nas houre in al the day or nyght,
Whan he was there as no wight myght [hym] here,
465 That he ne seyde, 'O lufsom lady bryght,
How have ye faren syn that ye were here?
Welcome, ywys, myn owene lady dere' –
But welaway, [al] this nas but a maze;   *delusion*
Fortune his howve entendeth bet to glaze.

470 The lettres ek that she of old tyme
Had hym y-sent, he wolde allone rede
An hundred sithe atwixen noon and pryme,

---

440 high and low. 443 *of: or.* 446 play in harmony (with the others); *at: as.*
449 what good is all this. 455 *festeynge: festenynge.* 454 so clearly recalling to
his mind. 459 *on: ony.* 464 was in a place where nobody. 466 *here: there.*
469 the better to deceive him.

Refigurynge here shap, here womanhede,
Withinne his herte, and every word and dede
475 That passed was, and thus he drof to an ende
The ferthe day, and seyde he wolde wende.   *leave*

And seyde, 'Leve brother, Pandarus,
Intendestow that we shul here bleve   *stay*
Til Sarpedoun wol forth congeyen us?   *turn us out*
480 Yet were it fairer that we tok oure leve.   *more fitting*
For Godes love, lat us now sone at eve
Oure leve take, and homward lat us torne;
For, trewely, I wol not thus sojourne.'

Pandare answered, 'Be we comen h[i]der
485 To fecchen fyr and rennen hom ayen?
God help me so, I kan not tellen whider
We myghten gon, yf I shal sothly seyn,
Ther ony wyght is of us more fayn
Than Sarpedoun, and yf we hens hye   *hurry away*
490 Thus sodeynly, I holde it vilonye.   *ill-bred*

'Syn that we seyden that we wolde bleve
With hym a wowke, and now thus sodeynly –
The ferthe day – to take of hym oure leve:
He wolde wondren on it trewely!
495 Lat us holde forth oure purpos fermely;
And syn that ye bihighten hym to byde,   *promised, stay*
Hold forward now, and after lat us ryde.'

Thus Pandarus, with al[le] peyne and wo,
Made hym to dwelle, and at the wykes ende
500 Of Sarpedoun thei toke here leve tho,
And on here wey they spedden hem to wende.
Quod Troylus, 'Now God me grace sende
That I may fynde at myn hom comynge
Criseyde comen' – and therwith gan he synge.

505 'Ye, haselwode!' thoughte this Pandare,
And to hymself ful so[ft]elich he seyde,

473 Representing (to himself) her figure and womanly excellence; *shap*: *shap
and*. 475 From the past . . . got through. 478 Do you propose. 484 *hider*:
heder. 485 make (only) a brief stay. 497 Keep (to your) agreement. 498 the
very greatest difficulty. 501 hastily got ready to leave. 505 A likely story! 506
softelich: *sobrelich*.

'God wot, refreyden may this hote fare
Er Calkas sende Troylus Cryseyde.'
But natheles he japed thus and [pl]eyde,
510 And swor ywys his herte hym wel byhight
She wolde come as soone as evere she myghte.

Whan they unto the paleys were y-comen
Of Troylus, thei down of here hors alight,   *their horses*
And to the chambre here wey than han thei nomen;
515 And into tyme that [it] gan to nyghte,   *grow dark*
They spaken of Criseyde the brighte;
And after this, whan that hem bothe leste,
Thei spedde hem fro the soper unto reste.   *went quickly*

O-morwe, as soone as day bygan to clere,
520 This Troylus gan of his slep t'abreyde,   *start out*
And to Pandare, his owene brother dere,
'For love of God,' ful pitously he seyde,
'So go we seen the paleys of Criseyde;   *let us*
For syn we yet may have no more feste,
525 So lat us seen here paleys at the leste.'

And therwithal, his meyné forto blende,   *mislead*
A cause he fond in towne forto go,
And to Criseyde[s] hous thei gonnen wende:
But lord, this sely Troylus was wo!   *wretched*
530 Hym thoughte his sorweful herte brast atwo,
For[r] whan he saugh here dores sperid alle,   *barred*
Wel neigh for sorwe adown he gan to falle.   *Very nearly*

Therewith whan he was war and gan byholde
How shet was every wyndowe of the place,
535 As frost, hym thoughte, his herte gan to colde;
For which with chaunged deedlych pale face,   *deathly*
Withouten word he forth bygan to pace;   *move on*
And as God wolde, he gan so faste ryde
That no wight of his contenaunce aspide.

540 Than seyde he thus: 'O paleys desolat   *deserted*
O hous of houses whilom best y-hight,

507 hot behaviour will cool off. 509 spoke cheerfully; *pleyde: seyde.* 524 no
greater pleasure. 533 As soon as he recovered himself. 538 *God: gold.* 539
No one could see how he looked. 541 formerly known as the best of all.

O paleys empty and disconsolat,   *forlorn*
O thou lanterne of which queynt is the light,   *put out*
O paleys whilom day, that now art nyght: *once*
545 Wel oughtestow to falle, and I to dye,
Syn she is went that wont was us to gye!   *govern*

'O paleys, whilom crowne of houses alle,
Enlumyned with the sonne of alle blysse,
O ryng fro which the ruby is out falle,
550 O cause of wo, that cause hast ben of lysse.   *comfort*
Yet syn I may no bet, fayn wold I kysse
Thi colde dores, dorst I for this route;
And farewel shryne of whom the seynt is oute!'*   *has left*

Therwith he caste on Pandarus his eye
555 With chaunged face, and pitous to byholde;
And whan he myght his tyme aright aspye,
Ay as he rod to Pandarus he tolde   *All the time*
His newe sorwe and ek his joyes olde,
So pitously, and with so dede an hewe,
560 That every wight myghte on his sorwe rewe.

From then[ne]sforth he rideth up and doun,
And every thing cam hym to remembraunce,   *into his*
As he rod forth by places of the toun
In whiche he whilom hadde al his plesaunce:
565 'Lo yende saugh I myn owene lady daunce,   *over there*
And in that temple with here eyen clere
Me kaught first my right lady dere.   *true*

'And yender have I herd ful lustily   *joyfully*
My dere herte laughe, and yender pleye
570 Saugh I here ones ek ful blysfully;
And yender ones to me gan she seye:
"Now goode swete, love me wel, I preye."
And yond so goodly gan she me byholde,
That to the deth myn herte is to here holde.   *faithful*

575 'And at that corner, in the yonder hous,
Herde I myn alderlevest lady dere   *very dearest*
So wommanly, with voys melodious,

---

550 *lysse: blysse.* 551 can do no better. 552 were it not for the people around
me. 569 enjoy herself. 573 she looked upon me so graciously.

Syngen so wel, so goodly, and so clere,
That in my soule yet me thenketh I here
580 The blisful soun, and in that yonder place,
My lady first me tok unto here grace.'

Thanne thought he thus: 'O blisful lord Cupide,
Whanne I the proces have in memorie
How thow me hast w[er]ryed on every syde,
585 Men myght a book make of it, lyk a storie.
What nede is the to seke on me victorie,
Syn I am thyn, and holly at thi wille?
What joye hastow thyn owene folk to spille?

'Wel hastow, lord, y-wroke on me thin ire,   *avenged*
590 Thow myghty god, and dredful forto greve.   *offend*
Now mercy, lord, thow wost wel I desire
Thi grace most of alle lustes leeve,
And leve and deye I wol [in] thi byleeve;   *live, faith*
For which I n'axe in guerdon but a bone:
595 That thow Criseyde ayen me sende soone.

'Distreyne here herte as faste to retorne   *Constrain*
As thow dost myn to longen here to se;
Than wot I wel that she nyl not soiorne.   *delay*
Now blisful lord, so cruwel thow ne be
600 Unto the blod of Troye, I preye the,
As Juno was unto the blood Thebane,
For which the folk of Thebes caught here bane.'*

And after this he to the yates wente,
There as Criseyde out rood a ful good paas,   *briskly*
605 And up and doun ther made he many a went,
And to hymself ful ofte he seyde, 'Allas,
From hen[ne]s rood my blysse and my solas!
As wolde blisful God now, for his joye,
I myghte here seen ayen come in[to] Troye.

610 'And to the yonder hill I gan here gyde,
Allas, and there I tok of here my leve;

583-4 I remember, in their sequence, the attacks you made on me; *werryed*: *waryed* ('cursed'). 586 need have you to strive to conquer me. 587 completely subjugated by you. 592 above all (other) dear pleasures. 594 I ask only a (single) favour in return. 598 *soiorne*: *soiourne*. 602 were doomed to die. 605 walked many times.

And yond I saugh here to hire fader ryde,
For sorwe of which myn herte shal to-cleve;   *split*
And heder hom I com whan it was eeve,
615 And here I dwelle, out-cast from alle joye,
And shal til I may se here eft in Troye.'

And of hymself ymagyned he ofte
To ben defet, and pale, and woxen lesse   *grown thinner*
Than he was wont, and that men seyde softe,
620 'What may it be? Who kan the sothe gesse
Whi Troylus hath al this hevynesse?'   *sorrow*
And al this nas but his malencolye,
That he hadde of hymself swich fantasye.*

Another tyme ymagynen he wolde
625 That every wight that wente by the weye
Had of hym routhe, and that thei seyen sholde,
'I am right sory Troylus wol deye.'
And thus he drof a day yet forth, or tweye,
As ye have herd – swych lyf right gan he lede,
630 As he that stood bytwixen hope and drede.

For which hym liked yn hise songes shewe   *to reveal*
Th'encheson of his wo as he best myghte,   *reason for*
And make a song of wordes but a fewe,
Somwhat his woful herte forto lyghte;
635 And whan he was from every mannes sighte,
With soft voys he of his lady dere,
That was absent, gan syngen as ye may here:

[*Canticus Troili*]

'O sterre, of which I lost have al the light,
With herte sor wel oughte I to bewayle,
640 That evere derk in torment, nyght by nyght,
Toward my deth with wynd in stere I sayle;   *following*
For which the tenthe nyght, if that I fayle   *lack*

614 returned home here. 618 changed in appearance. 620 What can the
reason for it. 628 got through a day or so. 634 to make less heavy. 637 *gan:*
gan to.

Th[e] gydyng of thi bemes bright an houre,
My ship and me Carybdes wol devoure.'*

645 This song whan he thus songen hadde, soone
He fyl ayen into his sikes olde;   *fell, usual*
And every nyght as was his wone to done,   *habit*
He stod the bryght mone to byholde,
And al his sorwe he to the mone tolde,
650 And seyde, 'Iwys, whan thow art horned newe,
I shal be glad, yf al the world be trewe.

'I saugh thin hornes olde ek by the morwe
Whan hen[ne]s rod my ryght lady dere,
That cause is of my torment and my sorwe;
655 For whiche, O bright Lathona* the clere,
For love of God, ren fast aboute thi spere!
For whanne thyn hornes newe gynne sprynge,   *grow*
Than shal [s]he come that may m[y] blisse brynge.'

The dayes more, and lengere every nyght,   *longer*
660 Than thei be wont to be, hym thoughte tho;
And that the sonne went his cours unright
By lenger wey than it [wa]s wont to go;
And seyde, 'Iwys, me dredeth evere mo,
The sonnes sone, Pheton, be on lyve,   *still lives*
665 And that his fadres cart amys he dryve.'*

Upon the walles faste ek wolde he walke,
And on the Grekes ost he wolde se,   *gaze*
And to hymself right thus he wolde talke:
'Lo, yender is myn owene lady fre,
670 Or elles yonder there tho tenten be,   *tents*
And then[ne]s comth this eyr that is so soote,   *sweet*
That in my soule I fele it doth me bote.   *good*

'And hardely this wynd, that more and more   *certainly*
Thus stoundemele encreseth in my face,
675 It is of my ladyes depe sikes sore.
I preve it thus: for in noon othere place

---

643 *The: Thi.* 650 you are newly crescent. 652 waning crescent. 656 move
quickly through your orbit. 658 *my: me.* 661 followed the wrong path. 662
was: is. 665 is driving his father's chariot badly. 674 grows stronger as time
goes by.

Of al this town, save onlyche in this space,
Fele I no wynd that sowneth so lyk peyne:
It seyth, "Allas, why twynned be we tweyne?" '   *parted*

680 This longe tyme he dryveth forth right thus,
Til fully passed was the nynthe nyght;
And ay bysyde hym was this Pandarus,   *at his side*
That bysily dide alle his fulle myght
Hym to comforte and make his herte lyght,
685 Yevynge hym hope alwey the tenthe morwe   *Giving*
That she shal come, and stynte al his sorwe.   *put an end to*

Uppon the tother side ek was Criseyde,   *opposite*
With wommen fewe among the Grekes stronge;
For whiche ful ofte a day, 'Allas,' she seyde,
690 'That I was born! Wel may myn herte longe
After my deth, for now lyve I to longe.   *For*
Allas, and I ne may it not amende,   *improve matters*
For now is wors than evere yet I wende.

'My fader nyl for no thing do me grace
695 To goon ayen, for [n]ought I kan hym queme;   *cajole*
And yf so be that I my terme passe,
My Troylus shal in his herte deme   *suppose*
That I am fals, and so it may wel seme:
Thus shal I have unthank on every side –   *ill-will*
700 That I was born, so weylawey the tyde!

'And yf that I me putte in jupartie
To stele awey by nyght, an[d] it byfalle
That [I] be caught, I shal be holde a spie;   *regarded as*
Or elles, lo, this drede I most of alle:
705 Yf in the hondes of som wrecche I falle,
I am but lost, al be myn herte trewe:
Now myghty God, thow on my sorwe rewe.'*

Ful pale y-woxen was here brighte face,   *grown*
Here lymes lene, as she that al the day   *thin*
710 Stod whan she dorste and loked on the place
The[r] she was born and she dwelt hadde ay;

683 diligently did his very utmost. 693 I would ever have imagined; *is: it is.*
694–5 will not on any account allow me to return. 696 go beyond the time
that I fixed. 701–2 embark upon the dangerous course of stealing away.

And al the nyght wepynge 'Allas!' she lay:
And thus, despeired out of alle cure,   *beyond any remedy*
She ladde here lyf, this woful creature.

715 Ful ofte a day she syked for destresse,
And in hereself she wente ay portraynge   *representing*
Of Troylus the gret worthinesse,
And alle his goodly wordes recordynge,   *recalling*
Syn first that day here love bygan to sprynge.   *grow*
720 And thus she sette here [wo]ful herte afyre
Thorugh remembraunce of that she gan desire.

In al this world ther nys so cruwel herte
That here had herd compleynen in here sorwe,
That nolde han wopen for here peynes smerte;   *wept*
725 So tendrely she wepte bothe eve and morwe,
Here nedede no teris forto borwe.
And this was yet the worste of al here peyne:
Ther nas no wight to whom she dorste hire pleyne.   *no-one*

Ful rowfully she loked upon Troye,   *sorrowfully*
730 Byheld the toures heyghe and ek the hall[y]s:
'Allas,' quod she, 'the plesaunce and the joye,
The wh che that now al torned into galle ys,
Have I had ofte withinne tho yonder wallys!
O Troylus, what dost[ow] now?' she seyde;
735 'Lord, where yet thou thenke upon Criseyde!   *whether*

'Allas, I ne hadde trowed on yowre lore,
And went with yow as ye me radde er this;   *advised*
Thanne had I now not siked half so sore.
Who myght have seyd that I had don amys,
740 To stele awey with swich on as he is?   *such a one*
But al to late cometh the letuarye,   *medicine*
Whan men the cors unto the grave carye.

'To late is now to speke of this matere:
Prudence, allas, oon of thyn eyen t[hre]
745 Me lakked alwey er that I cam here:
On tyme y-passed wel remembred me,

730 *hallys: halles.* 734 *O: Of.* 736 if only I had trusted your advice. 739 could have maintained that I did wrong. 744 *thre: two.* 746 I clearly remembered past times.

And present tyme ek koude I wel y-se;
But futur tyme, er I was in the snare,
Koude I not seen – that causeth now my care!*

750 'But natheles, bytyde what bityde,
I shal tomorwe at nyght, b[y] est or west,
Out of this ost stelen on som manere syde,   *armed camp*
And go with Troylus wher as hym lest.
This purpos wol I holde, and this is best:
755 No fors of wykked tonges janglerye –
For evere on love han wrecches had envye.

'For whoso wold of every word take hede,
Or rewelyn hym by every wightes wit,
Shal he nevere thryve, out of drede,
760 For that that somme blame[n] evere yit,
Lo, other manere folk commenden it.   *approve*
And as for me, for al swych variaunce,
Felicité clepe I my suffisaunce.

'For which withouten ony wordes mo,
765 To Troye I wole as for my conclusion' –
But God it wot, er fully monthes two,
She was ful fer fro that entencion;   *purpose*
For bothe Troylus and Troye toun
Shal knotles thorughout here herte slyde,
770 For she wol take a purpos for t'abyde.   *decide*

This Diomede, of whom yow telle I gan,
Gooth now withinne hymself ay arguynge,
With al the sleighte and al that evere he kan,
How he may best with short[est] taryinge   *least delay*
775 Into his net Criseydes herte brynge.
To this entent he koude nevere fyne: *desist from*
To fysshen here he leyde out hook and lyne.

---

751 *by*: be. 752 at some place or other. 753 wherever pleases him. 755 No
matter for the chattering of malicious tongues. 758 guide . . . everyone else's
judgment. 760 what some . . . always; *blamen*: han blamed. 762 diversity (of
opinions). 763 I will be satisfied with happiness (alone). 772 constantly
debating in his mind.

But natheles, wel in his herte he thoughte
That she nas not withoute a love in Troye;
780 For nevere, sithen he here then[ne]s broughte   *since*
Ne koude he sen here laughen or make joye.
He nyste how best here herte for t'acoye,
'But forto assaye,' he seyde, 'it nought ne greveth;
For he that nought n'assayeth nought n'acheveth.'

785 Yet seide he to hymself upon a nyght,
'Now am I not a fool, that wot wel how
Hire wo for love is [of] another wight,
And hereupon to gon assaye here now?
I may wel wite it nyl not ben my prow;   *advantage*
790 As wys folk in bokes it expresse:
"Men shal not wowe a wight in hevynesse."   *pay court to*

'But whoso myghte wynnen swych a flour   *perfection*
From hym for whom she morneth nyght and day,
He myghte seyn he were a conquerour' –
795 And right anoon, as he that bold was ay,
Thoughte in his herte, 'Happe how happe may,
Al sholde I deye, I wole here herte seche:
I shal no more lesen but my speche.'

This Diomede, as bokes us declare,   *tell*
800 Was in his nedes prest and corageus,
With sterne voys and myghty lymes square,
Hardy, testyf, strong and chevalrous   *bold, headstrong*
Of dedes, lyk his fader Tideus;
And som men seyn he was of tunge large;
805 And heyr he was of Calydoyne and Arge.

Criseyde mene was of here stature,   *of medium height*
Therto of shap, of face, and ek of chere,
Ther myght ben no fayrer creature;
And oft tyme this was here manere,
810 To gon y-tressed with here heerys clere
Doun by here coler at here bak byhynde,
Which with a thred of gold she wold bynde.

782 didn't know ... entice. 783 there is no harm ... in trying. 796 Come
what may. 797 I will make trial of her affection. 800 prompt and bold in
(satisfying) his desires. 804 boastful of speech. 807 (And) in addition, in figure.

And save here browes joyneden y-fere,
Ther nas no lak, in ought I kan espyen;   *blemish*
815 But forto speke of hire eyen clere,
Lo, trewely, thei writen that here syen,   *saw*
That Paradys stood formede in here eyen;
And with here riche beauté everemore
Strof love in here ay, which of hem was more.

820 She sobre was, ek symple and wys withal,   *demure, modest*
The beste y-norisshed ek that myghte be,   *bred*
And goodly of here speche in general;
Charitable, estatlyche, lusty and fre,   *dignified*
Ne nevere mo ne lakkede here pyté:
825 Tendre herted, slydynge of corage –
But trewely, I kan not telle here age.

And Troylus wel woxen was in highte,
And complet formed by proporcion   *perfectly, in*
So wel, that Kynde it not amenden myghte: *improve*
830 Yong, fresch, strong, and hardy as lyon;
Trewe as stel in eche condicion;   *quality*
On of the beste entecched creature   *disposed*
That is, or shal, whil that the world may dure.

And certaynly in storye it is founde
835 That Troylus was nevere unto no wight,
And in his tyme, in no degre secounde
In dorrying don that longeth to a knyght.
Al myghte a geaunt passen hym of myght,   *surpass*
His herte ay with the ferste and with the beste
840 Stod paregal, to dorre don that hym leste.*

But forto tellen forth of Diomede:
It fil that after on the tenthe day   *happened*
Syn that Criseyde out of the cité yede,
This Diomede, as fressh as braunche in May,
845 Com to the tente there a[s] Calkas lay,
And feyned hym with Calkas han to done
(But what he mente I shal yow telle soone).

---

813 apart from the fact that . . . met together. 819 Contended . . . greater. 825
unfixed in (her) affections. 837 daring to perform (all deeds) proper to. 840
absolutely equal . . . what he wished. 846 pretended to have business with.

Criseyde, at shorte wordes forto telle,
Welcomed hym, and doun hym by here sette –
850 And he was ethe ynowh to maken dwelle!   *easy*
And after this, withouten more lette,   *delay*
The spices and the wyn men forth hem fette,
And forth thei speke of this and that y-fere,
As frendes don – of which som shal ye here.   *a part*

855 He gan first fallen of the werre in speche
Bytwyxen hem and the folk of Troye toun,
And of th'assege he gan here ek byseche
To telle hym what was here opynyon;
Fro that demaunde he so descendeth doun   *then went on*
860 To asken here yf that here straunge thoughte
The Grekes gyse, and werkes that they wroughte;

[An]d whi here fader tarieth so longe
To wedden here unto som worthi wight.
Criseyde, that was in here peynes stronge   *severe*
865 For love of Troylus, here owene knyght,
As ferforth as she konnynge hadde or myght,
Answered hym tho; but as of his entente,
It semede not she wist what he mente.

But natheles this ilke Diomede
870 Gan in hymself assure, and thus he seyde:
'If ich aright have taken of yow hede,
Me thenketh thus, O lady myn Criseyde,
That syn I first hond on youre brydel leyde,
Whan ye out come of Troye by the morwe,
875 Ne koude I nevere sen yow but in sorwe.

'Kan I not seyn what may the cause be
But if for love of some Troian it were –
The which right sore wolde athynken me
That ye, for ony wight that dwelleth there,
880 Sholde spille a quarter of a tere,
Or pitously youreselven so bygile –   *delude*

855 began to talk about. 861 customs . . . deeds they performed. 866 To the
extent of her knowledge or power. 870 Gained confidence. 871 have observed
you correctly. 878 I would very greatly regret.

For dredles, it is nought worth the while.

'The folk of Troye, as who seyth, alle and some,
In preson ben, as ye youreselven see;
885 Fro then[ne]s shal not oon on lyve come
For al the gold bytwixen sonne and se;
Trusteth wel and understondeth me,
Ther shal not on to mercy gon on lyve,
Al were he lord of worldes twyes fyve.

890 'Swych wreche on hem for fecchyng of Eleyne
Ther shal be take, er that we hen[ne]s wende,
That Manes, which that goddes ben of peyne,*
Shul ben agast that Grekes wol hem shende;
And men shul drede, unto the worldes ende,
895 From hen[ne]s forth [to ravysshen any queene]:
So cruel shal oure wreche on hem ben sene.   *vengeance*

'And but yf Calkas lede us with ambages –
That is to seyn, with double wordes sleye,
Swich as men clepe a word with two visages –   *faces*
900 Ye shul wel knowen that I nought ne lye,
And al this thing right sen it with youre ye,
And that anoon – ye nyl not trowe how soone;   *promptly*
Now taketh heed, for it is forto done.

'What! wene ye youre wyse fader wolde   *do you imagine*
905 Han yeven Antenor for yow anoon   *exchanged*
If he ne wiste that the cité sholde
Destroyed ben? Whi nay, so mote I gon!   *as I may live*
He knew ful wel ther shal not skapen on
That Troian is – and for the gre[te] fere,
910 He dorste not ye dwelte lengere there.

'What wole ye more, lufsom lady dere?
Lat Troye an[d] Troian fro youre herte pace;
Dryf out that bittre hope and make good chere,
And clepe ayen the beauté of youre face   *call back*
915 That ye with salte terys so deface.   *disfigure*

---

883 every one of them. 888 not one (of them) survive to obtain mercy. 890
revenge . . . the abduction. 893 afraid . . . will put them to shame. 895 *to
ravysshen any: the ravesshynge of a.* 897 unless . . . is misleading us with
ambiguities. 903 bound to come about. 910 dared not have you remain.

For Troye is brough[t] in swych a jupartie,   *peril*
That it to save is now no remedye.

'And thenketh wel ye shal in Grekes fynde
A more parfit love er it be nyght,
920 Than ony Troian is, and more kynde,
And bet to serven yow wol don his myght;   *better*
And yf ye vouche sauf, my lady bryght,   *permit*
I wol ben he to serven yow myselve   *be the one*
Ye, levere than be lord of Greces twelve.'   *more gladly*

925 And with that word he gan to waxen red,
And in his speche a litel wight he quok,
And cast a litel wight asyde his hed,   *turned*
And stynte a while, and afterward awook,
And sobrelych on here he threw his look,
930 And seyde, 'I am – al be it yow no joye –
As gentil man as ony wight in Troye.   *nobly born*

'For yf my fader Tideus,' he seide,
'I-lyved hadde, I hadde ben er this
O[f] Calydoyne and Arge a kyng, Criseyde,
935 And so hope I that I shal yet, ywys.
But he was slayn, allas (the more harm is!)
Unhappyly at Thebes al to rathe,
Polymyte and many a man to skathe.*

'But herte myn, syn that I am youre man,   *vassal*
940 And ben the ferste of whom I seche grace
To serven yow as hertely as I kan,   *sincerely*
And evere shal whil I to lyven have space,
So er that I departe out of this place,
Ye wol me graunte that I may tomorwe
945 At bettre leyser tel yow my sorwe.'

What shold I telle his wordes that he seyde?
He spak ynow for o day at the meste.   *most*
It preveth wel: he spak so that Criseyde   *turns out*
G[r]aunted on the morwe at his requeste
950 Forto speke with hym at the leste,   *at any rate*

---

924 *be*: *the*. 926 his voice trembled a little. 928 paused . . . then recovered
himself. 937 Ill-fatedly . . . all too soon. 938 To the harm of Polynices and
many another. 942 *shal*: *I shal*.

So that he nolde speke of swych matere;
And thus she to hym seyde as ye may here,

As she that hadde here herte on Troylus
So faste, that there may non it arace;   *root it out*
955 And straungely she spak, and seyde thus: *distantly*
'O Diomede, I love that ilke place
Ther I was born, and Joves for his grace
Delivere it soone of al that doth it care!
God for thi might so leve it wel to fare.   *grant*

960 'That Grekes wolde here wraththe on Troye wreke
If that thei myghte, I knowe it wel, ywys.
And it shal not bifallen as ye speke,
And God toforn, and ferther over this,   *before, beyond*
I wot my fader wys and redy is;   *alert*
965 And that he me hath bought, as ye me tolde,
So dere, I am the more unto hym holde.   *indebted*

'That Grekes ben of heigh condicio[u]n   *noble*
I wot ek wel, but certeyn, men shal fynde
As worthi folk withinne Troye toun,
970 As konnyng, [and] as parfit, and as kynde,   *wise*
As ben bitwixen Orcades an[d] Inde.
And that ye koude wel youre lady serve,
I trowe ek wel, here thank forto deserve.

'But as to speke of love, ywys,' she seyde,
975 'I hadde a lord, to whom I wedded was,
The whos myn hert al was til that he deyde;   *wholly*
And other love, as helpe me here Pallas,
Ther in myn herte nys ne nevere was –
And that ye ben of noble and heigh kynrede,   *birth*
980 I have wel herd it tellen, out of drede.

'And that doth me to han so gret a wonder,   *makes*
That ye wole scornen ony womman so.
Ek God wot love and I be fer asonder;   *apart*
I am disposed bet, so mot I go,   *more inclined*
985 Unto my deth to pleyne and maken wo.

951 As long as he would not. 958 Free it quickly from all that oppresses it.
962 turn out as you say (it will).

What I shal after don I kan not seye;
But, trewely, as yet me lyst not pleye.

'Myn herte is now yn tribulacion,   *a turmoil*
And ye in armes b[isy] day by day.
990 Hereafter, whan ye wonnen han the town,
Paraunter thanne so it happen may,
That whan I se that I nevere er say,   *saw before*
Than wole I werke that I nevere wroughte:
This word to yow ynough suffisen oughte.

995 'Tomorwe ek wole I speke with yow fayn,
So that ye touchen nought of this matere.
And whan yow lyst, ye may come here ay[a]yn;
And er ye gon, thus muche I seye yow here:
As helpe me Pallas with [hire] heres clere,
1000 Yf that I sholde of ony Grek han routhe,   *take pity*
It shulde be youreselven, by my trouthe.

'I sey not therfore that I wol yow love,
Ne sey not nay – but in conclusion,
I mene wel, by God that sit above.'   *enthroned*
1005 And therwith[al] she cast here ey[en] down,
And gan to syke, and seyde, 'O Troye town,
Yet bidde I God in quiete and in reste   *I pray*
I may yow sen, or do myn herte breste.'   *cause to*

But in effect, and shortly forto seye,   *fact*
1010 This Diomede as fresshly newe aye[y]n,
Gan pressen on, and faste here mercy preye;
And after this, the sothe forto seyn,
Here glove he tok, of which he was ful fayn,
And fynally, whan it was woxen eeve,
1015 And al was wel, he ros and tok his leeve.

The bryghte Venus* folewede and ay taughte   *showed*
The wey there brode Phebus doun alighte;   *set*
And Cynthea here char-hors overraughte

---

987 I have no inclination to love; *not: not to.* 989 all the time engaged in
fighting; *bisy: ben.* 991 It may then perhaps come about. 993 act as I have
never done (before). 994 ought wholly to satisfy you. 996 As long as you don't
bring up this subject. 997 *ayayn: ayeyn.* 1004 My intention is sincere. 1006
O: *O Troylus and.* 1018 reached out over the horses of her chariot (to urge
them on).

To whirle out of the Lyon yf she myghte;
1020 And Sygnyfer his candeles shewed bryghte,   *the Zodiac*
Whan that Criseyde unto here bedde wente
Inwith here fadres faire bryghte tente,   *Inside*

Retornyng in here soule ay up and doun   *Turning over*
The wordes of this sodeyn Diomede,   *impetuous*
1025 His gret estat, and peril of the toun,
And that she was allone and hadde nede
Of frendes help; and thus bygan to brede   *grow*
The cause whi, the sothe forto telle,
That she tok fully purpos forto dwelle.

1030 The morwe come, and gostly for to speke,   *truly*
This Diomede is come unto Criseyde;
And shortly lest [that] ye my tale breke,   *interrupt*
So wel for hymself he spak and seyde,
That alle here sore sykes adoun he leyde;   *dispelled*
1035 And fynally, the sothe forto seyne,
He refte here of the grete of al here peyne.

And after this the story* telleth us
That she hym yaf the fayre baye stede,   *gave*
The which he onys wan of Troylus;
1040 And ek a broche (and that was litel nede)
That Troylus was, she yaf this Diomede;
And ek the bet from sorwe hym to releve,
She made hym were a pencel of here sleve.

I fynde ek in storyes ellyswhere,   *other chronicles*
1045 Whan thorugh the body hurt was Diomede
Of Troylus, tho wepte she many a tere,
Whan that she saugh his wyde wowndes blede,
And that she tok to [kepen] hym good hede,
And forto helen hym of his sorwes smerte
1050 Men seyn – I not – that she yaf hym here herte.*

But, trewely, the story telleth us,
Ther made nevere womman more wo

1019 the sign of Leo. 1025 powerful status. 1029 completely decided to
remain. 1032 *tale: tales.* 1036 relieved her of most of. 1039 had earlier taken
from. 1040 hardly necessary. 1043 her sleeve as a pennon. 1048 nursed him
carefully. 1050 I'm not sure.

Than she, whan that she falsede Troylus.
She seyde, 'Allas, for now is clene ago
1055 My name of trouthe in love for everemo!
For I have falsede on the gentilest   *one of*
Tha[t] evere was and on the worthyest.

'Allas, of me unto the worldes ende,
Shal neyther ben y-writen nor i-songe   *sung*
1060 No good wo[r]d, for these bokes wol me shende:
O, rolled shal I ben on many a tonge;
Thorughout the world my belle shal be ronge;
And wommen most wol hate me of alle:
Allas, that swych a cas me sholde falle!   *fate, befall*

1065 'Thei wole seyn, in as muche as in me is,
I have hem don dishonour, weylawey!
Al be I not the firste that dide amys,
What helpeth that to do my blame awey?   *dispel*
But syn I se ther is no bettre wey,
1070 An[d] that to late is now me to rewe,
To Diomede algate I wol be trewe.   *at all events*

'But Troylus, syn I no beter may,   *can do*
And syn that thus departen ye and I,
Yet preye I God, so yeve yow right good day,
1075 As for the gentileste, trewely,
That evere I say, to serven feythfully,   *saw*
And best kan ay his lady honour kepe' –
And with that word she brast anon to wepe.

'And certes, yow [ne] haten shal I nevere;
1080 And frendes love, that shal ye han of me,
And my good word al myght [I] leven evere.   *report*
And trewely, I wolde sory be
For to sen yow in adversité;
And giltles, I wot wel, I yow leve;
1085 But al shal passe, and thus take I my leve.'

1053 was unfaithful to. 1054 wholly destroyed. 1055 reputation for. 1057
That: Thas. 1060 *word: wood.* 1062 *Thorughout: Thorugh ought.* 1065 to
the full extent of my powers. 1067 Even though . . . sinned. 1070 to be sorry
for what I have done. 1074 give you the best of fortune. 1078 at once burst
out crying. 1079 *ne: to.* 1081 *myght I: myghty.* 1084 I know well that you
are blameless.

But trewely, how longe it was bytwene,   *until*
That she forsok hym for this Diomede,
Ther is noon auctor telleth it, I wene.*
Tak every man now to hise bokes hede:
1090 He shal no terme fynd, out of drede.   *period of time*
For though [that] he gan forto wowe here soone,
Er he here wan, yet was there more to done.

Ne me ne lyst this sely* womman chyde   *I don't wish*
Ferthere than th[e] story wol devyse:
1095 Here name, allas, is punysshed so wyde,   *reputation*
That for here gilt it ou[gh]t inow suffise.
And yf I myght excuse here ony wyse,   *to any extent*
For she sory was for here untrouthe,   *infidelity*
Iwys, I wolde excuse here yet for routhe.

1100 This Troylus, as I byforn have tolde,
Thus dryveth forth as wel as he hath myght;   *carries on*
But often was his herte hot and cold,
And namely that ilke nynthe nyght,   *especially*
Which on the morwe she hadde hym byhight
1105 To come ayeyn. God wot, ful litel reste
Hadde he that nyght – nothing to slepe hym leste.

The laurer-crouned Phebus with his hete
Gan yn his cours ay upward as he wente,
To warmen of the Est See* the wawes wete;
1110 And Nisus doughter* song with fressh entente,   *cheerfully*
Whan Troylus his Pandare after sente;   *sent for*
And on the walles of the toun they pleyde,
To loke if they kan sen ought [of] Criseyde.

Til it was noone thei stoden forto se
1115 Who that ther come; and every maner wight
That kam fro fer thei seyden it was she,
Til that thei koude knowen hym aright.
Now was here herte dul, now was it light;
And thus by-japed stonden forto stare   *deluded*
1120 Aboute nought, this Troylus and Pandare.

1094 More than the (authoritative) source directs; *the: this.* 1117 identify him properly. 1118 gloomy . . . cheerful.

To Pandarus this Troylus tho seyde,
'For ought I wot, byfor noon, sykerly,
Into this town ne cometh nouht Criseyde.
She hath ynow to done, hardyly,
1125 To twynnen from here fader, so trowe I;   *separate*
Here olde fader wole yet make here dyne
Er that she go; God yeve hys herte pyne!'

Pandare answered, 'It may wel be, certeyn,
And forthi lat us dyne, I the byseche,   *therefore*
1130 And after noon thanne mayst thou come aye[y]n.'
And hom thei go withoute more speche,   *debate*
And comen ayen; but longe may they seche
Er that thei fynde that thei after cape: *peer*
Fortune hem bothe thenketh forto jape.   *deceive*

1135 Quod Troylus, 'I se wel now that she
Is taried with here olde fader so,
That er she come it wol neygh even be.   *almost night*
Come forth – I wole unto the yate go:
This[e] porterys ben unkonnynge everemo;   *ignorant*
1140 And I wol don hem holde up the yate,
As nought ne were, although she come late.'

The day goth faste, and after that come eeve,
And yet com nought to Troylus Criseyde.
He loketh forth by hegge, by tree, by greve,   *thicket*
1145 And fer his hed over the wal he leyde.   *craned*
And at the laste he torned hym and seyde,
'By God, I wot hi[re] menynge now, Pandare:
Almost, ywys, al newe was my care.

'Now, douteles, this lady kan here good;
1150 I wot she meneth ryden pryvely.
I comende hire wysdom, by myn hood:
She wol not maken peple nicely
Gaure on here whan she comth, but softely   *Gawp at*

1122 As far as I can tell. 1124 Indeed, she has great difficulty. 1136 Has had
to hang about for so long. 1140 get them to keep the gate open. 1141 Without
fuss. 1147 *hire: his.* 1148 Truly, my sorrow was very nearly renewed. 1149
knows what is her best course. 1152 allow people foolishly. 1153 *whan: whan
that.*

By nyghte into the toun she thenketh ryde.   *means to*
1155 And dere brother, thenk not to longe to abyde: *wait*

'We han not ellys [for]to don, ywys,   *nothing*
And Pandarus, now woltow trowen me?
Have here my trouthe: I se here! Yond she is!   *There*
Heve up thyn eyen man – maystow not se?'   *Lift*
1160 Pandare answerede, 'Nay, so mot I the!   *prosper*
Al wrong, by God: what seystow man? wher arte?
That I se yond nys but a fare carte.'

'Allas thow seist right soth,' quod Troylus;
'But hardely it is not al for nought   *assuredly*
1165 That in myn herte I now rejoyse thus;
It is ayen som good I have a thought –   *portending*
Not I not how, but syn that I was wrought,
Ne felt I swich a comfort, dar I seye;
She comth tonyght – my lyf that dorste I leye.'

1170 Pandare answered, 'It may be wel yno[ug]h.'
And held with hym of al that evere he seyde;   *agreed*
But in his herte he thoughte and softe lough,
And to hymself ful sobrely he seyde,   *earnestly*
'From haselwode there joly Robyn pleyde,*   *dallied*
1175 Shal come al that that thow abydest here:
Ye farewel al the snow of fern yere!'   *yesteryear*

The wardeyn of the yates gan to calle
The folk which that withoute the yates were,   *outside*
And bad h[e]m dryven in here bestes alle,
1180 Or al the nyght they most b[l]even there.   *remain*
And fer withinne the nyght, with many a tere,
This Troylus gan homward forto ryde;
For wel he seth it helpeth nought t'abyde.

But natheles he gladed hym yn thys: *took comfort*
1185 He thoughte he mysacounted hadde his day,
And seyde, 'I understonde have al amys;
For thilke nyght I last Cryseyde say   *saw*
She seyde, 'I shal ben here, yf that I may,

1162 cart (for merchandise). 1166 *lt: lit.* 1167 I don't know why it is. 1170
ynough: ynowh. 1175 Is (the only place) where you'll get what you're expecting.
1179 *hem: hym.*

Er that the mone, O dere herte swete,
1190 The Lyon passe, out of this Ariete.

'For which she may yet holden al here byheste.'　　*keep*
And on the morwe unto the yate he wente,
And up and down, by west and ek by este,
Upon the walles made he many a wente;
1195 But al for nought – his hope alwey hym blente;　　*deceived*
For which at nyght yn sorwe and sykes sore,
He wente hym hom withouten ony more.　　*further delay*

His hope al clene out of his herte is fledde:　　*completely*
He nath wheron now lengere forto honge;
1200 But for the peyne hym thoughte his herte bledde,
So were hise throwes sharpe and wonder stronge.　　*attacks*
For when he saugh that she abood so longe,
He nyst what he juggen of it myght,
Syn she hath broken that she hym byhyght.

1205 The thridde, ferthe, fyfthe, sixte day
After tho dayes ten which I tolde,
Bytwyxen hope and drede his herte lay,
Yet somwhat trustynge on here hestes olde.
But whan he saugh she nolde he[re] terme holde,
1210 He kan now sen noon other remedye
But [forto] shape hym soone forto dye.

Therwith the wykked spyrit, God us blesse,　　*At which*
Which that men clepeth wode jalousye,*　　*crazed*
Gan yn hym crepe yn al this hevynesse;
1215 For which, bycause he wold soone dye,
He ne eet ne dronk, for his malencolye,
And ek from every compaignye he fledde;
This was the lyf that al the tyme he ledde.

He so defet was, that no maner man　　*disfigured*
1220 Unnethe myght hym knowe ther he wente;
So was he lene, and therto pale and wan,
And feble, that he walketh by potente;　　*crutch*
And with his ire he thus hymselven shente.　　*destroyed*

1194 turned many times. 1199 no longer has any (hope) to cling on to. 1203
didn't know how to interpret it. 1208 her past promises. 1209 appointed time.
1212 (from which) God protect us. 1213 *wode: the wode.* 1220 Could easily
recognize. 1223 *ire: Iire.*

But who so aske[d] hym wherof hym smerte,
1225 He seyde his harm was al aboute his herte.   *malady*

Pryam ful ofte, and ek his moder dere,
His bretheren and his sustren gonne hym freyne,   *question*
Why he so sorwful was in al his chere,
And what thyng was the cause of al his peyne –
1230 But al for nought: he nolde his cause pleyne,
But seyde he felte a grevous maledye
Aboute his herte – and fayn he wolde dye.

So on a day he leyde hym doun to slepe,
And so byfel that yn his slep hym thoughte   *it seemed to*
1235 That in a fforest faste he welk to wepe   *strode*
For love of here that hym these peynes wroughte;
And up and doun as he the forest soughte,   *went through*
He mette he saugh a bor with tuskes grete,   *dreamed*
That slepte ayeyn the bryghte sonnes hete.   *in*

1240 And by this bor, faste in hi[re] armes folde,
Lay, kyssyng ay, his lady bryght, Criseyde.*   *all the time*
For sorwe of which, whan he it gan byholde,
And for despit, out of his slep he breyde,   *anger, started*
And loude he cride on Pandarus and seyde,
1245 'O Pandarus, now knowe I crop and rote: *everything*
I nam but ded – ther nys noon other bote.

'My lady bryght, Criseyde, hath me bytrayed,
In whom I trusted most of ony wight;
She elliswhere hath now here herte apayed –
1250 The blysful goddes, thorugh here grete myght,
Han in my drem y-shewed it ful right.   *revealed*
Thus yn my drem Criseyde I have byholde' –
And al this thing to Pandarus he tolde.

'O my Criseyde, allas, what subtilté,   *cunning*
1255 What newe lust, what beauté, what science,   *craft*
What wratthe of just cause have ye to me?
What gilt of me, what fel experience,   *evil*

1224 *asked: asketh.* 1230 would not specify (the real) cause of his (grief). 1240
hire: his. 1249 Her heart has now taken its pleasure in another.

Hath fro me raft, allas, thyn advertence?
O trust, O feyth, O depe asseuraunce!
1260 Who hath me reft Criseyde, al my plesaunce?   *deprived of*

'Allas, whi leet I you from hennes go,
For which wel neigh out of my wit I breyde?   *went mad*
Who shal now trowen on ony othes mo?
God wot I wende, O lady bright, Criseyde,   *believed*
1265 That every word was gospel that ye seyde.
But who may bet bigile, yf hym lyste,
Than he on whom men weneth best to triste?

'What shal I don, my Pandarus, allas?
I fele now so sharp a newe peyne,
1270 Syn that ther is no remedye in this cas,
That bet were it I with myn hondes tweyne
Myselven slowh [than alwey] thus compleyne.
For thorugh my deth my wo shal han an ende,
Ther every day with lyf myself I shende.'

1275 Pandare answerede and seyde, 'Allas the while
That I was born! Have I not seyd er this
That dremes many a maner man bygyle?
And why? for men expounden hem amys.   *interpret them*
How da[r]stow seyn that fals thi lady is
1280 For ony drem, right for thyn owene drede?
Lat be this thought – thow kanst no dremes rede.

'Paraunter there thow dremest of this bor,
It may so be that it may signyfie,
Hire fader, which that old is and ek hor,   *grey*
1285 Ayen the sonne lith o poynt to dye,
And she for sorwe gynneth wepe and crye,   *weeps*
And kysseth hym there he lyth on the grounde:
Thus shuldestow thi drem arigh[t] expounde.'

'How myght I than do,' quod Troylus,
1290 'To knowe of this – ye were it nevere so lite?'   *little*

1258 diverted . . . your attention. 1259 deeply sworn promise. 1266–7 who is
better able to deceive . . . than the one who seems most trustworthy. 1272 *than
alwey*: *alwey than.* 1274 Whereas each day I go on living destroys me. 1277
deceive all kinds of people. 1280 solely on account of. 1281 don't know how
to interpret any dream. 1285 lies at death's door. 1288 This is the right way
to interpret.

'Now seystow wysly,' quod this Pandarus:
'My reed is this, syn thow kan[st] wel endite, *compose*
That hastely thow a lettre here write,
Thorugh which thow shalt wel brynge it aboute,
1295 To knowe a soth of that thou art in doute.

'And se now why: for this I dar wel seyn,
That if so is that she untrewe be,
I kan not trowen that she wol write aye[y]n. *back*
And yf she write, thow shalt ful soone se
1300 As wheyther she hath ony liberté
To come ayen, or ellys yn som clause, *part (of it)*
Yf she be let, she wole assigne a cause.

'Thow hast not wreten here syn that she wente,
Nor she to the, and this I dorste leye:
1305 The[r] may swych cause ben in here entente,
That hardely thow wolt thiselven seye
That here abod the beste is for yow tweye. *delay, two*
Now write here thanne and thow shalt fele soone
A sothe of al – there is no more to done.'

1310 Accorded ben to this conclusioun *Agreed*
(And that anoon) these ilke lordes two:
And hastely sit Troylus adoun,
And rolleth yn his herte to and fro, *turns over*
How he may best discryven here his wo; *describe to*
1315 And to Criseyde, his owene lady dere,
He wrot right thus, and seyde as ye may here.

[Litera Troili]*

'Right fresshe flour, whos I ben have and shal,
Withouten part of elliswhere servise, *love-service*
With herte, body, lyf, lust, thought and al,
1320 I, woful wight, in every humble wyse
That tonge telle or herte may devyse, *contrive*
As ofte as matere occupieth place,
Me recomaunde unto youre noble grace.

1298 *ayeyn: ayen.* 1302 is prevented (from coming), she will tell (you) why; *Yf: And yf.* 1308-9 will quickly perceive the whole truth (of the matter). 1323 I commend myself.

'Liketh it yow to wite, swete herte,
1325 As ye wel know how longe tyme agon
That ye me lafte yn aspre peynes smerte,   *bitter*
Whan that ye went, of which yet bote noon   *relief*
Have I noon had, but evere wers bygon
Fro day to day am I, and so mot dwelle,   *remain*
1330 While it yow lyst, of wele and wo my welle.

'For which to yow with dredful herte trewe   *fearful*
I wryte, as he that sorwe dryfth to wryte,   *compels*
My wo that every houre encreseth newe,   *afresh*
Compleynynge as I dar or kan endite.
1335 And that defaced is, that may ye wyte
The terys which that fro myn eyen reyne,
That wolden speke, yf that they koude, and pleyne.

'Yow first biseche I, that youre eyen clere
To loke on this defouled ye not holde,   *defiled*
1340 And over al this, that ye my lady dere,   *beyond*
Wol vouche sauf this lettre to byholde.
And by the cause ek of [my] cares colde,
That sleth my wit, yf ought amys m'asterte,   *destroys*
Foryeve it me, myn owene swete herte.

1345 'Yf ony servant dorste or oughte of right
Upon his lady pytously compleyne,
Than wene I that ich ought be that wyght,
Considered this: that ye these monethes tweyne
Han taried, there ye seyden, soth to seyne,   *whereas*
1350 But ten dayes ye nolde in ost sojourne –
But yn two monethes yet ye not retorne.

'But for as muche as I mot nedes lyke
Al that yow lyst, I dar not pleyne more,
But humbely, with sorwful sykes syke,
1355 Yow wryte ich myne unresty sorwes sore,   *restless*
Fro day to day desyring everemore

1324 May it please you to know. 1328 always in a worse state. 1330 For as
long as pleases you, the source of my well-being and sorrow. 1335 is damaged,
as you may see, by. 1343 anything wrong escapes from me. 1345 at all had
the right to. 1350 with the (Greek) army. 1354 distressed sighs.

To knowen fully, yf it youre wil were,
How ye han ferd and don whyl ye be there;

'The whos welfare and hele ek God encresse
1360 In honour swych, that upward in degre
It growe alwey so that it nevere cesse;
Right as youre herte ay kan, my lady fre,
Devyse, I pray [to] God so mot it be;   *Imagine*
And graunte it that ye soone on me rewe,
1365 As wysly as yn al I am yow trewe.

'And yf yow lyketh knowen of the fare
Of me, whos wo there may no wight discryve,
I kan no more, but, chyste of every care,   *receptacle*
At writynge of this lettre I was on lyve,
1370 Al redy out my woful gost to dryve;   *expel*
Which I delaye, and holde hym yet in honde,
Upon the sight of matere of youre sonde.

'Myn eyen two, yn veyn with which I se,
Of sorweful teres salte arn woxen wellys;   *springs*
1375 My song, yn pleynte of myn adversité;   *into*
My good yn harm, myn ese ek woxen helle ys,
My joye yn wo – I kan sey yow nought ellys,
But turned ys – for which my lyf I warye –   *curse*
Everych joye or ese in his contrarye.

1380 'Which with youre comynge hom ayen to Troye
Ye may redresse, and more a thousand sithe
Than evere ych hadde, encressen yn me joye:
For was there nevere herte yet so blythe
To han his lyf as I shal ben as swythe   *soon*
1385 As I yow se; and though no manere routhe
Commeve yow, yet thynketh on youre trouthe.

'And yf so be my gilt hath deth deserved,
Or yf you lyst n[amo]re upon me se,
In guerdon yet of that I have you served,   *payment*

1360-1 it perpetually, without ceasing, grows higher. 1366-7 how things have
gone with me. 1369 At (the time of). 1371 still restrain it. 1372 Awaiting . . .
sending. 1376 peace of mind. 1381 set right . . . times. 1383-4 so delighted
to go on living. 1385-6 even if you are not moved by any compassion. 1388
namore: no manere.

1390 Biseche I yow, myn hertes lady fre,
     That hereupon ye wolden wryte me,
     For love of God, my righte lode sterre,
     Th[at] deth may make an ende of al my werre.   *strife*

     'If other cause aught doth yow forto dwelle,
1395 That with youre lettre ye me recomforte;
     For though to me youre absence is an helle,
     Wit[h] pacience I wole my wo comporte,   *endure*
     And with youre lettre of hope I wol desporte.
     Now writeth, swete (and lat me thus not pleyne)
1400 With hope – er deth delyvere me fro peyne.

     'Iwys, myn owene dere herte trewe,
     I wot that whan ye next upon me se,
     So lost have I myn hele and ek myn hewe,
     Criseyde shal nought konne knowe me.   *be able to*
1405 Iwys, myn hertes day, my lady fre,
     So thursteth ay myn herte to biholde
     Youre beauté, that my lyf unnethe I holde.   *barely*

     'I sey no more, al have I forto seye   *even though*
     To you wel more than I telle may;
1410 But w[h]eether that ye do me lyve or deye,
     Yet pray I God, so yeve yow right good day.
     And fareth wel, goodly, fayre, fresshe may,
     As ye that lyf and deth me may comaunde;
     And to youre trouthe ay I me recomaunde.

1415 'With hele swych [that, but] ye yeven me
     The same hele, I shal noon hele have.
     In you lyth, whan yow lyst that it so be,
     The day yn which me clothen shal my grave.   *cover*
     In yow my lyf, in yow myght forto save   *(the) power*
1420 Me from dysese of alle peynes smerte;
     And fare now wel, myn owene swete herte.

                    ['*le vostre T.*']

1393 *That: There.* 1398 take comfort. 1403 health . . . colour. 1415 *that but:*
but that. 1417 You have the power (to determine). 1420 *dysese: dyshese.*

This lettre forth was sent unto Criseyde,
Of which here answere yn effe[c]t was this: *essentially*
Ful pytously she wrot ayen and seyde,
1425 That also soone as that she myght, ywys,
She wolde come, and mende al that was mys.   *put right*
And fynally she wrot and seyde hym thanne,
She wolde come, ye, but she nyst whanne.   *indeed*

But yn here lettre made she swych festes,
1430 That wonder was, and swereth she loveth hym best,
Of which he fond but botmeles byhestes;
But Troylus, thou mayst now, est or west,
Pype yn an ivy lef yf that the lest.
Thus goth the world – God shylde us fro myschaunce,
1435 And every wight that meneth trouthe avaunce.

Incresen gan the wo fro day to nyght
Of Troylus, for taryinge of Criseyde,
And lessen gan his hope and ek his myght,
For which al doun he yn his bed hym leyde;
1440 He ne eet, ne dronk, ne slep, ne [no] word seyde,
Ymagynynge ay that she was unkynde –
For which wel neigh he wax out of his mynde.

This drem, of which I told have ek byforn,
May nevere [come] out of his remembraunce;
1445 He thought ay wel he hadde his lady lorn,
And that Joves, of his purveyaunce,
Hym shewed hadde in sleep the signyfyaunce
Of hire untrothe and h[is] disaventure,   *misfortune*
And that the bor was shewed hym yn figure.

1450 For which he for Sibille* his suster sente,
That called was Cassandre ek al aboute,
And al his drem he tolde here er he stente,   *had done*
And here bisoughte assoylen hym the doute
Of the strong bor with tuskes stoute;   *mighty*
1455 And fynally, withinne a lytel stounde,

1423 *effect*: effett. 1429 paid (him) such compliments. 1431 empty promises.
1433 Whistle in the wind, if you feel like it. 1435 prosper all sincere (lovers).
1444 *come*: ek. 1448 *his*: here. 1449 as an emblem. 1453 begged her to relieve
him of (his) fear. 1455 short space (of time).

Cassandre hym gan right thus hys drem expounde:

She gan first smyle, and seyde, 'O brother dere
If thow a soth of this desirest knowe,
Thow most a fewe of olde storyes here,
1460 To purpos how that Fortune overthrowe   *demonstrate*
Hath lordes olde, thorugh which withinne a throwe*
Thow wel this bor shalt knowe, and of what kynde
He comen is, as men yn bokes fynde.

'Diane, which that [wroth] was and yn ire
1465 For Grekes nolde don here sacrifice,
Ne encens upon here auter sette afyre.   *altar*
She, for that Grekes gonne here so dispise,
Wrak here in a wonder cruwel wyse;
For with a bor as gret as oxe yn stalle,
1470 She made up frete here corn and vynes alle.   *eat up*

'To sle this bor was al the contre reysed,   *up in arms*
Amonges which ther com this bor to se,
A mayde, on of this world [the] beste y-preysed;
And Meleagre, lord of that contre,
1475 He lovede so this fressh mayde fre,
That with his manhod, er he wolde stente,   *valiantly*
This bor he slow and here the hed he sente.

'Of w[h]ich as olde bokes tellen us,
Ther ros a contek and a gret envye;   *strife, hatred*
1480 Of this lord descendede Tydeus,
By ligne (or ellys olde bokes lye);   *Lineally*
But how this Meleagree gan to dye
Thorugh his moder,* wol I yow not telle,
For al to longe were it forto dwelle.'

1485 She told ek how Tydeus, er she stente,   *had finished*
Unto the strong cité of Thebes,
To cleyme kyngdom of the cité, wente
For his felawe, daun Polymytes,   *companion*
Of which the brother, daun Ethyocles,
1490 Ful wrongfully of Thebes held the strenghthe: *might*
This told she by proces al the lengthe.

1461 a short time. 1462-3 family he is descended; *of: ek of.* 1464 *ire: lire.*
1491 fully in sequence.

She told ek how Hemonydes asterte   *escaped*
Whan Tydeus slowh fyfty knyghtes stoute;*
She told ek al the prophesies by herte,
1495 And how that sevene kynges with here route   *followers*
Bysegeden the cité al aboute;
And of the holy serpent and the welle
And of the Furyes – al she gan hym telle:

   a *Associat profugum Tideo primus Polimitem;*
   b *Tidea legatum doceat insideasque secundus;*
   c *Tercius Hemoduden canit et vates latitantes;*
   d *Quartus habet reges ineuntes prelia septem;*
   e *Mox Furie Lenne quinto narratur et anguis;*
   f *Archimori bustum sexto ludique leguntur;*
   g *Dat Graios Thebes et vatem septimus umbris;*
   h *Octavo cecidit Tideus, spes vita Pelasgis;*
   i *Ypomedon nono moritur cum Parthonopea;*
   j *F[ul]mine percussus decimo Capaneus superatur;*
   k *Undecimo sese perimunt per vulnera fratres;*
   l *Argiva flentem narrat duodenus et ignem;*

Of Archymoris bur[i]ynge and the pleyes,   *(funeral) games*
1500 And how Amphiorax f[i]l thorugh the grounde,
How Tydeus was slayn, lord of Argeys,
And [how] Ypomedon y[n] lytel stounde
Was dreynt, and ded Parthonope of wounde;   *drowned*
And also how Cappaneus the proude
1505 With thonder dynt was slayn, that cryde loude.   *boasted*

She gan ek telle hym how that eyther brother,   *each*
Ethyocles and Polymyte also,

Between 1498 and 1499 The first (book) links the exiled Polynices with Tydeus;
the second teaches (us about) Tydeus the ambassador and the ambush; the third
sings of the son of Haemon and the prophets who hide (what they know); the
fourth has the seven kings going into battle. Soon (after that) the Furies and the
serpent of Lemnos are told of in the fifth; the cremation of Archimorus and
the (funeral) games read about in the sixth; the seventh gives the Greeks to
Thebes and the prophet (Amphiorax) to the Underworld; in the eighth Tydeus
fell, the hope (and) life of the Greeks; in the ninth, Ypomedon dies together
with Partonopeus; in the tenth, struck by a thunderbolt Capaneus is overcome; in the eleventh, the brothers destroy each other with wounds; the twelfth
tells of the weeping Argia and the fire. j *Fulmine: Flumine* (by a river).
1500 *fil: ful.*

At a scarmych eche of hem slowh other,   *skirmish*
And of Argyves wepynge and here wo,
1510 And how the town was brent she told ek tho;
And so descendeth doun from gestes olde
To Diomede – and thus she spak and tolde:

'This ilke bor bytokeneth Diomede,
Tydeus sone, that doun descended is
1515 Fro Meleagree that made the bor to blede;
And thi lady, wher that she be, ywys,
This Dyomede here herte hath, and she [h]is:
Wep if thow wolt, or leef, for out of doute,   *refrain*
This Diomede is inne and thow art oute.'

1520 'Thow seyst not soth,' quod he, 'thou sorceresse –
With al thi fals gost of prophesie!   *spirit*
Thow wenest ben a gret devyneresse;
Now seystow not this fol of fantasye
Peyneth here on ladyes forto lye?
1525 Awey,' quod he, 'ther Joves yeve the sorwe!   *may*
Thow shalt be fals, paraunter, yet tomorwe.*

'As wel thou myghtest lyen on Alceste,
That [was] of creatures, but men lye,   *unless*
That evere weren, kyndest and the beste:
1530 For whanne hire housbonde was in jupartie   *danger*
To dye hymself but yf she wolde dye,
She ches for hym to dye and go to helle,   *instead of*
And starf anoon, as us the bokes telle.'*   *died at once*

Cassandre goth, and he with cruwel herte
1535 Foryat his wo ffor angre of here speche,
And from his bed al sodeynly he sterte,
As though al hol hym hadde made a leche.   *doctor*
And day by day he gan enquere and seche
A sooth of this with al his fulle cure;   *endeavour*
1540 And thus he drieth forth his aventure.   *endures, fate*

Fortune – which that permutacion   *alteration*
Of thinges hath, as it is here commytted

1511 moves on from histories of ancient times. 1522 think you are a great
prophetess. 1523 this imaginative fool. 1524 Tries hard to slander. 1526 may
be (proved) false.

Thorugh purveyaunce and disposicion   *planning*
Of heyghe Jove, as regnes shal ben fl[y]tted
1545 Fro folk yn folk, or whan they shal ben smytted –
Gan pulle awey the fetheres [brighte] of Troye
Fro day to day til thei ben bare of joye.

Among al this the fyn of the parodye   *end, life-span*
Of Ector gan approchen wonder blyve;   *fast*
1550 The fate wolde his soule sholde unbodye,
And shapen hadde a mene it out to dryve;
Ayeyns which fate [hym] helpeth not to stryve;
But on a day to fyghten gan he wende,
At which, allas, he caught his lyves ende.

1555 For which me thenketh every manere wight
That haunteth armes oughte to bywaylle   *practises*
The deth of hym that was so noble a kn[y]ght:
For as he drough a kyng by th'aventaylle,
Unwar of this, Achille thorugh the mayle   *Unexpectedly*
1560 And thorugh the body gan hym forto ryve;   *pierce*
And thus this worthi knyght was brought of lyve.

For whom, as olde bokes tellen us,
Was mad swych wo that tonge may it not telle;
And namely the sorwe of Troylus,   *especially*
1565 That next hym was of worthinesse welle;
And yn this wo gan Troylus to dwelle,
That, what for sorwe, and love, and [for] unreste,   *distress*
Ful ofte a day he bad his herte breste.   *urged*

But natheles, though he gan hym dispeyre,
1570 And dradde ay that his lady was untrewe,   *feared*
Yet ay on here his herte gan repeyre;   *went back to*
And as these loveres don, he soughte ay newe
To gete ayen Criseyde, bryght of hewe;   *win back*
And in his herte he wente here excusynge,
1575 That Calkas causede al here taryinge.

And ofte tyme he was yn purpos gret,
Hymself[ven] lyk a pylgrym to degyse   *disguise*

1544 (rule over) kingdoms shall be moved; *flytted: fletted.* 1545 disgraced.
1546 *brighte: out.* 1550 leave his body. 1551 contrived a way of forcing it out.
1558 pulled ... by the neck armour. 1576 seriously intended. 1577
hymselven: hymself.

    To sen here – but he may not contrefete   *imitate*
    To ben unknowen of folk that weren wyse,
1580 Ne fynde excuse aright that may suffise,
    Yf he among the Grekes knowen were;
    For which he wep ful ofte many a tere.

    To here he wrot yet ofte tyme al newe   *afresh*
    Ful pitously – he lefte it nought for slouthe –   *neglected*
1585 Bisechyng here [that], syn that he was trewe,
    That she wolde come ayeyn and holde here trowthe.
    For which Criseyde upon a day for routhe –
    I take it so – towchynge this matere,
    Wrot hym ayeyn, and seyde as ye may here:

                   [*Litera Criseydis*]*

1590 'Cupides sone, ensample of goodlihede,   *pattern*
    O swerd of knyghthod, sours of gentilesse,
    How myght a wyght in torment and in drede
    And he[l]eles, yow sende as yet gladnesse?
    I herteles, I syke, I yn distresse –
1595 Syn ye with me nor I with yow may dele,   *have dealings*
    Yow neyther sende ich herte may nor hele.

    'Youre lettres ful, the papir al y-pleynted,
    Conseyved hath myn hertes pi[e]té;   *Comprehended*
    I have ek seyn with terys al depeynted   *stained*
1600 Youre lettre, and how that ye requeren me   *ask*
    To come ayen, which yet may not be.
    But why, lest this lettre founden were,
    No mencion ne make I now for fere.

    'Grevous to me, God wot, is youre unreste,
1605 Youre haste, and that the goddes ordenaunce   *plan*
    It semeth not ye take it for the beste;
    Nor other thyng nys yn youre remembraunce   *mind*

1579 Not to be recognized by discerning people. 1580 would be adequate (to
explain his position). 1593 without any good thing. 1594 deprived of love.
1597 filled with complaint. 1598 heart's compassion. 1602–3 I won't give a
reason at this time for fear that. 1607 *nys: nys not.*

(As thenketh me) but oonly youre plesaunce.
But beth not wroth – and that I yow byseche:
1610 For that I tarye is al for wykked speche.

'For I have herd wel more than I wende,   *expected*
Towchynge us two, how thynges han y-stonde;
Which I shal with dissimulynge amende –
And (beth nought wroth) I have eke understonde
1615 [How] ye ne don but holden me in honde;   *deceive me*
But now no fors – I kan not in yow gesse   *no matter*
But alle trouthe and alle gentilesse.   *complete*

'Come I wole, but yet in swich disjoynt   *difficulties*
I stonde as now, that what yer or what day,
1620 That this shal be, that kan I not apoynte.   *fix*
But yn effect I prey yow as I may,
Of youre good word and of yowre frendship ay;
For trewely, whil [that] my lyf may dure,   *last*
As for a frend ye may in me assure.   *rely on*

1625 'Yet preye I yow [o]n yvel that ye ne take   *amiss*
That it is short which that I to yow write;
I dar not, there I am, wel lettres make,   *properly*
Ne nevere yet ne koude I wel endite.
[Ek] gret effect men write yn place lite:
1630 Th'entent is al and nought the lettres space.   *length*
And fareth now wel. God have you in his grace.

[*La vostre C.*]

This lettre this Troylus thoughte al straunge,
Whan he it saugh, and sorwefully he sighte;
Hym thoughte it lyk a kalendes of chaunge.
1635 But fynally he ful ne trowen myghte   *wholly*
That she now wolde hym holden that she highte:
For with ful yvel wil lyst hym t[o] leve
That loveth wel, yn swich cas, though hym greve.

1610 for fear of malicious gossip. 1612 Concerning what has passed between.
1613 set right by dissembling. 1625 *on: an.* 1629 *Ek: Of.* 1634 the beginning
of. 1636 would now keep the promise she had made to him. 1637 he is very
reluctant to give up; *to: te.* 1638 it is painful to him.

But natheles, men seyn that at the laste,
1640 For ony thing, men shal the sothe se;
And swych a cas bytidde (and that as faste)
That Troylus wel understod that she
Nas not so trewe as that here oughte be;
And fynally he wot now, out of doute,   *for certain*
1645 That al is lost that he hath gon aboute.   *undertaken*

Stod on a day in his malencolye
This Troylus, and yn suspecion
Of here for whom he wende forto dye.
And so bifel that thorughout Troye town,
1650 As was the gyse, y-bore was up and down   *carried*
A manere cote arm[ur]e, as seyth the storye,
Byfore Deiphebe yn signe of victorye.

The which cote, as telleth Lollius,*
Deiphebe it had y-rent from Diomede   *torn*
1655 The same day; and whan this Troylus
It saugh, he gan to taken of it hede,
Avysyng of the lengthe and of the brede,   *Studying*
And al the werk – but as he gan byholde,
Ful sodeynly his herte gan to colde,   *chill*

1660 As he that on the coler fond withinne   *inside*
A broch that he Criseyde yaf that morwe
That she from Troye moste nedes twynne,
In remembraunce of hym and of his sorwe;
And she hym leyde ayen here feyth to borwe
1665 To kepe it ay – but now ful wel he wiste,
Hys lady nas no lengere on to tryste.

He goth hym hom and gan ful soone sende
For Pandarus; and al this newe chaunce,   *occurrence*
And of this broche he told hym word and ende,
1670 Compleynynge of here hertes variaunce,   *fickleness*
His longe love, his trouthe, and his penaunce;
And after deth, withouten wordes more,   *for*
Ful faste he cride, his reste hym to restore.

1640 In spite of everything, the truth will come out. 1649 it came about. 1651
sort of short embroidered coat. 1652 *of: of his.* 1662 had of necessity to part.
1664 she in return pledged her word to him. 1667 *hym: hym forth.*

Thanne spak he thus: 'O lady myn, Criseyde,
1675 Wher is youre feyth, and wher is youre byheste?   *promise*
Wher is youre love? Wher is youre trouthe?' he seyde.
'Of Diomede have ye now al this feste?
Allas, I wolde have trowed, at the leste,
That syn ye nolde yn trouthe to me stonde,   *remain*
1680 That ye thus nolde han holden me in honde.

'Who shal now trowe on ony othe[s] mo?
Allas, I nevere wolde han wend er this
That ye, Criseyde, koude han chaunged so,
Ne, but I hadde a-gylt or don amys,
1685 So cruwel wende I not yowre herte, ywys,
To sle me thus – allas, youre name of trouthe
Is now fordon, and that is al my routhe.   *destroyed*

'Was there noon other broche yow lyste lete
To feffe with youre newe love,' quod he,
1690 'But thilke broche that I with terys wete
Yow yaf, as for a remembraunce of me?
Non other cause, allas, ne hadde ye
But for despit – and ek for that ye mente   *scorn*
Al outrely to shewe youre entente.

1695 'Through which I se that clene out of youre mynde
Ye han me cast, and I ne kan nor may,
For al this world, withinne myn herte fynde
To unloven yow a quarter of a day.
In cursed tyme I born was, weylaway!
1700 That ye that do me al this wo endure
Yet love I best of ony creature.

'Now God,' quod he, 'me sende yet the grace
That I may meten with this Diomede;
And trewely, yf I have myght and space,   *opportunity*
1705 Yet shal I make, I hope, his sides blede.
O God,' quod he, 'that oughtest taken hede
To fortheren trouthe and wronges to punyce –   *support, punish*
Why nyltow don a vengeaunce on this vice?

1677 Do you now take all your pleasure in Diomede? 1681 *othes: other.* 1684
Without my having sinned or misconducted myself. 1688–9 you were prepared
to give up to endow your. 1694 Unambiguously to make your meaning plain.
1698 stop loving you for.

'O Pandar[e] that in dremes forto triste

1710 Me blamed hast, and wont art ofte upbreyde –   *reproach*

Now maystow se thiselve, yf that thow lyst,

How trewe is now thi nece, bryght Cryseyde!

In sondry formes, God it wot,' he seyde,   *various*

'The goddes shewen bothe joye and tene   *affliction*

1715 In slep, and by my drem it is now sene.

'And certaynly, withoute more speche,

From hen[ne]sforth, as ferforth as I may,

Myn owene deth yn armes wol I seche;

I recche not how soone b[e] th[e] day.   *care*

1720 But trewely, Criseyde, swete may,   *maiden*

Whom I have ay with al my myght i-served,

That ye thus don, I have it nought deserved.'

This Pandarus that alle these thynges herde,

And wist wel he seyde a soth of this,

1725 He nought a word ayen to hym answerede;

For sory of his frendes sorwe he is,

And shamed for his nece hath don amys,

And stant astoned of these causes tweye,   *dumbfounded*

As stille as ston – a word ne koude he seye.

1730 But at the last thus he spak and seyde:

'My dere brother, I may the do no more.

What shuld I seyn? I hate, ywys, Criseyde,

And God wot, I wol hate here everemore!

And that thou me bysoughtest don of yore,

1735 Havynge to myn honour ne my reste

Right no reward, I dede al that the leste.

'If I dede ought that myght lyken the,   *please*

It is me lef; and of this treson now,

God wot that it a sorwe is unto me;

1740 And dredles, for hertes ese of yow,

Right fayn wolde I amende it, wist I how.

And fro this world, almyghti God I preye,

Delyvere here soone – I kan no more seye.'

1709 *Pandare*: Pandarus. 1717 to the full extent of my powers. 1719 *be the*: by this. 1724 spoke the truth about this. 1734 long ago implored me to do. 1736 regard ... pleased you. 1738 I am glad of it. 1740 to give comfort to your heart.

Gret was the sorwe and pleynt of Troylus;
1745 But forth hi[re] cours Fortune ay gan to holde.   *kept to*
Criseyde loveth the sone of Tideus,
And Troylus mot wepe in cares colde.
Swich is this world, whoso it kan biholde;
In eche estat is litel hertes reste;   *condition*
1750 God leve us forto take it for the beste!

In many cruwel batayle, out of drede,
Of Troylus, this ilke noble knyght,
As men may in these olde bokes rede,
Was sene his knyghthod and his grete myght;
1755 And dredles, his yre day and nyght,
Ful cruwel[y] the Grekes ay a-boughte:*   *paid for*
And alwey most this Diomede he soughte.

And ofte tyme I fynde that they mette
With blody strokes and with wordes grete,*   *threatening*
1760 Assayinge how here speres were whette;
And God it wot, with many a cruwel hete   *onslaught*
Gan Troylus upon his helm to bete.
But natheles, Fortune it nought ne wolde   *not permit*
Of otheres hond that eyther deyen sholde.

1765 And yf I hadde y-taken forto wryten   *undertaken to*
The armes of this ilke worthi man,
Than wold I of hise batayles endite[n];
But for that I to write first bygan
Of his love, I have seyd as I kan
1770 (H[i]se worthi dedes, whoso list hem here,
Red Dares – he kan telle hem alle y-fere),*

Bysechynge every lady bryght of hewe,
And every gentil womman, what she be,   *whoever*
That al be that Criseyde was untrewe,   *although*
1775 That for that gylt she be not wroth with me.
Ye may here gilt in othere bokes se;
And gladlyer I wol write, yf yow leste,
Penolopees trouthe, and goode Alceste.*

1745 *hire: his.* 1747 must go on weeping in bitter sorrow. 1748 (the way of)
this world, whoever is able to perceive it. 1754 was made manifest. 1760
Putting to the test the sharpness of their spears. 1765–6 had undertaken to
write about the (feats of) arms. 1770 *Hise: Hese.*

Ne I sey not this al only for these men,
1780 But most for wommen that bytraysed be   *chiefly*
Thourgh false folk; God yeve hem sorwe, amen!
That with here grete wit, and subtiltee
Bytrayse yow; and this commeveth me   *compels*
To speke, and yn effect yow alle I preye,
1785 Beth war of men, and herkeneth what I seye.

Go, litel bok; go, litel myn tr[a]gedie,
Ther God thi makere yet, er that he dye,   *May, creator*
So sende myght to make yn som comedye;
But litel bok, no makyng thow n'envye,
1790 But subgit be to alle poesye,   *submissive*
And kys the steppes there as thow seest pace   *go by*
Virgile, Ovyde, Omer, Lukan, and Stace.*

And for ther is so gret dyversité
In Englyssh, and yn wrytyng of oure tonge,   *language*
1795 So preye I God that noon myswryte the,
Ne the mysmetre for defaute of tonge.
And red wherso thou be, or elles songe,
That thow be understonde, God [I] beseche –
But yet to purpos of my rathere speche:

1800 The wraththe, as I began yow forto seye,*
Of Troylus, the Grekes boughten dere;
For thousandys h[i]se hondes maden deye,
As he that was withouten ony pere,   *equal*
Save Ector yn his tyme as I kan here.
1805 But, weylaway – save only Goddes wille! –
Dispitously hym slowh the fiers Achille.*   *In anger*

And whan that he was slayn yn this manere,
His lighte gost ful blysfully i[s] went   *soul*
Up to the holwghnesse of the [eigh]the spere,*   *concavity*
1810 In convers lettynge every element;
And there he saugh with ful avysement   *total clarity*

1786 *tragedie: tregedie.* **1789** don't be envious of any (other) poetic composition. **1795–6** carelessly copy or versify you through lack of linguistic skill. **1799** the matter of which I spoke earlier. **1802** *hise: hese.* **1805** were it not the will of God. **1808** *is: it.* **1809** *eighthe: seventhe.* **1810** Leaving every (one of the four) element(s) on its reverse side.

Th'erratyk sterres, herkenynge armonye   *wandering*
With sownes ful of hevenyssh melodye.

And doun from thens faste he gan avyse   *perceive*
1815 This litel spot of erthe that with the se
Embraced is, and fully gan despise   *scorn*
This wrecched world, and held al vanite
To respect of the pleyn felicité
That is yn hevene above; and at the laste,
1820 Ther he was slayn his lokyng doun he caste.

And yn hymself he lough right at the wo
Of hem that wepten for his deth so faste,
And dampned al oure werk that folweth so   *condemned*
The blynde lust, the which may not laste;
1825 And shuld al oure herte on hevene caste.   *turn*
And forth he wente, shortly forto telle,
There as Mercurye sorted hym to dwelle.*   *assigned*

Swich fyn hath, lo, this Troylus for love;   *Such an end*
Swych fyn hath al his grete worthynesse;
1830 Swich fyn hath his estat real above;
Swich fyn his lust, swych fyn hath his noblesse;
Swych fyn hath false worldes brotelnesse: *fragility*
And thus bygan his lovynge of Criseyde,
As I have told, and yn this wyse he deyde.

1835 O yonge fressh folkes, he or she,
In which that love up groweth with youre age,
Repeyreth hom from worldly vanyté,   *springs*
And of youre herte up casteth the visage   *Return*
To thilke God that after his ymage   *in*
1840 Yow made, and thynketh al nys but a fayre
This world, that passeth soone as floures fayre.

And loveth hym the which that right for love
Upon a cros oure soules forto beye,   *redeem*
First starf, and ros, and sit yn hevene above;
1845 For he nyl falsen no wight, dar I seye,   *betray*
That wole his herte al holly on hym leye.   *commit to*

1818 Compared with the complete bliss. 1820 To where ... his gaze. 1830 his
exalted royal status. 1835 of both sexes. 1838 turn up the face. 1840 passing
show. 1844 died, and was resurrected, and sits.

And syn he best to love is, and most meke,
What nedeth feyned loves forto seke?

Lo here, of payens corsed olde rytes;
1850 Lo here, what alle hire goddes may avaylle;
Lo here, these wrecched worldes appetites;
Lo here, the fyn and guerdon for travayle
Of Jove, Appollo, of Mars – of swych rascaylle!   *riff-raff*
Lo here the forme of olde clerkes speche
1855 In poetrie, yf [ye] here bokes seche.   *look up*

O moral Gower, this boke I directe   *dedicate*
To the, and [to] the, philosophical Strode,*
To vouchen sauf, ther nede is, to corecte,   *where*
Of youre benygnitees and zeles goode;
1860 And to that sothfast Crist that starf on rode,
With al myn herte of mercy evere I preye;   *for*
And to the, Lord, right thus I speke and seye:

Thow oon, and two, and thre, eterne on lyve,
That regnest ay yn thre, and two, and oon,
1865 Uncircumscript, and al mayst circumscryve,
Us from visible and invysible foon   *enemies*
Defende, and to thi mercy, ev[e]rychon,
So make us, Jhesus, for thi grace digne,   *worthy*
For love of mayde and moder thyn benigne. Amen.

E[x]plicit liber Troili et Criseide

1849 accursed religious practices of pagan antiquity. 1850 what good all their gods may do. 1852 the end and reward for labouring (in the service). 1854-5 of the poetic language of learned men of old. 1860 true . . . cross. 1864 rule perpetually. 1865 Impossible to contain and able to contain all things. 1869 Virgin . . . gracious.

NOTES

Book One

6: In the *Thebaid* the fury Tisiphone is generally invoked to stir up strife, whether alone or in conjunction with her sisters Megaera and Allecto (mentioned in TC IV.22–4): see *Theb.* I.59ff. Boccaccio self-consciously invokes his lady at this point, and not the muses or gods (as he says he has done in the past (F I. 1–2)).

21–3: This is the only part of Chaucer's proem that stands close to its Boccaccian counterpart (in F I. 5–6):

> Tuo sia l'onore e mio sarà l'affanno,
> s'e detti alcuna laude acquisteranno.

> E voi, amanti, priego ch'ascoltiate
> ciò che dirà'l mio verso lagrimoso,
> e se nel core avvien che voi sentiate
> destarsi alcuno spirito pietoso . . .

> [Yours be the honour and mine the toil, if what I say gains any praise. And you lovers: I pray that you listen to what my tearful verse will say, and if it happen that you should feel any compassionate spirit awaken in your heart . . .]

But the context is quite different; here it is Boccaccio's lady (and not any other lover) who is to get the 'honour', and the other lovers are subsequently to pray to Love for the poet's sake (not remember their past misfortunes). Boccaccio had already equated his own love with that of Troiolo in his (prose) *Proemio*, and in F I.3–5. See Introduction, p.xviii.

36–7: Despair was traditionally an off-shoot of the sin of sloth, which implied the deliberate refusal of God's offered love. In the context of secular love, it implies the refusal to believe that one's lady could be merciful. While the narrator presents dying in a state of amorous despair as a blessed release (and not a deadly sin against the lady) in TC I.41–2, Pandarus is more severe in I. 778–81 (while the lady lives the lover may always hope for her grace) and in I.813 (lovers much worse off than Troylus still refrain from despair). Troylus has more serious grounds for despair in IV. 954 when he knows that Criseyde must be returned to her father, and in V. 1569 when he is virtually certain that she is unfaithful to him and will never come back, and after this his physical death proves not merely a release but a revelation: see V.1814–25.

70: Benoit tells how Calkas had been warned by the oracle of Apollo at Delphi to go to the Greek fleet; he does this under the guidance of Achilles (RT 5817–58); compare TC IV.1411.

138–40: The influence of Fortune upon the fighting of the Greeks and Trojans becomes heavily weighted against the latter in TC V.1546–7. The subjection of Troylus to Fortune has already been implied in I.3–4 and is explicitly stated in IV.1–11; see also I.837–54. The ultimate subjection of Fortune herself to God is made clear in III.617–19 and V.1542–4.

146: Dares and Dictys claimed to have been present at the Trojan war (the first on the Trojan side, the second on the Greek); their accounts of it have survived in full only in Latin versions of the sixth and fourth centuries AD, respectively: the De Excidio Troiae Historia, and the Ephemeris Belli Troiani. Dares begins his history with an account of the voyage of the Argonauts, their first destruction of Troy, and its later rebuilding by King Laomedon; Dictys ends his by describing the adventures of the Greek leaders on their way home from Troy. The two histories are combined by Benoit in his Roman de Troie, and in Guido's Historia Destructionis Troiae of 1287; it is in Benoit that Briseida (Criseyde) first appears. Following the letter prefixed to Dares, both Benoit and Guido express grave doubts about Homer's reliability as a historian, and accept the claims of the two pretenders. Neither Benoit nor Guido is mentioned by Chaucer in Troylus, although Guido turns up in a list of historians of the Trojan war in his Hous of Fame (HF)1466–9, along with Homer, Dares, Tytus (Dictys), and Lollius (see notes to I.394 and V.1653).

153: The Palladium was a divinely-sent image that preserved Troy from destruction until delivered into the hands of Antenor by the priest Thean, its venal guardian (RT 25615–59).

171: This has been interpreted as an allusion to Anne of Bohemia, married to Richard II in 1382.

211–31: One of the most remarkable of all Chaucer's expansions of a single stanza in F (I.25). This reads:

O ciechità delle mondane menti:
Come ne seguon sovente gli effetti
Tutti contrarii a' nostri intendimenti!
Troiol va ora mordeno i difetti
E' solliciti amor dell'altre genti,
Sanza pensare in che il ciel s'affretti
Di recar lui, il quale Amor trafisse
Più ch'alcun altro, pria del tempio uscisse.

[O, blindness of worldly minds: how often do the results (of our plans) turn out quite contrary to our intentions! Troilus is now going about mocking the weaknesses and careworn love of other people, without suspecting what heaven is hastening to bring upon him. Which Love transfixed him more than anyone else, before he left the temple.]

218: Bayard was the horse given by Charlemagne to Renaud, and as such provides an appropriate counterpart to Troilus in line 218. But by the later fourteenth century the name was applied mockingly to much less exalted breeds of horse: see *Canterbury Tales*, Fragment A 4115 and, more generally, the entry for **baiard** n.(1) in MED. In any case line 220 of the stanza makes it clear that the war-horse is very soon demoted to a draught horse (even if one who is the leader of a team), with the corollary that Troilus the aristocratic (and arrogant) individualist, declines into a human being who must put up with the limitations of his condition like everyone else.

394: The best explanation of the name Lollius remains that of G. Latham, which rests upon the misreading of the opening lines of the second epistle of Horace's first book; in these a reference to the 'writer of the Trojan war' (Homer) is juxtaposed to the poet's invocation of 'Maxime Lolli' (Maximus Lollius). Latham concluded that Chaucer (whether accidentally or not) took all this to mean that 'Lollius' was the greatest authority on the Trojan war. See also Root 1926: xxxvi–xl; Windeatt 1984: 111.

400–20: These lines translate the eighty-eighth sonnet of Petrarch; each of the three stanzas of Chaucer's *canticus* corresponds to one of its principal sections:

S'amor non è, che dunque è quel ch'io sento?
Ma, s'egli è Amor, per Dio che cosa e quale?

Se bona, ond'e l'effetto aspro mortale?
Se ria, ond'è si dolce ogni tormento?

S'a mia voglia ardo, ond'è 'l pianto e lamento?
S'a mal mio grado, il lamentar che vale?
O viva morte, o dilettoso male,
Come puoi tanto in me, s'io no'l consento?

E s'io'l consento, a gran torto mi doglio.
Fra si contrari venti in frale barca
Mi trovo in alto mar, senza governo,
Si lieve di saver, d'error si carca,
Ch'i'medesmo non so quel ch'io mi voglio;
E tremo a mezza state, ardendo il verno.

[If it is not Love, what then is it that I feel? But, if it is Love, dear God, what is it, and of what kind? If it is good, from whence comes this bitter, deadly consequence? If evil, how is it that all [my] torment is so sweet?

If I willingly burn [in love], why [such] weeping and lamentation? If misfortune pleases me, what is the point of deploring it? Oh living death, oh, delightful harm: how can they [exist] so strongly in me, if I do not consent to it?

And if I do consent, I am very wrong to grieve [about it]. Between such opposed winds in a fragile boat, I find myself on the high seas without a rudder, so light in wisdom, so weighed down with error, that between the two I do not know what I want for myself. I shiver in the midst of summer, and [am] burning in winter.]

455: Both Benoit and Guido describe at length the courting of the Greek Helen by the Trojan Paris, and of the Trojan Polyxena by the Greek Achilles. The second of these affairs proves fatal to both characters, and the account of its earlier phases may have suggested to Boccaccio some things in the same part of his story of Troiolo and Criseida (which both Benoit and Guido wholly omit).

472: At the corresponding point in F I. 45 Boccaccio follows two lines closely akin to TC I. 470–1 with:

> ... dagli amorosi
> pensieri però niente il rimovieno;

[however did not at all take him away from his love-reveries.]

548: In F II.1, Pandaro is introduced as young, well-born, and very dashing ('molto coraggioso'); Chaucer's label 'frend' brings to mind the character of the same name in the Guillaume de Lorris part of the

Romaunt of the Rose (RR) who is sought out by the Lover when depressed and in need of support (RR 3343–8).

561–7: Compare IV. 428–34, also meant to excuse an insensitive response on Pandarus's part: see note to IV. 414–34.

654: In Ovid's *Heroides*, V. Oenone writes a letter of complaint to Paris after he has deserted her for Helen.

677: The mention of Helen here shows Pandarus to be as capable of excess as the Narrator; Pandaro makes no such offer in the corresponding F II. 12.

699: Niobe wept for the loss of her seven sons and seven daughters, and was finally turned into stone from which (as in line 700 here) her tears still flowed (Ovid, *Metamorphoses* VI. 312).

890–6: The first of two stanzas that are traditionally included in the text of TC but are not present in the Morgan copy or in other texts of its group. Unlike the second such stanza (IV. 708–14), it is expendable from the point of view of sense, but the final line is of interest in opposing 'hap' and 'grace': 'hap' ('chance', 'fortune') is defined by Philosophy in *Consolation of Philosophy* (CP) V. prosa 1 just before the discussion with Boethius of free will and God's providence of which a substantial part is taken over as TC IV.974–1078.

932–5: In TC II.507–53 Pandarus tells Criseyde of an earlier discovery of Troylus's secret, in which he had needed no prompting to make an act of contrition to the god of Love for his past sins against him.

939–66: These four stanzas, which have no counterpart in Boccaccio, exemplify the down-to-earth tone and density of proverbial wisdom characteristic of Chaucer's Pandarus.

1072–85: These stanzas are Chaucer's addition; their celebration of the ennobling effects of love anticipates that of III. 1772–806, also placed at the end of the book in which they appear.

Book Two

8: The invocation of Cleo, the Muse of History, goes naturally with the Narrator's claim in II.12–18 to be faithfully reproducing an authoritative source.

29–49: The excuse made here for the way in which Pandarus goes to work on the hero's behalf also underlines the Narrator's concern with 'historical' accuracy.

64: Procne was the wife of Tereus (Tireux, 69), who raped and mutilated her sister Philomela. In the Ovidian version of the story (*Met.* VI. 412–674) this act is avenged by the sisters' murder and butchery of Procne's son, and their feeding of him to his unsuspecting father; subsequently all three of the principal characters are transformed into birds. The story was later told by Chaucer in the *Legend of Good Women* (LGW) 2228–393, but here the need to present Philomela as the innocent victim of masculine vice brings the narrative to a halt well before the sisters take their revenge upon Tereus, and before the transformation of Procne into a swallow, that is evoked in the present line.

104–5: Amphiaraus was the Greek prophet who foresaw the disastrous end of the expedition against Thebes, took part in it unwillingly, and while slaughtering the enemy on a heroic scale fell into the Underworld while still alive (*Theb.* VII.794–823): see also TC v. 1498 g. The Oedipus and Laius of lines 101–2 had appeared so much earlier in the story of Thebes as to make it impossible that they could have been read about in the same session as the 'bishop', without much skipping of intervening matter.

113–19: Compare the response which Criseyde makes to Diomede's advances in V.974–87.

157–8: The claim that Troylus was second only to Hector is also made in II.644, III.1774–5, and V.1803–4.

190–203: This account of the military exploits of Troylus is part of a significant expansion of Boccaccio's narrative at the beginning of TC II. As usual, his feats of arms are presented in very general terms, and so in sharp contrast to Benoit's normal practice.

384: In courtly love-literature, 'Daunger' is perhaps the most effective weapon in the lady's armoury. Its force is essentially negative: that of a holding back, not a thrusting forward. The allegorical technique of the *Romaunt* makes possible the communication of both senses. On the literal level the action of Daunger in leaping out at the lover when he asks to be given the rosebud seems aggressively 'masculine'; on the allegorical level it stands for the more 'feminine' breaking off of all significant contact (3130–66). For other mentions of 'Daunger' in TC, see II.399, 1243, and 1376, and III. 1321.

416: The inclusion of the Greek Achilles in this list reminds us of Benoit's account of his love for the Trojan Polyxena. While mostly passive and reticent, she had bitterly resented the murder of her lover by her brother Paris (RT 22435–60).

425: Pallas Athene, the virgin goddess, is also invoked by Criseyde at moments of stress in V.977 and 999.

507–53: Pandarus's account of this first discovery of the hero's love is not foreshadowed at the appropriate point in Book I (as the account of the second discovery of it in II.554–74, is in I.547ff.), and it could seem an off-the-cuff invention on the part of its narrator. But it cannot have been Chaucer's invention as well, as it is already present in F II.56–61.

610–58; This episode validates Pandarus's eulogy of Troylus in II.157–61. It is quite lacking in F, nor does it have any precise equivalent in Benoit, since in RT 10201–18 it is Hector, not Troilus, who returns from battle (and severely wounded) to Troy, and is given a hero's welcome. Chaucer's scene also invites comparison with the later scene in which Pandarus deliberately arranges the sighting of Troylus by Criseyde: see note to II.1247–74.

617–18 The gate named in honour of Dardanus (Dardanides) was one of six set in the walls of Troy (and named in the Prologue to Shakespeare's *Troilus and Cressida*, lines 16–17). The parallels with six-gated fourteenth-century London would have made it natural for the ancient city to be conceived in terms of the medieval one, both by Chaucer (who lived above the Aldgate for about twelve years) and by many of his readers.

680–3: The seventh 'house' was the one of the twelve divisions of the skies most associated with matters of love and marriage, and the presence of the beneficent planet within it promises well for the love-affair, especially since other, potentially hostile, planets are favourably placed in relation to Venus.

816: Neither these nieces nor their names appear in Boccaccio or Benoit; Antigone, the only one to play a significant part in the story, bears the same name as the heroine of the *Thebaid* of Statius, but her function there is to help administer funeral rites to her brother (*Theb.*

XII.349ff.), and not (unwittingly) to help along any love affair, as in TC II.827–96, or serve as Criseyde's lady-in-waiting, as in TC II.1563, 1716 and III.597.

827–75: General parallels with Antigone's song have been found in a number of the lyrics of Guillaume de Machaut (c. 1300–77), in which ladies sing in praise of love in general and their lovers in particular.

918: Philomela is transformed into a nightingale at the end of Ovid's version of the story, see note to II.64. Criseyde is herself compared to a nightingale in III.1233–9.

925–31: For a partial source for this dream see note to V. 1234–41 and Introduction, p.xx. In Chaucer's *Parlement of Foules* (PF) the first of the three eagles is presented as an ideal royal suitor (393–9); in its total deference to its lady (414–41) it is much more like Troylus than is the eagle here.

1062: Minerva was the goddess of wisdom.

1109–13: Here, as in II.1692–701, matters of public concern are made to serve as a cover for the love-affair.

1217: 'Disdayn' is the natural associate of 'Daunger'; the two personifications are explicitly linked in the warning inscription over the gate leading into the garden of love in PF 136.

1247–74: This scene had been planned in II.1010–20. Like the earlier (unplanned) riding by of Troylus in II.610–58, it has no real parallel in Boccaccio, who instead supplies, between lines corresponding to TC II.980 and 981, an account of how Troiolo goes with Pandaro to see the reaction of Criseida (at her window) to the disclosure of the hero's love to her. This proves favourable (F II.81–2).

1331–4: These lines do not appear at the same point in F (II.130) but had turned up earlier as the first half of II.85 (of which the narrative context was broadly similar), which had not then been taken over by Chaucer:

> Ma come noi, per continua usanza,
> Per più legne veggiam foco maggiore,
> Cosi avvien, crescendo la speranza,
> Assai sovente ancor cresce l'amore.

[But as we see constantly, the more wood, the greater the fire, so it comes about that as hope increases so too, very often, does love.]

1398: Deiphebus was the third son of Priam and Hecuba; his close association with Helen throughout the rest of this scene brings to mind the claim made by Dictys that he became her husband after the death of Paris (Frazer 1966: 101, 113). For the complex relationship of his function in TC II and in F VII see Introduction, pp. xx–xxi.

1422–8: This encouraging reaction is supported by the later conduct of Deiphebus in II.1485–91, of Helen in 1604–10 and 1674–80, and by the sentiments ascribed to Hector in 1450–6.

1467: The character of Poliphete and the story of his lawsuit against Criseyde are Chaucer's invention. To the reader he is blackened by his association with Antenor, traditionally the betrayer of Troy (see note following), but from the Trojan point of view the real traitor at this stage in the narrative would be Calkas, and the persecution of his daughter likely enough on 'patriotic' grounds, Hector or no Hector.

1473–5: The treachery of Antenor is made explicit in IV.203–5; in the medieval histories of Troy, Æneas is associated with him as an advocate of peace with the Greeks, but is more ambivalent in his dealings with them. After the murder of Achilles, he even manages to save Polyxena's life for a time, by hiding her from the Greeks (RT 26190–4); later, her discovery and handing over to Agamemnon by Antenor (RT 26420–7) causes him to be banished after the fall of the city (RT 27240–9). But he is never the man that he had been in the *Æneid*.

1735–6: In F II.134–5, the only 'corona' mentioned is that of Criseida's virtue, but while this might have suggested Chaucer's 'corounes tweyne', it does not explain them, nor do the 'corones two' of lilies and roses that are brought to Cecilia and Valerian in the *Second Nun's Tale* (CT G.221). Two abstract qualities are presumably meant; of those that have been suggested, Pity and Generosity ('Bounté') would be particularly apt.

1750: Pandaro is even more insistent in F II.142. Here only he and Criseida are involved, but some time has still to pass before the affair is consummated. In the text of TC contained in Bodleian Library MS Rawlinson Poet. 163, after two lines corresponding to II. 1576–7, Pandarus continues his exhortations in a stanza that is found in no other copy, and of which the authenticity is disputed:

> For ye must outher chaungen [now] your face,
> That is so ful of mercy and bountee,

Or elles must ye do this man sum grace;
For this thyng folweth of necessytee,
As sothe as God ys in his magestee.
That crueltee, with so benigne a chier,
Ne may not last in o persone yfere.

1752: Despite a wide range of suggested etymologies, 'kankedort' has never been decisively explained. The general context suggests that it meant something like 'difficult situation', 'uncomfortable state', or 'predicament'; the specific address to lovers and the final question recall the end of the first part of the *Knight's Tale* (CT A.1347–54), where the narrator sets the 'loveres' in his audience a genuine problem to solve (which of the two heroes of the story is having the worse time of it).

Book Three

1–42: See Introduction, pp. xix–xx for the transposition of these stanzas from a point corresponding to III.1744 (F III.74). This was probably suggested by the invocation of 'Fulvida luce' (Brilliant light), in F III.1. Both Chaucer and Boccaccio blend astrology and mythology throughout the passage; see note to III.712–21.

3: Venus is meant here; mythologically the daughter of Jove, and astronomically the companion of the sun through the heavens.

15: Other texts read 'effectes' here; the sense would then be closer to that of the opening lines of F III.76:

Tu Giove prima agli alti effetti lieto,
Pe' quai vivono e son tutte le cose,
Movesti.

[You first impelled Jove to delight in those noble impulses through which all things live and have their being.]

20: See III.722–3 for one of the 'formes' assumed by the amorous god (here that of the bull, when he seduced Europa).

35: The image of the fish-trap ('were') had already been used by Chaucer in PF 138–9 to express the dangers of being in love. In the present line it rounds off a typically colloquial and lively expansion of Boccaccio's original:

. . . che fai maravigliare
Chi tua potenza non sa ragguardare. (III.78)

[which causes wonder in whoever does not know how to estimate your power.]

43–9: At the same point, Boccaccio cites Hercules as proof that no one can defend himself against the power of love (F III.80). There then follows a run of stanzas in praise of love, Venus, and Criseida (F III.81–9); after which come the stanzas in praise of Troiolo that are found at the same point in TC III.1772–806.

45: The invocation of Calliope, the sweet-voiced muse of epic poetry, implies that the poem now aspires above the (allegedly) fact-bound 'history' implied by the invocation of Cleo at the beginning of the second book.

76–9: Troylus's confusion is understandable in that the 'lordship' that is naturally his in the everyday world (and will certainly be useful in checking the evil Poliphete) has been completely surrendered to Criseyde in their private relationship; see also III. 169–75.

185–6: Pandarus's gloss in the second line is necessary in a work in which Christian and pagan ideas of divinity are sometimes juxtaposed or confused: see Introduction, p.xxx.

374–82: Troylus will in fact later be killed by Achilles, although not as the result of any breach of secrecy in love: see V.1806. Unlike Agamemnon, Achilles is not named by Boccaccio in the source of this passage (F III.15).

410: Cassandra is not included in Troiolo's offer at the same point in F (III.18).

468: Since Criseyde is a widow this comment would support the view – ascribed to the Countess of Champagne by Andreas Capellanus – that true love was impossible within marriage (Parry 1941:106–7).

501–4: No such admission is made by Boccaccio here or elsewhere.

536–46: A further example of the use of religious and political concerns to mask the real point of the hero's actions.

575–8: Here again the auctour is made to seem remiss; Boccaccio had in fact noted that the news that Troiolo was out of town was most grievous to Criseida (F III.22).

592–3: Pluto was lord of the Underworld and abductor of Proserpina (mentioned in IV.473); the story of Tantalus is briefly mentioned in Chaucer's translation of Boethius (CP III.metrum 12).

595–603: Criseida herself arranges the meeting with Troiolo, in her own house, at a time when some at least of her servants will be absent, and later ensures that those who remain go quickly to bed (F III.26; compare TC III.654–8).

614: In the Middle High German *Kudrun* Wate plays an important part as a skilful navigator who leads the expedition to win a bride for his master Hetel. See Gillespie 1973: 138–9 for fuller details of this story, and for English allusions to (and traditions of) Wade.

624–5: A rare planetary conjunction that actually occurred in May 1385, and could represent the earliest date at which TC could have been composed: see Root 1926: xvi–xviii and 475; Windeatt 1984: 283. It is also relevant to any attempt at establishing the chronology of the love-affair itself: see note to V.8–14.

712–21: Like much else around them, these lines have no equivalent in Boccaccio, and exemplify the double aspect of Venus as goddess and as planetary influence. In the first capacity she is both an object of prayer and a very human figure (who has herself felt the power of love, in her passion for Adonis); in the second, she is a cosmic force for good (unless thwarted by the sun, or by Mars or Saturn, the great malevolent planets).

726–7: Pursued by Apollo (Phebus), Daphne is saved by being transformed into a laurel tree.

729–30: In Ovid, Pallas was angry not with Herse, but with her venal and envious sister Aglauros, whom she punishes by turning into stone. This story is followed in *Met.* II by that of Jupiter and Europa, evoked in TC III.722–3.

797: There is no trace of such a character in F; the name may be a variant of that of Orestes ('Horeste' in Gower, *Confessio Amantis* III.2176).

813–33: These three stanzas derive from Boethius, CP II.prosa 4. It is ironical that these sentiments should be expressed by Criseyde; her 'brotel' in line 820 looks forward to the 'brotelnesse' of V.1832, in a stanza wholly unsympathetic to the love affair.

890: Under MED **hasel** n. 2(b) 'haselwode' is glossed 'foolishness, nonsense' and 'shaken haselwodes', 'to do something foolish'. See also TC V.505 and 1174.

931–3: Two propositions of the first book of Euclid are confused here: Criseyde alludes to the forty-seventh, with its two-horned figure; Pandarus mistakes this for the fifth (the 'fuga miserorum').

1046: In mentioning these two ways of clearing herself Criseyde recalls Gottfried von Strassburg's Isolde, who really is guilty of infidelity and has publicly to undergo both tests (Hatto 1960: 245–8).

1086–92: The fainting of Troylus here, and his reviving in III.1114–20 derive from the later account in F IV.18–21 of his collapse after hearing of the decision to give back Criseida to her father. See also note to TC IV. 176–203.

1254–67: The first of these stanzas again exemplifies the blending of Venus the goddess with Venus the planet; the second, while chiefly indebted to Dante's hymn to the Virgin in *Paradiso* XXXIII.13–18 (more extensively reproduced in the Prologues to the *Prioress's Tale* and *Second Nun's Tale*) begins with the very Boethian concept of Love as a universally binding force: see TC III.1744–71 and CT A.2991–3.

1316: In F III.32 Boccaccio had written 'd'amor sentiron l'ultimo valore' (they experienced the power of love to the full), and followed this with an admission of his own inability to express the lovers' joy: compare TC III.1310–11. While Chaucer is less specific at this point, his earlier account of the lovers' foreplay in III.1247–53 is physical to a degree nowhere approached by Boccaccio.

1370–2: This incident, not found in F. seems to have been suggested by Troylus's much later discovery of the brooch he had given Criseyde on Diomede's coat of arms (TC V.1660–2; F VIII.9–10).

1384: Not an allusion to wine (MED **red** n. (2) (i)) but to gold (ibid., (j)). At the same point (F III.39), Boccaccio says that such misers will lose their wealth ('denar perderanno').

1389–91: Bacchus bestowed upon Midas the fatal gift of turning everything touched into gold (and later withdrew it, at the king's request); Crassus, less fortunate, died through being forced to drink molten gold (Gower, *Confessio Amantis* V.141–320, 2068–224).

1420: 'Fortuna Maior' was one of the figures of geomancy (a mode of divination based on the random setting down of dots); it may also denote a group of stars in the constellations of Aquarius and Pegasus roughly akin to this figure.

1428: When Jove took the place of Amphitryon, the husband of Alcmena, to beget Hercules, the length of the night was miraculously extended.

1450–70: In their colloquial detail and high-handed tone, these stanzas are sometimes unexpectedly close to Donne's *The Sunne Rising*.

1464: There is confusion here between Titan (the sun) and Tithonus, the mortal lover of Aurora (the dawn), who was granted immortality but not eternal youth.

1600: Of the other rivers of Hades, Styx is mentioned (but as a pit) in TC IV. 1540.

1691: In V. 1818, 'felicité' denotes the bliss of heaven and dismisses all that earth can offer as trivial when set beside it. In the present line the Narrator sets the harmony that Troylus has now achieved with Criseyde as a joy beyond the power of words to express it. The noun is also used by Criseyde in V.763, but in a less obviously exalted sense.

1695–708: The relation of these two stanzas to F is complex. From one point of view they are an expanded version of a single stanza there (III.70):

> Ma il nemico giorno s'appressava,
> come per segno si sentiva aperto,
> il qual ciascun cruccioso biastemiava,
> parendo lor che el si fosse offerto
> più tosto assai ch'offrirsi non usava:
> il che doleva a ciascun per lo certo,
> ma poi che più non si poteva allora,
> ciascun su si levò sanza dimora.

> [But the hostile day hastened on, as was clearly perceived from (various) signs, and this each of them cursed angrily, since it seemed to them that it had come much earlier than it was used to do, which truly was grievous to both of them. But since there was nothing else to be done, each of them quickly got up.]

But the reference in TC 1702–5 to the unusual speed of the horses of the sun owes something to the later F V.68, which is also expanded upon at the corresponding point in TC: see note to V.659–65.

1805: The three of the seven deadly sins that are not explicitly named are Gluttony, Lechery, and Sloth. The first is unthinkable in Troylus; the second might raise problems in a celebration of extra-marital love (Gower replaced it by Incest as one of the major divisions of his *Confessio*); Sloth is more of a danger, being the sin against which Pandarus had explicitly warned both lovers, and with Despair as one of its most important offshoots (I.36–7, II.1008, III.896); see note to I.36–7.

1807: Venus is meant here.

1809: Elycone seems here to refer to a spring rather than a mountain (in Boeotia); its placing near Parnassus is also inexact: compare HF 521–2.

1814–16: These lines derive from a later point in F (IV.24):

> Io ho infino a qui lieto cantato
> il ben che Troiol senti per amore,
> come che di sospir fosse mischiato.

> [Until now I have gladly sung of the happiness that Troilo experienced through love, though it was mingled with sighs.]

But their impact is very different there, as they come after the scene in which the exchange of Criseida is determined by the Trojan parliament, and form part of a sequence of three stanzas in which Boccaccio complains to his own lady of the grief which he feels on her account, and urges her to return to him.

Book Four

1–28: In the Morgan and Corpus texts (and two others) these four stanzas are used to conclude the third book; in Boccaccio the equivalent of the first of them also stands in final position (as F III.94), but there is nothing to correspond to the other three.

15–21: These lines would have been more apt at the head of the fifth book, which is the only one lacking an extended proem.

25: Quirinus was another name for Romulus, traditionally the founder and first king of Rome.

32: Hercules is associated with the sign of Leo here by his killing of the Nemean lion.

50–4: This detailed catalogue of Trojan warriors contrasts sharply with the impressionistic style of the preceding stanza, and brings to mind the manner of Benoit and Guido. In fact it derives from F IV.3, although Chaucer has added the name 'Phebuseo', and, by inserting

'Maugré' at the head of line 51, corrected Boccaccio's statement that Polydamas and the rest were taken prisoner along with Antenor. In RT 12551–65 Polydamas is outraged by the loss of his companion-in-arms and wishes to avenge it, but is prevented from doing so.

120–6: Not in F; in RT 25920–3, Neptune is said to have built the walls, and Apollo to have consecrated them.

124: Laomedon, Priam's father, had ruled over Troy at the time of its first destruction; this was caused by the refusal of the Trojans to give hospitality to Hercules and Jason on their way to win the Golden Fleece (RT 1037–60), and not because they had denied the gods their wages, as is stated here.

138: In Benoit it was Thoas (not mentioned in F IV.13) who was exchanged for Antenor (RT 13080–5); Criseida was subsequently sent back to Calchas because Priam did not wish any of the kinsfolk of the traitor to remain in Troy (RT 13116–20).

162–8: The opposition of Love and Reason is very important in the scene in the *Romaunt* which follows the Lover's rebuff by 'Daunger' (for which see notes to II.384 and 1217). 'Resoun' makes a long speech urging him to give up his misguided pursuit (RR 3219–304), but her advice is rejected. See also TC IV.573–4.

176–203: In F IV.19, Hector's concern is not with Criseida, but with Troylus, who has fainted away on hearing of the exchange; in consequence, there is no outcry from the people, and no reproach of these last by the Narrator. At roughly the same point in RT (12963–992) Hector had instead objected to the excessive length of the truce proposed by the Greeks. See also note to III.1086–92.

197–201: The claim that very few people know how to separate what is to their advantage from what is not comes at the beginning of Juvenal's Tenth Satire.

239–45: The image of the bull is taken over from F IV.27, where it was borrowed from the description of the Minotaur in Dante, *Inferno* XII.22–4. Such violence is unexpected in Troylus, but the image itself balances that of Diomede as a boar in the following book: see note to V.1234–41.

300–1: Oedipus blinded himself on discovering that he had killed his father and married his mother (*Theb.* I.46–52). For other events in the story of Thebes see II.104–5 and V.1485–510.

323-6: Compare the Narrator's own invocation of happy lovers in TC I.22-8 (which never suggests that their bliss may not last).

351-7: Compare the first intrusion of Pandarus upon the grief of Troylus (TC I.547ff.); this time it is more difficult to think of an effective way of putting an end to it.

391-2: This also brings the earlier scene to mind, since Pandarus had also noted there that Fortune is 'commune' (I.843-4). But while both passages convey her unpredictability, the first is given an optimistic gloss quite lacking in the second.

414-34: The first two stanzas amplify a single one in Boccaccio (IV.49), the third is completely new, inserted to soften the cynical tone of the others. The sentiment expressed in 415 comes from F IV.49 and has as its ultimate source Ovid, *Remedia Amoris* 462. The Zauzis of 414 (not mentioned by Boccaccio) has not been satisfactorily explained; in the *Physician's Tale* it is used as a name for a painter, presumably the Athenian Zeuxis (CT C. 16).

473: The reference to Prosperpyne is Chaucer's addition; see also the *Merchant's Tale* (CT E.2229-33).

533-5: The rape of Helen by Paris is more explicitly set out as a precedent for violent action in IV.608-9.

589-90: Pandarus's contempt for excessive 'courtly' deliberation contrasts sharply with the kind of advice he had given Troylus in I.810-19 and elsewhere, and reflects the fact that time is running out for both Troylus and Troy.

618: This claim brings to mind the proverb 'Who shal yeve a lovere any lawe', quoted by Arcite in the *Knight's Tale* (CT A.1164).

624-7: These lines also contrast violently with the mood of the earlier books, replacing the harmonious social intercourse characteristic of Troy with the prospect of the bloodiest kind of civil strife.

659: This description of Fame derives from F IV.78; see HF 1360-92 for a more comprehensive view of the goddess.

708-14: The second of the stanzas omitted from the Morgan copy and others in the same group. It is less expendable than I.890-6, since not only do its first two lines derive from F IV.84, but the content of the stanza as a whole is picked up in the one that follows.

762: Neither Benoit nor Boccaccio mentions Criseyde's mother; Argia is the wife of Polynices in TC V.1509.

789: Compare Ovid's 'arva piorum' (fields of the godly), where the ghost of Orpheus is at last reunited with Eurydice (*Met.* X.61–3).

927: In the *Squire's Tale* Cambyuskan is presented with a magic sword which gives wounds with its edge that will be cured when they are stroked with the flat of it (CT F 160–5).

954: See note to I.36–7.

974–1078: The whole of this section is based upon the first part of the long speech that Boethius assigns to himself after Philosophy has set out the case for supposing that human free will can co-exist with God's foreseeing of all events (CP V. prosa 3). Troylus does not reproduce all that Boethius has to say at this point, and wholly omits the later arguments with which Philosophy contests this view in proses 4–6. The soliloquy is not present in manuscripts belonging to Root's α group, Windeatt's Ph*etc.* group.

1079–85: This stanza reverses Boethius's slightly later conclusion that prayer is pointless because everything is preordained (ibid. prosa 3).

1085–120: While temperamentally unable to offer Troylus the kind of consolation that Philosophy had offered Boethius, Pandarus at least seems a little less cynical here than in IV.400–27.

1116: No mention is made at any point in *Troylus* of the hostility of Juno towards the Trojans, although her cruelty towards the Thebans is noted in V.601–2.

1138–9: Myrrha, made pregnant by her father, begged the gods to change her into some other shape, and was transformed into a myrrh tree, through the bark of which her tears dropped as gum (*Met.* X.298–502). Compare IV.228–9 in which Troylus is metaphorically imprisoned in this way.

1156–211: The story of Pyramus and Thisbe offers the best-known classical example of how the lover's mistaken belief that his lady is dead drives him to suicide (not, in this case, prevented in time): see Chaucer, LGW 823–52.

1188: Minos passes judgment on the souls of the dead in the Underworld (see Dante, *Inferno* XIII.94–6).

1296–414: The account of Criseyde's scenarios for coping with the new situation is over twice as long as its original in F IV.128–136.

1338–41: Contrast Diomede's much more realistic assessment of Calchas's motives in TC V.904–7.

1348: This could imply the handing back to the Trojans of Priam's sister Hesione, captured by the Greeks at the time of their first destruction of Troy (see note to TC IV.124), and kept by them in spite of Antenor's plea that she should be returned (RT 3455–62).

1368–9: In RR 181–206 and 349–412 images of Covetousness and Old Age are among those set on the outer walls of the Garden, as a sign of their total incompatibility with the kind of love that is celebrated within it. 'Elde' is also mentioned in TC II.399.

1459: Argus's head was set round with a hundred eyes, two of which rested while the others stayed open (*Met*, I.625f.).

1538–40: Athamas, King of Thebes, was sent mad by the fury Tisiphone on the orders of Juno (*Met*. IV.416–562); Styx is a river of hell, not a pit.

1548: Symoys is a tributary of the Scamander, not mentioned in either F or RT; the present passage fuses material from two passages from Ovid (*Amores* I.15.10 and *Heroides* V.29.30).

1576–82: Ironically, these fears are realized by a very different course of action by Criseyde: see V.1058–68.

1591–2: That is, before the moon has passed from her present position in Aries through the three intervening signs to Leo. This would take ten days, by which time it would appear as a crescent.

Book Five

1–14: These two stanzas are not found in F, but contain material drawn from the opening lines of Boccaccio's *Teseida* IX and II respectively.

2–4: Here the Fates have replaced the Goddess Fortune as the intruments of the divine will.

8–14: The first four of these lines translate *Tes*. II. 1–3, which immediately precede the return of Teseo to Athens:

Il sole avea due volte dissolute
le nevi en gli alti poggi, e altrettante
Zeffiro aveva le frondi rendute . . .

[The sun had twice melted the snows of the high hills, and as often Zephirus
had brought back the leafy branches . . .]

Taken in conjunction with other passages that help to fix the chronology of the affair (TC I.156, II.56, III.624–5), the passage suggests that Troylus and Criseyde had been lovers for 'some fourteen months' (Root 1926: xxxiv). Nothing so precise can be inferred from any of the statements made by Boccaccio.

88: For Tydeus see lines 803–5, 932–8 (and note), 1485–93 (and note), 1498 a, b, h., 1501.

207–8: Boccaccio at the same point (F V.17) makes only a general reference to 'the gods and goddesses'. As the deities of corn and wine, Ceres and Bacchus seem out of place in Chaucer's list; perhaps he was recalling their close association with Venus in PF 275–7 (as in *Tes.* VII.66).

212: Ixion was bound in Hades to a constantly revolving wheel.

281–7: For once in the narrative, matters of public concern really do take precedence over the demands of the love-affair.

298–315: The funeral arrangements set out in these lines are Chaucer's addition; those mentioned in 302–8 are characteristic of the classical epic. See also the brief allusion to the funeral games of *Theb.* in TC V.1499.

319: Ascalaphus was changed into an owl for betraying Prosperpina and preventing her return to Elysium (*Met.* V.533ff).

321: One of Mercury's functions was to guide the souls of the dead to the Underworld. See also note to V.1827.

358–78: The various categories of dreams, and the extent to which each is worthy of serious attention, are discussed by W. C. Curry 1960: 195–240, but they are not precisely differentiated by Chaucer either here or in the much fuller list given in HF 1–48. This imprecision seems in line with more general fourteenth-century usage: MED records the senses of 'dream', 'dream-vision', 'prophetic dream' for **sweven**.

403: No further details about Sarpedon are provided by Chaucer or Boccaccio. Benoit records that he had brought a large body of troops to the help of his kinsman Priam (RT 6686–94), and was killed by Palamedes during the twelfth battle (RT 18784–818).

411–3: Pandarus had played upon Troylus's fear of being thought a coward in I.799–805; his tactic is less plausible here, as it is now a time of truce: see IV. 1312–14.

551–3: This is the most extreme 'exaltation' of Criseyde in the whole of TC; there is nothing to correspond in F.

601–2: The anger of Juno against the Thebans was motivated by the affairs of Jupiter with the Theban Semele and Alcmena: see *Theb.* I.12, 256–8, II.292–3, X.67, 282–4. These are also implied in the *Knight's Tale* (CT A.1329–31 and 1543–62).

617–23: What is imagination here becomes fact in V.1219–32, where Troylus looks so ill as to become an object of general concern.

644: Charybdis was a whirlpool opposite the coast of Sicily.

655: Latona was in fact the mother of Diana and Apollo; the word is glossed 'luna' (the moon) in one copy of TC; two others emend to Lucyna.

659–65: The corresponding stanza in F is V.68; as noted, this had already contributed to the expansion of F III.70 that lay behind TC III.1695–708:

> Li giorni grandi e le notti maggiori
> oltre all'usato modo gli parieno;
> el misurava dalli primi albori
> infino allor che le stelle apparieno;
> e dicea 'l sole entrato in nuovi errori,
> né i cavai come già fer corrieno;
> della notte diceva il simigliante,
> e l'una, due, diceva tute quante.

[The days seemed to him longer and the nights more drawn out than they were used to be. He measured from the dawn right up to when the stars appeared; and said that the sun had become once more mistaken, nor did the horses (of its chariot) run as they had formerly done; and he said the same thing of the night, and counted all the hours twice as long.]

701–7: Compare V.1576–82, where Troylus considers (and rejects) the possibility of crossing the enemy lines.

744–9: The three eyes of Prudence correspond to the three qualities ascribed to that virtue by Cicero (*De Inventione* II.53,160); 'memoria', 'intelligentia', 'providentia'.

799–840: Portraits of Diomede, Briseida and Troilus are found in the same order in Benoit, but are there separated by descriptions of a number of other characters (RT 5211–24, 5275–88, and 5393–446). Some of the particular detail in TC recalls the versions of these portraits given by Joseph of Exeter in the fourth book of his *Frigii Daretis Ylias*; as in Dares, these occur in the sequence Troilus (lines 61–4), Diomede (124–7) and Briseis (156–62).

892: Originally spirits of the dead and subsequently, of the family dead, the Manes were later identified as gods of the Underworld, and of retribution.

932–8: See also TC V.805. In fact, Tydeus had been exiled from Calidon for murdering his brother (*Theb.* I.402–3), and his last moments on earth are unedifying (he is eating the severed head of his enemy Melanippus at the time (*Theb.* VIII.751–66)). See also note to V.1485–93.

1037 The references to 'story(es)' in 1037, 1044 and 1051 imply a historical source, and it is Benoit, not Boccaccio, who tells how Diomede fights with Troilus on Briseida's account, unhorses him, and then presents her with the captured steed (RT 14286–300). She warns him that Troilus will avenge himself very soon (14336–46), but in fact it is Polidamas who defeats him and sends his horse as a present to Troilus (14409–32). Before lending it to Diomede, Briseida taunts him with his imprudence in passing on to her a horse that he would later have need of himself (15093–119).

1044–50: These details are again drawn from RT, where Briseida visits the badly wounded Diomede often, in defiance of her father's prohibition. In contrast to TC V.1050 she is unambiguously said to have given him 's'amor, son cuer e son pensé' (her love, her heart and her mind (20202–28)). See also note to TC V.1758–9.

1086–8: While Benoit sets no figure on the time Briseida took in giving her love to Diomede, he does note the length of the battles and truces that separate their first meeting from her final surrender. See Root 1926:549–50.

1093: 'Sely' is a word of wide semantic range in the later fourteenth century, with the senses 'happy', 'blessed' (as in TC IV.503) at the one extreme, and 'weak', 'poor', 'simple', 'foolish' at the other. In TC it is applied to Troylus in I.871 and II.683, and for each of these examples 'poor' would be an apt translation. When applied metaphorically to Criseyde (as a lark) in III.1191, 'innocent' or 'harmless' would do, but the present example suggests 'wretched' (given as sense 3.(a) for seli in MED).

1109: The mention of a sea to the east of Troy is surprising; see also LGW 1425–6 in which the Isle of Colchis (in the Black Sea) is located 'beyonde Troye, estward in the se'.

1110: The daughter of Nisus was Scylla, who betrayed her city to Minos, its besieger, and was then changed into the bird 'ciris' (Met. VIII. 11–151); Chaucer may have found this glossed as lark.

1174: The reference is to the shepherd hero of a number of songs in dialogue form, and of Adam de la Halle's dramatic pastoral Le Jeu de Robin et de Marion (c. 1283).

1213: Compare Criseyde's own denunciation (and discussion) of jealousy in III. 1016–43.

1234–41: The boar had been more actively violent in F VII.23–4:

> ché gli parea, per entro un bosco ombroso,
> un gran fracasso e spiacevol sentire;
> per che, levato il capo, gli sembiava
> un gran cinghiar veder che valicava.
>
> E poi appresso gli parve vedere
> sotto a' suoi piè Criseida, alla quale
> col grifo il cor traeva, ed al parere
> di lui, Criseida di così gran male
> non si curava, ma quasi piacere
> prendea di ciò facea l'animale.

[It seemed to him that, within a shady wood, he heard a great and hideous crashing; it (also) seemed to him when he raised his head that he saw a great boar crossing through.
    And after that he thought he saw under its feet Criseida, whose heart it drew out with its tusk, and it seemed to him that Criseida was unconcerned at so great a hurt, and almost took pleasure in what the creature did.]

See Introduction, p. xx for the earlier use of part of this dream by Chaucer.

1317–421: Chaucer here radically alters the (longer) letter which Troilo writes at this point (F VII.52–75), making it at once more submissive and less querulous. Troiolo had gone so far as to suggest that Criseida had become 'quasi greca' (almost a Greek), and that she now loves someone else (53, 56–8).

1450: 'Sibille' here is a 'female prophet'; the application of the word to Cassandra is made quite explicit in Gower's *Confessio* V.7451–5.

1459–61: These lines recall the subject-matter of such compendia as Boccaccio's *De Casibus Virorum Illustrium* (which Lydgate translated as *The Fall of Princes*) and Chaucer's own *Monk's Tale*. But Fortune plays no explicit part in the stories that she goes on to tell.

1482–3: Meleager died when – in revenge for his killing of her two brothers (*Met.* VIII.511–24) – his mother cast on the fire the log of which the life-span exactly matched his own.

1485–93: In Argos the exiled Tydeus had become the companion of Polynices (himself exiled by the refusal of his brother Eteocles to honour their agreement to rule over Thebes in alternate years). Tydeus goes to Thebes to remind Eteocles of his obligations (*Theb.* II.391–409); the latter contrives an ambush for Tydeus, and it is here that the 'fifty knyghtes stoute' are slain; Hemonydes alone survives to report the massacre to Eteocles, before killing himself (*Theb.* III.58–91). See also TC V. 1498 a-c.

1520–6: On the personal and private level this stanza replicates the disbelief and outrage that the more public prophecies of Cassandra had always produced in her unwilling audience (RT 4931–6, 10447–54). At the same point in F, Troiolo fears that she may be divinely inspired in finding out about the love-affair (VII.88), but still resolutely denies the truth of what she says (VII.91).

1527–33: Another brief account of the story of Alceste is given in LGW [G] 499–504, and in [G] 530–2 the god of Love presents her as a much more worthy subject for Chaucer than Criseyde ever was. The Narrator anticipates this comparison in TC V.1777–8.

1653: This time 'Lollius' must stand for Boccaccio, who tells how Deifobo returns from battle:

con uno ornato vestimento,
a Diomede gravemente offeso
tratto. (F VIII.8)

[with an ornate garment, torn from the seriously wounded Diomede.]

1751-6: Here 'batayle' implies 'combat(s)' rather than any of the large-scale encounters distinguished and numbered by Benoit. Troilus had much earlier been warned by Hector against acting with unnecessary rashness in the field (RT 7758-72).

1758-9: At the same point F VIII.26 mentions the 'rimproveri cattivi e villani' (malicious and offensive insults) of the rivals; RT 20080-102 had already given an example of one such insult in the scene in which Troilus, after severely wounding Diomede, denounces the infidelity, both present and to come, of Briseida. Chaucer briefly narrates the hero's wounding of his rival in TC V.1045-6, but never allows him to humiliate Criseyde in public.

1771: No such accounts are found in either Dares (too laconic) or Dictys (too pro-Grecian). Benoit has much more to say on this point, even if his Troilus is not uniformly successful in battle: see note to V.1037.

1777-8: Penelope had remained faithful to Odysseus during his long absence at the Trojan war; for Alceste, see V.1527-33 and note.

1786-92: In F IX.5 Boccaccio instructs his own book humbly to commend him to his lady. The five poets named in the final line are described at more length in HF 1456-66 and 1477-502; what they have in common is not their status as authorities on the Trojan war (though Virgil and Homer are that as well), but their literary excellence, and – with the exception of Ovid – their preeminence as epic poets. Calliope is very much the presiding muse here.

1800: 'As I began yow forto seye' obliquely acknowledges that five stanzas have been interpolated between Boccacio's closely linked VIII.26 and 27 (TC V.1758-64 and 1800-6).

1806: At the same point in F (VIII.27) the adverb is *miseramente*; Benoit – following Dares rather than Dictys – tells how, after a vigorous defence against the Myrmidons, Troilus is beheaded by their master, Achilles, and his body dragged at the tail of his horse (RT 21402-50).

1809: The reading 'eighthe' (against the 'seventhe' of most of the surviving copies) is supported by the 'ottava' of the corresponding line in *Tes.* XI. 1. If the planets of medieval cosmology are numbered outwards from the earth, the eighth sphere would be that of the fixed stars; if numbered in the reverse direction, it would be that of the moon; the nearest 'planet' in the medieval system and the one from which events on earth might most plausibly appear visible. But in the part of PF that also encourages a contempt for worldly things and selfish actions, the super-terrestrial vantage point is a 'sterry place' (line 43).

1827: The reference to Mercury, taken over verbatim from the third of the stanzas mentioned above, consorts oddly with the dismissal of other classical gods as 'rascaylle' less than four stanzas later. See also note to V.321.

1856-7: The epithet 'moral' is more clearly justified by Gower's works in French (*Le Mirour de l'Omme*) and Latin (the *Vox Clamantis*) than by the *Confessio*. Ralph Strode's legal career in London was preceded by a period as a fellow of Merton college, Oxford, when he wrote some important philosophical books.

GLOSSARY OF NAMES

In the Pierpont Morgan copy there is considerable variation in the spelling of the names of the principal characters; this is sometimes produced by the demands of rhyme or metre, but by no means always: see the variant forms of Criseyde's name. Only a few examples of the dominant forms are given; minority spellings are recorded more fully. Genitive forms are indicated thus: (g).

ACHILLES   II.416, III.374, ACHILLE V.1559, 1806
ADOON   Adonis III.721
AGAMENOUN   Agamemnon III.382
AGLAWROS   Aglauros III.730
ALCESTE   Alcestis V.1527, 1778
ALETE   Allecto, a Fury IV.24
ALMENA   Alcmena III.1428
AMETE   Admetus I.664
AMPHIORAX   Amphiaraus II.105, V.1500
ANTENOR II.1473, IV.50, 133, etc., ANTENORE IV.665
ANTIGONE   II.816, 824, 887, etc.
APOLLO   III.543, 546, APPOLLO I.72, II.843, III.541, etc.; A.
   DELPHEBUS I.70: see also PHEBUS
ARCHYMORIS   Archemorus's (g.) V.1499
ARGE   Argos V.805, 934, ARGEYS V.1501
ARGYVE   Argia IV.762; ARGYVES (g.) V.1509
ARGUS   IV.1459
ARIETE   (zodiacal sign of) Aries IV.1592, V.1190
ATHAMANTE   Athamas IV.1539
ATTROPOS   one of the Fates IV.1208, 1546

BACUS   Bacchus V.208
BAYARD   I.218
BOLE   (zodiacal sign of) Taurus II.55

CALYDOYNE   Calydon V.805, 934
CALIOPE   Calliope III.45

CALKAS   Calchas I.66, 71, 87, etc.; (g.) IV.663
CANCRO   (zodiacal sign of) Cancer III.625
CAPPANEUS   Capaneus V.1504
CARYBDES   Charybdis V.644
CASSANDRE   Cassandra III.410, V.1451, 1456, 1534
CERBERUS   I.859
CERES   V.208
CYNTHEA   Diana IV.1608, V.1018
CIPRES   Venus III.725, CIPRIDE IV.1216, CIPRYDE V.208
CITHEREA   Venus III.1255
CLEO II.8
CRASSUS   III.1391
CRISEYDE   *passim*, CRISEIDE III.507, V.176, CRYSEYDE III.85, 1173,
   IV.292 etc., CRISEYDA I.169, II.1644, CRISEYD III.1238, CRESEYDE
   IV.479
CRIST   Christ V.1860
CUPIDE   III.186, 1808, V.207, CUPIDO III.461; CUPIDES (g.) V.1590

DANE   Daphne III.726
DARDANUS   II.618
DARES   I.146, V.1771
DEIPHEBUS   II.1402, 1408, 1422, etc., DEYPHEBUS II.1398,
   DEIPHEBE V.1652, 1654
DELPHOS   IV.1411
DIANE   Diana III.731, V.1464: see also CYNTHEA
DIOMEDE   Diomedes IV.11, V.37, 46, etc., DYOMEDE V.15, 1517
DYONE   Dione III.1807
DITE   Dictys I.146

ECTOR   Hector I.110, 113, 471, etc.
ECUBA   Hecuba V.12
EDYPPUS   Oedipus II.102, EDIPPE IV.300
ELEYNE   Helen I.62, 455, 677, etc.
ELYCONE   Helicon III.1809
ELYSOS   Elysium IV.790
ENEAS   Æneas II.1473
ERUDICE   Eurydice IV.791
ESCAPHILO   Ascalaphus V.319
EST SEE   ? V.1109
ETHYOCLES   Eteocles V.1489, 1507
EUROPE   Europa III.722

FLEGITON   Phlegethon III.1600
FLEXIPPE   II.816
FORTUNE   *passim*; FORTUNES (g.) III.1625

GOWER   V.1856
GRECE   Greece I.88, 609, V.123

HERMONYDES   V.1492
HERCULES   (g.) IV.32
HERYNES   the Furies IV.22
HIERSE   Herse III.729
HORASTE   ? Orestes III.797, 806

IMENENUS   Hymen III.1258
INDE   India V.971
YPOMEDON   Ipomedon V.1502
IXION   V.212

JANUS   II.77
JOVE   III.625, 722, etc., JOVES II.1607, V.2; (g.) I.878, III.3
JUNO   IV.1116, 1538, 1594, V.601
JUPPITER   Jupiter II.233, IV.669, 1683
JUVENAL   IV.197

KYNDE   Nature I.238, II.1374, etc.

LATHESIS   Lachesis, one of the Fates V.7
LAYUS   Laius II.101
LAMEADOUN   Laomedon IV.124
LATHONA   Diana, the Moon V.655
LEON   (zodiacal sign of) Leo IV.1592, LYOUN IV.32, LYON V.1019,
   1190
LOLLIUS   ? V.1653, LOLLYUS I.394
LUCIFER   the day star III.1417
LUCYNA   the Moon IV.1591
LUKAN   Lucan V.1792

MANES   gods of the Underworld V.892
MARS   (the god) II.593, 630, etc., MARTE II.435, 988; MARTES (g.)
   III.437; (the planet) III.716
MEGERA   Megaera, a Fury IV.24
MELEAGRE   Meleager V.1474, MELEAGREE V.1482, 1515
MERCURYE   Mercury III.729, V.321, 1827
MYDA   Midas III.1389

MYNERVA   Minerva II. 1062, MYNERVE II.232
MYNOS   Minos IV.1188
MYRRA   Myrrha IV.1139
MONESTEO   Mnestheus IV.51

NEPTUNUS   Neptune II.443, NEPTAMUS IV.120
NIOBE   I.699, 759
NISUS   (g.) V.1110

OENONE   I.654
OMER   Homer I.146, V.1792
ORCADES   the Orkneys V.971
ORPHEUS   IV.791
OVYDE   Ovid V.1792

PALLADION   Palladium I.153, 164; PALLADIONES (g.) I.161
PALLAS   II.425, III.730, V.308, 977, 999
PANDARUS   *passim*, PANDARE *passim*
PARCAS   the Fates V.3
PARYS   Paris I.63, 653, II.1449, IV.608
PARNASO   Parnassus III.1810
PARTHONOPE   Partonopeus V.1503
PENELOPEES   (g.) Penelope's V.1778
PHEBUS   Phœbus (the god) I.70, 659, etc.; (the sun) II.54, III.1495,
    etc.
PHEBUSEO   ? IV.54
PHETON   Phaeton V.664
PIROS   Pyrois III.1703
PLUTO   III.592
POLYDAMAS   Polidamas IV.51
POLYMYTES   Polynices V.1488, POLYMYTE 938, 1507
POLYNESTOR   Polimestor IV.52
POLIPHETE   ? Polyphoetes II.1616, 1619, POLYPHETE II.1467
POLYTE   Polites IV.53
POLIXENE   Polyxena I.455, III.409
PRYAM   Priam III.791, IV.139, etc., PRIAMUS IV.1393; (g.) I.2;
    PRYAMUS IV.57
PROIGNE   Procne II.64
PROSERPYNE   Proserpina IV.473

QUYRYNE   Quirinus (Romulus ?) IV.25

ROBYN   Robin V.1174

RUPHEO   Ripheus IV.53

SANTIPPE   ? Antipus IV.52

SARPEDON   IV.52, V.403, SARPEDOUN V.431, 434, 435 etc.

SATURNE   Saturn (the god) SATURNUS (g.) IV.1538; (the planet) III.625, 716

SYGNYFER   the zodiac V.1020

SYMOYS   Simois IV.1548

STACE   Statius V.1792

STIX   Styx IV.1540

STRODE   V.1857

TANTALUS   III.593

THARBE   II.816, TARBE II.1563

THEBES   II.84, 100, etc.

THESIPHONE   Tisiphone, a Fury I.6, THESYPHONE IV.24

TICIUS   Tityos I.786

TYDEUS   V.88, 1480, 1485, 1493, 1501, TIDEUS V.803, 932, 1746

TIREUX   Tereus II.69

TYTAN   Titan / Tithonus III.1464

TOAS   Thoas IV.138

TROY   IV.1343, TROYE I.2, 68, 74 etc.; TROYES (g.) I.100; TROYES (pl.) II.977

TROYLUS   passim, TROILUS 936, etc., TROYLES III.1443, 1498

VENUS   (the goddess) I.1014, II.234, etc: see also CIPRES; (the planet) II.680, III.715, etc.

VIRGILE   Virgil V.1792

WADE   Wate III.614

ZAUZIS   Zeuxis IV.414

ZEPHIRUS   Zephyr V.10

SUGGESTIONS FOR FURTHER READING

Facsimile

Ruggiers, P.G., (ed.): *The Pierpont Morgan Library Manuscript M.817*; introduction by J. Krochalis. The Facsimile Series of the Works of Geoffrey Chaucer, vol. 4 (Oklahoma: Pilgrim Books, 1986).

Chaucerian Texts

Benson, L. D., (gen. ed.): *The Riverside Chaucer* (Oxford: OUP, 1988). For texts of the *Romaunt of the Rose, Parlement of Foules, Consolation of Philosophy, Legend of Good Women* and *Canterbury Tales*, as well as of *Troylus*.

Root, R. W., (ed.): *The Book of Troilus and Criseyde by Geoffrey Chaucer* (Princeton U.P., 1926). Eccentric text, very full notes.

Windeatt, B. A., (ed.): *Troilus and Criseyde: A New Edition of the 'The Book of Troilus'* (London: Longman, 1984). Offers parallel texts of *Il Filostrato* and *Troylus*, with copious interpretative and textual notes.

——, (trans.): *Troilus and Criseyde*. World's Classics (Oxford: OUP, 1998). Translation into prose with introduction and explanatory notes.

Other Texts

Constans, L., (ed.): *'Le Roman de Troie' par Benoit de Sainte Maure*. Société des Anciens Textes Français. 6 vols (Paris: Librairie de Firmin-Didot, 1904–12). Volumes II and III contain the whole of the Troilus-Briseida story.

Frazer, R. M., (trans): *The Trojan War: The Chronicles of Dictys of Crete and Dares the Phrygian* (Bloomington: Indiana U.P., 1966).

Hatto, A. T., (trans.): *Gottfried von Strassburg: 'Tristan'*, Penguin Classics (Harmondsworth: Penguin, 1960).

Havely, N. R., (trans.): *Chaucer's Boccaccio*, Chaucer Studies V (Cambridge: D. S. Brewer, 1980). Translations of the whole of the *Filostrato*, and of excerpts from Benoit and Guido, as well as from the *Teseida*.

Innes, M. M., (trans.): *The Metamorphoses of Ovid*. Penguin Classics (Harmondsworth: Penguin, 1955).

Macaulay, G. C., (ed.): *The English Works of John Gower*. Early English Text Society Extra Series, 81, 82. (Oxford: OUP, 1900–1). Complete text of the *Confessio Amantis*.

Meek, M. E., (trans.): '*Historia Destructionis Troiae*': *Guido delle Colonne* (Bloomington: Indiana U. P., 1974).

Melville, A. D., (trans.): *Statius, 'Thebaid'* (Oxford: Clarendon Press, 1992). Translation into (mostly) blank verse; introduction and notes by D. W. T. Vessey.

Muir, K., (ed.): Shakespeare, *Troilus and Cressida* (Oxford: Clarendon Press, 1982).

Parry, J. J., (trans.): '*The Art of Courtly Love*' by Andreas Capellanus (New York: Columbia U.P., 1941). The twelfth-century guide to proper behaviour in love.

Rickard, P. (ed.), *Chrestomathie de la langue francaise au quinzième siècle* (Cambridge U. P., 1976).

Critical Anthologies

Barney, S. A., (ed.): *Chaucer's 'Troilus': Essays in Criticism* (London: Scolar Press, 1980).

Boitani, P., (ed.): *The European Tragedy of Troilus* (Oxford: Clarendon Press, 1989). Wider ranging than the other collections, with the texts studied extending from classical antiquity to the late twentieth century.

Benson, C. D., (ed.): *Critical Essays on Chaucer's 'Troilus and Criseyde' and his Major Early Poems* (Milton Keynes: Open University Press, 1991).

Schoeck, R. J., and Taylor, J., (eds): *Chaucer Criticism II: 'Troilus and Criseyde' and the Minor Poems* (Indiana: Notre Dame Press, 1961).

Salu, M., (ed.): *Essays on 'Troilus and Criseyde'* (Cambridge: D. S. Brewer, 1979).

Between them, these collections give access to some of the best *Troylus*-criticism, and with relatively little duplication of individual essays.

Literary and Textual Studies

Anderson, D., *Before the 'Knight's Tale': Imitation of Classical Epic in Boccaccio's 'Teseida'* (Philadelphia: University of Pennsylvania Press, 1988). The relation of the *Teseida* to the *Thebaid*.

Benson, C. D., *The history of Troy in Middle English Literature* (Woodbridge: D. S. Brewer, 1980). Groups the major texts into historical and literary categories.

Bradley, A. C., *Shakespearean Tragedy*, 2nd edn (London: Macmillan, 1905). Still valuable for its discussion of the construction of the plays.

Burrow, J. A., *Ricardian Poetry* (London: Routledge and Keegan Paul, 1971). Sets Chaucer in relation to his major literary contemporaries.

Curry, W. C., *Chaucer and the Medieval Sciences*, 2nd edn (London: George Allen and Unwin, 1960). Dream-lore and predestination are considered in detail.

Dinshaw, C., *Chaucer's Sexual Poetics* (University of Wisconsin Press, 1989). Interrogates Chaucer's critics as well as his characters.

Gordon, I. L., *The Double Sorrow of Troilus* (Oxford: OUP, 1970). Concerned with the ambiguities of the poem.

Hanly, M. G., *Boccaccio, Beauvau, Chaucer: 'Troilus and Criseyde'*. (Oklahoma: Pilgrim Books, 1990). Concedes that Chaucer's use of Beauvau remains unproven; gives brief excerpts from the latter with translations.

Kolve, V. A., *Chaucer and the Imagery of Narrative* (London: Arnold, 1984), For the images of the prison and the garden in the *Knight's Tale*.

Lawton, D., *Chaucer's Narrators* (Cambridge: D. S. Brewer, 1985). For the Narrator as neutral voice rather than separate character.

McAlpine, M. E., *The Genre of 'Troilus and Criseyde'* (Ithaca: Cornell University Press, 1978). Considers modes of tragedy and comedy in *Troylus*.

Minnis, A. J., *Chaucer and Pagan Antiquity*. Chaucer Studies 8 (Cambridge: D. S. Brewer, 1982).

——, *Medieval Theory of Authorship*, 2nd edn (Aldershot, Wilwood House, 1988). Both books discuss the attitudes of Chaucer and Gower to literary authority.

Miskimin, A. S., *The Renaissance Chaucer* (New Haven: Yale University Press, 1975). The development of the story of Troylus is used to throw light on Chaucer's poem.

Muscatine, C., *Chaucer and the French Tradition* (Berkeley: University of California Press, 1960). Discusses the mixture of styles in *Troylus*, and the ambiguity of Criseyde.

Nolan, B., *Chaucer and the Tradition of the 'Roman Antique'*. Studies in Medieval Literature 15 (Cambridge University Press, 1992). Considers Boccaccio's Narrator as well as Chaucer's.

Patterson, L., *Chaucer and the Subject of History* (London, 1991) For Chaucer's reflection of contemporary events and views of history.

Pearsall, D., *The Life of Geoffrey Chaucer* (Blackwell: Oxford, 1992). A fruitful interweaving of biography and literary criticism.

Propp, V., *Morphology of the Folktale*, 2nd edn (Austin: University of Texas Press, 1968). Translated by L. Scott and with an introduction by A. Dundes. Classic account of literary structures.

Seymour, M. C., *A Catalogue of Chaucer Manuscripts I: Works before the 'Canterbury Tales'* (London: Scolar Press, 1995). Includes descriptions of all the manuscript copies of *Troylus*; sceptical about previous attempts at grouping them.

Windeatt, B., *Troilus and Criseyde*, Oxford Guides to Chaucer (Oxford: Clarendon Press, 1992). Very detailed consideration of all major aspects of the poem.

Works of Reference

Davis, N., Gray, D., Ingham, P., Wallace-Hadrill, A., *A Chaucer Glossary* (Oxford: Clarendon Press, 1979).

Gillespie, G. T., *A Catalogue of Persons Named in German Heroic Literature (700–1600)* (Oxford: Clarendon Press, 1973).

Kurath, H., Kuhn, S. M., (first eds): *Middle English Dictionary* [MED] (Ann Arbor, Michigan: University of Michigan Press, 1954 –).

Book I

Calkas, a Trojan priest, foresees the fall of Troy and, fearing for his own life, defects to the rival Greek camp. He leaves behind his beautiful daughter, Criseyde, a young widow. Sympathising with Criseyde's fear and anxiety, Hector offers to protect her despite her father's treason. For his arrogant disdain of other men's weakness in love, prince Troylus is pierced by the god of Love's arrow upon his first sight of Criseyde. He continues mocking other knights for their devotion to women, but the image of Criseyde haunts him. Alone in his room, he resolves to dedicate himself to the service of his lady. In this state Troylus loses all other fear, and launches himself with renewed ferocity into battle with the Greeks in the hope of impressing her. His friend Pandarus discovers him lamenting his sorrow; Troylus reveals the cause of it, and Pandarus offers to convey Troylus's feelings to Criseyda, his niece. For how can a woman possibly return Troylus's love if she has no idea that his feelings even exist? Troylus is reinvigorated by the prospect of their meeting.

Book II

Pandarus visits Criseyde and praises Troylus highly, before revealing the young prince's love for her. He expresses the fear that Troylus will die if his love remains unrequited. At first, Criseyde withholds her affection. Pandarus accuses her of cruelty, crying out that he too will perish should Troylus die. Wishing to preserve her uncle's life as well as her honour, Criseyde eventually agrees to show Troylus more kindness; watching him ride by her window in triumph following one of his battles she is amazed that such a man might die on her account. Her inner debate over the rightness of returning Troylus's feelings is largely resolved by a song from one of her nieces, in praise of love.

Pandarus informs Troylus that Criseyde will indeed love him if he courts her diligently, and there is an exchange of letters between the two lovers. Pandarus visits Troylus's brother Deiphebus, to ask his support for Criseyde, who has lawsuits pending against her. Deiphebus arranges for her to dine at his house with a gathering of his relations, including Troylus. Pandarus instructs him to arrive early, then plead illness, and retire to bed. Thus he provides the opportunity for Troylus and Criseyde to speak privately while gaining the family's support and respect for her – and preserving their ignorance of the relationship.

Book III
Troylus declares his love to Criseyde; she accepts it on condition that he preserve her honour. Later Pandarus also pleads with Troylus to protect his niece's honour and to keep their love secret. Troylus and Criseyde snatch moments of conversation with each other, and Pandarus continues to act as a go-between. Soon he organises a meal for Criseyde at his own house, during which Troylus conceals himself in a closet. Criseyde dines and is entertained, but as she prepares to leave, the planets conspire to prevent her from doing so by sending a storm which keeps her and her attendants at her uncle's house. Pandarus arranges the sleeping quarters so that Criseyde and her waiting women are lodged separately. He reminds her that she has pledged herself to Troylus, and informs her that the latter has slipped into the house unnoticed, suffering because of a rumour that Criseyde loves another. Criseyde is disturbed by Troylus's lack of faith in her, but promises she will assure him of her love the following day. Pandarus chafes at this, saying that any delay could be disastrous. Criseyde relents, and Troylus is ushered into her bedchamber. She is startled by his sudden entrance, but reaffirms her love for him, and curses jealousy. Deeply chastened by her anger, Troylus falls into a swoon. Pandarus rushes to his side, and lifts him on to Criseyde's bed, begging her assistance in his attempts to revive him. Criseyde's words and caresses draw Troylus out of his faint, and Pandarus withdraws. The lovers then pass an ecstatic night together, grieving when the day breaks and they are forced to part. They continue to meet secretly with Pandarus's help.

Book IV
Following a savage battle between the Greeks and the Trojans, the Greeks take several prisoners of war and seek an exchange of their own people for these hostages. Calkas hears of the situation, and begs for one of the Trojan prisoners to be exchanged for his daughter Criseyde. Troylus's father, the King of Troy, agrees to the proposal.

Driven to despair by the news, Troylus retires to his palace where he throws himself against the walls in agony. Pandarus, hearing of the assembly's decision, rushes to Troylus, and tries to give comfort by suggesting that other women may take Criseyde's place. Troylus condemns the offer outright, preferring death to the betrayal of his love. Pandarus organises a meeting between the lovers. Criseyde is so ill with fear that she faints, and Troylus is unable to revive her. Believing her to be dead, he prepares to kill himself, and Criseyde revives just in time to save him.

The two discuss ways out of the situation, with Criseyde trying to reassure Troylus that they may not be parted for long. Troylus doubts the likelihood of Criseyde's early return from the Greek camp, but equally, Criseyde cannot accept the proposition that they run away together: her good name would be destroyed. Troylus gives way, and the lovers part in the belief that Criseyde will somehow effect her return in ten days time.

Book V

Diomede is sent to escort Criseyde from Troy to the Greek encampment. For fear of harming Criseyde Troylus restrains himself from killing Diomede, although furiously jealous at the sight of her in another man's care. Diomede attempts to charm Criseyde, sympathising with her predicament and declaring that she may command him at her leisure. Criseyde is unable to respond to him, and submits herself to the reunion with her father.

In Troy, Troylus locks himself away, sends for Pandarus and, believing the separation will kill him, begins to dictate his will. No festivity can divert him and the ten days pass slowly.

Criseyde for a time swears that she will return at the promised time, but her resolve soon weakens. Diomede considers how best to win her heart, and visits her in her father's tent, asks why Calkas has not married her to a man of standing, and tries to dissuade her from her attachment to her past. He asks if she will accept his love, and if he may visit her again the following day. Criseyde agrees, on condition that he does not speak of his love for her, but offers him hope by giving him her glove. On his subsequent visits she decides to become his mistress; she afterwards laments her unfaithfulness in love.

On the tenth day of their separation, Troylus waits in vain for Criseyde's return. Days pass, and finally he writes to her, pleading with her to return. Although her reply renews her promise, she is unable to predict when she will come. Troylus sends for the prophetess Cassandra to interpret a worrying dream in which Criseyde embraces a boar, but when she explains this as proof of Diomede's success in love, Troylus rejects her interpretation. He again writes to Criseyde.

Criseyde's subsequent letter to Troylus describes how his lack of faith hurts her, and claims that she is delaying her return in order to dispel rumours that the two of them are lovers. Troylus is suspicious, but wills himself to continue trusting Criseyde. Soon after this, an ornate surcoat is torn from Diomede in battle, and on its collar Troylus sees the brooch he gave Criseyde before they parted. Heartbroken Troylus re-enters battle with a lust for vengeance. He constantly seeks out Diomede, but although the two often meet in bloody combat neither kills the other and Troylus finally meets death at the hands of Achilles.

Ascending to the gods, Troylus's soul views his earthly love as folly, compared with the perfect bliss of heaven.

ACKNOWLEDGEMENTS

I wish to express my gratitude to the Director of the Pierpont Morgan Library, for permitting me to reproduce in edited form the copy of *Troylus and Criseyde* that is contained in Pierpont Morgan Library, New York. M.817, and for arranging that a microfilm of it should be made available to me.

I am also indebted to previous editors of *Troylus*, whose scholarship and dedication has made so much easier the preparation of the present edition; to Janet Edwards and Simon Meecham Jones for their helpful suggestions and criticisms; and, most of all, to dear Vivien for her lively interest in the early stages of a book she did not live to see finished.